THE PROMISE
OF INDIA

ADVANCE PRAISE FOR THE BOOK

'Bhagwati's book is refreshingly frank and fair. It is a magisterial effort, informed by his unique roles in India's government. It dissects India's governance issues both past and for the future with exceptional clarity. It is a must-read for the young and seasoned alike'—Nandan Nilekani, chairman and co-founder of Infosys and founding chairman of UIDAI (Aadhaar)

'A thoughtful and nuanced consideration of India's economic and foreign policies since Independence by a highly respected economist and diplomat with practical experience at the highest levels of government. By using the prism of leaders, namely, Indian prime ministers, this book makes great and significant issues accessible not only to the specialist and scholar but also to the general reader'—Shivshankar Menon, former foreign secretary and national security adviser

'With his versatile background, Bhagwati provides a bridge between news headlines and the reality of behind-the-scenes public policymaking under each of the prime ministers since Independence. This timely book is a fascinating insider's account of the interplay of politics, economics, diplomacy, administration and financial markets.

The Promise of India is unique in its sweep, providing insights not just on the past and present, but also on future possibilities. It is a must-read for leaders and laypersons, scholars and students of the social sciences'—Dr Y.V. Reddy, former governor, Reserve Bank of India, and chairman, Fourteenth Finance Commission

'An extraordinarily extensive bird's-eye survey of our post-Independence evolution. The number of facts cited bears witness to Bhagwati's range of knowledge, as his literary quotations do to his range of interests, all brought in with an admirable sense of values and lightness of touch. He must write several more books to help us digest the full feast for which this is a most enjoyable appetizer'—K.S. Bajpai, former ambassador

'A fascinating history of post-Independence India told with originality through studies of each prime minister individually by someone who has had an unusually wide experience of working for the Government of India'—Mark Tully, senior journalist and author of *No Full-Stops in India*

'A unique compendium of political and economic history, insightfully captured through the lens of one of India's finest diplomats. To truly understand India's progress over the years, Bhagwati's book is a must-read'—Deepak Parekh, chairman, HDFC Limited

THE PROMISE OF INDIA

HOW **PRIME MINISTERS** NEHRU TO MODI
SHAPED THE NATION (1947–2019)

JAIMINI BHAGWATI

PENGUIN
VIKING
An imprint of Penguin Random House

VIKING

USA | Canada | UK | Ireland | Australia
New Zealand | India | South Africa | China

Viking is part of the Penguin Random House group of companies
whose addresses can be found at global.penguinrandomhouse.com

Published by Penguin Random House India Pvt. Ltd
4th Floor, Capital Tower 1, MG Road,
Gurugram 122 002, Haryana, India

Penguin
Random House
India

First published in Viking by Penguin Random House India 2019

ISBN 9780670089826

Typeset in Adobe Garamond Pro by Manipal Digital Systems, Manipal
Printed at Replika Press Pvt. Ltd, India

www.penguin.co.in

MIX
Paper from
responsible sources
FSC® C016779

CONTENTS

PROLOGUE

The Promise of India Endures

In the last few years, I have thought every now and then about writing on why I love India and yet why I am infuriated by it. I have been fortunate to have worked on both sides of Rajpath[1] in New Delhi—in the Ministry of External Affairs to the south of Rajpath and the Ministry of Finance to the north. I decided that perhaps I do have something of interest to say about the background to and consequences of the path taken by India at the crucial crossroads since Independence.

The geographical region called India has endured through the ages but was raided repeatedly, plundered, splintered, colonized, and eventually brought together as one nation. Independent India has progressed impressively on several fronts. The ironies of the country's successes and many abject failures have been delightfully satirized through the decades in the facial expressions and dilemmas of the average man and his wife in R.K. Laxman's cartoons. It is the common people who have brought post-Independence India back on track time and time again by participating enthusiastically in large numbers in the elections.

After Independence, India started on the task of building a new country out of the depths of its colonial past. From then on, there have been periods of promise, and there have been several setbacks. With rising awareness, the masses among the electorate are likely to seek greater accountability from India's political elites. This should help the country in its continuing quest to achieve a fuller expression of its soul. Such an indefinable goal may be too ambitious, yet it tugs at the heartstrings of Indians as they yearn for a future which is consistent with the teachings of India's ancient past.

After 1947, India has been shaped to a significant extent by decisions taken by its prime ministers (PMs), and they have been responsible for uplifting and even soaring successes as well as depressing failures. I use the words 'soaring' and 'depressing' because those are precisely the emotions I feel when I reminisce about crucial Indian decisions. The focus of this book, then, is primarily on the role played by India's PMs, and to some extent, by cabinet ministers, senior officials and the judiciary. At a birthday celebration for Dr Shankar Acharya[2] at the India International Centre in Delhi, Mark Tully, the former bureau chief of the BBC in India, challenged me to condense the central contents of this book into one sentence. I gulped for a moment, collected my thoughts and said that the book tracks the extent to which India's political leadership at the apex level had raised optimism or cynicism among Indians. To place this assessment in perspective, the India that each PM inherited and subsequently bequeathed to the successor is outlined at the beginning and end of each chapter.

The book covers over seventy-one years of India's foreign and economic policies and practices. Each chapter, focusing on one or a couple of the short-lived PMs, includes factual narratives to provide the context for observations and conclusions. India, as a federation of states,[3] has a written constitution which gives exclusive jurisdiction to the Central government in foreign affairs, national security and borrowings in foreign exchange. The Central government shares responsibilities on economic issues with state governments, but it sets the country's overall agenda on tax and spending issues. In the Indian cabinet system of government, the PM chairs various cabinet committees, the more important of which are on economic, security and political affairs.[4] These committees take all crucial decisions on foreign and economic policy issues.[5] The Central government's annual budgets have to be approved by the PM and by the Lower House of Parliament—the Lok Sabha.

Deriving its powers from the Indian Constitution, the Central government headed by the PM, even compared to the combined weight of all state governments, continues to have a predominant say in running the country. Shivshankar Menon is of the view that there is a 'determinant role of the Prime Minister in India'.[6] Menon is referring to foreign policy decisions but this is equally true about India's economic policies.

The prime minister, as primus inter pares in the Central government, is the key decision maker in all important appointments. The PM, as the head of government and the chairman of the Appointments Committee of the Cabinet (ACC), is the final arbiter in the selection of the chief election commissioner (CEC), comptroller and auditor general (CAG), all Indian ambassadors and high commissioners around the world, and all secretary-level officers of the Central government including the chairman of the Atomic Energy

Commission, the heads of the Indian Space Research Organisation (ISRO) and Defence Research Development Organisation (DRDO). The heads of the three wings of the armed forces are also selected by the ACC, as are the heads of financial-sector regulatory agencies such as the Reserve Bank of India (RBI), the Securities and Exchange Board of India (SEBI), and the deputy chairman of the erstwhile Planning Commission.[7] The PM recommends the appointment of Supreme Court and high court judges to the President based on the suggestions of the Supreme Court's collegium.[8]

Each major government decision taken by India's PMs must have been preceded by careful weighing of pros and cons from the perspective of the nation, the party in power and the personalties involved. It is difficult long after the fact to take into account the circumstances and comprehend the full range of economic and other constraints. Consequently, it is impossible to even mention, let alone discuss, all the details that influenced decisions taken by India's PMs in a single book. Nevertheless, I have attempted to piece together significant events and decisions, and their consequences for the country.

At the beginning of the twentieth century, Argentina was seen as a country of the future. It has abundant natural resources, and the expectation was that Argentina would catch up and even outstrip the larger European countries in standards of living. However, unrepresentative, military-led governments and the cynicism of its elite resulted in Argentina performing way below its potential. In a somewhat similar manner, although India started out extremely well, it has had its share of missed opportunities. Hence, a recurring theme in this book is the slow pace of development for the poorest sections of the Indian people. A large proportion of the disadvantaged in India are engaged in subsistence agriculture or work in low-paying menial jobs in urban areas, and live in cramped and unhygienic conditions. An oft-repeated refrain on how to improve the lot of these two groups of Indians is that they must be provided better education and opportunities to improve their skills. The central and state governments in India provide free to highly subsidized education in government schools, and there are vocational training centres around the country. However, progress in real terms has been too slow.

Taking a step back to reflect, perhaps the processes which result in sustainable development are 80 per cent heart and only 20 per cent brain. In other words, those who teach and train in primary schools or skill development centres have to be sincere about their work which can often be tedious and is usually low paid. No amount of tinkering with technical solutions will suffice if those who are responsible for teaching and training lack motivation. If average Indians feel optimistic about their future, they are likely to fulfil their own accountabilities diligently and honestly. It follows that a defining quality in the political leadership of India, and hence that of PMs, has to include the ability to motivate teachers, trainers and those working at lower levels of administration. In a functioning democracy, the well-being of citizens is also dependent on what they collectively want, namely, whether they want to build a caring, participative and meritocratic nation. It is important, therefore, in evaluating the track records of India's PMs to assess whether the PMs have built an awareness of the country's history and shared future destiny among the people.

In the run-up to Independence and after 1947, several among the leaders of the freedom movement and the newly formed government were educated in England. Members of the political executive and Indian Civil Service (ICS) officials were fluent in English, and there was no controversy in running the affairs of the Central government in English. Over the years, as homespun leaders have emerged and headed state governments, English has been replaced by regional languages. This was inevitable and is a welcome development since Sanskrit and India's regional languages have a rich history of profound writings and literature. Somewhat less welcome is the chauvinistic chest thumping about a distant glorious past expressed self-consciously in the vernacular that is often closely correlated to a lack of familiarity with and understanding of documented history. There is an inchoate criticism against the powerful and well connected in so-called Lutyens's Delhi, which is also directed at those who are affluent, live in the megacities around the country, and speak among themselves mostly in English. This conveniently fails to acknowledge that those who flaunt the vernacular could also fail basic tests of honesty and decency and be wealthy beyond measure. Those who speak in English are referred to as belonging to a foreign ethos called 'India', while the homespun are from the real, indigenous 'Bharat'. Although this is a motivated and inaccurate distinction, Indians who speak mostly in English need to know at least one Indian language well. Otherwise they would remain poorer for having cut themselves off from the rich founts of knowledge and culture which abound in Indian writings and folklore.

In the book, PMs are assessed on whether they consciously or unconsciously promoted an elitist India. Alternatively, were they more homespun and pushed for an all-inclusive Bharat, or ideally, did they straddle both India and Bharat with equal comfort and moved into and out of each reality with ease.

Nehru was the longest-serving PM with an uninterrupted tenure of close to seventeen years, followed by Indira Gandhi—sixteen years, Manmohan Singh—ten years, Atal Bihari Vajpayee—six years, Rajiv Gandhi and Narasimha

Rao—about five years each. The PMs who were in office for five years or more are covered in greater detail. The short-lived coalition governments of Morarji Desai, Charan Singh, V.P. Singh, Chandra Shekhar, Deve Gowda and Inder Kumar Gujral were marked by shifting loyalties. The alignments and realignments of the various political parties to form these governments were driven by the ambition of the leaders of those years to be the PM, even if it was abundantly obvious that it would be for a short while. This mindset did little credit to them. The growing cynicism with which the short-lived PMs achieved their narrow objectives was illustrative of the gradual yet steady erosion in the accountability of Indian political figures.

The personal characteristics, or the three 'Cs', of India's PMs have been enumerated to compare performances across different points of time. The three Cs are Character, Competence and Charisma, in that order of importance. The qualities of compassion and commitment are deemed to be part of Character for the purposes of this book. No other quality in a leader can make up for deficiencies in Character, and that is why it has pride of place among the desirable Cs. Ideally, India's PMs need all three Cs to move India along to a better future. This evaluation is at the end of the 'Legacy' section for PMs with tenures of five years or more. The one exception is Lal Bahadur Shastri.

Why write this book?

Even when Richa Burman suggested I write a book for Penguin, I was hesitant although I had authored chapters in several books, a number of research papers and a regular column in the *Business Standard* for nearly fourteen years. Any number of books have been written about various aspects of India by those who have worked in crucial positions in the Central government, the private sector and as academics. Unfortunately, despite all the information in the public domain, Indians tend to make sweeping statements about past PMs. For example, India's current economic backwardness is often attributed to Nehru who passed away more than half a century ago. A nuanced picture of independent India which explains the multiple constraints which decision makers faced provides a better sense of why and how domestic developments and international events unfolded and impacted the country. Hopefully, this book will provide a measure of understanding as to why Indian politics has come to be so self-serving even as the country has made considerable progress towards higher standards of living.

Senior leaders in Indian political parties speak the truth about others but rarely about themselves. There is an exasperated look on the faces of Indian politicians when asked about why certain obvious decisions were not taken or distorted in implementation. The speeches and writings of those who have held high political or official positions, contrary to their strident claims, do not 'speak truth to power' without concern to where the pieces fall.

Academics, think-tank experts and journalists have written extensively about Indian PMs and their policies. Such writing has, for the most part, been fairly objective but not sufficiently probing. This could be because it is rare for writers among these three categories to have worked in senior ministerial or official positions in close proximity to PMs.

All things considered, there has been a tendency towards maintaining a conspiracy of silence about blatantly inappropriate PM-level decisions which had hugely negative consequences for the country. Self-promoters have highlighted achievements of PMs and whitewashed shortcomings, thus distorting the record. To rephrase what Blanche DuBois says wistfully in *A Streetcar Named Desire*, 'deliberate distortion of facts is unforgivable'.[9]

Readers will find that there are no overarching explanations within which PM-level policy decisions can be understood. India's foreign and economic policies have been messy in formulation and implementation, and the choppy nature of the narrative and analysis in the book is because that is how things were and are in India.

Indians are troubled by the glaring shortfalls between the ideals and hopes of the founders of independent India and today's ground realities. Several factors, mostly domestic and at times external, have impeded India's progress towards a more meaningful 'tryst with destiny'. Haphazard urbanization and human misery are most apparent in the slums in Indian cities.[10] Jean Dreze and Amartya Sen have been constrained to remark that 'India looks more and more like islands of California in a sea of sub-Saharan Africa'.[11] A few of today's super rich, while flying in and out of Dubai, London or New York, remark that it is impossible to live in India.

India takes pride in providing low-cost higher education, and this is a worthwhile objective. In practice, this has meant that some among the best educated seek higher living standards and settle in developed countries. Much remains to be achieved in nation-building, and it is disheartening at times to watch so many among the gifted give up on India. If we look around, there are specific achievements to cherish. For instance, post-Independence India has made significant advances in the fields of space and nuclear energy. At the same time, there is this gnawing doubt that by now, almost seventy-two years after Independence, we could have done more to reduce the poverty that is so starkly evident all around us.

A starting premise in *What Is History?*[12] is that all writings about the past are impacted by the choices of what to include and what interpretation to give to the so-called recorded facts. In Carr's words, history 'is a continuous process of interaction between the historian and his facts, an unending dialogue between the present and the past'. The film *Zorba the Greek*[13] was released in 1964, and when I saw it a few years later as a callow teenager, it made a lasting impression on me. The title character was played superbly by Anthony Quinn, and the British professor was played by Alan Bates. Towards the end of the film, when the professor asks Zorba for his opinion of him, Zorba responds, 'You have everything but a man needs a little madness or else he never dares cut the rope and be free.' I wish more of those who have written about decision making in the last seventy-two years had cut the rope to free us of distortions and half-truths.

I remind myself in the autumn of my life that there cannot be any despondency. As Nehru put it, 'God we may deny but what hope is there if we deny man.' And, as Dylan Thomas wrote, 'Do not go gentle into that good night, Old age should burn and rave at close of day, Rage, rage against the dying of the light.' That is sound advice, and I intend to rage constructively in this book about why India seems close to achieving the breakthroughs vital to ever-widening circles of well-being in the country but has not done so yet.

An ambition of this book is to help younger Indians, nowadays known as millennials,[14] to be discerning voters. Perhaps enthuse them to join a political party or even start one.[15] To this end, I have included the salient elements of India's economic and diplomatic history in the narrative.

I apologize to all who feel that the enormous scope of the book makes it omit and gloss over details, and is simplistic or erroneous in many of its conclusions. My attempt has been to focus on inflection points to enable readers to arrive at an uncluttered understanding of how and why India happens to be where it is in the middle of 2019.

All omissions and shortcomings in this book are my own.

Table 1
Prime Ministers since Independence

Prime Minister	Dates in Office	Tenure
Shri Jawaharlal Nehru	15 August 1947 to 27 May 1964	16 years 9 months
Shri Lal Bahadur Shastri	9 June 1964 to 11 January 1966	1 year 7 months
Smt. Indira Gandhi	24 January 1966 to 24 March 1977	11 years 2 months
Shri Morarji Desai	24 March 1977 to 28 July 1979	2 years 4 months
Shri Charan Singh	28 July 1979 to 14 January 1980	5 months
Smt. Indira Gandhi	14 January 1980 to 31 October 1984	4 years 9 months
Shri Rajiv Gandhi	31 October 1984 to 2 December 1989	5 years 1 month
Shri Vishwanath Pratap Singh	2 December 1989 to 10 November 1990	11 months
Shri Chandra Shekhar	10 November 1990 to 21 June 1991	7 months
Shri P.V. Narasimha Rao	21 June 1991 to 16 May 1996	4 years 11 months
Shri Deve Gowda	1 June 1996 to 21 April 1997	10 months
Shri Inder Kumar Gujral	21 April 1997 to 19 March 1998	10 months
Shri Atal Bihari Vajpayee	19 March 1998 to 22 May 2004	6 years 2 months
Dr Manmohan Singh	22 May 2004 to 26 May 2014	10 years
Shri Narendra Damodardas Modi	26 May 2014 to date	5 years till May 2019

Table 2
Foreign Ministers since Independence

No	Name	From	To	Political Party
1	Jawaharlal Nehru	2 September 1946	27 May 1964	Indian National Congress
2	Gulzarilal Nanda	27 May 1964	9 June 1964	Indian National Congress
3	Lal Bahadur Shastri	9 June 1964	17 July 1964	Indian National Congress
4	Sardar Swaran Singh	18 July 1964	14 November 1966	Indian National Congress
5	M.C. Chagla	14 November 1966	5 September 1967	Indian National Congress
6	Indira Gandhi	6 September 1967	13 February 1969	Indian National Congress
7	Dinesh Singh	14 February 1969	27 June 1970	Indian National Congress
8	Sardar Swaran Singh	27 June 1970	10 October 1974	Indian National Congress
9	Yashwantrao Chavan	10 October 1974	24 March 1977	Indian National Congress
10	Atal Bihari Vajpayee	26 March 1977	28 July 1979	Janata Party
11	Shyam Nandan Prasad Mishra	29 July 1979	13 January 1980	Janata Party (Secular)
12	P.V. Narasimha Rao	14 January 1980	19 July 1984	Indian National Congress
13	Indira Gandhi	19 July 1984	31 October 1984	Indian National Congress
14	Rajiv Gandhi	31 October 1984	24 September 1985	Indian National Congress
15	Bali Ram Bhagat	25 September 1985	12 May 1986	Indian National Congress
16	P. Shiv Shankar	12 May 1986	22 October 1986	Indian National Congress
17	N.D. Tiwari	22 October 1986	25 July 1987	Indian National Congress
18	Rajiv Gandhi	25 July 1987	25 June 1988	Indian National Congress

No	Name	From	To	Political Party
19	P.V. Narasimha Rao	25 June 1988	2 December 1989	Indian National Congress
20	V.P. Singh	2 December 1989	5 December 1989	Janata Dal
21	I.K. Gujral	5 December 1989	10 November 1990	Janata Dal
22	Vidya Charan Shukla	21 November 1990	20 February 1991	Samajwadi Janata Party
23	Madhav Singh Solanki	21 June 1991	31 March 1992	Indian National Congress
24	P.V. Narasimha Rao	31 March 1992	18 January 1993	Indian National Congress
25	Dinesh Singh	18 January 1993	10 February 1995	Indian National Congress
26	Pranab Mukherjee	10 February 1995	16 May 1996	Indian National Congress
27	Sikander Bakht	21 May 1996	1 June 1996	Bharatiya Janata Party
28	I.K. Gujral	1 June 1996	18 March 1998	Janata Dal
29	Atal Bihari Vajpayee	19 March 1998	5 December 1998	Bharatiya Janata Party
30	Jaswant Singh	5 December 1998	23 June 2002	Bharatiya Janata Party
31	Yashwant Sinha	1 July 2002	22 May 2004	Bharatiya Janata Party
32	K. Natwar Singh	22 May 2004	6 November 2005	Indian National Congress
33	Manmohan Singh	6 November 2005	24 October 2006	Indian National Congress
34	Pranab Mukherjee	24 October 2006	22 May 2009	Indian National Congress
35	S.M. Krishna	22 May 2009	26 October 2012	Indian National Congress
36	Salman Khurshid	28 October 2012	26 May 2014	Indian National Congress
37	Sushma Swaraj	27 May 2014	May 2019	Bharatiya Janata Party

Table 3
Finance Ministers since Independence

No	Finance Minister	Tenure
1	Liaquat Ali Khan	1947
2	R.K. Shanmukham Chetty	1947–49
3	Dr John Mathai	1950–51
4	Dr C.D. Deshmukh	1951–57
5	T.T. Krishnamachari	1957–58
6	Jawaharlal Nehru, P.M.	1958–59
7	Morarji R. Desai	1959–64
8	T.T. Krishnamachari	1964–65
9	Sachin Choudhury	1966–67
10	Morarji R. Desai, Dy. P.M.	1967–69
11	Smt. Indira Gandhi, P.M.	1969–70
12	Y.B. Chavan	1971–74
13	C. Subramanian	1975–77
14	H.M. Patel	1977–78
15	Charan Singh, Dy. P.M.	1979
16	H.N. Bahuguna	1979
17	R. Venkataraman	1980–82
18	Pranab Mukherjee	1982–84
19	V.P. Singh	1984–86
20	Rajiv Gandhi, P.M.	1987
21	N.D. Tiwari	1987–88
22	S.B. Chavan	1988–89
23	Madhu Dandavate	1989–90
24	Yashwant Sinha	1990–91
25	Dr Manmohan Singh	1991–96
26	Jaswant Singh	1996
27	P. Chidambaram	1996–98
28	Yashwant Sinha	1998–2002
29	Jaswant Singh	2002–04
30	P. Chidambaram	2004–08
31	Pranab Mukherjee	2009–12
32	P. Chidambaram	2012–14
33	Arun Jaitley	2014–19

Table 4
Strength of Ruling Party and Coalition Partners in Lok Sabha and Rajya Sabha

Prime Minister	Ruling Party		Coalition Partners	
	Lok Sabha	Rajya Sabha	Lok Sabha	Rajya Sabha^
Shri Jawaharlal Nehru	398/543	186/232 (1954–56)	NA	NA
	403/534	164/236 (1960–62)	NA	NA
	394/540	162/238 (1962–64)	NA	NA
Shri Lal Bahadur Shastri	394/540	166/238 (1964–66)	NA	NA
Smt. Indira Gandhi	303/553	107/243 (1970–72)	NA	NA
	372/553	146/244 (1974–76)	NA	NA
Shri Morarji Desai	302/557 (a)	106/244 (1976–78) (m)	44/557 (b)	5/244 (1976–78)^
Shri Charan Singh	*	*	*	*
Smt. Indira Gandhi	377/566	152/244 (1982–84)	NA	NA
Shri Rajiv Gandhi	426/567	141/245 (1986–88)	NA	NA
Shri Vishwanath Pratap Singh	142/534	38/245 (1988–90)	149/534 (c)	51/245 (1988–90)^
Shri Chandra Shekhar				
Shri P.V. Narasimha Rao	252/555	85/245 (1994–96)		
Shri Deve Gowda	46/551 (i)	9/245 (1996–98)	287/551 (j)	89/245 (1996–98)^
Shri Inder Kumar Gujral	31/551 (k)	9/245 (1996–98)	302/551 (l)	89/245 (1996–98)^
Shri Atal Bihari Vajpayee	183/546	47/245 (1996–98)	82/546 (g)	27/245 (1996–98)^
	189/568	45/245 (2002–04)	115/568 (d)	41/245 (2002–04)^
Dr Manmohan Singh	159/586	71/245 (2008–10)	139/568 (e)	34/245 (2008–10)^
	211/560	72/245 (as in 2013)	116/560 (f)	47/245 (as in 2013)^
Shri Narendra Damodardas Modi	281/542	56/245 (as in 2017)	54/542 (h)	16/245 (as in 2017)^

Source: Lok Sabha website, Rajya Sabha Statistical Information 1952–2013.
^: these figures only include the seats of coalition partners that were explicitly stated in official documents; Rajya Sabha seats of smaller parties are usually cited in official documents as 'Others'—these small parties' seats have not been counted here.
*: Charan Singh government never faced the Lok Sabha.

ACKNOWLEDGEMENTS

Several of my former colleagues in government and friends were generous with their time and spoke to me at length about their perceptions of government decisions on significant issues. I thank all who provided background briefings. For instance, former Foreign Secretary and Ambassador M. Rasgotra, Ambassadors K.S. Bajpai, Chinmaya Gharekhan, Chandrashekhar Dasgupta, Kuldip Sahdev, Ronen Sen and former Foreign Secretary and National Security Adviser Shivshankar Menon.

Former Foreign Secretary and Ambassador Shyam Saran, former Secretary (Economic Affairs), Chief Economic Adviser and Deputy Governor RBI Dr Rakesh Mohan, former Chief Economic Adviser Dr Shankar Acharya and well-known chairman of *Business Standard* and journalist T.N. Ninan took the time to look through the manuscript and provide detailed comments.

Ambassador Rakesh Sood and Manoj Raman are friends from my student days. Rakesh and I were first together at St Stephen's College and then in the Indian Foreign Service. Manoj studied with me at Tufts University and is widely read. Both have done me the favour of reading through the manuscript and putting me right on a number of issues.

Most of this book was written while I was the Reserve Bank of India chair professor at the Indian Council for Research on International Economic Relations (ICRIER). I thank Shuheb Khan, Mohit Srivastava, Ramakrishna Reddy, Barkha Gupta and Akshaya Aggarwal, research associates at the ICRIER, for assisting me in tabulating the numbers.

This book would not have been possible without the active encouragement of my wife Rita, former Reserve Bank of India and World Bank economist, and daughter Jahnavi, an investment banker with a flair for poetry. Rita painstakingly read through the manuscript line by line and made detailed suggestions both on content and idiom. My younger brother Dr Satyakam Bhagwati is a neurologist based in New York, and he gave me useful feedback.

I dedicate this book to my father Bijoy Chandra Bhagwati who spent over seven years of his youth, on three separate occasions, in jails in Assam[1] during India's freedom struggle. Among his achievements in pre-independent India was the mobilization of Assam tea garden labour to form trade unions. These unions were later able to successfully bargain with tea estate owners to obtain pensions, healthcare and education benefits. The Assam Chah Karamchari Sangh (Tea Workers' Union) was set up on 9 February 1947 in Tinsukia in upper Assam. This trade union was and continues to be headquartered in Dibrugarh, and they have erected a monument, in front of the deputy commissioner's office, in my father's name with his bust in stone. He was the first president of the Chah Karamchari Sangh.[2]

Assam narrowly escaped becoming part of East Pakistan at the time of Partition. Gopinath Bordoloi was the premier of Assam and was in correspondence for some time with Nehru about this matter. Jinnah argued strenuously that Assam, with a higher proportion of Muslim population, should belong to East Pakistan. It is likely that Jinnah was also swayed by the consideration that Assam, with its lower density of population, tea gardens, coal, bamboo and oil, would complement East Pakistan demographically and economically. Bordoloi wrote several times to Nehru and was concerned that Jinnah may win the argument. On 17 December 1946, Bordoloi sent Mahendra Mohan Choudhury[3] and my father to Noakhali to appeal to Gandhi (Gandhi was then in Noakhali to douse communal fires). Gandhi's only question to Choudhury and my father was whether an overwhelming majority of the people of Assam wanted to be part of India. Since their reply was in the affirmative, Gandhi remarked that Assam needed to 'lodge its protest and retire from the Constituent Assembly. It will be a kind of Satyagraha against the Congress for the good of the Congress.'[4]

Gandhi asked my father to draft a note which would explain the Mahatma's advice in this matter. Subsequently, this note appeared in the press on 23 December 1946.[5] Nehru is said to have shown the Mahatma's advice to Jinnah who then gave up on Assam. It was by that slender thread of chance that Assam is today proudly a part of India.

My father was elected unopposed to the Lok Sabha from Tezpur in Assam in 1957, 1962 and then in 1967 by a considerable margin. Later he was a member of the Rajya Sabha from 1971 to 1977 and was the president of the Indian National Trade Union Congress (INTUC) from 1971 to 1988.

I also offer this book as homage to my mother Bimal Bhagwati, a tireless perfectionist, who wrote widely read short stories in Assamese and translated *The Spirit's Pilgrimage*, the 1960 autobiography of Madeleine Slade,[6] into Assamese. She won a Sahitya Akademi award for translating V.S. Khandekar's Jnanpith award-winning 1959 Marathi novel *Yayati* into Assamese.

INTRODUCTION

Each Indian prime minister inherited a set of advantages and constraints. In the case of independent India's first PM, Jawaharlal Nehru, a defining advantage at home was an environment of sacrifice and honesty of purpose engendered by the examples of Mahatma Gandhi and other leaders of the freedom movement. Most of the leading freedom fighters were well educated—several had trained as lawyers in the UK—and spoke and wrote English fluently, and were admired for their integrity as individuals.

The following sections set out the economic, strategic and social context in which Nehru assumed office.

Colonial Era and Indian Resurgence

The British came to India under the aegis of the East India Company in the seventeenth century. They drained capital out of India for almost two centuries after the victory of Robert Clive in the Battle of Plassey in 1756 till Indian independence, causing a steady decline in the relative size of the Indian economy. In 1820 India had 20.1 per cent of the world's population and 16 per cent of its economic output. By 1950 India's share of population came down to 14.2 per cent, but the size of its economy fell more sharply to 4.2 per cent of world output.[1]

Over time the technical skills, and consequently the productivity of Indians, eroded in comparison to those of workers in Western nations. Of course, India as it was territorially constituted in 1947, did not exist in 1820. It can be argued that India, with different ethnicities, multiple scripts and varying cultures, would never have banded together as one country without unified colonial administration. Irrespective of such speculation, it is a fact that the economic benefits of the Industrial Revolution did not spread deep or wide enough in British-ruled India.

In the social sphere, the British exacerbated differences between Hindus and Muslims through various policies including the Minto–Morley reforms. The Indian Councils Act of 1909—or the reforms enacted by Secretary of State John Morley and Viceroy Lord Minto—included provisions for assured representation for Muslims. In personal correspondence, on 28 May 1906, Minto wrote to Morley: 'I have been thinking a good deal lately of a possible counterpoise to Congress aims. I think we may find a solution in the Council of Princes . . .' On 23 November 1906, Morley wrote back to Minto: 'I incline to think that the admission of a Native, whether to your Council or to mine, or to both, would be the cheapest concession we could make.'[2] Clearly, the British looked for the 'cheapest' way for them to accommodate the desire of 'Natives' to be represented in the governance of British India. Britain has never had separate seats for local bodies or the House of Commons based on religion, race or economic backwardness. Consequently, the conclusion has to be that this was a way for the British to counter the Congress objective of working towards self-rule and ultimately full independence.

For probably the same reason of creating durable fissures in Indian society and thus delaying independence, the Scheduled Castes (SCs) and Tribes (STs) were also granted separate constituencies under the Government of India Act of 1935 and were referred to by the British as Depressed Classes. A *Journal of Asian Studies* paper by Francesca R. Jensenius titled 'Mired in Reservations: The Path-Dependent History of Electoral Quotas in India'[3] and her doctoral dissertation in the University of California, Berkeley,[4] traces reservations for religious minorities and Dalits since the beginning of the twentieth century.[5] The British provided for separate constituencies for Dalits, ostensibly to help them overcome disadvantages stemming from centuries of social and economic discrimination. However, B.R. Ambedkar felt that reservation of seats for Dalits (SCs) in joint electorates was not helpful since elected Dalit candidates remained beholden to the majority communities. Nevertheless, the Constituent Assembly approved reserved seats for Dalits (SCs) with joint electorates. Reservation of seats for Muslims or other minorities was not approved.[6]

Commenting on the adverse consequences of the separation of electoral constituencies, Nehru wrote in *The Discovery of India*[7]

There were vested interests enough in India created or preserved by the British Government. Now an additional and powerful vested interest was created by separate electorates . . . There came into existence [much later] separate Muslim trade unions and students' organisations and merchants' chambers. [The separate electorates] . . . created divisions and ill feeling where there had been none previously, and it actually weakened the favoured group by increasing a tendency to depend on artificial props and not to think in terms of self-reliance. The obvious policy in dealing with groups or minorities which were backward educationally and economically was to help them in every way to grow and make up these deficiencies, especially by a forward educational policy . . . The whole argument centred in petty appointments in the subordinate public services, and instead of raising standards all round merit was often sacrificed. These electorates, first introduced among Muslims, spread to other minorities and groups till India became a mosaic of these separate compartments.

The counter view is that reservations of electoral constituencies, and subsequently jobs in the government and public sector, and seats in educational institutions, were and are still needed. The argument that centuries, if not millennia, of caste-based discrimination has made the lower castes and marginalized communities unable to participate equally in open competition is valid up to a point.

Reservations for SCs and STs was followed by additional reservations for 'Other Backward Classes' (OBCs), implemented in 1993. In recent years, various groups have sought to be included in this category of OBCs or even Scheduled Castes/Tribes. The National Democratic Alliance (NDA) headed by Narendra Modi had introduced an additional 10 per cent reservations for 'Economically Weaker Sections' (EWSs) without reference to caste or religion. Parliament had passed the required legislation, and the Indian President signed the legislation amending Articles 15 and 16 of the Constitution to provide for this quota for EWSs. With this latest addition, the total for all reservations has risen to 59.5 per cent.

According to a Supreme Court ruling, quotas cannot exceed a ceiling of 50 per cent since that would be inconsistent with equality for all Indian citizens as articulated in the Constitution. As of May 2019, the Supreme Court had not yet ruled on whether this latest legislation granting 10 per cent reservation for EWSs is consistent with the Indian Constitution or not. Irrespective of arguments for and against reservations and what could be better ways to help those who are 'backward' because of their caste, social and economic background, the fact is that this issue has become intensely politicized. The approach of several segments among those who benefit and those who do not is quite cynical. This book tracks the levels of cynicism that influences the government's policies, and Indian society in general, and hence this brief discussion about this highly controversial issue.

Mahatma Gandhi took charge of the 'Swaraj' or self-rule campaign at the start of the 1920s, and as it spread all over the country, it was combined with social reform causes. To undermine this push for independence, the British promoted doubts about the viability of India as one nation. The logic was that given the multiplicity of languages, cultures and religions, and the fact that it had never been one country with the cartographical contours of British India, such a nation could not hold. Spokesmen for the British government also conjectured whether democracy would be the appropriate form of government.

Although several divisive colonial-era policies had adverse long-term consequences, the British did set up educational institutions in South Asia which fostered pioneering scientific work. For example, Satyendra Nath Bose (of Bose–Einstein statistics fame) did most of his research in quantum mechanics in the 1920s in Dacca. Meghnad Saha, an astrophysicist (known for the Saha ionization equation), worked in Allahabad and Kolkata from the 1930s till the 1950s. C.V. Raman taught in Kolkata and won the Nobel Prize for physics in 1930 for his work on scattering of light.

British-built structures in India, funded fully by locally raised revenues, were grand in design and execution to emphasize colonial might. In Delhi, the President's house (built for the British viceroy), the office complexes of North and South blocks and the Parliament house were completed by 1929. Independent India has built little to compare with precolonial India or British-built structures in its large cities or cantonment towns.

Roots of India's Stable Democracy

It was apparent to Bal Gangadhar Tilak, Gopal Krishna Gokhale, Mahatma Gandhi, Nehru and other leaders of the Indian freedom movement that the effort to dislodge the British had to include Indians developing a sense of unity and dignity about themselves and their history. To provide a more self-assured picture to internal and external audiences, stalwarts of the freedom struggle spoke and wrote prolifically about India's long history of scientific, architectural, spiritual and cultural achievements. The divisive elements in today's India often forget just how difficult it was to forge this sense of unity and self-respect among Indians across the country.

The suspicions and animosities born out of ages of internecine and debilitating infighting across Indian sub-nationalities due to differences in wealth, social and religious practices had contributed in large part to India's colonial bondage. Mahatma Gandhi's humility and empathy enabled him to perceive the inner peace, resilience and unifying elements in the mosaic of India's toiling and impoverished millions. Gandhi was able to enthuse the masses and motivate better-placed Indians and also a host of exceptionally gifted and driven leaders who could relate intellectually and emotionally to his ideals.

Gandhi believed that India lives in its villages, and we can only speculate as to why he felt Nehru from the urban elite should lead the Congress party and become India's first PM. Maybe because although there is wisdom and continuity in India's villages, there is also much that is backward, including extreme forms of social discrimination and prejudice towards lower castes, religious minorities and women. Gandhi was able to encourage the Indian masses to band together against the injustices of British colonialism. It is likely that Gandhi sensed that independent India needed a PM who would continue with the task of leading the people to rise above partisan politics of community, caste and religion. He judged that Nehru had the required qualities of head, and most importantly, heart, to build a prosperous India at peace with itself and the rest of the world. Since Nehru was Gandhi's choice, his position as first among equals was readily accepted by Sardar Patel and other leaders of the freedom struggle.

Given the trying experience of long jail terms during British rule, India's first cabinet included leaders who were used to facing adversity with dignity and self-discipline. However, most ministers had limited administrative experience. Their individual success was determined by the ability to build competent teams at a time when there were few Indian professionals with technical or senior managerial experience. In 1937 the Congress party formed governments in seven provinces under the Government of India Act of 1935. The following year, the Congress, led at that time by Subhas Chandra Bose, set up a National Planning Committee with Nehru as its chairman. The need for socialist planning was emphasized by several Congress leaders of that era, including Bose. Before Independence, the non-agriculture part of the Indian economy consisted mostly of textiles, jute products, coal, iron and steel. The Second World War gave a boost to the production of chemicals and shipbuilding.

Continuing Dependence on a Partisan UK

In the run-up to the partition of India, senior UK officials felt that it would be ideal if the two newly independent countries were to cooperate with the UK. However, if that was not possible, 'the majority of our [UK's] strategic requirements could be met, though with considerably greater difficulty by an agreement with Pakistan alone'.[8]

At Independence, India had little autonomy in defence matters as most of its military hardware was from the UK, and petroleum supplies were obtained via UK companies. The top generals in the Indian Army were British when confrontations took place with Pakistani raiders and irregulars in Kashmir. Specifically, the Indian Army was headed by Field Marshal Auchinleck, and the commander in chief was General Lockhart. General K.M. Cariappa took over as the first Indian chief of army staff five months after Independence on 15 January 1948. The air[9] and naval[10] wings were headed by British officers who continued to be based in India for many more years till March 1954 and April 1958 respectively.[11]

The importance of air power and oil as the fuel of choice had become evident during the course of the Second World War. Consequently, by 1947 the discovery of huge oil deposits in the Gulf and West Asia had enhanced the importance of these regions. The fact that these oil-rich regions were made up of Muslim-majority countries had a bearing on the British and later US tilt towards Pakistan on the Kashmir issue. Another reason for the UK and the US siding with Pakistan was that it was smaller than India, and they felt that it would seek third-power intervention in disputes with India or others, and would be more amenable to providing military bases on its territory. British officers who continued as heads of the armed forces of India and Pakistan after Independence were often in touch with each other through cables and phone calls without keeping the prime ministers of India and Pakistan informed. India's attitude towards West Asia and the Gulf region too was influenced by concern about Arab sentiment which was against the partition of Palestine. India received Israel's formal request for recognition in May 1948 and then took over two years to recognize Israel by September 1950.

In a nutshell, Nehru started with a country which had never existed with the geographical boundaries India came to have at Independence. British India was torn apart into India and Pakistan—the latter included parts of Punjab (West) and Bengal (East)—in the wake of communal violence in 1946 and 1947. About a million people were killed and many millions displaced during Partition mostly in Punjab and Bengal. The thousands of cases of forced conversions and rape inflamed passions on both sides. On the Pakistani side, it was felt that the Indian government's armed interventions in Hyderabad and Junagadh were stage-managed and unfair. There was bickering at the working levels of the two governments on how the assets of British India would be shared. Among the populations at large, the feelings of antipathy between India and Pakistan have festered and persisted; this continues to be true particularly in northern India, where refugees from West Pakistan had settled. The total number of refugees who came to India from West and East Pakistan was around 15 million. Partition was a cataclysmic event that continues to impact postcolonial India's South Asian and international interactions till today.

I

PANDIT JAWAHARLAL NEHRU

Unparalleled Nation Builder, Caring Yet Distant Leader

On 21 June 1954, about ten years before he passed away, Jawaharlal Nehru[1] penned his last Will and Testament. The following are a few lines from that Will:

'. . . A handful of my ashes be thrown into the Ganga at Allahabad to be carried to the great ocean that washes India's shore . . . The major portion of my ashes . . . be carried high up into the air . . . And scattered from that height over the fields where the peasants of India toil, so that they may mingle with the dust and soil of India and become an indistinguishable part of India.'

On 2 September 1946, with Gandhi's blessings and popular acclaim, Jawaharlal Nehru became the vice-president of the Viceroy's Executive Council. He took over as PM on 15 August 1947, taking charge of the first-ever pan-India government headquartered in Delhi, three months short of reaching fifty-eight years of age. The retirement age in the Indian government till 1998 was fifty-eight. Given the incessant travel to distant locations in the Indian subcontinent by train, car and on foot, lengthy jail terms and the tensions of being one of the leaders of the freedom movement, Nehru must have felt older than the average fifty-eight-year-old Indian in 1947.

Nehru had not held a job nor practised law for any length of time. He had no experience of administering a small office, let alone overseeing the management of India's development while maintaining internal security in the country and guarding against external threats. Nehru was elected thrice to the Lok Sabha in 1952, 1957 and 1962, and each time he won from the Phulpur constituency in Uttar Pradesh (UP).

1

The preservation of the unity and integrity of India was uppermost in Nehru's mind all through the years that he was PM. This was an issue he repeatedly touched upon during every address he made on Independence Day from the ramparts of the Red Fort. It sounds trite today, but even eleven years after Independence on 15 August 1958, he felt the need to ask the nation to 'take up the challenge of all forces which might seek to weaken the country's unity and freedom'.[2] Although English was the dominant language in decision-making circles in India at that time, Nehru did set a tradition of PMs speaking in Hindi on 15 August from the Red Fort.

At Independence, the provinces and princely states of the colonial era had yet to be integrated into one country. The difficulties that the newly formed Indian government had to overcome to forge the country territorially into one nation have been much discussed in many publications. What is less remembered is that in August 1942, the British had put into effect the Armed Forces Special Powers Ordinance to put down the Quit India movement. This was the precursor to the Armed Forces (Special Powers) Act (AFSPA) of 1948. This Act was repealed in 1957 but was re-enacted in 1958. The Nagas had declared independence in 1951 and boycotted the first general election in 1952. AFSPA's origins lie in the Central government's determination to maintain territorial integrity by keeping rebellious areas of the North-east within India.

In 1947 India did not have the structures, institutions and mechanisms which are at the core of a democracy. Nehru and his colleagues started from scratch to achieve consensus in the deliberations of the Constituent Assembly to adopt a forward-looking Constitution. One important element was the supremacy of the political executive over the armed forces. It was clear from the start that the armed forces would report to the defence minister, and through that office to the PM. The heads of the three services, namely army, air force and navy, were made co-equals. And Nehru as PM took over the residence of the former British commander in chief at Teen Murti House.

Administration after Independence

After India was partitioned, there was continuing violence within India as it was being put together, and there were external threats. Two of the several stalwarts in Nehru's cabinet were Sardar Vallabhbhai Patel and Dr B.R. Ambedkar. Sardar Patel, who was born in 1875, was fourteen years older than Nehru and was from a humbler economic background in rural Gujarat. Patel was self-taught, and by the time he was thirty-six years old, had saved enough to study law at Middle Temple Inn in London. He returned to practise law in Ahmedabad and joined the freedom struggle in 1917.

At seventy-two years of age in 1947, Sardar Patel was India's first minister for home and the states. He was the pragmatic, strong-willed and undisputed architect of the integration of India. As is well known, there were several hiccups; for example, the incorporation of Junagadh and Hyderabad and the battle for Kashmir. Additionally, integrating the provinces with the princely states looked like an impossible task at Independence.[3] Post 1947, Patel's relationship with Nehru was marked by 'frankness and loyalty'.[4]

After Gandhi was assassinated on 30 January 1948, Sardar Patel was criticized for not having provided adequate security to the Mahatma in the heart of New Delhi. Three days after Gandhi's death, Nehru wrote to Patel on 3 February 1948: 'My dear Vallabhbhai, with Bapu's death, we have to face a different and more difficult world. I have been greatly distressed by the persistence of whispers about you and me, magnifying out of all proportion any differences we may have . . . I think it is my duty, and I may venture to say yours also, for us to face it together as friends and colleagues, not merely superficially but in full loyalty to one another and with confidence in one another.' Sardar Patel responded two days later on 5 February, 'I am deeply touched, indeed overwhelmed by . . . your letter. The paramount interests of our country and our mutual love and regard, transcending such differences of outlook and temperament as existed, have held us together. I had the good fortune to have a last talk with Bapu for over an hour just before his death. His opinion also binds us both.'[5]

Patel was frank in conveying on which issues he disagreed with Nehru. Patel's loyalty to Nehru was based on his clear-headed understanding that for the government to function efficiently, Nehru's decisions as the head of government had to be respected. Although Patel suffered a major heart attack in March 1948, just seven months after Independence, he was indispensable till he passed away in December 1950.

The story of how Dr B.R. Ambedkar pulled himself up from his discriminated and deprived social and economic background is not only inspirational but magical. He went for his higher studies to the UK and the US and earned doctoral degrees from reputed institutions. Dr Ambedkar's contributions as one of the principal authors of the Indian Constitution, and as a social reformer, are folklore in India.

Among the other senior figures, C. Rajagopalachari became the minister for home affairs after Patel passed away, and he held that office till October 1951. Thereafter, he left for Tamil Nadu, his home state, due to differences with Nehru on relations between the Congress party and the communists and sundry other issues. This divergence of views between the two leaders may have been due to a south-north difference in perception about the left parties. By the early 1950s, the communists had established an electoral presence in Tamil Nadu and Kerala and were nowhere nearly as significant in the northern states.

During Nehru's years as PM, the Congress party had a comfortable majority in the Lok Sabha and Rajya Sabha. Nehru was his own foreign minister for the seventeen years that he was PM and was also the minister for atomic energy.

One of the many immediate difficulties that the new Indian government was confronted with was an extreme shortage of competent officers and technical experts. On the civil administration front, an important question was about what was to be done with the Indian Civil Service (ICS), which used to be referred to as the 'steel frame' which had kept India together. In 1947 there were about 980 ICS officers and of these 468 were British. Most of the well qualified among the British went back to the UK. Of the remaining 512 ICS officers, 101 were Muslim and ninety-five of them opted for Pakistan.

It is evident from the memoirs of ICS officers[6] that the two overriding concerns of the pre-1947 British administration were timely collection of land revenue, taxes and prevention/prosecution of crime. However, despite the much-vaunted abilities of the ICS and their politically appointed British supervisors, they were spectators to the communal violence in Punjab and Bengal between 1946 and 1948. Nehru had remarked in his 1936 autobiography that among 'those who have served in the Indian Civil Service or other imperial services there will be many, Indians or foreigners, who will be necessary and welcome to the new order. But of one thing I am quite sure: that no *new* [emphasis added] order can be built up in India so long as the spirit of the Indian Civil Service pervades our administration and our public services.' In *The Discovery of India*, Nehru commented that 'they [ICS] had no training to function democratically and could not gain the goodwill and cooperation of the people . . . it was extraordinary how unfit they were for the new tasks that faced them.'

Opinion was divided in the Constituent Assembly about allowing ICS officers to continue in government after Independence. Sardar Patel was vehemently in favour of honouring the agreement that the Congress party had reached with the British government. The Indian Independence Act passed by the British Parliament contained service protection clauses for the ICS, and Sardar Patel argued in favour of retaining the ICS in the following terms at the Constituent Assembly discussions.

'I wish to place it on record in this House that if, during the last two or three years, most of the members of the services had not behaved patriotically and with loyalty, the Union would have collapsed . . . Is there any Premier in any province who is prepared to work without the Services? What did Gandhiji teach us? You are talking of Gandhian ideology and Gandhian philosophy and Gandhian way of administration. Very good. But you come out of jail and then say—these men put me in jail. Let me take revenge. That is not the Gandhian way. It is going far away from that . . .'[7]

The inconsistency in Sardar Patel's logic was that the ICS, which had felt little empathy for the freedom struggle, was now to be entrusted with development in independent India, and was deemed capable of supervising and overruling specialists. These specialists were, for example, engineers of the Central Public Works Department (CPWD was set up in 1854 and took its present form in 1930), surveyors and architects of the Indian Army, scientists from the regional laboratories and the Council for Scientific and Industrial Research (CSIR was set up in 1942). This issue about generalists and specialists had been debated since 1857 within the administrative circles of British India. The British finally decided that overall, in other words politically and financially important, decisions should be left to generalist administrators. This worked well for the British in transferring wealth back home. To an extent, ICS officers continuing in senior positions in the central and state governments was inevitable and less harmful than experimenting with newly recruited officers who had no experience of working in government or regulatory positions. However, India persisting with exactly the same administrative structures and practices left by the British sapped efforts to build a new country focused on development. Nehru and others in the Central and state governments needed to put together teams of administrators and specialists who cared deeply about development for all Indians.

Mark Tully, the long-time BBC bureau chief in India, is now living in Delhi. On the unfortunate similarity between the pre-Independence ICS and Indian Police (IP), and post-Independence Indian Administrative Service (IAS) and the Indian Police Service (IPS) respectively, Tully has commented[8] that:

The world's largest democracy is still governed and administered by the institutions of the British Raj. The Indian Administrative Service, which dominates the administration, is a carbon copy of the Raj's ICS, and the Indian Police Service is a carbon copy of the Indian Police. Macaulay's Penal Code is still in force. The hired witnesses who used to testify in favour of the Raj now testify before magistrates in favour of independent India's police . . . The poor [destitute] regard the police and courts as their oppressors.

Although Tully's observations are somewhat sweeping, they hold a kernel of truth. Many officers become indifferent to the plight of the marginalized because of the inefficient, uncaring administrative and legal framework within which they work, but there are substantial differences at the individual level.

The British administration's policies in India were tailored to maintain law and order rather than push economic and social development. Post Independence, it is the implementation of development programmes which has been inadequate. Human development indicators such as literacy, infant mortality, life expectancy and per capita income were very low in 1947. Political leaders such as Nehru at the Centre in Delhi and chief ministers (CMs) in the states were well aware of the formidable challenges ahead in improving these indicators for the masses. However, implementation of government policies was in the hands of administrators, and the ICS did not have adequate understanding or empathy to push the everyday agenda of safe drinking water and primary education.

The political service, which was entirely reserved for British nationals before independence, was converted to the Indian Foreign Service (IFS). From 1947 to 1950, selection to the IFS was done mostly through word-of-mouth recommendations. In those early years, Nehru personally interviewed new entrants to the Foreign Service. Consequently, Nehru knew IFS officers personally and would often walk from his office on the first floor of South Block (Rashtrapati Bhawan end) across (in the Vijay Chowk direction) to the offices of secretaries in the foreign office.

In former Foreign Secretary M. Rasgotra's[9] opinion, too many ICS officers were inducted into the Indian Foreign Service. About Nehru's ambassadorial appointments, he feels that Vijaya Lakshmi Pandit[10] was a success in the UK but not in the USSR or the US. Rasgotra's sense is that Nehru was an idealist but lacked experience in 'realpolitik'. A counter to that point of view could be that during the freedom struggle, many compromises had to be made by the Congress with the British and Nehru had participated in that give and take. Former Ambassador K.S. Bajpai feels[11] that the ICS was too influenced by the British world view. Coming from him, this was a startling observation since his father Sir G.S. Bajpai joined the United Provinces (Uttar Pradesh) cadre of the ICS in 1915.

A fair alternative would have been to give ICS officers the choice of leaving in 1947 or serving for fifteen years till 1962, with generous retirement benefits under both options. Fifteen years would have been enough time for fresh recruits selected through Union Public Service Commission (UPSC) examinations and lateral entrants with specialist skills to bring themselves up to speed.

Most of the institutions basic to parliamentary democracy were set up after Independence. For instance, the Election Commission (25 January 1950), the Supreme Court (28 January 1950) and the Reserve Bank of India (RBI)[12] (January 1949) were established at arm's-length from government and made functionally autonomous.

Nehru's first visit to the Soviet Union in 1927, along with his father, wife and sister, Vijaya Lakshmi Pandit, seems to have convinced him about the benefits of centralized planning. On the Russian example, Nehru said in one of his circular letters to CMs dated 15 August 1949 that 'Russia gives us a very complicated picture, much of which we like and much of which we dislike [lack of democracy]'. In the same letter, Nehru mentions that 'it is careful planning that both Russia and Japan have to teach us', and 'the State should help in this planning on a large scale, even though a great part of our national economy be left to private enterprise'.

Accordingly, the Planning Commission was set up with the PM as chairman on 15 March 1950 under a cabinet resolution. That is, it did not have a statutory or constitutional status. Among the reasons for the resignation of the then Finance Minister John Mathai after the presentation of the budget in 1950 was the setting up of the Planning Commission. Mathai felt that this commission would dilute the powers of the finance ministry.

Deputy chairpersons of the Planning Commission were usually well-known political figures and only occasionally economists. As the end purpose of the Planning Commission was to make the allocation of funding goal-oriented, it would have made sense to rely more on technocrats rather than serving politicians. The definitive political input was provided by Nehru anyway since he chaired the Planning Commission's meetings. However, after Nehru, the commission gradually lost its initial sheen, and its voice was drowned out in the din of the shorter-term considerations of the PM in office.

The first Finance Commission (FC), a constitutional body, was set up in 1952. The FC is not a standing body, and its members are changed and terms of reference are set every five years. The FC's primary task is to allocate tax revenues between the central and state governments. Over the decades, the FC became increasingly mindful and more sophisticated about considerations such as population and per capita income.[13]

The National Development Council (NDC) was set up by Nehru in 1952, under a decision taken by the Union cabinet. This council consisted of the PM as chairman and the entire Central government cabinet and all CMs as members. This was another demonstration of Nehru trying to reach out to all shades of opinion within the Central government and all corners of the country to formulate effective national development policies. In the seven years between 1952 and 1959, the NDC held thirteen meetings, but over the decades, the meetings have decreased in frequency, coming down to less than one a year by 2014.[14]

Several other well-known institutions which have served India well in the collation and analysis of economic data were set up during the Nehru years. For example, the Indian Statistical Institute (ISI), National Council for Applied Economic Research (NCAER), Indian Institute for Public Administration (IIPA), Central Statistical Organisation (CSO) and National Sample Survey. The University Grants Commission (UGC) was set up under an Act of Parliament in 1957.

Turning to heavy industry, the 1955 and 1964 steel plants at Bhilai in Jharkhand and at Bokaro in Chhattisgarh were set up in collaboration with the USSR. The UK helped set up the Durgapur steel plant in West Bengal in 1955, and the Rourkela steel plant in Orissa was set up in 1959 with assistance from Germany. The US was conspicuous by its absence from collaborative efforts in heavy industry or infrastructure during the Nehru years. It may be that the Bokaro plant was offered to the US first, but since it was to be set up in the public sector the US side refused.

The British had left behind an extensive network of railway tracks. Table 1.1 in the Appendices details the increase in the length of tracks from 1947 till 2016. In summary, from a total of 55,000 kilometres of tracks, this number increased over seventeen years, from Independence till Nehru passed away in May 1964, to about 88,970 kilometres. That is an increase of 62 per cent. By March 2016, the length of tracks had risen to 119,630 kilometres, which is an increase of just 35 per cent in the fifty-two years since 1964.

As for electricity generation and irrigation, the Hirakud dam, close to Sambalpur in Orissa, was inaugurated by Nehru in 1957. The plans for the Bhakra dam were conceived prior to Independence, and this hydroelectric project was completed in October 1963. In words that continue to resonate, Nehru called Bhakra one of 'the temples' of modern India. Work on the Nagarjuna dam on the Krishna river in Andhra Pradesh began in 1955 and was completed by 1967. The Damodar river had a history of over a century of causing severe flooding in West Bengal and Jharkhand, and the Damodar Valley Corporation (DVC) was set up in 1948 and was modelled on the Tennessee Valley Authority in the US. DVC constructed dams on the Damodar river, and power generation began by 1953. These are a few examples of the long-gestation projects which were either initiated or completed during Nehru's tenure as PM.

Economic Inheritance

Despite evidence to the contrary, an abiding incorrect perception about Nehru's economic policies is that he alone was the initiator of protectionism in India and that he single-handedly set up a highly damaging socialist model with centralized planning as the mainstay. A little history will help in clearing this misunderstanding. Prior to Independence, the first Indian Fiscal Commission appointed in 1921 recommended protection for select industries.[15] Subsequently, between 1923 and 1939, in an era of administratively determined exchange rates, the Indian Tariff Board's deliberations led to higher import duties for a variety of items including iron and steel, cotton textiles, sugar, paper and gold thread. For some of these products, cheap raw material was first sourced from India. It was in this environment of colonial economic exploitation that the Congress party leaders became followers of the Swadeshi movement led by Gandhi. It was considered a national duty to promote local production of cloth, textiles and other products to generate employment and retain a greater share of the value added within the country.

The image on page 10 is an advertisement from a shop in Lahore in the 1930s. After Independence, the Congress party continued to mistakenly perceive import substitution as a patriotic duty that promoted local employment.

In 1947, India was a country of about 350 million people, an overwhelming majority of whom lived on subsistence agriculture, with relatively little manufacturing or industrial development. Nehru was convinced that the road out of poverty for India's masses was by adopting a government-driven, but not a totally government-owned, economic model. In the Constituent Assembly debates, Nehru had affirmed that his government would not nationalize existing Indian or foreign private-sector firms. Even a cursory examination of Nehru's writings indicates that he wanted the state to take charge of what the private sector could not or did not want to get into.

Several well-known economists of that era were doubtful about the prospects of trade-led growth for developing countries. For instance, the well-known Argentinian economist Raul Prebisch, first head of UNESCO (United Nations Educational Scientific and Cultural Organization), felt that terms of trade would be unfavourable for products from developing countries. The Prebisch Singer hypothesis[16] was that the prices of primary commodities decline over time compared to manufactured items, and hence the terms of trade deteriorate for developing countries that produce primary commodities. Nehru's scepticism about trade was based on this line of thinking in the specialist circles of that time.

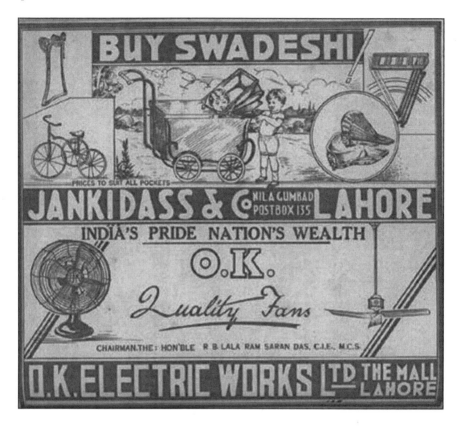

The major Indian business houses such as the Birlas and Tatas had gradually come to be identified with the freedom struggle. Gandhi consulted them often and accepted their support. A couple of years before Independence, in 1944, several leading industrialists of that time, including J.R.D. Tata, G.D. Birla, Lala Shri Ram, Purshottam Thakurdas, Ardeshir Dalal, Kasturbhai Lalbhai and John Mathai came up with what came to be known as the Bombay Plan.[17] This plan conceived of raising economic growth rates through government investment for long-gestation projects. Effectively, the captains of private industry, who were the authors of the Bombay Plan, indicated that they did not have the capital or the risk appetite to make the required investments to push growth above pre-Independence levels.

The Indian private sector also pushed the infant industry argument for protective tariff and non-tariff import barriers. As scarcities persisted and there was enough evidence of hoarding, the environment of permits, licences, controls and foreign exchange restrictions of the Second World War years was continued or tightened after 1947. The fact that the private sector of that time looked to the government to take the lead in raising investment levels indicates that Nehru had less elbow room than is currently claimed, and had to necessarily plan for a large role for government in the economy.

Several of the draconian pieces of economic legislation post Independence had their origins in the Defence of India Act of 1915 which was further tightened in its 1939 version. During the Second World War, in the UK the government ran several of the utilities, including power, water and public transport. Consequently, towards the end of the war, the thinking in UK government circles, even among the Conservatives, including Churchill, was that in post-war Britain, not just the private sector but also 'state enterprises', should play an important role in providing employment and rebuilding the country. In a paper in the *Journal of Comparative Economics*, Rakesh Mohan and Vandana Aggarwal have linked the origins of industrial licensing in India to the controls imposed during the war years.[18]

The Labour party came back to power in the UK in 1945, and this government nationalized coal, iron and steel, railroads, utilities and international telecommunications. The Bank of England (central bank) was nationalized in 1946. The UK's Labour party borrowed the term 'commanding heights' of the economy, which is attributed to Lenin by Daniel Yergin and Joseph Stanislaw in their 1998 book.[19] That is, Britain moved sharply towards the left in the wake of the Second World War, and this must have influenced the thinking of the British-educated Indian elite.

Licence–Permit Raj, Socialism and Planning

Nehru is often charged as the villain of the piece for instituting the so-called 'licence–permit' raj. This accusation is made by many among today's Indian elite with little patience to look up the circumstances and constraints under which India was born. It bears repeating that Indians were deeply scarred in the decade prior to Independence by economic distress, communal killings and physical displacement caused by the Bengal famine, the Second World War and Partition. India was at abysmally low levels of public health, literacy and per capita income. The average life expectancy was about thirty-two years, literacy was 12 per cent, and per capita income was Rupees 247.5 in 1950–51.[20]

The subsequent two decades through the 1950s and the 1960s were marked by food scarcities and constant worries about pockets of starvation. All things considered, it was to the fledgling Indian government's credit that there was no widespread famine anywhere in India during Nehru's years as PM.

To put matters in perspective, renowned economists often disagree vehemently with each other about should have been done and when. As for the rest of the world, they mock economists for their collective lack of foresight, for example, about the 2008 financial-sector breakdown. This was yet another instance of market failure which has resulted in a decline in economic growth rates in developed Western countries from trend levels for more than a decade now and counting.[21]

During the Nehru years, economic activity was mostly in the private sector. Therefore, the assertion that Indian growth rates were low during the first two decades after Independence because a high proportion of the economy was government owned is factually incorrect. For instance, agriculture was and for that matter even in May 2019 remains mostly private. Only with the nationalization of banks in 1969 did the public sector come to have a substantial share of the services sector. Railways was mostly in the public sector from before Independence. In manufacturing, the public-sector units engaged in the production of steel, power, cement and fertilizers gained in size only from the late 1950s onwards. It is from the late 1960s, after Nehru's demise, that the share of the public sector in the national economy rose to sizeable proportions.

At Nehru's request, a committee of economists presented their *Report on the Economic Situation in India* to the cabinet[22] on 22 August 1948. That is, within a year of Independence, this committee took stock of the economy and provided their recommendations. The report was classified 'Secret', and such a classification can be questioned. However, some of the recommendations involved market-sensitive information; for instance, that interest rates should be raised (this was an era when interest rates were driven by the government's views). The relevant point to note is that Nehru tried to consult Indian economists from around the country.

In the committee's assessment, the most important 'aspect of the economic crisis' that the country faced was 'rising prices'. Among the principal reasons for this were 'continuous inflation of the currency during the war period', and 'continued budget deficits at the Centre on both revenue and capital accounts . . . aggravated by deficit budgets in most of the Provinces during the current year', and 'unplanned removal of *controls* on prices and distribution of essential goods' (emphasis added). Among the remedies suggested to boost government's access to private savings was to make small savings attractive by offering a 'higher rate of interest than that now given on negotiable bonds of equal duration . . . export controls should be exercised'. In addition, the committee recommended that there should be a freeze on salaries and wages, and a new system of 'controls of prices and distribution of cotton and cloth should be elaborated'. As for industry, the suggestion was that 'Government should lay down for each major industry and establishments therein a programme of production and production targets'. It is evident that this group of eminent economists of that time was in favour of extensive government controls on interest rates, production and prices.

With remarkable swiftness, just a day later, Nehru wrote to all premiers (later called chief ministers) on 23 August 1948 detailing the recommendations of this report and adding his own thoughts. It is a reflection of Nehru's inclusive thinking that he mentioned in this letter, 'We invited a number of prominent economists from all over the country . . . the economists . . . represent different schools of thought.' In other words, Nehru did try to reach out to all shades of expert opinion around the country. Based on the prevailing circumstances and the understanding of well-known Indian economists of that time, the unequivocal advice was to set up a government-run economy.

It is surprising that some among those who shout from the rooftops that Nehru's socialism set India back by decades ignore just how difficult it must have been to have agreed policies actually implemented on the ground all around the country. Under most circumstances a country's economic progress has more to do with honest implementation rather than perfect economic policies. And, the state has to first provide physical security, safe drinking water, primary healthcare and basic education. No government can do this, irrespective of its political complexion, without honesty of purpose—not just among the political executive but also at the level of field-workers and the people at large.

Nehru's understanding was that major inputs for industries needed to be built or acquired by the public sector since the government needed to be in charge of strategic industries. He was acutely conscious that in developed countries a few mega private companies—by being in charge of large public works and utility companies—exercised enormous influence on not just government's economic but also social and foreign policies. Nehru felt that the better option for India was for public-sector firms to add to steel production and build power stations, while encouraging the private sector to produce inputs such as cement and aluminium.[23] Consequently, Nehru promoted central and state government-funded production of steel and power with the financial and technical support of Western governments and the Soviet Union.

On the surface, Nehru's use of the word socialism and espousal of policies in support of an economy which would be competitive appears to be contradictory. He was convinced that economic autonomy was important for India to retain its independence of action in the foreign policy space. He probably felt that the freedom of the country would be circumscribed if India did not set up its own heavy and defence industries. The Congress party included leaders with views across the political spectrum from the left to the right. It is likely that Nehru's choice of a mixed-economy path was a reflection of a middle-of-the-road compromise within the party.

Nehru sought acceptance of his economic plans by state governments by communicating with CMs through fortnightly letters. One of his earliest letters dated 19 December 1947 mentions that India's 'basic problem [is] of poverty,[24] which we had temporarily put in second place amidst the preoccupations of communal disorder'. Nehru reiterated to CMs in 1953 that mere nationalization of existing companies did not serve any useful purpose since no new assets are created, and this only resulted in transfer of ownership. His sense was that the rigid set of beliefs developed in Europe by Marx in the nineteenth century did not apply to India in the twentieth century. Further, according to Nehru, communism develops large and powerful bureaucracies, and there is an absence of democracy. It was clear to Nehru that much faster economic growth was required, and he thought that rigid socialism was not the way forward. What is less apparent, even with the benefit of Nehru's considerable volumes of writings and speeches, is exactly how he intended to achieve faster growth along with poverty reduction with his mixed-economy model. It is likely that it was not all that clear to him either, and he and his ministerial colleagues were learning by doing.

In a letter to CMs dated 24 December 1954 Nehru mentioned 'that the Lok Sabha, in considering the economic policy resolution, unanimously passed an amendment laying down that the pattern of society to be aimed at should be socialistic'. However, in the same letter, Nehru said that 'socialistic' did not mean that the 'State should own everything, but it must own or control all strategic points'. Next month, in January 1955, the Congress party's manifesto at its annual session at Avadi mentioned the need for a 'socialist pattern [of society]'. In a perceptive observation, C.D. Deshmukh, finance minister from 1950 to 1956, has mentioned in his autobiography[25] that Nehru had a 'theoretical commitment to socialism', while Patel was a 'realist' and aware of the 'foibles of human nature', and hence aware of the 'limitations' of socialism.

Although Nehru did not suggest complete exclusion of the private sector from any industry, the repeated use of the word socialism in Congress party circles must have rung warning bells for private investors within India and in the developed West. It would have helped to attract foreign private investment if Nehru had clarified more forcefully that his government's efforts were geared towards achieving equality of opportunity and not equality of outcomes. John Kenneth Galbraith, ambassador of the US to India from 1961 to 1963, understood that India was not a socialist state and downplayed the prevalence of public enterprises in India as a small part of the overall economy to audiences in the US.

On the mix between public and private sectors and state support for the poor, Walter Crocker, Australia's high commissioner in Delhi in two stints, 1952–55 and 1958–62, understood the ground realities in India. Crocker knew Nehru personally and was a frequent guest at Teen Murti House. According to Crocker,[26] a significant complication in efficient implementation of government economic policies was that some ministers were intellectually or even financially dishonest. Crocker empathizes with Nehru's view that with so many desperately poor and unemployed in India, some form of state support was required. That is, although India needed to grow faster to reduce poverty, Crocker agreed that focusing on growth alone would not be sufficient.

At times, analysts tend to overemphasize Adam Smith's 'invisible hand'— that self-interest is the most efficient way of promoting growth and equality. An extension of that logic is that any form of government intervention in economic decision making results in inefficiencies without compensating benefits. Smith was also the author of *The Theory of Moral Sentiments*. In that earlier work of Smith's, an important facet of morality was sympathy, and, as Jesse Norman puts it, 'thanks to sympathy . . . human beings have the capacity of self-conscious introspection'.[27] And, every now and then, there is a rethink on the balance between the disembodied invisible hand and man's capacity for sympathy for others.[28]

In short, the left-oriented economic policies including the setting up of a large public sector, in ex ante terms, were not viewed with disdain as a sure recipe for lower growth. Given their own exemplary commitment to the country, Nehru and his generation of Indian leaders probably felt that they could motivate and inspire a majority of government officials, public-sector management and workers to behave ethically and with empathy for the less fortunate.

The world of the 1940s and 1950s would not have forgotten so soon about the damage done to hundreds of millions of lives in the interwar years of the 1930s by the Great Depression in the US. A superb study titled *The*

Lords of Finance: 1929, The Great Depression, and the Bankers Who Broke the World by Liaquat Ahamed[29] details the suspicions that the US, the UK, France and Germany had of each other's central bank policies in those economically difficult interwar years. Further excesses of Wall Street were sought to be prevented by the enactment of the 1933 Glass–Steagall Act in the US which segregated commercial from investment banking. The prolonged suffering of destitute, out-of-work agricultural workers during the depression years in the US is described with heart-wrenching feeling in Nobel Prize-winning author John Steinbeck's 1939 novel *The Grapes of Wrath*.

It is small wonder, therefore, taking into account market, central bank and government failures in the West in the 1930s, that a number of Indian economists from the 1950s into the 1970s favoured planning. Nehru's left-leaning views were reinforced by a majority of development economists, barring a few. Among well-known foreign economists who supported planning and visited India and spent time at the Indian Statistical Institute (ISI) in the 1950s were Nicholas Kaldor, Joan Robinson, Gunnar Myrdal, Paul Rosenstein-Rodan, Oskar Lange, John Kenneth Galbraith, Tjalling Koopmans, Jan Tinbergen and Ragnar Frisch. Myrdal is reported to have commented that 'grand-scale national planning' is 'unanimously endorsed by governments and experts in the advanced countries'.[30] They felt that government planning was required to raise investment levels in poorer countries, and funding shortfalls could be met through foreign aid.

Like many of his generation, Nehru was impressed with the Soviet Union's progress in heavy industries including sharply enhanced levels of steel production. The high economic and political cost to average USSR citizens was not yet fully apparent to the rest of the world. The fact that the USSR was not involved in any large-scale colonization made it appear less predatory to newly independent countries as compared to the UK, France (North and West Africa), Belgium (Congo), and the US (overwhelming influence in Latin America; grabbing of Guantanamo Bay from Cuba; military bases in Japan, South Korea, Philippines, Vietnam and Guam). Czarist Russia's annexation of contiguous Central Asian territories and the USSR's absorption of its neighbouring areas or domination of the Comecon[31] countries was condoned, and not condemned in equal measure as colonization. Perhaps because economic conditions, including the availability of consumer goods and living conditions in the Russian republic, were not that different from those in the other Soviet republics and the satellite Comecon countries.

The third Finance Minister John Mathai resigned in June 1950 because of differences with Nehru about allocation of funds and planning.[32] In 1958–59

Mathai observed that 'Pandit Nehru in his approach to problems laid more emphasis on formulating a programme for future rather than providing solutions for immediate difficulties. He was following the instincts of the true politician rather than the man of affairs intent on fulfilling the job in hand. He and I, for instance had many long arguments about setting up of the Planning Commission at a time when conditions were so fluid that no data of any permanent value could be collected and when general scarcity of money and materials made it difficult to implement any new plans.'[33] Contrary to John Mathai's comments, along with constant firefighting on domestic and international fronts, Nehru did try to have economic data gathered more systematically. Professor Mahalanobis, who was in charge of the ISI in Calcutta, was at the forefront of this effort.

The First Five Year Plan was ad hoc, and covered the period 1951–56. The focus was on food sufficiency, cotton and jute, price controls, reduction of rural unemployment, and increased availability of power and transportation. It is ironic and disturbing that except for the reference to jute, these could well be India's objectives today. Rural employment could have been given a boost by promoting the setting up of small to medium enterprises (SMEs) by the private sector. And, this could have been encouraged by facilitating access to not just domestic but also foreign capital.

Domestic production of competitively priced *consumer* goods did not get the attention it deserved in the First Plan. The comparative advantage of low-cost Indian labour could not be immediately used since skill levels were inadequate, and hence productivity was low. Facilitating the entry of multinationals in the consumer space would not have diluted political autonomy and would have expedited gaining of skills and promoted exports. It seems that no concerted effort was made to attract foreign direct investment (FDI) to produce consumer products locally.

Nehru exhorted CMs to tour their states to explain the First Five Year Plan. In his idealism, Nehru saw this as a cooperative effort which would boost unifying forces since the Plan would be seen as a partnership between the centre and the states. In this First Plan period, quantitative restrictions on imports were minimal. The average growth rate of net national product (NNP) over the five years was 3.5 per cent despite the administrative and financial burden of rehabilitating refugees from West and East Pakistan.

Milton Friedman visited India in the last quarter of 1955 at the invitation of the Ministry of Finance. This was part of the effort to seek the views of prominent Western economists. One of his suggestions[34] for India was that not enough was being thought through or budgeted for to improve human resources.

And while government inevitably has to fund education, health and social development programmes designed to benefit the needy and underprivileged, the actual delivery could be bid out to private parties.[35] Similar suggestions have been made by many others too, over the last six decades. A second point Friedman made was that growth comes from promoting an environment in which 'small and medium enterprises (SMEs)' thrive and not just the giants such as the Tatas. A third issue, which is of contemporary relevance, referred to by Friedman as 'the Achilles heel of the Indian economy' is the 'artificial and unrealistic (high Rupee) exchange rate'.[36]

The central and state governments during the Nehru years were well aware of the need to raise literacy and numeracy levels particularly in villages and remote areas. And, the numbers of schoolteachers in government schools have grown hugely over time. However, on average, teachers were either not adequately motivated, or qualified enough, to teach. The task was daunting since average literacy levels in rural and semi-urban areas was probably even lower than the national average of about 12 per cent at independence.

A glaring omission in Nehru's steady stream of letters to CMs is that these missives did not emphasize how implementation of government's goals in spreading elementary education and primary health were key to development. Nehru does refer to vocational training but not the underlying requirement— sound primary education. In short, effective and consistent implementation of these objectives was not monitored diligently enough. Mao's China was able to deliver basic reading and writing skills to its impoverished millions through communist fiat by the early 1970s. Comparatively, higher education received greater attention in India, and Deshmukh became the first chairman of the University Grants Commission (UGC) after he resigned from his position as finance minister in 1956.

As for Friedman's suggestion about helping SMEs to grow, this sector did not receive the attention it deserved in the 1950s. The emphasis at that time was on heavy industry and mega-power projects mostly in the public sector and occasionally on a project-specific basis large private investments.

An overvalued rupee has been a recurring problem in India. Between 1951 and 1966, Indian consumer price inflation was about 3 per cent. Given higher Indian inflation compared to the US, and since in those early years Indian productivity was lower than that in richer countries, the rupee should have been devalued much before June 1966. Over the decades, the incorrect understanding among many in the Indian political executive has been that a strong national currency means the economy is doing well.

The boost given to the appetite for imports by an overvalued rupee was sought to be dampened by a complex set of import restrictions. Subsidies were provided for exports, and thus the trade sector came to be riddled with inefficiencies from the late 1950s onwards. Such policies were not unique to India in those years of US dollar shortages. For instance, Japan too had imposed a set of import entitlements. However, Japan did not have an overvalued currency at that time. An overvalued rupee created an incentive to over invoice exports as the 'effective export subsidy exceeded the black market premium charged for illegal foreign exchange'.[37] Distortions in pricing, including for exchange rates, inevitably brought financial corruption in their wake.

Taking a step back in time, even before Independence the Indian government was concerned about conserving foreign exchange reserves. Consequently, under the Import-Export Control Act 1947,[38] domestic suppliers of import substitutes were protected by high tariff barriers. The private companies of that era used the same reasoning that some Indian private firms offer even today. Namely, that they were not in a position to compete against large Western companies as they did not have the required capital to achieve economies of scale. And, that they needed time to build expertise and size.

The Second Five Year Plan over the years 1956–61 was focussed on setting up or completing on-going heavy industry projects. As expenditure on imports of machinery ate into sterling balances, reducing the outflow of foreign exchange became an overriding priority. A supplementary strategy should have been boosting of exports and promotion of FDI. Instead of the Indian economy opening up as compared to the period of wartime controls, it started closing down from the late 1950s. B.R. Shenoy was the only economist among those who worked on the Second Five Year Plan to submit a dissent note. Shenoy was prescient in that he felt government would not have the resources to fund the capital investments of the Second Plan, and he was critical about import substitution.

By 1957–58, India's foreign exchange reserves were dwindling fast, and import and export licensing requirements resulted in India's share of global exports shrinking from 2.2 per cent in 1951 to 0.7 per cent in 1970 (see Table 1.2 in the Appendices). And imports plus exports decreased from a total of about 15–16 per cent of GDP in 1950–51 to about 8–9 per cent in 1968–69.

In the first fifteen years after 1947 India's trading relationship with the Soviet Union did not overwhelm that with the Western countries, even though India paid for imports from the USSR in rupees since 1954. By 1961, Indian exports to the USSR amounted to just 5 per cent of total exports, and this number rose to 16 per cent in 1966, two years after Nehru had passed away.[39] The average NNP[40] annual growth rate over the Second Plan 1956–61 years, despite the scarcity of hard currency, was 4 per cent, which was higher than the average growth rate of 3.5 per cent during the First Plan period.

On export pessimism, the following exchange in 1956 between I.G. Patel and C.D. Deshmukh[41] illustrates the lack of risk-taking ability even at the level of the finance minister. At that time, I.G. Patel was a deputy economic adviser in the Ministry of Finance, and according to Patel, 'Sir Arthur Lewis[42] had suggested that since India had a comparative advantage in steel production it should aim to increase production from one to 10 million tons, much of it for export.'[43] T.T. Krishnamachari had taken over as the industry minister and was keen to raise steel production to 6 million tons. In Patel's first meeting with Deshmukh, the latter ridiculed the idea of raising steel production, saying, 'Those people [Ministry of Industry] do not know what steel is and where it can be used. I have asked them to tell me how much of each variety of steel they want produced and where [and] in what quantity would each variety be consumed. It would take months to answer these queries and in the meanwhile the whole thing will be forgotten.' This attitude of the finance minister who started his career as an ICS officer was perhaps symptomatic of those who had joined the civil services prior to Independence. In an environment in which availability of financing for fresh investments was limited, ICS officers were perhaps used to raising doubts about the merits of proposals till these were no longer viable.

The State Trading Corporation (STC) was set up at the start of the Second Plan period in 1956 for trade in all so-called canalized items. At the time it was set up, the STC was meant to facilitate India's trade with the Soviet Union and East Europe. Initially, it dealt with imports and exports of bulk agricultural products such as wheat, pulses and edible oils. The STC has been deservedly criticized for misusing its monopoly power and the scarcities and price distortions caused by it. It focused on those imports which were highly profitable in terms of resale value in India. However, even by 1965, it accounted for only 5 per cent of India's total two-way trade in goods. Although this was a small fraction of total trade at that time, the mindset created by canalization created the conditions for subjective and corrupt decision making. The same avoidable mistake was repeated in setting up the Mineral and Metals Trading Corporation (MMTC) in 1963 and the Metal Scrap Trade Corporation (MSTC) in 1964.

The Third Plan's growth rate for the years 1961–66 was just 2.8 per cent. The loss of morale post the 1962 war with China, Nehru passing away in May

1964, the India–Pakistan war in 1965 and drought conditions in 1965–66 were among the causal factors. India had to depend on import of foodgrains from the US in the mid-1960s. It became increasingly evident that the country should have started much earlier on collaborating with the US to experiment with higher-yielding strains of wheat and rice.

The Table 1.3 below lists the GDP growth rates over the three Plan periods. The average rate of NNP growth in pre-independent India from 1900–47 was about 0.8 per cent. In comparison, the first two Plan periods recorded four to five times that rate of growth. Even the low growth in the third Plan period of 2.8 per cent was more than three times the 1900–47 number.

Table 1.3
Net National Product (NNP) and Per Capita Income
Growth Rates during the First Three Plans[44]
(Annual average – per cent)

Plans	Target Rates of Growth	Realized Average Annual NNP Growth Rates	Annual Average Rise in Per Capita Incomes
1st Plan 1951–1956	2.5	3.5	1.6
2nd Plan 1956–1961	5.0	4.0	1.8
3rd Plan 1961–1966	6.0	2.8	0.6

Industry, Foreign Investment, Trade, Agriculture, Exchange Rate and Taxation

The prevailing view in the Indian government, even prior to Independence, was that industrial workers needed to be protected and that large corporates should not be allowed to acquire monopoly powers. And food self-sufficiency was necessary to ensure that scarce foreign exchange was used to build heavy industry.

The Industrial Disputes Act which came into force four months before Independence in April 1947 was meant to protect labour interests, but ended up inhibiting the formation of large companies which benefit from economies of scale. Under this Act, it became virtually impossible to dismiss employees of a firm with more than fifty permanent workers. It was and is still seen as worker friendly in some circles. However, over time this legislation has had the unintended effect of inhibiting formal hiring of workers.[45]

The following year the 1948 Industrial Policy Resolution placed arms and ammunition, atomic energy and railways exclusively in the public domain. However, existing private-sector coal, iron and steel and shipbuilding companies were allowed to continue, with the condition that further development of these areas would be in the public sector. In other sectors, private companies could continue to bring in fresh investment and expand.

In Nehru's understanding the role of the public sector had to be expanded to increase employment opportunities in the formal sector. To that end, the 1956 Industrial Policy Resolution was adopted, and Schedules A, B, and C were drawn up. All industries included in Schedule A, for example, defence equipment, atomic energy, iron and steel, heavy machinery, mineral oil and coal were reserved exclusively for the government and the public sector. For areas under Schedule B, for instance, aluminium, machine tools, pharmaceutical products and chemical fertilizers, the government would take the lead and the private sector could play a supporting role.

All economic activities which were not part of A or B were deemed to fall under Schedule C, and these areas were left to the private sector. However, even for investments deemed to be part of Schedule C, licences were needed for new industries or for expansion of production. The unrealistic thinking which led to these three Schedules plus inducements for investments in economically backward areas was based on the misplaced understanding that this would necessarily lead to a reduction in economic disparities across regions. Concurrently, the feeling in Central government circles was that cottage and small-scale industries should be supported to boost employment opportunities in traditional occupations. It is likely that this was perceived to be consistent with Gandhi's support for village-level economic activities. These SMEs did provide employment, but their cottage industry, manual labour-intensive nature, could not be scaled up. Without adequate mechanization and economies of scale, consumer products could not be competitively priced for international markets.

The contributions of the various sectors to Indian GDP at ten-year intervals from 1950 to 2018 are shown in Table 1.4 in the Appendices.

It is apparent from Table 1.4 that up to about 70 per cent of the Indian economy was in the private sector during the Nehru years since agriculture was in private hands and also a significant portion of the services sector. If the span of industries for the private sector had not been restricted by the Industrial Policy Resolution of 1956, the industry component of the economy may have risen faster.

Irrespective of whether the private sector would have stepped up to the plate, it is abundantly clear again with the benefit of hindsight that the 1948 and 1956 Industrial Policy Resolutions were counterproductive. While investment in infrastructure and heavy industry had to come from government, it did not follow that industrial licensing was necessary. And, the emphasis should have been on promoting larger units of production to achieve economies of scale, not just for industry but also for consumer goods.

Although there was no explicit prohibition on attracting smaller foreign firms or large multinational corporations (MNCs), there was no concerted effort to conclude tie-ups with foreign private companies. In addition to the restrictions imposed by licensing requirements, the then small size of consumer markets in India was the reason for low levels of FDI. Another factor which restricted FDI was that Indian companies did not want to share access to India's small consumer markets with foreign companies.

Jagdish N. Bhagwati and Padma Desai have analysed investment and trade policies, during the Nehru era and the first few years that Indira Gandhi was PM, in their seminal publication titled *India: Planning for Industrialization: Industrialization and Trade Policies since 1951.*[46] In the concluding section of this book called 'Lessons', Bhagwati and Desai state that 'Indian planning for development suffered from excessive attention to targets down to product level, and a wasteful physical approach to setting and implementation thereof, along with a generally inefficient framework of economic policies designed to regulate the growth of industrialization'. In the same section, they add that 'the inefficiencies in planning that we have highlighted in this volume were probably inevitable: there is *no escape from learning by doing* and it is pertinent to remember that *few, if any, critics and least of all laissez faire advocates, grasped the full dimensions of the planning and developmental problems faced by India around 1950*' (emphasis added).

Arvind Panagariya has quoted extensively from this study in a piece he wrote for the NCAER's (National Council of Applied Economic Research) Golden Jubilee volume.[47] Panagariya mentions in this NCAER article that 'in the 1950s, India enjoyed a relatively liberal trade and foreign investment regime. The import regime began to tighten up only towards the end of the 1950s, while the foreign investment regime remained open until at least the mid-1960s.'

Turning to agriculture, since before Independence the issues of land–agrarian reform and improved functioning of panchayati samitis were very much on the minds of Congress leaders. As PM, Nehru wondered how best to abolish 'jagirdaris and zamindaris' such that land reform enhanced the purchasing power of the tiller. At times in the 1950s, courts were obstructionist and high courts set aside state-level laws as inconsistent with the right to property enshrined in the Constitution. Despite the opposition from the landed rich, land ceiling laws were passed in some states. For instance, in UP, Chaudhary Charan Singh was able to get a landholding law passed for the state in 1960. This law reduced the ceiling on landholdings and also made it uniform throughout UP. Although similar laws were enacted in several states, there were differences from state to state, and implementation on the ground was patchy.

Even though the British colonial administration had focused little on universal literacy and primary healthcare, attention was given to providing loans to farmers. For instance, the Cooperative Credit Societies Act of 1904 was enacted for this purpose. Subsequently, the RBI Act of 1934 provided for the setting up of an agricultural credit department. In 1951, RBI conducted an All-India Rural Credit Survey, and one of Nehru's objectives in nationalizing the State Bank of India in 1955 was to promote lending to farmers. Notwithstanding the availability of some credit to the agriculture sector, it remained mired in practices which were too dependent on manual labour. Even though agriculture is a state subject in the Indian Constitution, the Central government could have pushed harder to increase land under assured irrigation.

Scarcities in food items continued after Independence. By the start of the 1950s, one of the major concerns of the Central government was shortage of foodgrains. The population increased steadily due to improvements in healthcare, and domestic production of foodgrains could not keep pace with it. Wheat had to be imported from the US and the USSR (the latter provided the shipping too), and rice was imported from Burma and Siam. Concern was repeatedly expressed by Nehru and others at government meetings about the outflow of foreign exchange in making these purchases. Prices were sought to be kept down by holding stocks, and self-sufficiency in foodgrains remained an important objective through the first three decades after Independence.

The possibility of pockets of starvation due to a lack of roads to remote areas was also a constant concern. For instance, in 1957 the rains were well short of the annual average, leading to firefighting measures around the country to transport foodgrains to the worst-affected areas. Intermediaries were accused of making unconscionable profits by hoarding commodities. It was in this environment of recrimination that the Essential Commodities Act of 1955 was made applicable all over India. This Act was meant to prevent hoarding or profiteering in the sale of foodgrains, fertilizers, pulses and edible oils, pharmaceutical and petroleum products. In practice, as should have been anticipated, the law was misused by officials for rent-seeking purposes.

At Independence the Indian economy's linkages with that of the UK were extensive, and a high proportion of India's foreign trade was denominated in pound sterling. India's foreign exchange reserves were all in sterling, and only a small fraction was fully convertible. It would have made sense from a foreign exchange risk-management perspective to exchange the convertible portion of India's sterling balances to US dollar soon after Independence. The US was clearly the pre-eminent economic power after the Second World War, and the UK government's finances were evidently under stress. The pound sterling was devalued by about 30 per cent in 1949,[48] and the value of India's convertible sterling holdings was reduced by the same proportion. The Ministry of Finance made the mistake of pegging the rupee to the sterling at the rate of one rupee equal to one shilling, sixpence at Independence. Although currency pegs[49] were the norm at that time, a precise—that is, inflexible—equivalence with the British pound made downward adjustments to the value of the rupee to maintain export competitiveness more difficult. The rupee could have, instead, been adjusted downwards at periodic intervals to reflect the difference in productivity between developed Western countries and India.

The Indian Income Tax Act was first adopted in 1922 and in the 1950s, income tax rates were not based on efficiency of compliance. For instance, tax rates (Table 1.5 in the Appendices) for the highest income slab were around 80 or 70 per cent from the 1950s onwards till the mid-1970s, and this had to lead to tax evasion.

Despite a recommendation from Nicholas Kaldor, professor of economics at Cambridge, to reduce personal income tax, Nehru's government decided to retain high income taxes and also levied a wealth tax. High personal and wealth tax rates were the result of the prevailing left-oriented sentiments in the rank and file of the Congress who probably wanted to soak the rich, most of whom had stayed aloof from the freedom struggle.

In the years from 1950 to 1964 there was a gradual increase in the share of direct taxes as a fraction of GDP, and this number moved up from 2.2 per cent to 3.1 per cent[50] over this period. In comparison, the share of indirect taxes in GDP rose faster from 3.8 per cent to 7.3 per cent.[51] Defence expenditure increased from about 1.4 per cent of GDP in the mid-1950s to nearly 3 per cent by the mid-1960s, reflecting the anxieties about defence preparedness post the 1962 and 1965 wars with China and Pakistan.

Foreign Assistance—Bilateral and Multilateral

Bilateral aid is invariably tied to donor country priorities. For Nehru, alternatives to bilateral sources of funding were preferable, and the cost of that capital was a secondary consideration since maintaining national autonomy was more important. The feeling in India's decision-making circles was that bilateral aid was not a favour from developed countries since India would had to 'give' in some way to receive such assistance.

Although C.D. Deshmukh's autobiography *The Course of My Life*[52] is mostly personal, useful insights can be gleaned about the context and content of India's interactions with the Bretton Woods institutions. For instance, a lot of behind-the-scenes efforts had to be made to ensure that India's quotas in the World Bank and the International Monetary Fund (IMF) were adequate for it to nominate its own executive directors to the boards. Over the decades, the volumes of private capital flows to emerging economies have become much higher than loan amounts from the World Bank and its soft lending window, the International Development Association (IDA).[53]

The policies of import licensing and an overvalued rupee took their toll, and India needed loans and grants from the World Bank[54] and the US. Multilateral assistance from the World Bank was less tied to conditionalities than bilateral loans but needed extensive consultations, and, at times, it takes years for disbursements of each loan tranche to be made. The total nominal volume of cumulative lending by the World Bank to India from 1945 to 2015 amounts to US $52.7 billion IBRD loans and US $49.4 billion IDA loans. This combined total is higher than for any other recipient country.[55] These are not large volumes in today's terms. However, in the late 1950s hard currency loans from the World Bank were essential in meeting the Second Plan's import requirements of heavy machinery.

India's first World Bank loan in 1949 was for the railways.[56] During the First Five Year Plan period India had adequate foreign exchange reserves, and reliance on foreign financial assistance was marginal. However, the picture changed dramatically by the late 1950s. An Aid India Consortium which included the US and other Western countries plus the World Bank was formed in 1958 to help India tide over its balance of payments difficulties. The following World Bank note dated 10 July 1968[57] looks back at events a decade earlier from 1958 onwards. This note is quoted at considerable length as it details the difficulties India was facing in raising hard currency financing and the coordinated response of Western countries.

World Bank Note dated 10 July 1968

The consortium for India first met in August 1958. It came together to deal with something of an emergency. India was about midway in her Second Five-Year Development Plan and was in imminent danger of running out of foreign exchange with the main development projects only partly completed. The Plan had been started in a flush of enthusiasm . . . But the cost of the new Plan proved to have been considerably underestimated and the reserves [as sterling balances] began to melt away . . . By July 1958 the deficit in the balance of payments was running at $1.0 million a week and on August 8, 1958 Indian foreign exchange reserves stood at $647 million, including $247 million in gold. It was feared that unless immediate remedial steps were taken, India's foreign exchange reserves would be wiped out by the end of 1958. Furthermore, it was estimated that the uncovered foreign exchange gap for the last three years of the Second Plan, even after taking into account curtailments effected in the Plan, would be $1,317 million. The estimate was that, this gap could be further reduced to about $930 million through import cuts and increased exports together with additional drawings on the reserves. There was not much more the Indian Government could do to reduce this gap any further. There was no reason to expect a significant increase in the estimated export proceeds and there was no room for further adjustments in the Plan that would reduce the prospective import bill. Something had to be done quickly. Either foreign expenditures had to be drastically cut, thus starving industry of raw materials and leaving resources tied up in incomplete projects, with severe damage to the Plan and the economy, or large new resources had to be made available from outside. As a major lender to India the IBRD—which up to 1958 was contributing to the financing of the Second Plan at an average rate of approximately $100 million a year—accepted the task of consulting with countries interested in giving development assistance to India with a view to finding among them enough additional aid to permit the central core of the Plan to be carried out.

At the instance of the IBRD, Canada, Japan, the UK and the US met and agreed to provide financial aid to India, in addition to what they were already doing. The note adds, 'These were the non-communist countries . . . in which India had placed most of her orders for projects under the Plan. Canada had been providing aid on a grant basis to India under the Colombo Plan. In the spring of 1958, the Federal Republic of Germany had postponed its claims against India amounting to about $160 million which were due during the remainder of the Second Plan.

Japan had, in February 1958, extended its first credit to India to the tune of $50 million in Yen to assist the Second Plan. The United Kingdom had been extending development aid to India under the Export Guarantees Act while the United States and the IBRD were India's biggest source of development finance.'

B.K. Nehru, an ICS officer, was the Indian executive director at the World Bank in 1949 and minister (economic) in the Indian Embassy in Washington DC in 1954. In his understanding, total Western financial assistance including that of the World Bank and the US was substantial in the funding of the Second and Third Five Year Plans.[58] For the Second Plan years 1956–61 external assistance amounted to US $284 million and the same number for the Third Plan period 1961–66 was US $825 million.[59] It is evident that India had painted itself into a corner by the end of the 1950s. That is, India had ambitious investment plans for the Second and Third Five Year Plans but did not have adequate financial resources to go through with the intended investments.

The perception within Western governments was that India was gaming the two sides in the Cold War era since the West felt compelled to provide concessional financing bilaterally and via multilateral agencies to prevent India from turning communist. Despite this sense of grievance at being gamed, expressed in no uncertain terms by Walter Crocker[60] and others, the West felt that it had to assist India. A.M. Rosenthal[61] wrote a caustic yet illuminating piece in the *New York Times* of 7 January 1958 on India's financial predicament and the considerable economic support it received from the West. According to Rosenthal, the attitude of 'most informed Americans' towards financial assistance to India could be described as follows:

'India's perpetual edginess, her strange acceptance of the respectability of the Communists, make her a difficult country to get close to, and a difficult country to help . . . But India as she stands remains a road block against a Communist Asia, and if no aid is given the likelihood of that road block being destroyed is large. It is a negative equation, but an important one.'

This sentiment about why the US and hence the West needed to help India was the dominant view in Western capitals at that time. Given Rosenthal's profile, the Indian Embassy in Washington DC, the Indian executive director to the World Bank or the Permanent Mission of India to the United Nations must have sent this article with comments to the Ministry of External Affairs and the Ministry of Finance. India was never on the verge of becoming a one-party communist state, and that rationale in Rosenthal's article was stretched. However, the charge of 'edginess' was true, and Nehru and others in India (in particular V.K. Krishna Menon) needed to take note. The bottom line was that despite prodigious efforts at home and assistance provided by the Soviet bloc in adding to India's heavy industry capacities, India had to turn to the West and its multilateral institutions in its hour of need.

During the McCarthy and John Foster Dulles years (1947–59), the US had adopted the 'if you are not with us you are against us' attitude. The US had made Pakistan its ally in its strategic manoeuvres against the USSR. Nations rarely express gratitude in public. Notwithstanding the US defence relationship with Pakistan and its sense of superiority, it would have been in India's interest if Nehru had expressed India's appreciation for the loans and grants received from the West.[62] For instance, Nehru could have publicly mentioned to his host President J.F. Kennedy when he visited the US in November 1961 that Second Plan investments would have been cut down but for the financial support received from the West.

Strengths and Fault Lines in External Relations

A country's foreign policies are driven by its history, geography, relative size of economy, strength and sophistication of its armed forces and equipment, location and size of population.[63] Indians were reminded of the country's historical strengths by the leaders of the freedom struggle. In 1947 India's economy was small by comparison with most Western countries and its manufacturing and technical capabilities were limited. In comparison, India's armed forces were well disciplined due to British training. India's stock around the world was relatively high despite the small size of its economy, and in today's terminology India had a large soft power footprint. Here was a country that had successfully wrested freedom from the clutches of a pre-eminent colonial power through non-violent non-cooperation.

Nehru gave more than warranted weight to India's physical size and large population of 350 million in 1947. That is, he had an exaggerated sense about a manifest role for India in international relations. In 1948, Nehru happened to mention that 'India had become the fourth or fifth most influential country in the United Nations'.[64] This was surely an exaggerated claim since a year earlier, in 1947, India had to withdraw its candidature for the United Nations Security Council (UNSC) when 'Ukraine got more votes than India in seven successive ballots on the same day'.[65] Soft power has to be backed by hard economic and military strength, both of which India did not possess at the time.

In contrast to domestic economic policies, which were discussed widely within India and with foreign experts, external affairs remained exclusively the domain of Nehru and his close advisers. Written examinations for the Indian Foreign Service started in 1950, and ICS officers who had opted for the foreign office were the dominant providers of inputs for the entire duration of Nehru's years as PM. Among the non-ICS, Krishna Menon and Gopalaswami Parthasarathy were important sounding boards.

Of the foreign ambassadors who were stationed in Delhi in the 1950s, Australian High Commissioner Walter Crocker was a keen observer of Nehru and his policies. Crocker mentions that in the Nehru era, 'India was a status society and not a money-nexus society'.[66] This could be interpreted to mean that status derived from learning, parentage and position was given importance while wealth alone did not confer the same respect. In Crocker's words, Nehru was a true liberal, not a crypto-communist, since communists were too doctrinaire. And that Nehru was impatient with caste, obscurantist religion and poverty. It was on public record that Nehru was also a committed democrat and spent hours in the Lok Sabha listening to the relatively few opposition MPs criticizing him on his domestic and foreign policies. Hence the posture of some in government circles in the US who projected Nehru as a closet communist was not based on reality but on their obsession about demonizing the USSR and any country that chose to have close relations with it.

Many a time, domestic issues have implications for external security. For instance, on 15 August 1960, Master Tara Singh a seventy-six-year-old Akali leader began a fast unto death to demand a Punjabi 'Suba' (separate state for Punjab). Punjab borders Pakistan, and in his Independence Day speech from the Red Fort on the same day, Nehru exhorted everyone in the country including the Sikhs and Hindus in Punjab 'to not lose themselves in petty squabbles over caste, region, religion or language'.[67] The States Reorganisation Commission had started work in 1953, and the Akali demand for a separate state was subsequently tactically changed for one on the basis of the Punjabi language. After the States Reorganisation Act of 1956 ceded the Punjabi-speaking parts of Patiala and East Punjab States Union (PEPSU) to Punjab, Nehru was able to defuse the situation in this sensitive border state.[68] It was Nehru's careful handling of the situation that prevented Pakistan from meddling in the affairs of Punjab as it did post 1980.

After the Second World War, Europe and Japan were struggling economically. Although the USSR could match the US in nuclear and conventional weaponry, the economies of the Soviet Union and satellite countries in East Europe were relatively small and unable to produce quality consumer goods. China was nowhere in the picture economically. The US economy amounted to about 30 per cent of world GDP, and the sophistication of its military hardware and strategic reach around the globe was unparalleled.

In the 1950s the US had little patience for Indian leaders who perceived neocolonialism as a greater danger than socialism or communism. It was inevitable, therefore, that there would be sharp differences of opinion between the establishment in the US and Nehru on affairs around the globe. Nevertheless, the US arming of Pakistan, and its ill-considered military interventions in Korea and Vietnam, and the setting up of military bases around the world need not have interfered with India promoting inward FDI from the US and West European nations. In other words, despite the fact that the US talked down to India, Nehru needed to focus more on national economic interests rather than act as a standard-bearer for newly independent and developing countries.

Sardar Patel could have oriented Nehru towards somewhat more practical policies in foreign affairs. Unfortunately for India, he suffered a heart attack in 1948 and passed away in 1950. In the first decade after Independence, India's defence forces and the economy had extensive supply of equipment and technology dependencies on the UK. At that early stage, India needed someone with administrative experience who could maintain these supply relationships with UK-based firms on an even keel as the Indian government diversified its sources of defence supplies and machinery. An article titled 'A Serious Menace to Security: British Intelligence, V.K. Krishna Menon and the Indian High Commission in London, 1947–52' by Paul M. McGarr[69] casts serious doubts about Menon's capability to hold any office with administrative or policymaking responsibilities. Given the British establishment's deep suspicions about Krishna Menon he was an extremely poor choice as India's first high commissioner to the UK.[70]

During the 1950s and early 1960s, Nehru had a blind spot when it came to Krishna Menon. J.B. (Acharya) Kripalani, a veteran leader of the freedom struggle, felt strongly that Menon should not continue as the defence minister,[71] and on 11 April 1961 he made a withering speech against him in the Lok Sabha.[72] Even though Kripalani's usual constituency for the Lok Sabha was Samastipur in Bihar, he stood against Menon from a Bombay constituency. Nehru and the Congress party pulled out all stops, and Menon won that election.

In Ambassador K.S. Bajpai's view,[73] the choice of Krishna Menon as defence minister led to disastrous results in the war with China in 1962. According to Bajpai, Nehru made things difficult for himself and tended to be 'theoretical and unworldly'. Bajpai was referring to Nehru's world view in which the US was not dealt with sensitively enough as the foremost economic and military power of that time. It was an error of judgement on Nehru's part to disregard the widely acknowledged fact that despite Menon's brilliance, he aroused deep antagonism domestically, and in the West, thus harming national interest.

An example of the mutual finger pointing of that era was that Western democracies commented openly that India's harsh treatment of Naga separatists was inconsistent with its criticism of their actions in the Congo. On India's part it had reason to be suspicious that Belgium, a former colonial power in the Congo supported by the US, was trying to retain its hold over that country's immense natural resources.[74] Decolonization was an important objective for Nehru which brought him into conflict with Western powers. For instance, it must have coloured his mind against the US that the 14 December 1960 UN Declaration on Granting of Independence to Colonial Countries and Peoples was opposed by Western nations and supported by the USSR.

Reading between the lines of the writings by various foreign observers and officials who worked with him, Nehru spent more time than warranted on visits abroad, in the foreign office and with visitors from abroad.[75] Nehru should have appointed a full-time foreign minister to enable him to spend more time on domestic issues. Walter Crocker recounts an amusing incident when Australian students had come to Delhi and requested him to seek a meeting for them with Nehru. By the time the Australian High Commission informed the students that such a meeting would not be possible, the students responded that they had already met Nehru, having sought a meeting directly through his office.

Atomic Energy and Strategic Implications

Nehru set up the Indian Atomic Energy Research Committee in 1946 with nuclear physicist Homi Bhabha as chairman. Thereafter, the Atomic Energy Act was proposed by Nehru to the Constituent Assembly. This piece of legislation was similar to the corresponding Act in the UK, but the provisions for secrecy were even tighter, and all aspects of atomic energy were confined to government and reserved for the public sector. After the Act was passed, the Atomic Energy Commission was set up in August 1948 with Bhabha in charge. A Department of Atomic Energy was formally created in 1954, and Bhabha become the first secretary of this department which reported to the PM.

In response to questions raised domestically about the need for extreme secrecy, Nehru said that this was necessary for issues related to atomic energy but not for fundamental research. Nehru clarified that since peaceful uses of atomic energy cannot be distinguished from defence applications, all aspects of the production of atomic energy would be kept secret. At about the same time, the US proposed controls on fissile materials at the United Nations. The US suggested the setting up of an international atomic development authority, which would oversee the ownership and production of all nuclear facilities which could be used to produce nuclear weapons. Nehru's sister, Vijaya Lakshmi Pandit, was the Indian delegate at those UN deliberations, and she emphasized that India would retain autonomy over its programmes in the fields of nuclear energy and related technologies.

In 1951, India signed a nuclear energy cooperation agreement with France. In retrospect, it was only a matter of time before India's plans to strike out on its own in matters related to atomic energy would be in conflict with US non-proliferation objectives.[76] US concerns about non-proliferation were first expressed in the early 1960s, probably with China in mind. However, China was able to conduct its nuclear test in 1964, and that led to the discriminatory Non-Proliferation Treaty (NPT) of 1 July 1968.

Nehru has to be credited for his longer-term understanding of national interest that though the horrific aspects of nuclear bombs were evident in Hiroshima and Nagasaki, India needed to build its own institutional structures and expertise in this area. He was prescient in selecting Homi Bhabha to lead the effort. Bhabha proved that he had the technical and administrative abilities to lay the solid foundations on which the Department of Atomic Energy, ancillary institutions and excellence in research were built.

Kashmir Saga

Some of today's Indian television channels compete with each other in spreading factually inaccurate jingoism about Pakistan and its role in Kashmir. Even in educated circles, Indians seem to be dimly aware about the circumstances under which a portion of Kashmir was occupied by Pakistan and how the matter came to be referred to the United Nations. At the same time, there is little hesitation in blaming Nehru.

Around August 1946, a year before Independence, armed intruders from West Punjab and the North-West Frontier Province (NWFP), both areas now in Pakistan, began to infiltrate into Kashmir. However, it was more than a year later on 1 October 1947, about six weeks after Indian and Pakistani independence, that the Maharaja of Kashmir sought military equipment from India to resist the advancing trained Pakistani 'irregulars'. Kashmir had not yet acceded to India or Pakistan at that time.[77]

The firm resolve of Sardar Patel, the home minister, and Baldev Singh, defence minister, to help the Maharaja of Kashmir was frustrated by the then

British heads of the Indian armed forces as they insisted that no arms could be spared. On 24 October 1947, the Kashmir state made frantic appeals to the Indian government for arms in the face of an invasion of the Jhelum valley by Pakistani militia. The specific dates of these developments have a bearing on who was accountable for what and when in the tortured history of Kashmir and India–Pakistan relations.

In October 1947, defence-related decisions, including on how best to counter the dangers posed by the invasion of Kashmir by Pakistan, were not taken by the Union cabinet headed by Nehru. The Defence Committee of the Indian government, which was the highest decision-making body in defence matters, was headed by the then Governor General Mountbatten. And, Mountbatten and British generals were reluctant to send military support to the Maharaja. Thus continuing British influence delayed Indian military action to clear what is now called Pakistan Occupied Kashmir (PoK) of the raiders. The international community, which was still reeling from the consequences of the Second World War, supported the British position that ostensibly did not want a full-scale war between India and Pakistan on Kashmir.

At meetings of the Defence Committee on 25 October 1947, Mountbatten objected to India coming to the assistance of Kashmir till this princely state had formally acceded to India. In the meantime, Pakistani forces were approaching Baramulla and would have reached Srinagar in two days. The only option left to resist the armed Pakistani invaders was to airlift an Indian Army contingent to Srinagar. Mountbatten and the British chief of the Indian Army continued with their objections, and in desperation the Maharaja acceded to India on 26 October 1947. The Maharaja was concerned about his personal physical safety if the invading marauders were to reach Srinagar. The Maharaja also agreed that after accession, Kashmir would have a National Conference government headed by its founder Sheikh Abdullah. The instruments of accession were accepted by Mountbatten, and an Indian battalion was airlifted to Srinagar on 27 October 1947. By the evening of that day, Indian forces were able to occupy the heights at Pattan and thus control the road to Srinagar.[78]

By the end of October 1947, frustrated by its inability to capture Srinagar, Pakistan was prepared to go to war with India. The British head of the Pakistani Army reminded the civilian Pakistani leadership of the 'stand-down' instructions for British officers. That is, in case of an open outbreak of hostilities between the two countries, the British officers on both sides were required to resign.

At around this time, the feedback sent by the British high commissioner in Pakistan to London was that if India were to gain control of PoK that would give India direct access to the North West Frontier Province (NWFP). This would in turn give India the ability to create mischief for Pakistan in the Pathan region and even create openings for the USSR. The fact that British policy favoured Pakistan on the Kashmir issue was not lost on Nehru and his cabinet from the time that Kashmir acceded to India.[79] Although the Nawab of Junagadh had acceded to Pakistan, it was determined through voting that most people in this Hindu-majority area wanted to be part of India. Mountbatten's suggestion was that in similar fashion, the will of the Kashmiri people should be determined through a plebiscite even though the Hindu Maharaja of majority-Muslim Kashmir had acceded to India.

Pakistan disagreed with the suggestion that troops of both countries should leave Kashmir before a plebiscite. Pakistan probably felt that Sheikh Abdullah's pro-India stance would tilt such a vote against them. Nehru was comfortable with a plebiscite and said so publicly, in the Indian Parliament and in a telegram to the prime minister of Pakistan. The conjecture was that without the intimidating presence of Pakistani forces, it was highly likely that Sheikh Abdullah and his supporters, who formed a majority in Kashmir, would vote to remain in India. Sheikh Abdullah's National Conference party was close to the Congress, and Abdullah had a close, friendly relationship with Nehru.

In the face of the stalemate on the issue of a plebiscite, Mountbatten suggested that the stand-off in Kashmir should be referred to the UN. Nehru initially resisted Mountbatten's proposal. However, given India's multiple dependencies on the UK for spares for military equipment and a host of civilian supplies, the British view prevailed. Once Nehru made a reference to the UN, the consequences were predictably negative. The duplicitous manoeuvring of Noel-Barker, the British representative at the UN, favoured Pakistan.[80]

The extent of Indian dependence on the UK is evident from the fact that most of the equipment in use with the Royal Indian Air Force (RIAF), and the Indian Army at that time was of British and, in a few instances, US origin. It is highly probable that if India was seen as intransigent on the Kashmir issue by the UK, spares for military equipment and technical assistance for repairs would not have been forthcoming. Specifically, the Royal Indian Air Force (RIAF) had a total of six fighter squadrons with twelve Tempest (British) fighters each, twenty Spitfire (British) aircraft, seven Dakota (US) transport aircraft and four Harvard (US) trainer aircraft. The army had 260,000 troops consisting of eleven infantry regiments, fourteen cavalry units and eighteen artillery regiments and supporting engineering, signals, supply and ordnance corps. The tanks were Second World War Stuart (British) and Sherman (US) vintage and the army also had some Daimler Ferret Scout (US) cars.

The infantry was equipped with .303 bolt-action rifles, Sten carbines and Bren machine guns (all British).[81]

Faced with domestic criticism, despite financial and military constraints, Nehru did consider sending the Indian Army into Pakistan to stop their continued assistance to irregular forces in PoK. He wrote to British PM Clement Attlee that India may have no option but to take military action in its 'right of self defence'. Attlee advised Nehru that India would prejudice its position at the UN if it 'took unilateral action'. Nehru-baiters are of the opinion that he should have ignored British objections and authorized the Indian Army to clear PoK of Pakistani infiltrators. This suggested line of action overlooks India's military and overall dependence on the UK and the West.

The ceasefire terms set out by the United Nations Commission for India and Pakistan (UNCIP) resolution of 13 August 1948 called for the withdrawal of Pakistani troops from all of Kashmir, and this was rejected by Pakistan. John Foster Dulles, who was the US delegate to the UN, informed his government in November 1948 that the 'present UK approach to the Kashmir problem appears extremely pro-government of Pakistan as against the middle ground that we have sought to follow'.[82] From this dispatch, it appears that in 1948 Dulles did not perceive India as too preachy or leaning towards the USSR. Subsequently, in the mid-1950s, when Dulles was the secretary of state, the US moved closer to Pakistan as India turned to the USSR for food aid and for support in setting up heavy industry.

The on and off hostilities between India and Pakistan on Kashmir continued till the end of December 1948 and ceasefire was finally declared on 1 January 1949. This ceasefire line became the Line of Control (LoC) after the Shimla Agreement was signed between India and Pakistan in 1971. To sum up, a majority of the Kashmiri people felt that the governments installed by Maharaja Hari Singh discriminated against Muslims in government jobs and had done little to develop the state. Sheikh Abdullah, with secular and left-leaning credentials, emerged as the most popular leader in the Srinagar Valley and preferred India over Pakistan. However, Abdullah wanted autonomy for Kashmir which did not sit comfortably with many among the senior Congress leaders.[83]

One of the lessons for India of this de facto division of Kashmir was that the UN could not be expected to be even-handed. In August 1952, more than three years after the ceasefire, Nehru informed the Indian Parliament that if Pakistan were to embark on an aggression in Kashmir again, there would be 'all-out war not in Kashmir only but elsewhere too'.[84] This is exactly what happened in 1965 when Lal Bahadur Shastri directed the Indian Army to cross into West Pakistan to relieve the pressure of a Pakistani attack into Kashmir.

One of the initial reforms of Sheikh Abdullah's government in Kashmir was to bring in a ceiling of 23 acres for landholdings under the Big Landed Estates Abolition Act, 1950. Holdings of more than 23 acres were confiscated and distributed among the landless. No compensation was paid, and the Indian Constitution did not apply in that state at that time. By contrast, the Indian Constitution had incorporated a fundamental right to property.[85] As the minority-Hindu community in Kashmir owned about 30 per cent of the land under cultivation, they lost substantially in the redistribution of land. While this move by Abdullah was immensely popular locally, it was seen as anti-Hindu by elements within the Congress and in the rest of the country.

Syama Prasad Mukherjee, who was a member of the Constituent Assembly, was the minister for industry and supply in Nehru's cabinet post Independence. He resigned in April 1950 to protest against the Delhi Pact[86] between Nehru and Pakistani PM Liaquat Ali Khan and founded the Jana Sangh in 1951. Mukherjee was opposed to this Pact because he felt that it amounted to a policy of appeasement, and he held East Pakistan responsible for the large number of Hindu refugees who felt compelled to migrate to West Bengal at the time of Partition. Mukherjee was also against Article 370 in the Constitution which provides for the special status and autonomy of Kashmir. Subsequently, Mukherjee went to Srinagar to agitate against the ban on non-Kashmiri ownership of property in Kashmir. He was arrested and passed away in detention in June 1953.[87] Hindu opinion in Delhi, including within Congress circles, was inflamed. It is under these circumstances that the following development was used by Abdullah's local Kashmiri opponents to oust him.

On 3 May 1953, Abdullah met with the US Senator Adlai Stevenson who was on a fact-finding mission in Kashmir. According to Indian media reports, Abdullah was suspected of having hinted that he may be prepared to accept US support for an independent Kashmir, and it is possible that the US would have favoured such an arrangement. A strategically located country the size of Kashmir would need foreign assistance and may have been amenable to providing military bases or listening-post facilities to the US.[88]

Sheikh Abdullah was dismissed as head of government of Kashmir in August 1953 and was arrested soon thereafter for alleged anti-state activities. It is not clear whether Abdullah's alleged meetings with foreign interlocutors were to establish an independent Kashmir or for colluding with Pakistan. Irrespective of the provocation, Abdullah's arrest undermined Nehru's reputation as a liberal democrat in the West.[89]

Ominously for the future of Kashmir, Abdullah was summarily replaced as chief minister by Bakshi Ghulam Mohammed. Acquiescing in the appointment of B.G. Mohammed was a more serious failure on the part of Nehru than the arrest of Abdullah. Among the factors which have alienated a significant proportion of Kashmiris from the rest of India has been this legacy of Delhi's support for unpopular administrations in Kashmir since the 1950s.[90]

India does not appear to have ever sought surface connectivity with Afghanistan in the many rounds of discussions on Kashmir with Pakistan during Nehru's years as PM. One of the consequences of Pakistan-occupied Kashmir is that India's land border with Afghanistan, and through it, albeit via difficult mountainous terrain, to Central Asia was lost. India has a rich history of connections with Central Asia. The first Mughal emperor Babur came from the Fergana valley in Uzbekistan. Bairam Khan who served Babur, Humayun and Akbar as a military commander and regent was probably from modern-day Turkmenistan. The Patna-born poet Abdul Qadir Bedil (of Central Asian descent) is venerated in Tajikistan and wrote in Persian. He is buried across the street from Purana Quila (Old Fort) in New Delhi. The huge reservoirs of oil and gas in Central Asian republics had not been discovered yet. However, it is surprising that Indian negotiators, without giving up the claim on PoK, did not seek a land corridor through it. Perhaps such a linkage could have been sought by India, as a quid pro quo as the upper riparian, at the time the Indus Waters Treaty was signed in Karachi in September 1960 by Nehru and Pakistani general turned president, Ayub Khan.

Given the armed conflict in Kashmir from 1946 to 1948, Nehru paid close attention to relations with Pakistan. He supported many rounds of discussions to resolve differences alternately in Pakistan and India. On occasion, there was limited progress with backsliding in the very next round of negotiations. The bottom line was and is that Pakistan wants not just PoK but the rest of Kashmir to be part of Pakistan. To the extent that there were no further armed confrontations with Pakistan after 1948, Nehru was able to ring-fence the contentious Kashmir issue all through his remaining years as PM till 1964.

Smaller Neighbours

Pakistan had not yet shrunk due to the breaking away of Bangladesh during the Nehru era. Apart from China and undivided Pakistan, other neighbours were considerably smaller in population and size. In relations with Bhutan and Nepal, Nehru ensured that India was seen as a logical successor to British India. For instance, India quickly signed a treaty with Bhutan in August 1949 which permitted India to guide foreign and defence policies in continuation of the relationship Bhutan had with British India. Of course, Buddhist Bhutan's concerns about being overwhelmed by the larger Buddhist community in Tibetan China helped and continues to buttress Bhutan's ties with India.

In July 1950, India signed a Treaty of Peace and Friendship with Nepal which allows free movement of people and goods between the two countries. However, India's relations with Nepal have been tinged with differences since the 1950s. Nehru chose to give King Tribhuvan refuge in the Indian Embassy in Kathmandu in 1951, ending a hundred years of exploitative rule of the Ranas. Koirala took over in November 1951 as the PM in Nepal and soon thereafter found fault with India for his domestic political reasons. Surprisingly, the cynicism among the Nepali elite was such that demonstrators were encouraged to throw stones at a delegation of Indian MPs who were on a visit to Kathmandu as far back as June 1952.

Although Nepal looked for a scapegoat in India for its own problems, Nehru was patient and supported development projects that would help both countries. As late as 5 May 1964,[91] Nehru inaugurated the Gandak[92] barrage project located close to Gorakhpur (Uttar Pradesh) along with the king of Nepal. The project was meant to provide power and irrigation on both sides of the border. Immediately after the inauguration ceremony, with scant consideration for Nehru who was visibly unwell, the Nepalese king gave him a note seeking changes in the terms of the Gandak project contract between the two countries. This has been par for the course in India–Nepal relations with after-the-fact second-guessing in Nepalese decision-making circles on how to improve on bilaterally agreed Indian offers. A Hindu-majority Nepal probably worries that it could be assimilated into a much larger Hindu-majority India if it does not keep a prickly distance from its larger neighbour.

Turning to Burma (now called Myanmar), it had become a part of British India in 1866. Indian trading businesses established themselves there, and Indian labour also moved to that part of the British empire well before 1947. After the British withdrew from Burma in January 1948, the Indian government persuaded the newly independent Burmese to allow Indian shopping establishments and manual labour to continue to operate in that country. After the military coup in Burma in 1962, this Buddhist country turned increasingly inwards and relations with India remained cordial but distant.

Sri Lanka which was called Ceylon earlier obtained Dominion status from the British in February 1948. The newly independent southern neighbour is separated from India by about 20 kilometres of water and posed no serious bilateral issues for India during the years that Nehru was PM. However, Sri Lanka did go through its internal convulsions and was racked by conspiracy theories after Prime Minister S.W.R.D. Bandaranaike was assassinated at his residence on 25 September 1959.

Missed Opportunities

Nehru's strong anti-colonialism sentiments were logical prior to Independence. And, post Indian Independence, Western academics and liberals—as distinct from their governments—understood India's reluctance to take sides in the US–USSR and US–China stand-offs. All things considered, Nehru's interactions with government leaders in the US could have been warmer. For instance, one of Nehru's meetings during his visit to the US in 1949 at the invitation of President Truman was with Dean Acheson (US secretary of state 1949–53). According to Acheson's[93] memory of that meeting, Nehru was in a 'prickly mood', and he sharply criticized the colonial behaviour of France in Indo-China and the Netherlands in Indonesia. This was counterproductive, as was Nehru's suggestion to US leaders that the Kuril Islands be returned to the Soviet Union and Formosa to China.

Post his visit to India in 1952, US vice-president Nixon commented that Nehru had lectured him on the presence of US troops in Japan. Nehru's concern about the US role during the Korean War and in Japan could have been tempered, at least in bilateral discussions, by expressing disquiet about Chinese action in Tibet. The US Secretary of State John Foster Dulles visited India in 1954 and again in 1956. The conversations with Nehru were mostly about the dangers of war and little was achieved on closer economic cooperation between the world's two largest democracies. Dulles suggested to Nehru that India join the Bangkok-headquartered South East Asia Treaty Organization (SEATO).[94] Nehru refused to have anything to do with military alliances including the Central Treaty Organization (CENTO)[95] which was based initially in Baghdad and later in Ankara. Nehru was more than justified in taking this view since the experience of the first fifty years of the twentieth century had amply demonstrated that mutual defence pacts did not prevent wars.

The political environment in the US was rabidly anti-communist in the mid-1950s. Even Hollywood stars such as Charlie Chaplin and scriptwriter Dalton Trumbo[96] were hounded. Incidentally, Nehru met Charlie Chaplin in Burgenstock and in a small village called Cossier, in Switzerland in June 1953.[97] Gundevia recalls Nehru's courtesy call on the Swiss President Philipp

Etter in Berne. In the course of their conversation, Etter happened to mention to Nehru, 'Such a long border with Communist China Mr. Prime Minister, must be a matter of some anxiety to you.' In Gundevia's words, 'that set Mr. Prime Minister off on a lovely tirade', and Nehru, responding to Etter, said that 'China is no danger to anybody. China is a gigantic country and they are going to be very busy settling down after the Revolution . . .' and Nehru went on and on till he was fifteen minutes late for his next meeting.

Of course, Nehru did not need to be cowed by the US paranoia about China (likely that a summary of the discussion between Nehru and Etter found its way to US diplomats based in Berne) or be irritated by their obtuse insensitivity in driving a comic genius like Chaplin out of the US. However, keeping Indian economic interests in mind, Nehru could have chosen to tread a bit more lightly on the absurd fears of US business and political elites which resulted in the setting up of committees to investigate anti-American activities in the 1950s.

Nehru was strenuously against US involvement in Vietnam post the French withdrawal from South East Asia, particularly after their definitive loss to the communist Viet Minh at Dien Bien Phu in 1954. It could be a spurious correlation with Nehru's criticism of US policies, but in the mid-1950s the US turned down India's request for F-104 fighter jets even on full payment. The US logic was that the F-104s were too costly for India. At around the same time, responding to an Indian request, the UK, possibly in coordination with the US, said that India did not need submarines.[98]

In contrast to India, Pakistan was an eager member of both SEATO and CENTO and provided military base facilities to the US in Peshawar. Given the history of Pakistan's relations with India, it probably felt threatened by its bigger neighbour. Pakistan's close ties with Saudi Arabia and Iran, two close allies of the US, would have also made it veer towards the US. This Peshawar facility was used by the US to fly U-2[99] surveillance flights over China and the USSR. Pakistan received a steady supply of armaments from the US in return for its collaboration against communist states.[100]

After Pakistani Army chief Ayub Khan took over as President, the talk of Pakistan partnering the US to contain communism was ratcheted up. Consequently, in conversations between India and the US, more so during the Republican administration of Eisenhower than that of Democratic President J.F. Kennedy, the persistent US suggestion was that India needed to be mindful of the smaller[101] neighbour Pakistan's interests. For example, India needed to be generous about the sharing of Indus waters,[102] be sensitive to Pakistan's security concerns and resolve the Kashmir issue.

Nehru's obituary speech after the death of Stalin in 1953 was probably too warm for the US. Although Nehru's criticism of the UK and France on their invasion of Egypt in October 1956 post the nationalization of the Suez Canal was justified, it must have irked those two countries. Subsequently, Western countries got their own back by comparing Nehru's stance on the Suez Canal with his silence on the putting down of the Hungarian uprising by the Soviet Union in early November 1956.

In the past few years, Nehru has been criticized often for his government's 'mistaken' policies. One specific criticism is that he refused an offer from the US for India to become a permanent member of the United Nations Security Council. The fact is that on 27 September 1955 Nehru denied that any offer was ever made to India in response to a short-notice question in the Lok Sabha. Nehru is on record as having said, 'There has been no offer, formal or informal, of this kind. Some vague references have appeared in the press about it which have no foundation in fact. The composition of the Security Council is prescribed by the UN Charter, according to which certain specified nations have permanent seats. No change or addition can be made to this without an amendment of the Charter. There is, therefore, no question of a seat being offered and India declining it. Our declared policy is to support the admission of all nations qualified for UN membership.' At the same time, Nehru demonstrated his concern about not annoying China by adding that, 'India has repeatedly supported the People's Republic of China being given its legitimate place in the United Nations.'[103] Namely, that India did not covet the UNSC seat which should legitimately go to China.

A fuller understanding of Nehru's China-related policies is not possible without close examination of the security environment and potential loss of territory in the areas which are now part of Arunachal Pradesh, Nagaland, Manipur and Mizoram. India's relationship with Sikkim too could have evolved on a different trajectory if China had taken a decidedly anti-India attitude from the mid-1950s onwards. Despite Nehru's overtures of friendship towards China, the relationship deteriorated to the point of a war with that country in 1962. All things considered, Nehru was too sensitive about Chinese concerns that India may be siding with the West.

Eisenhower visited India in December 1959. No other US President had visited India till then. Nehru had visited the US in October–November 1949 and again in December 1956. A return visit by the US President was due and it is also likely that that the US was mindful that Soviet assistance in heavy industry was influencing Delhi. Negotiations between India and the USSR on arms purchases had also probably started in the latter half of the 1950s. President

Eisenhower came to Delhi after visiting Pakistan and Afghanistan. Large crowds greeted him, and the discussions he had with Nehru centred on China. As Bruce Riedel suggests,[104] the US President was well aware of the ground-level situation on the India-China border because of the reports he received on the Central Intelligence Agency's (CIA's) covert operations and the U-2 surveillance flights.

B.K. Nehru was the Indian ambassador to the US for seven years from 1961 to 1968. He was Nehru's nephew and his autobiography has ample references to Nehru's meetings with JFK during the Indian PM's last visit to the US in November 1961.[105] Nehru was accompanied by Indira Gandhi and the visit began with a stay at Jacqueline Kennedy's home in Newport, Rhode Island. President Kennedy joined for informal meetings with Nehru at Newport and it appears from the time and attention that JFK paid to Nehru's visit that he was serious about India outstripping communist China as a successful democracy. Unfortunately for India, Nehru's meetings with Kennedy did not go well. According to those who were present at these meetings, Nehru was distracted and responded to JFK in monosyllables.

John K. Galbraith was the US ambassador in Delhi in 1961 and had direct access to JFK. Nehru, a cerebral head of government, Galbraith an erudite ambassador and Kennedy, a Democrat who was inclined to temper the pro-Pakistan line of earlier US administrations, was a good combination to improve India–US relations. This triumvirate could have set India on the path that China took ten years later in 1971.[106]

For the reasons spelled out in the section on China below, it should have been clear to India by 1961 that China was an imminent military threat. That is, it was high time to set India–US economic and defence ties on mutually agreed platforms which would not be shaken much by changes in political leadership in either country. However, Nehru was probably uncomfortable about the CIA-supported April 1961 Bay of Pigs attempt to dislodge Cuban President Fidel Castro and the growing involvement of the US in Vietnam.

During the same visit to the US, Nehru happened to meet some of the heads of the largest US companies. At this meeting, Nehru was told by one of the businessmen, in a self-congratulatory manner, that Nehru was in the presence of fifty billionaires. A billion dollars was a lot of money in the early 1960s, but Nehru was appalled and did not react favourably.[107] Nehru's qualities of self-abnegation and indifference to wealth were necessary for him to make the contributions he did to the Indian freedom struggle. However, this mindset was a serious handicap in dealing with self-important US business tycoons.

As a result of the April 1956 Industrial Policy Resolution, defence and heavy industries were mostly the preserve of the public sector. In comparison, most heavy and armaments industries in the US were in the private sector. It was difficult for the public sector in India to do business with the private sector in the US. It may have been possible to dilute the pro-Pakistan tilt of the US if India had made significant volumes of arms purchases to feed the 'military-industrial complex'[108] in the US after J.F. Kennedy became President. All things considered, the time between Nehru's visit to the US 6-10 November 1961 and JFK's assassination on 22 November 1963 could have been better used to place India–US relations on firmer ground. Opportunities for closer economic ties were lost and as the much poorer of the two, in per capita income terms, India was the bigger loser.

The border war with China in 1962 ended in a humiliating defeat for India, and Nehru's reputation at home and abroad was in tatters. In panic mode, Nehru wrote two letters to JFK on 19 November 1962.[109] In the first letter, Nehru thanked JFK for the small arms and ammunition already received and sought 'air transport and jet fighters to stem the tide of Chinese aggression'. Nehru mentioned in this letter to JFK that he was writing a similar letter to the British PM Harold Macmillan. In Nehru's second letter to JFK he emphasized that Chinese forces were threatening the entire Brahmaputra valley and that he was concerned about aggression into Kashmir. Nehru felt that the only way of checking the Chinese was to use air power, and India needed twelve US squadrons of supersonic all-weather aircraft. And that the US personnel would have to fly the fighters and man the radar stations till Indian personnel could be trained. Nehru also sought two squadrons of B-47 bombers and confirmed that these fighters and bombers would be used only against China, not Pakistan. Just two days after Nehru had sent these written requests to the US President, China declared a unilateral ceasefire on 21 November 1962. We will never know whether the US would have sent the fighters and bombers and air force personnel if Chinese forces had moved southward into Assam. It is likely that China's decision to declare a unilateral ceasefire was influenced by their assessment that the US and other Western countries were on the verge of providing substantial military and technical assistance to democratic India against communist China.

Engagement with UN and Europe

India's experience with the UNSC on Kashmir was that the deliberations of this body were driven mostly by the interests of the UNSC permanent members. However, in the era in which the UN was set up, even the non-veto-wielding members felt it was worth having such a forum. Nehru took the UN seriously, and the cynicism today that the UN is a mere talk shop had not yet set in.[110] In September–October 1960 Nehru was in New York for a month to attend meetings at the UN. Even without knowing just how effete the UN would gradually become over the coming decades, a month was way too much time for an Indian PM to be away from priorities at home.

Nehru met General Secretary Khrushchev of the Soviet Communist Party at the Russian consulate during this trip. M. Rasgotra was present at this meeting and has mentioned in his autobiography[111] that Khrushchev remarked, 'You, Mr Nehru, are the world's hope for peace.' Nehru must have seen through this unctuous flattery, but the lack of equals within the Indian government or in the Congress party who could speak frankly to Nehru made timely course correction on foreign policy less likely.

Amid rising tensions with China, the first conference of non-aligned countries took place in Belgrade in 1961. Unexceptionably, Nehru's understanding of non-alignment was for India to be free to make up its own mind. Nehru's prominent 'non-aligned' friends were Nasser of Egypt, Sukarno of Indonesia, Nkrumah of Ghana and Tito of Yugoslavia. Fear of neocolonialism was a binding factor. However, India lost credibility with liberals in the West because these four countries were not democratic at home. The irony was that developed Western democracies had no difficulty in forging close strategic and economic linkages with dictatorships in Latin America, Africa or Asia.

Despite the extraction of huge economic and manpower contributions from the colonies, the two World Wars took a heavy toll on the UK's economy and youth. Somehow, till at least the late 1950s, the UK managed to punch way above its weight in its relations with India. For one, there was considerable nostalgia among the elite in the Central government since many had studied in the UK. Unfortunately for India, the UK took a shorter-term tactical approach to India–Pakistan relations. It was inevitable that the UK would favour oil-rich Muslim-majority monarchies, oligarchies and dictatorships, and by extension Pakistan. This was and is because the UK had and continues to have wider and deeper economic and exports of defence equipment interests in these countries as compared to India. It also did not help India–UK relations that the UK has a long history of giving asylum to political and high-net-worth economic refugees. For instance, from 1956 onwards, Angami Zapu Phizo the Naga leader masterminded his separatist activities out of London.

In Gundevia's view, Nehru was swayed more than warranted by arguments presented by the British government and particularly in matters relating to arms purchases. For instance, Nehru allowed himself to be convinced by Mountbatten to buy tanks from the UK as a counterweight to Pakistan buying tanks from the US without sufficiently exploring other options. India also bought a rundown Second World War aircraft carrier and Midge fighter aircraft from the UK. Over time, as ties with the UK inevitably weakened, India's defence and commercial relations with France and Germany started strengthening.

As of 1960, despite the anachronistic nature of its claim, Portugal wanted to cling on to Goa. At that time Portugal was under the authoritarian rule of Salazar. In two key Western bastions of democracy, namely the US and the UK, the sentiment was, ironically, pro-Portugal. An obvious reason was that since 1949 Portugal was a founding member of the US-dominated inter-governmental military alliance called the North Atlantic Treaty Organization (NATO). Portugal also provided an extremely useful, from a cold-war perspective, airbase facility to the US at its Lajes airfield in the Azores archipelago in the north Atlantic region.

The widespread Western support for Portugal can be gauged from Crocker's illogical assertion that Portugal's claim to Goa was similar to India's stand on Kashmir. In December 1961 Nehru authorized Indian Army action to take over Goa, this last European colony on the Indian subcontinent.[112] This was consistent with growing domestic sentiment against continued Portuguese occupation of Goa and was popular with Indian voters. The US, the UK, France and Turkey[113] called for immediate withdrawal of Indian troops and sponsored a United Nations Security Council (UNSC) resolution to this effect. Adlai Stevenson was particularly vitriolic against India. The USSR vetoed this UNSC resolution and was perceived as standing by India in its hour of need.

Soviet Bloc

Stalin was said to have remarked derisively that India was not really independent even after August 1947 since it still had British generals heading its armed forces. Perhaps for that or other reasons, Stalin chose not to meet with Vijaya Lakshmi Pandit, Nehru's younger sister and India's first ambassador to the USSR, during her three-year term in Moscow from 1947 to 1949. However, Stalin did meet India's second ambassador to the USSR S. Radhakrishnan who was stationed in Moscow from 1949 to 1952. Perhaps Radhakrishnan was seen as favourably disposed towards the Soviet Union and in some circles in the UK he was derided as the Soviet ambassador to the West. The fact is that Radhakrishnan did push for closer India–USSR relations and for India to make critically needed foodgrain purchases from Russia.[114]

Nehru first visited the Soviet Union in 1927 at the invitation of the Communist Party of the Soviet Union (CPSU) on the tenth anniversary of the October 1917 revolution. This was twenty years before Independence. The Soviet leadership was prescient since they could not have known that Nehru would necessarily be the PM as and when Indian gained independence. Nehru's writings and speeches must have marked him out in Soviet decision-making circles as someone worth keeping in touch with.

After becoming the Indian PM, between the two superpowers Nehru chose to visit the US first in 1949, and he visited the USSR six years later in June 1955. Ergo Nehru did try to reach out to the West in his own didactic way before he turned to Moscow. Nehru was met at the airport in Moscow by the entire CPSU Politburo and extended unprecedented courtesies throughout his visit.

Nehru was shown around and was duly impressed with the Soviet Union's industrial progress. On 21 June 1955 Nehru met with a phalanx of senior Soviet leaders (Bulganin, Khrushchev, Kaganovich, Mikoyan, Gromyko and Kuznetsov). At this and other meetings, Nehru exchanged views on the international situation, developments in the Far East and what would be discussed at the Four Power Conference which was to be held the following month.[115] Khrushchev remarked that the 'Soviet Union was trying to draw up the iron curtain but the requisite help was not forthcoming from the other side'.[116] Comparatively little was said about bilateral trade or FDI. In fact, Mikoyan commented that the 'Soviet Union did not look for foreign markets'. It was a sign of the times that top government leaders mostly discussed international affairs, and it is also likely that the Soviets did not have much to say about India's ongoing development efforts with a mixed-economy model.

Nehru's visit to the USSR in the summer of 1955 was followed by Khrushchev's trip to India in November 1955. The Soviet Union had provided technical and financial assistance in the setting up of a steel production unit in Bhilai, and Khrushchev visited this plant during his stay in India. These visits to and from Russia and the cooperation must have got the attention of the US. It was probably a confirmation for the West that India was playing the two sides to extract the maximum possible assistance from both sides. This line of Western reasoning mistakenly assumed that opinions within the Indian government were uniformly against the US and favoured the Soviet Union. Ministers such as Morarji Desai were well disposed towards the US.

India's immediate recognition of Fidel Castro's government in Havana after the kleptocratic government of the Cuban dictator Fulgencio Batista was overthrown on 1 January 1959 must have been another source of irritation for the US government. It must have been noticed in the US State Department and particularly by the intensely anti-Castro Cuban émigrés in Florida that the Cuban revolutionary hero Che Guevara visited Delhi in July 1959. Although Nehru did not approve of communist dictatorships, he and many others in India viewed the leadership of countries such as Cuba, which had thrown off the yoke of foreign domination, with admiration.

Prime Minister Jawaharlal Nehru in a happy mood after receiving a box of cigars as a gift from the Cuban delegation led by Che Guevara on 1 July 1959. Photograph courtesy: Photo Division, Government of India.

East and South East Asia

Japan got the better of Russia in their war of 1905 and acquired the image of a resurgent Asian country. However, Japan's brutality in Korea and China before and during the Second World War years was viewed with discomfort in India. So much so that the Congress party organized a boycott of Japanese goods in 1939, and Nehru visited China in that year. Subsequently, given that Japan was bludgeoned into submission by the US through the use of nuclear weapons, there was sympathy again for that country.[117]

The US and forty-seven other countries signed a Japanese Peace Treaty in San Francisco in September 1951 to end the US occupation of Japan. India chose not to be a party to this treaty and arrived at a separate bilateral agreement with Japan in June 1952. Among the reasons for India's refusal to be a party to the San Francisco treaty was that Taiwan was not to be returned to China and the jurisdiction of the Soviet Union over the Kuril and Sakhalin islands was not recognized. During Nehru's years in office, Japan had not recovered from the destruction of the war years and remained firmly under US tutelage.

After Indonesia obtained its independence from the Dutch in 1949, Sukarno became its first President and remained in power till 1965 overlapping for most of that time with Nehru. Sukarno was one of the leaders who attended the first non-aligned summit meeting in Belgrade in 1961. Earlier, India's participation in the 1955 Afro-Asian Conference at Bandung (Indonesia) was Nehru's way of showing solidarity with newly emerging and independent countries of these two continents. The rest of South East Asia was still finding its feet during Nehru's years as PM, and he was somewhat critical of SEATO members such as Thailand and the Philippines for opting to be firmly in the US camp, and that too, so soon after regaining their independence from colonial powers. For instance, in a conversation with Indian ambassadors to South East Asian countries in the summer of 1963, Nehru remarked that there was not much in common between India and Thailand. Upon being asked to clarify, Nehru dismissively said that 'the PM of Thailand is an important personality in the Coca Cola company'.[118] The ASEAN grouping of nations was formed post Nehru in 1967.

Military Defeat against China Was Game Changing

The people-to-people and trade relations with China go back thousands of years. The Silk Road, which enabled trade between China and the Mediterranean nations, had a southern branch which entered India via Lahore. This 'road' is credited with resulting in highly profitable trade for India and China and also the spread of Buddhism from India to China and beyond.

More recently, from the nineteenth century onwards, the British East India Company and its successor British India actively promoted the sale of opium grown in India to China.[119] During the Second World War, leaders of the Indian Congress party such as Nehru sided with China and were critical of the harsh Japanese occupation of Shanghai and Nanjing. After Indian

Independence, it was one of the first countries to recognize the PRC and break ties with Taiwan.

After the Second World War, the communists led by Mao Tsetung came to power in China in October 1949. Soon thereafter, in June 1950 hostilities broke out between North and South Korea with the military involvement of the US in support of the South, and China–USSR on the side of the North. It is estimated that up to 2 million civilians were killed in the two Koreas. About 200,000 Chinese soldiers were killed, and the US lost 40,000 of its armed forces personnel. Nehru voiced his concern that the world may slip into a Third World War, and India's medical missions to the Korean peninsula were praised by the Western media and intellectuals. However, India's protestations that the combatants on both sides disengage ended up annoying both the US and China.

China is currently (as of May 2019) in possession of the Aksai Chin area in the west, which, as per the Macartney–MacDonald line,[120] should have been part of India. In the east, the Line of Actual Control (LAC) is roughly consistent with the McMahon Line. The LAC is not a border since the two countries have not yet agreed on the precise location of the border. A corridor of about 20 kilometres width, effectively no man's land, used to lie between the Indian and Chinese armies along the LAC.[121]

More than three decades before Indian independence, a Shimla Convention was held in July 1914 to agree on borders between British India, Tibet and China. While this convention was signed by the Tibetan and British representatives it was initialled by the Chinese delegate. It is only post October 1950, after the PRC invaded and occupied Tibet that China became a neighbour. After this takeover of Tibet, China has worked ruthlessly towards eliminating any vestige of independent Tibet.

Nehru felt that the British had wronged China just as it had in colonizing India and dominating other territories around the globe. It is apparent from one of Nehru's letters to chief ministers that he was convinced that no practical purpose would be served by holding on to rights of access and stationing of personnel that the British were able to impose on China in 1914. In any case, Nehru appears to have concluded that India did not have the military capability to challenge China in Tibet.

In the context of China's occupation of Tibet, Sardar Patel's letter of 7 November 1950 to Nehru cautioning him about Chinese intentions remains a much-discussed document till today.[122] It is likely that the letter was drafted by Sir G.S. Bajpai who was the secretary general in the Ministry of Foreign Affairs at that time. Patel's contention in this letter was that the Chinese had managed to instil in the Indian ambassador to China, K.M. Panikkar,[123] a false sense of confidence in their professed desire to settle the Tibetan problem by peaceful means. It does not appear that India's ambassadors in the capitals of the five permanent members of the UNSC raised any red flags (no pun intended) about China. PMs do not have the luxury of passing on the blame for their decisions to others. The responsibility for the choice of ambassadors, and consequently the quality of the information they transmitted back to Delhi, rested with Nehru.

The armed occupation of Tibet should have triggered an Indian rethink about China's intentions. Nehru would have known about the fighting abilities of China's army after the bloody nose the US got from the Chinese in the battle of the Yalu-river during the Korean War. And, later in 1954, during Nehru's visit to China, Mao had shocked him by expressing indifference to the potential death of millions of Chinese were his country to be attacked by the US with nuclear weapons. Nehru's overall strategy was based on avoidance of war. However, this vision overlooked the possibility that India may be forced to go to war to defend its borders. Given the long record of conflicts between nation states on border issues, there was no reason to expect that China necessarily shared India's hope for an Asian revival driven by cooperation between these two large countries.

The 1954 visit of Chinese premier Zhou Enlai to India, and the acceptance of a trade and transit treaty with Tibet (effectively accepting it as part of China) and the Panchsheel ideals of peaceful coexistence, are consistent with the speculative thought that Nehru was buying time to settle matters in India's north-east. The 'Agreement between the Republic of India and the People's Republic of China on Trade and Intercourse between the Tibet region of China and India' was signed in Peking (Beijing) on 29 April 1954. Under this agreement, the Indian mission in Lhasa was reduced to a consulate general, and trade agencies were opened in Gyantse, Gangtok and Yatung. Reciprocally, China opened a consulate in Bombay and trade agencies in Kalimpong, New Delhi and Calcutta. The British-era practice of Indian military escorts in Tibet was withdrawn. At around this time, India suggested to the West that the People's Republic of China should be accepted as a member of the UN. The concessions with regard to Tibet and the friendly gesture of advocating membership of the UN for PRC should have been significant enough to extract a mutually satisfactory recognition of India's entire border with China.

The Dalai Lama was concerned about the loss of Tibetan autonomy, and he visited India in 1956 and would have liked to stay on. By that time, there was a seventeen-point agreement between Tibet and China, and the latter was in physical control of most of Tibet including Lhasa. Of course, this seventeen-point agreement had been agreed to by the Dalai Lama under duress when he was just fifteen years of age. The agreement guaranteed the right of Tibetans to follow their way of life and respect for Buddhist beliefs and clergy. Zhou Enlai chose to visit India in 1956, and he committed China to respecting the seventeen-point agreement. Nehru advised the Dalai Lama to return to Lhasa, probably because he felt China would accuse India of interfering in Tibet if His Holiness were to be granted refuge in India.

Delhi must have been aware that there were minor incidents between the two armies along the border every year between 1955 and 1958. However, the Parliament was not informed of these skirmishes. It is unlikely that China could have built the Sinkiang–Tibet road via Aksai Chin without anyone in India coming to know. It is likely that India kept a lid on this information as it needed time to get more entrenched in the North-east.

In March 1959, nine years after China had occupied Tibet, a mass uprising broke out in Lhasa against the brutalities of Chinese occupation, desecration of Tibetan monasteries and persecution of Buddhist monks. In the ensuing confusion the Dalai Lama fled to India. According to Bruce Riedel,[124] His Holiness was escorted by a CIA operative who remained in radio contact, throughout the journey, with CIA headquarters in the US in McLean, Virginia.

Gyalo Thondup, who was born in 1928, is seven years older than his younger brother the Dalai Lama. Thondup's fascinating autobiography titled *The Noodle Maker of Kalimpong* is about Tibet's troubled history from the time he was a child.[125] Thondup emphasizes in his account that Tibetan monks and the population at large had extremely low levels of literacy and awareness in the early twentieth century. According to him, the Tibetan nobility and religious leadership did not understand the danger to Tibet's autonomy after the British passed on their rights in Tibet to India. Official circles in India are sceptical about the veracity of some of the details in Thondup's book. The facts are that Thondup married a Chinese lady with influential family connections and he met the top Chinese leadership at frequent intervals on his visits to China and Taiwan over seventy years.[126]

In his account of those times, Thondup refers to his meetings in India with Nehru and director of the IB, B.N. Mullick.[127] The details in Thondup's account raise intriguing questions without shedding any conclusive light on the answers. For instance, Thondup mentions that the CIA was involved in the training of Tibetan resistance fighters from the mid-1950s till 1966 to use the Morse code, and in the use of arms in camps located in East Pakistan and Mustang in Nepal. Small bands of trained Tibetans would dart back into Tibet and confront Chinese patrols, and, on occasion, were able to come back with official Chinese documents containing valuable information. The obvious question is to what extent were the Indian authorities aware of CIA activities in and around India. It is likely that Indian intelligence and hence Nehru would have known about this. It must have been apparent to Nehru that a handful of Tibetan resistance fighters could not overcome the Chinese army. On the downside for India, China would have perceived the involvement of the CIA, with or without the tacit agreement of the Indian government, as interference in Tibetan and hence China's internal affairs.

As Chinese armed presence in Tibet gradually became a stranglehold, the local population resented their loss of autonomy and particularly the violation of the seventeen-point agreement. When the Dalai Lama finally left for India in 1959, it was in the midst of an army crackdown on protesters in Lhasa and on resistance fighters. Thondup asserts that the Chinese were fooled into thinking the Dalai Lama was still in Lhasa when he had already escaped disguised as a Tibetan army soldier. Even if this is factually correct, it may have been possible for the Chinese to have intercepted the Dalai Lama on his the long journey to Arunachal in India. The team members of His Holiness were using Morse signals to communicate with Tibetan émigrés in Darjeeling and those signals were possibly intercepted by Chinese agencies. Perhaps China chose not to stop His Holiness because there was a higher probability of Tibetan resistance regrouping in Lhasa if it were to be centred on the person of the Dalai Lama. According to Thondup, about a hundred thousand Tibetans were killed by the Chinese army and many thousands fled Tibet to India as refugees. This Tibetan suffering may have been less if Nehru had allowed the Dalai Lama to stay on in India in 1956.

After the Dalai Lama was given refuge in India Nehru met him in Mussoorie on 24 April 1959. Subsequently, His Holiness gave frank, anti-China responses to questions at a press conference on 20 June 1959.[128] The Indian government immediately advised the Dalai Lama that he should not carry out any political activities in India that may be seen as anti-China.

Zhou Enlai visited India again in April 1960. During this visit, he offered a settlement of the border in the east including Arunachal in exchange for Aksai Chin. Around this time, a White Paper on the boundary issue had been released by the Indian government. This was counterproductive since it unleashed uninformed nationalistic passions in India. Nehru was inclined to accept the Chinese offer, but sentiment in India had turned against China and an important opportunity was missed. As for defence preparedness, despite the tensions with China, most of India's troops were stationed on the border with Pakistan.

Much has been said by domestic and foreign commentators about Nehru's so-called 'forward policy' at the India–China border. It consisted of forty-two new Indian check posts in the no-man's land between the two countries, and this was decried by China as provocative. China may have felt by the late 1950s that India would have known about the CIA's U-2 spying missions out of the Kumaritola airbase (close to Dacca, now Dhaka) in East Pakistan and the US supply of guns and communication equipment to Tibetan rebels. According to Riedel,[129] Indian interactions with US intelligence prior to 1962 included a meeting between then director of IB, Mullick, and CIA officials in Hawaii. These alleged contacts with US agencies may have fed into China's paranoia about Western machinations against China.

Articles in Indian news magazines have suggested CIA involvement with the construction of an airfield at Charbatia, 35 miles from Cuttack, in Orissa. The suggestion is that in the early 1960s the CIA wanted to fly spying missions out of this airfield, but after some dilly-dallying Nehru finally turned down this US request.[130] It is likely that this CIA move was after the 1962 war when decision-making circles in India may have been more receptive to the US using an airbase in Orissa to spy on China. It is possible that Indian agencies would have gained technical expertise from collaborating with US agencies. In any case, within nine years, by 1971, Richard Nixon, the US President, and Henry Kissinger, his national security adviser, were literally pleading with China for collaboration in an effort to contain the Soviet Union.

Bilateral differences with India and internal developments fed into China's preparations since around 1959–60 for a war with its southern neighbour. Mao's Great Leap Forward at the end of the 1950s was an economic and human disaster. By some estimates, as many as 20 million people died of starvation. In 1959 the *People's Daily* (presumably on Mao's directive) had carried the incredible suggestion that India intended to build a greater empire in South East Asia. That is, well before the 1962 war, Chairman Mao chose to air China's absurd propaganda about India's expansionist intentions. Mao possibly needed an assured quick victory in war to rally support for himself domestically. And, to put down a potential competitor in Asia with democratic credentials which irritatingly for China's leadership received accolades in liberal circles in the West.

On 22 October 1962, two days after China had launched full-scale attacks on 20 October 1962 against Indian positions on the eastern and western borders, Nehru wrote to N.S. Khrushchev, chairman of the council of ministers of the USSR.[131] In this seven-page letter, Nehru explained at length the exchanges between India and China and why India would have to 'resist if the Chinese continued this new aggression in the Eastern sector'. There is a certain make-believe tone to this letter since forty-eight hours after China had started overrunning Indian positions with overwhelming military force, Nehru sounds as if he is still not totally clear about Chinese intentions.

It appears from this letter to Khrushchev that Nehru did not wish to convey any sense of Indian helplessness and that it did not expect the Soviet Union to side with India. The ground reality was that by this time India did need help, and the Soviet Union could have been asked to defuse the situation by using its influence with China although it was waning by this time. In this letter Nehru expresses his surprise about a reference in an official Soviet note 'to those who are interested in intensifying world tension, who wish to line their coats by military clash between India and China', to 'forces of war' and 'imperialist circles' and how they 'dream in their sleep of ways of disturbing the friendship of the Soviet Union with India and with China'. It is obvious that the Soviet note was referring to the United States trying to create problems in the relationships between India–USSR and India–China. Clearly, Nehru is disappointed with the contents of the Soviet note but chose not to say so explicitly. The overall sense of the letter is that Nehru does not expect any specific help or even a statement in favour of India from the USSR. So much for India consistently and justifiably criticizing US military involvement around the world while being careful not to step on Soviet sensitivities.

It would surprise non-specialists that Nehru and Zhou exchanged letters[132] about the border even as hostilities continued between the two armies. Zhou wrote to Nehru on 24 October, suggesting PM-level talks between him and Nehru. Zhou suggested that China and India withdraw to the north and south respectively of the LAC. The Chinese were prepared to respect the McMahon Line in the east but wanted the 'traditional' border in the middle and the west. Nehru responded to Zhou on 27 October that it was not clear where the LAC was and whether the two sides would withdraw to prior to 8 September 1962 positions. Nehru's reply mentioned that '. . . nothing in my long political career has hurt and grieved me more than the fact that the hopes and aspirations for peaceful and friendly neighbourly relations . . . which we worked so hard since the establishment of the PRC should have been shattered by the hostile and unfriendly twist given to India–China relations during the past few years.'[133]

It was natural for Nehru to feel betrayed. In the following passage from *The Discovery of India*, which Nehru had completed by 1946, he was sentimentally hopeful about India's future relations with China:

'And now the wheel of fate has turned full circle and India and China look towards each other again and past memories are in their minds; again pilgrims of a new kind cross or fly over the mountains that separate them, bringing their messages of cheer and goodwill and creating fresh bonds of a friendship that will endure.'

Zhou wrote back on 4 November that China could not agree to the prior to 8 September 1962 positions. On his birthday on 14 November, Nehru responded that for India to accept China's suggestions meant that in the middle section China's border would extend to the south of the Himalayan crest, which was never the case in the past. Effectively, according to Nehru, this would leave 'the Indian frontier defenceless and at the mercy of any fresh invasion by an aggressive and arrogant neighbor'.[134]

On 19 November, Zhou summoned the Indian chargé d'affaires in Beijing and harangued him about the military aid and advice India was receiving from the US, and that imperialistic countries were intriguing to separate India and China. On 20 November, India's chargé d'affaires was summoned again and told that China's unilateral ceasefire would start from 22 November. The fact that the US had ordered the aircraft carrier Enterprise into the Bay of Bengal may have alerted the Chinese to the possibility that the US may mount air assaults against forward Chinese positions.

A day after China had put into effect its announcement of a ceasefire, Nehru wrote to all CMs and the prime minister of J&K state on 23 November 1962.[135] This letter was an attempt to explain briefly (the letter is just one page) that although India 'cannot object to their [Chinese] withdrawal . . . we cannot admit even indirectly to their claim to parts of our territory'. The letter also states the obvious that India's 'war [in the future] effort essentially means greater production in agriculture and industry . . . concentration of certain basic aspects of our Third Five Year Plan'. Nehru also mentions that 'it is of utmost importance that we should not let defeatist rumours to spread'.

This letter is disappointing in several ways. First, Nehru was not upfront about his own limited understanding of China and its intentions, and the numerous opportunities that were missed to reach a border settlement. Although it never helps to be defeatist, a call from Nehru to bolster the country's defences and immediate replacement of the entire complacent top brass in the armed forces, Ministry of Defence and the Ministry of External Affairs would have been in order. The reference to the implementation of the Third Five Year Plan (1961–66) made little sense when the implementation of the Second Plan needed considerable bilateral and multilateral financial assistance from the West. And, the total resources for the Third Plan, even though this plan period had started in 1961, had yet to be fully identified at the end of 1962. On 23 November 1962, the country would have been better served if Nehru had sought the nation's understanding as the government re-evaluated all its options to strengthen both the economy and its defence preparedness.

According to journalist Bertil Lintner,[136] China took at least three years to obtain detailed intelligence, from Tibetan-speaking informants on both sides of the border who knew local dialects, about the terrain and logistical details in Arunachal. Lintner mentions that Indian prisoners of war, on return, said that at the border there were Chinese interpreters who spoke Tamil, Bengali and other Indian languages. If Lintner's information is correct, China was preparing for war with India for several years before 1962. After China declared a ceasefire, the de facto border in the west continued to include Aksai Chin in China, and in the east, Chinese forces withdrew out of Arunachal to pre-war borders.

The following extract from declassified minutes of a meeting between Nixon and Kissinger with Chinese premier Zhou Enlai almost a decade later on 23 February 1972 in Beijing demonstrates that Nehru's sentiments were not at all reciprocated by Chinese leaders. In fact, several of the remarks are factually incorrect, and the derisive tone of both the Americans and the Chinese about India is vicious.

Even allowing for Nixon's dislike for Indira Gandhi, his laughing at the sheer effrontery of Zhou calling India a 'bottomless hole' is surprising. Zhou's deliberate lie (parroting Mao's line of 1959) that Nehru advocated a greater India encompassing 'Malaysia, Ceylon . . . Tibet etc.' was heavy spin doctoring. Both sides must have assumed that the contents of their conversation would never be made public.

In 1972 Zhou's angst towards India was probably because China had been upstaged. That is, China could not help its client state Pakistan by preventing the creation of Bangladesh. In the early 1970s, China was still a poor, ideologically driven country yet wanted other nations to look up to it. Nehru's extensive and fluent writings in English, gave him a global audience and larger-than-life image even well after he had passed away. This despite India's poverty and relative lack of military strength, must have rankled with Mao and Zhou. Nehru's misreading of the minds of China's leaders was extremely costly for India and the consequences are playing out till now.

MEMORANDUM

THE WHITE HOUSE

WASHINGTON

~~TOP SECRET~~/SENSITIVE/EXCLUSIVELY EYES ONLY

<u>MEMORANDUM OF CONVERSATION</u>

PARTICIPANTS: The President
Dr. Henry A. Kissinger, Assistant to the
    President for National Security Affairs
John H. Holdridge, NSC Staff
Winston Lord, NSC Staff

Prime Minister Chou En-lai
Ch'iao Kuan-hua, Vice Minister of Foreign Affairs
Chang Wen-chin, Director of Western Europe, North
    American, and Australasian Affairs, Ministry of
    Foreign Affairs
Wang Hai-jung, Deputy Director of Protocol
Chao Chi-hua, Ministry of Foreign Affairs
Chi Chao-chu, Interpreter
T'ang Wen-sheng, Interpreter
Two Notetakers

DATE & TIME: Wednesday, February 23, 1972 - 2:00 p.m. -6:00 p.m.

PLACE: The President's Guest House, Peking

(There were some opening pleasantries in which Prime Minister Chou
asked about Mrs. Nixon and the President said she was fine. He added
that she had been impressed with the acupuncture demonstrations she had
seen. The President noted that there were forecasts of snow and asked
if they would get to the Great Wall the next day. Chou responded yes.

Chou then referred to a mural hanging in the room painted in 1935 which
depicted a battle in which the Chinese Communists won a big victory over
Chiang Kai-shek, a very great turning point. The battle was near Tsunyi,
in Kweichow province, after which the Communist forces marched west
into Yunnan. In response to the President's question of whether this was
the battle in which the Communists crossed the river, Prime Minister Chou

~~TOP SECRET~~/SENSITIVE/EXCLUSIVELY EYES ONLY

TOP SECRET/SENSITIVE/EXCLUSIVELY EYES ONLY   -10-

Prime Minister Chou: And India actually is a bottomless hole. (President Nixon laughs)

President Nixon: When the Prime Minister referred to the problem India has with Bangladesh, as I look at India's brief history, it has had enough trouble trying to digest West Bengal. If now it tries to digest East Bengal it may cause indigestion which would be massive.

Prime Minister Chou: That's bound to be so. It is also a great pity that the daughter (Madame Gandhi) has also taken as her legacy the philosophy of her father embodied in the book Discovery of India (in English). Have you read it?

Dr. Kissinger: He was thinking of a great Indian empire?

Prime Minister Chou: Yes, he was thinking of a great Indian empire -- Malaysia, Ceylon, etc. It would probably also include our Tibet. When he was writing that book he was in a British prison, but one reserved for gentlemen in Darjeeling. Nehru told me himself that the prison was in Sikkim, facing the Himalayan mountains. At the time I hadn't read the book, but my colleague Chen Yi had, and called it to my attention. He said it was precisely the spirit of India which was embodied in the book. Later on when I read it I had the same thought.

President Nixon: When did Chen Yi die?

Prime Minister Chou: Just recently. Chairman Mao attended the funeral. He had cancer of the stomach. Do you have a way of curing cancer?

President Nixon: It is a serious problem. One of the programs we want to undertake this year is a massive research program on cancer. We hope to have such a program. Who knows when we will find the answer? Scientific genius is not natural any place in the world, and we don't know where to find it -- here, or there. But whatever money is required will now be provided for massive cancer research.

Prime Minister Chou: We can cooperate in that field.

President Nixon: We would approve of that. I was going to suggest it in the counterpart meetings if the question of medical research comes up. We will make all our facilities available on cancer, because research should not be for one country but for all the countries of the world.

TOP SECRET/SENSITIVE/EXCLUSIVELY EYES ONLY

Legacy

Nehru suffered a stroke in January 1964 during the Congress party's annual session in Bhubaneswar. Gundevia mentions in his book, *Outside the Archives*, that despite Nehru's difficulty in walking and slowness of speech, he kept working long hours. A few months later, Nehru passed away on 27 May 1964. I was in seventh grade in school at that time. My father was a junior minister in Nehru's cabinet, and I accompanied him as we filed solemnly past Nehru's body which lay in state in Teen Murti House. We also attended Nehru's cremation which took place at a spot, now called Shantivan, along the west bank of the Yamuna river close to Rajghat where Mahatma Gandhi was cremated. It took our (Ambassador) car several hours to reach the cremation grounds as we followed the slow-moving ceremonially decorated cortège on which Nehru's body was carried. My overwhelming memory of that non-air-conditioned car journey and the cremation ground is that I was extremely thirsty and there was a sea of people on foot all around us. The air was thick with grief, and it was spontaneous and palpable. Even so, the huge crowds were self-disciplined, and I do not remember any pushing or shoving at Shantivan.

Nehru was a towering figure in Indian politics for over four decades. His impact on the country overshadows that of all other PMs who have come after him till now. Nehru's successors did not have his level of wide reading (except P.V. Narasimha Rao), his capacity to reflect and write, or his ability to make moving speeches. For example, Nehru's speech at Independence and when Gandhi passed away, and *The Discovery of India*, written while he was in prison, are simple and yet relevant even today, and should be compulsory reading in high schools.

Nehru as the first head of India's Central government had the burden of reconciling a range of retrograde and poorly informed attitudes to forge consensus on forward-looking social legislation and government policies. The enormous domestic, foreign policy and security challenges that Nehru addressed all look simple to face with the benefit of hindsight. Memories have faded about the difficult environment in which India was put together in its present form.

First, a liberal and forward-looking Constitution was adopted based on Nehru's commitment and that of the freedom-fighting generation of leaders to democracy, which institutionalized legal structures against religious bigotry and feudal mindsets. Despite low levels of education and widespread illiteracy, basic norms of debate in the national Parliament and state assemblies were established. His contributions in setting up transparent precedents of governance are still basically intact despite the cynicism of several of his successors. Nehru had civil servants around him who were glad to slave for him. However, the circle was too small, mostly ICS officers, and hence somewhat inbred.

Nehru's legacy includes the holding of regular free and fair elections. This achievement alone, which involved the setting up of the Election Commission and all the attendant procedures, separates India from its neighbours to the east, west and north. In addition, parliamentary committees and the checks and balances of a well-functioning democracy, including a free press and independent judiciary, were institutionalized. Nehru's Congress won absolute majorities in the Lok Sabha in 1952, 1957 and 1962. R.K. Laxman's cartoon below says it all about the 'common' man's trust in Nehru.

During the Nehru years, educational and specialized institutions were headed by experts rather than those who were close to the ruling party in Delhi.

Of course, this had a lot to do with the optimism of a newly independent country. The foundations of India's leading scientific and technological institutions were laid during the 1950s. For example, the Bhabha Atomic Research Centre (BARC), Indian Institutes of Technology (IITs), All India Institute of Medical Sciences (AIIMS) and the Indian Space Research Organization (ISRO). The emphasis was on identifying academics or professionals with proven track records to head institutions of excellence, including in the social sciences. No other Indian PM has come close to Nehru's success in building quality institutions which have served the nation.

Nehru was able to enthuse Indian professionals with qualifications from technologically advanced countries including the US, the UK and Canada to return to India to participate in institution building. This sense among well-trained professionals of giving back to India continued through the 1950s and 1960s. From the 1970s onwards, academics, engineers and doctors went to developed countries for higher studies but increasingly they stopped coming back.

Nehru was fortunate to have highly gifted professionals and public figures around him who were solely driven by the motivation of nation-building. These included cabinet colleagues, chief ministers in various states, scientists and a host of other gifted contemporaries without whom several of India's achievements would not have been possible. The enthusiasm and idealism of the countless who worked in junior positions immediately after India's independence collectively constituted the pillars on which Nehru was able to start building the edifice of a forward-looking unified country.

Nehru is criticized for his so-called 'socialist' economic policies. The fact is that Nehru's mixed performance on the economic front was a huge improvement on that of British India. For instance, inflation was muted during the first ten years after Independence and severe food shortages were averted. Despite an acute shortage of capital, there was significant industrial growth. The following observation suggests that Nehru was not too theoretical or far removed from the practical realities of governance. John Mathai[137] commented around 1958 that 'Pandit Nehru like Mahatma Gandhi before him, combined political idealism with a keen sense of political expedience—not in any unworthy sense but in the realization that idealism bore no fruit unless men's eyes could be opened to it and their support enlisted in its behalf.'[138]

Well before Independence Nehru was convinced that India would play an important role in international affairs as a large country. At the same time, Nehru felt that India should not get sucked into taking sides between the West led by the US and the Soviet bloc of nations. However, the India economy would have modernized faster and growth would have accelerated earlier if he had not been so wary about forging closer economic linkages with the West. Nehru knew principal decision makers in Britain personally and was not sufficiently detached on matters involving the UK.

Developed democracies were piqued by Nehru's grandstanding on the world stage without commensurate economic or military weight. Communist China's leaders felt the same. And, Nehru blundered in the lead-up to the 1962 war with China. Nehru's default mode was to trust his own ability to convince others, and this did not necessarily work with heads of government of other countries.

Nehru did not intend that non-alignment would become a movement. It was his way of carving out foreign policy space for India. Subsequently, non-alignment came to be mistakenly seen in Western countries not so much as a desire for autonomy than as a banding together of countries with an anti-West agenda. This was more the doing of those who came after Nehru. However, during his years as PM, Nehru could have promoted the activities of not-for-profit Western bodies such as the Ford and Rockefeller Foundations more actively. Such institutions could have served as valuable partners in expediting universal primary education and efficiency in agriculture.

Despite the examples of conflicts based on personal ambition and religious and other seemingly irreconcilable differences around the world, Nehru retained an optimism that peaceful accommodation could prevail. This line of thinking was natural for Gandhi, Nehru, Patel and others leaders who had organized non-violent non-cooperation and voluntarily spent years in jail during the freedom struggle. This sense that truth would prevail found expression in independent India's idealistic motto 'Sayameva Jayate' (Truth Will Triumph). Moral conviction was a source of strength during the freedom struggle. It was on occasion a liability in India's foreign policy after Independence.

An extremely distressing error that various commentators deliberately or mistakenly make is to speak of Nehru and Indira Gandhi in the same breath. For instance, use of the phrase Nehru–Gandhi dynasty, as if similar values and principles governed decision making during the Nehru era and the Indira Gandhi years. Nehru's missteps were more in the realm of foreign policy and were just that—mistakes. Starting with Indira Gandhi and subsequently other PMs, decisions were often driven by personal, family or partisan interests. The only way that Nehru and Indira Gandhi were related was that he was a doting father and she a loving daughter. In everything to do with modes of governance, building of institutions, transparency and personal values they were as different as day and night.

After Nehru passed away in May 1964, Lal Bahadur Shastri was selected by the Congress members of Parliament (MPs) as the next PM. No one could have anticipated that Shastri would pass away in Tashkent in January 1966. Consequently, Nehru cannot be accused of foisting his daughter on India as PM after him. However, Nehru did acquiesce in Indira Gandhi becoming the Congress president in 1959 when there were several others with more valuable contributions during the freedom struggle and longer association with the party waiting in the wings.

After Patel's passing, other senior leaders in the Congress such as Rajagopalachari, Acharya Kripalani and Jayaprakash Narayan drifted away or joined other parties. Nehru was the crowd favourite, and he led the campaign in three general elections in 1952, 1957 and 1962. In each of these elections, the Congress was able to win more than 70 per cent of the seats in the Lok Sabha. Nehru was able to consistently lead the Congress to overwhelming victories in elections, and there were no co-equals within the party. This meant that despite the efforts Nehru made to consult widely, it was his individual understanding that dominated decision making and that was unhealthy.

Was Nehru a 'huge banyan tree' that did not allow anything to grow beneath it? From various accounts, it does seem that Nehru appeared worn out by 1959–60 by the pressures of office and particularly the road travel for electioneering. Unfortunately, no one close to him persuaded him to groom a successor. After 1957 he could have continued as Congress president but without the day-to-day responsibilities of head of government. The US instituted a two-term limit for Presidents after the three terms of F.D. Roosevelt. Although parliamentary democracies around the world do not have such term limits, it would have helped the cause of Indian democracy had Nehru persuaded Parliament to pass legislation that limits an Indian PM to two five-year terms or ten years in total if there are midterm elections. Such a move by Nehru would have probably sailed through and would have nipped in the bud the possibility of personality cults developing around any subsequent Indian PM.

Given Nehru's school and university education in England, he unwittingly perpetuated an English-speaking elitism. On 15 August 1947, as India awoke to freedom, Nehru made his brilliant and moving 'tryst with destiny' speech in the central hall in Parliament. My abiding memory of that speech is that I first saw it in a black-and-white grainy Films Division documentary with a squeaky soundtrack and yet found the words truly inspiring. The slow whirring of the old-style fans could be seen but not heard. Nehru probably overlooked the reality that less than 5 per cent of Indians would have understood his speech since it was delivered in English. Nehru could have had his speech recorded in English in his own voice and had it transmitted simultaneously over the air as he delivered it in Hindi. The speech could also have been read out on All India Radio in all major Indian languages.

The Indian elite in all walks of life, not just politics, was English speaking during the Nehru era. To the extent that the vernacular-speaking masses did not understand the English used by decision makers, there was bound to be a pushback in a representative democracy. The exclusive use of local languages for government forms and applications started in the south and has now gradually spread all over the country. This pride in India's well-developed regional languages and culture is natural. However, as it descends to chauvinism and rejection of English, average Indians risk losing this useful medium of communication with the rest of the world. Even as of mid-2019, no Indian language including Hindi has been accepted widely enough throughout the country for English to be fully displaced.

On Mahatma Gandhi's return to India from South Africa, he dressed exclusively in the most simple of Indian dresses—a single piece of white cloth called 'dhoti'. Sardar Patel too dropped his Western suit and chose the dhoti and kurta after he left his law practice and joined the freedom movement. The clothes of Gandhi, Patel and many others who were part of the struggle for freedom were made out of hand-spun cloth called khadi. Nehru chose the achkan (long buttoned coat) and churidar (calf-hugging pyjamas) as his dress as the PM. This dress is typical of the nobility in the north Indian state of Uttar Pradesh. It can be argued that the dress does not make the man, and Nehru's choice of dress had no relevance to his work as PM. However, a simpler, less elitist dress such as a white kurta and pyjamas would have certainly made him appear more approachable.

Although there was some erosion in the high levels of post-Independence optimism, particularly after the defeat in the war with China in 1962, the electorate continued to have faith in elected representatives. The average voter's faith in institutions, except perhaps the police, rose with the replacement of the British with Indians at the highest levels of administration and government.

India is the only democracy among all others around it which has had the same Constitution since Independence. Gratuitous predictions suggesting that India would break up have not come true. By contrast, several Asian and African regions which became independent countries in the twentieth century are now under military rule, totalitarian fiefdoms or one-party communist dictatorships.

Memoirs of civil servants close to Nehru suggest that he could be quick to anger yet democratic in his outlook and warm in personal interaction. Nehru's achievements and mistakes are better understood if he is humanized rather than put on a pedestal. He had several of the usual human weaknesses yet an immeasurable love for his country.

Nehru's conduct and decisions indicate that he had two out of the 3 Cs—Character and Charisma—in abundant measure. There can be no question about his Character given the many sacrifices in his personal life and unwavering commitment to the Indian people. It is in Competence that he may be faulted in some measure on foreign policy and national security matters. On economic policies, he followed what was the prevailing wisdom of the time and considered appropriate by a majority of domestic and internationally renowned economists. All said and done, it is likely that without Nehru at the start, there may still have been a continuing 'idea of India'[139] but not as an undivided, independent and democratic nation.

II

LAL BAHADUR SHASTRI

War and Peace during Short Tenure

Blessed are the meek:
for they shall inherit the earth

(Third verse of the Sermon on the Mount)

Lal Bahadur Shastri[1] rose within the Congress through the freedom struggle
and was the minister for railways and later minister for home affairs in Nehru's
cabinet. K. Kamaraj was the Congress president when Nehru passed away,
and the so-called 'Syndicate' within the Congress included Kamaraj and other
Congress leaders such as Atulya Ghosh of West Bengal, N. Sanjiva Reddy of
Andhra Pradesh, S. Nijalingappa of Mysore (Karnataka) and S.K. Patil from
Bombay (Mumbai). Shastri was fifty-nine years of age, and Morarji Desai was
nearing seventy in 1964, and the latter had more experience in government
than Shastri. However, the Syndicate preferred a conciliatory Shastri to Morarji
who was perceived to be too strong-willed and obdurate. Shastri took over as
PM on 9 June 1964, less than a month after Nehru passed away. Shastri, who
was a mild-mannered, gentle figure, nevertheless kept Desai out of his cabinet.

Shastri's positive inheritance from Nehru included absolute majorities
for the Congress party in both houses of Parliament. Most MPs were well
informed and disposed to work collegially across party lines in the various
parliamentary committees. Nehru had encouraged civil servants to think
afresh and also given them sufficient elbow room to function independent of
political compulsions. By the time Shastri took over, more than ten annual
cohorts of government officers had been selected since Independence through
competitive examinations. Effectively, a measure of predictability had soaked
into the staffing and working of government offices.

The Indian private sector had reconciled with the government's resolve to continue with planning and occupy the commanding heights of the economy. Imports were allowed liberally during the Nehru years till 1958 when balance of payments difficulties led the government to introduce restrictions. Investment licences were issued without serious allegations of graft, and multinational corporations were still welcome. In overall terms, the police, media, judiciary and the armed forces functioned reasonably well, overseen by an elected political executive which enjoyed credibility.

On external relations, the 1962 defeat and Nehru's letters to JFK seeking urgent military assistance had dented India's image. India was now perceived as a country which could not defend itself against China. Lyndon B. Johnson had taken over as President of the US after JFK was assassinated in November 1963, and he judged countries by the similarity of their foreign affairs positions with that of the US, particularly on Vietnam. In contrast to India, Ayub Khan's Pakistan was seen in Washington as a close ally in the Cold War against the Soviet Union. Given the post-1962 perception that India's armed forces were weak, Pakistan felt emboldened to make preparations for war over Kashmir.

Overall Direction and State of Economy

On 11 June 1964, in his inaugural speech, Shastri asserted that there would be 'no looking to right or left. Our way is straight and clear—the building up of a secular mixed-economy, democracy at home with freedom and prosperity, and the maintenance of world peace and friendship with select nations.'[2] Average GDP growth rates came down to 2.8 per cent between 1961 and 1966 compared to the target for the Third Plan of 6 per cent.[3] Import restrictions due to the foreign exchange shortages from 1958 onwards were an inhibiting factor in fresh investments. By 1964 India's population was close to 500 million, starting with 350 million at Independence. Growth in the agriculture sector was inadequate, and pockets of food scarcity were more widespread. In the aftermath of the 1962 debacle and growing tensions with Pakistan, Shastri had to be mindful of raising the allocation for defence. Defence expenditure was 1.87 per cent of GDP in 1960, and this number rose to 3.8 in 1963 and was at 3.6 per cent in 1965.

An example of Shastri's down-to-earth approach was his encouragement of milk production. Shastri visited Anand at the end of October 1964 and extended the government's support to Verghese Kurien, who was then the general manager of the Kaira district Cooperative Milk Producers Union (Amul). As a consequence, the National Dairy Development Board (NDDB) was set up at Anand in 1965. The rest, as they say, is history. In 1951 the total milk production in the country was a little over 15 million tons. This number went up to 20 million tons by 1970. With 'Operation Flood', milk production rose to 50 million tons by 1992 and 130 million tons by 2012. In time, the various government-run milk-bottling undertakings such as the Delhi Milk Scheme were absorbed into the NDDB.

In the prevailing situation of food-grain shortages, Shastri appointed C. Subramaniam as the agriculture minister. Subramaniam revamped the Indian Council of Agricultural Research, and US agricultural specialists were consulted to raise food-grain production with a greater sense of urgency. Although information about the high yields of Norman Borlaug's wheat seeds in Mexico was widely known, the Planning Commission resisted the use of these seeds in India.[4] These high-yielding varieties were finally planted in India in 1965–66, and the enormous success in raising output started the Green Revolution.

In order to involve the lay public, Shastri appealed to the Indian people to give up one meal a week, preferably on Monday evening. It was a sign of those less cynical times and the credibility of Shastri's personality that many around the country did give up a meal. This made little difference to the availability of food in tangible terms. However, government's credibility went up as it was a simple call which was widely understood in a country like India in which several religious occasions involve fasting.

The diversion of scarce resources to defence, continued policies of industrial licensing and promotion of investment in small-scale cottage industries meant stagnation in the growth of salaried employment. On the depleting foreign exchange front, Shastri left import restrictions in place and did not recognize the need for the rupee to be devalued even as the balance of payments situation weakened. In any case, Shastri's short-lived government was beset by the immediate problems of food scarcity and war with Pakistan and could not focus on economic policy issues.

1965 War and Tashkent Agreement

Pakistan had signed a Military Assistance Programme agreement with the United States in 1955. Under this agreement, Pakistan was eligible to receive tanks, fighter planes, transport aircraft and other defence equipment from the US. By 1965, the Pakistani Army had acquired US-built Patton tanks, self-propelled howitzers and jeep-mounted recoilless anti-aircraft guns. Pakistani soldiers were armed with 7.62 self-loading rifles (SLRs) while the Second World War .303 rifles of their Indian counterparts were still being gradually replaced by Belgian 7.62 SLRs. Pakistan's air force boasted of F-86 sabre jets, while

India had older British Hawker Hunters, French Mystères, Russian MiG-21s and Gnats built in Bangalore. Both air forces had British Canberra bombers. Pakistan had also received a few F-104 supersonic fighters from the US and the C-130 Hercules transport aircraft. In summary, the Indian armed forces were larger in numbers but most of their equipment was of older vintage.

After J.F. Kennedy was replaced by Johnson, the somewhat conciliatory US attitude towards India post the 1962 war with China faded away. Further, given the favoured status of Pakistan as a Western ally, Shastri faced pressures from the US and the UK for India to make concessions to Pakistan on Kashmir. The memories of this bullying and partisan behaviour in the mid-1960s during India's vulnerable years fuelled suspicions about these two permanent members of the UNSC in Indian ruling circles for decades. In March 1963, Pakistan and China ceded territories to each other in PoK. The areas ceded to China were of strategic significance and heralded the beginning of a Pakistan–China all-weather friendship. Consequently, Shastri had to face a Pakistan which had the military and tactical support of both the US and China.

In his first Independence Day speech on 15 August 1964, Shastri responded positively to Pakistani President Ayub Khan's call, in a radio talk two days earlier on 13 August, for tearing the veil of 'passion and prejudice' in India–Pakistan relations. The tradition of the PM speaking from the Red Fort in Hindi was maintained. It is interesting in retrospect that on the same day it was reported[5] that Lieutenant General S.H.F.J. Manekshaw and Lieutenant General Harbaksh Singh had been appointed as the GOC-in-C of the Eastern and Western Commands respectively.

About nine months into Shastri's tenure as PM, in March 1965, Sheikh Abdullah (he was released from prison in April 1964, a month before Nehru passed away) travelled to Mecca via London. On his way back, Abdullah stopped in Algiers and met Zhou Enlai. Given India's wariness about Pakistan and suspicions about China post the 1962 conflict, Abdullah was ill-advised to meet Zhou. Shastri had Abdullah put under house arrest on his return to Delhi. This was yet another complication for Shastri in Kashmir.

At about this time, Sant Fateh Singh started on a fast unto death demanding a separate state for Punjab with Chandigarh as its capital. Given the incipient signs of a possible confrontation with Pakistan, Shastri did not want disturbances and possibly street demonstrations in the border state of Punjab. Accordingly, Shastri wisely gave an assurance to Sant Fateh Singh, who had gone on fast in the past, that in due course Punjab would get a separate state.[6]

In Pakistan, President Ayub Khan and his egomaniacal foreign minister, Z.A. Bhutto, fancied their chances of capturing the Srinagar valley with their better equipment. In April 1965, less than a year after Shastri had assumed charge as PM, Pakistani forces crossed the border in the Rann of Kutch in a diversionary tactic. It was an intelligence failure that India had not anticipated this feint, and Indian troops had to fall back in Kutch.

The precise India–Pakistan border in the Rann of Kutch area in Gujarat state was not clearly delineated and agreed to by both sides at the time of Partition. In January 1965, Pakistani troops established a post in the Kanjarkot area. By mid-February, Pakistan's troops established themselves in this area which had been unoccupied by either side till then. India protested and moved in troops in March–April. There were small-scale battles, in which the Pakistani Army was able to penetrate Indian lines and in early April captured Briar Bet. Due to international pressure, a ceasefire was declared on 30 April. Surprisingly, given the UK's pro-Pakistan line, Shastri asked British PM Harold Wilson to mediate with Pakistan. By June, the British PM persuaded the United Nations to set up a tribunal. (A couple of years later, in February 1968, the UN India-Pakistan Western Boundary Case Tribunal awarded about 90 per cent of the 9100 square kilometres claimed by Pakistan to India.)

In the first week of August 1965, Pakistan launched Operation Gibraltar into the Indian side of Kashmir. Pakistani soldiers, along with irregulars, wriggled their way in and were meant to incite the local population to revolt against Indian rule. Operation Gibraltar was a failure because Kashmiris informed local authorities about the infiltrators, and the Indian Army and police picked up most of them.

A measure of China's hostile attitude towards India at that point of time can be gauged from the following extract from a 1965 Chinese note to India:

'So long as the Indian Government oppresses the Kashmiri people, China will not cease to support the Kashmiri people in their struggle for self-determination. So long as the Government of India persists in its unbridled aggression towards Pakistan, China will not cease supporting Pakistan in her just struggle against aggression. This stand of ours will never change, however many helpers you may have such as the US, the Modern Revisionists and the US controlled United Nations.'[7]

It is amazing 'revisionism', or flexibility if you like, in China's thinking that just six years later, in 1971, Mao and Zhou welcomed Nixon and Kissinger in Beijing. Communist China's leadership did not need to justify the move to engage with the capitalist US to its people. Totalitarian states can change foreign and domestic policies without concern about being voted out of office.

Despite the considerable uncertainties that decision makers in Delhi faced, Shastri finally upped the ante, and, referring to Pakistan's intention to forcibly annex Kashmir, announced 'force would be met by force'. The Indian Army retaliated and captured the strategic Haji Pir pass in PoK and also pushed towards Lahore in West Pakistan starting around 15 August 1965. This was an option that Nehru had consciously chosen not to use in 1948, but he had informed Parliament that India may be forced to do so in the future if Pakistan reinitiated hostilities over Kashmir.

Tank and air battles ensued with heavy losses of troops and equipment on both sides. India and Pakistan soon fought themselves to a standstill and agreed to a ceasefire in a little over a month on 23 September 1965. At the cessation of hostilities, India was in possession of the strategic Haji Pir pass and adjoining areas which are located in PoK. Shortly after this war was over, the first contingent of the Border Security Force (BSF) was raised on 1 December 1965 to ensure the security of India's borders. The BSF is currently deployed on the border with Pakistan in Rajasthan and points along India's border with other neighbouring countries including Bangladesh.

India had burnt its fingers in the past by taking up the Kashmir issue at the UN, and the US and the UK were suspect. Consequently, the Soviet Union was accepted as the host for the peace discussions between Shastri and Ayub Khan in the Uzbek capital, Tashkent. It is likely that the US and the Soviet Union were closely in touch before, during and after this India–Pakistan war in support of their own objectives.[8] The US did not allow its ally Pakistan to suffer any lasting damage or loss of self-image. The Soviet Union saw an opportunity to gain influence, not just with India but also with Pakistan. It is another matter that Pakistan, due to its dependence on the US, could not play the Soviet game, and the USSR swung towards India in the late 1960s and also during the war between India and Pakistan in 1971.

The Tashkent Agreement between India and Pakistan, which was signed on 10 January 1966, provided for the return of the Haji Pir pass and for both sides to return to their pre-war positions. India had claimed since 1948 that Pakistan had illegally occupied a part of Kashmir, and it would have been logical to argue that the Haji Pir pass in PoK should remain with India.

The following day, 11 January 1966, the nineteen-month term of Lal Bahadur Shastri came to an end with his sudden death due to a heart attack in Tashkent.

Legacy

Nehru's halo diminished after the beating India took in the 1962 war with China, and he looked visibly older. The question 'After Nehru Who' started appearing in the media. Clearly, there was no one in the Congress party who could measure up to him. However, predictions about instability in India after

Nehru's passing away in 1964 were proved wrong, and the Congress party unanimously selected Lal Bahadur Shastri as his successor. Despite Shastri's low profile during the Nehru years, he was able to capture the imagination of many with his simple slogan of '*Jai Jawan Jai Kisan*' (Victory to the Soldier and the Farmer). If Shastri had continued for another term after the general elections of 1967, the higher standards of honesty of thought and action of the freedom-fighter generation may have persisted in India for another decade.

The first MiG fighter aircraft and other arms purchases from the Soviet Union started from around the late 1950s. It was abundantly clear through the course of the 1965 war with Pakistan that India had fallen far behind in the quality of its defence equipment. Given that the US and the UK had favoured Pakistan both before and after the 1965 conflict, this war was a turning point for India as it stepped up its purchases of Soviet armaments. This closer defence relationship with the Soviet Union also led to comparatively higher dependency on that country.

Unfortunately, Shastri was not at the helm long enough to even begin to address the causal reasons for slower economic growth in the 1960s compared to the 1950s. The opportunity costs of the Shastri government's inadequate attention to correcting the overvalued rupee exchange rate can be summed up aptly by the metaphor 'a stitch in time saves nine'. Finance Minister T.T. Krishnamachari and P.C. Bhattacharya, the RBI governor[9] at that time, could and should have coordinated their efforts to convince Shastri to effect a much-needed devaluation of the rupee. The confidence in government continued to be high, particularly with Indian armed forces being able to hold their own against the better-equipped Pakistani forces.

On India versus Bharat, Shastri leaned very much towards Bharat. His usual dress was dhoti and kurta, the clothes of millions of his countrymen, and was usually made of hand-spun khadi. Shastri was fluent in Hindi and often chose to speak in this vernacular rather than English.

As for the 3 Cs, Shastri was a man of exceptional Character, which included compassion and commitment. He did not have the same level of Charisma as Nehru but that was too high a standard to meet. As for Competence, his tenure was not long enough for a fair assessment to be made. Shastri did handle the difficulties created by the war with Pakistan and the shortage of food-grains effectively. The talks leading to the Tashkent Agreement could have been managed better, and despite pressures from the US and the USSR, India could have insisted on conditions to be met on a continuing basis for the handing back of the Haji Pir pass to Pakistan. The simplicity of Shastri's life and of many around him helped to keep the electorate's optimism levels about elected representatives at around the same level as when Nehru had passed away.

III

INDIRA GANDHI

End of Innocence Yet Remarkable Achievements

Were the King to eat a single apple without paying for it, his staff will uproot the whole apple tree.[1]

(From 'Gulistan' by Persian poet–author Musharraf ud-Din Sa'di, 1213–1295, born in Shiraz and who, according to legend, travelled to many parts of West Asia, Central Asia and India.)

After Indira Gandhi (IG)[2] was separated from her husband Feroze Gandhi in the late 1940s, she moved in with her prime minister father Jawaharlal Nehru. Thereafter, she was the official hostess at Nehru's Teen Murti[3] House residence and accompanied him on trips abroad. She was appointed the Congress president in 1959 and was perceived as one of the prime movers in having the communist Kerala government dismissed and Governor's rule imposed.[4]

The interactions at high political levels at home and internationally gave Indira Gandhi a ringside view of governmental decision making. In June 1964, she accepted the junior position of minister for information and broadcasting in Lal Bahadur Shastri's government and held this portfolio till January 1966. According to Katherine Frank,[5] 'Nehru had never made any financial provision [for] his daughter's future. Apart from her father's possessions and the family home, Indira inherited only her father's royalties and these fluctuated and were never lucrative. Nor did she have a home in Delhi . . . A place in Shastri's cabinet provided her with both a salary and a roof over her head . . . she was assigned 1 Safdarjung Road where she would spend the next twenty years except for a three-year period in the late seventies.' Subsequently, when Sardar Swaran Singh was appointed as the foreign minister, Indira Gandhi vented her feelings publicly against Shastri to Inder Malhotra. She felt that, given her international exposure, she was the natural choice for the post.[6]

Shastri passed away on 11 January 1966, and the Congress president K. Kamaraj along with other senior Congress leaders again decided that they would not support Morarji Desai's candidature for PM. With general elections a little over a year away, given IG's name recognition and in the Syndicate's view greater pliability,[7] the decision went in her favour. Unlike when Shastri had become PM, on this occasion Morarji Desai sought a contest. At the Congress parliamentary party election for head of government, Indira Gandhi won convincingly by 355 votes to Desai's 169. This was a genuine election. In later years, elections for Congress party positions or for that of the leader in Parliament were stage-managed.[8] Indira Gandhi was just forty-nine years old when she was sworn in as PM by President Radhakrishnan on 26 January 1966, compared to Nehru and Shastri who were fifty-eight and fifty-nine years old respectively when they had taken over as PM.

IG's inheritance as PM was a Congress party which had majorities in both houses of Parliament. However, popular support was eroding by 1966 due to food scarcities caused by droughts in 1964 and 1965. Consumer price inflation was in double digits at 11 and 13 per cent in 1966 and 1967. The open-hearted optimism of the 1950s had eroded by the mid-1960s, with food shortages and defeat in the war with China in 1962.

Despite the comfortable margin of victory against Morarji Desai, there was significant dissent since 169 MPs had voted for him to be PM. Indira Gandhi could not expect the unqualified support within the party that Nehru had received. As for Shastri, although he did not have Nehru's stature, he had been a cabinet minister earlier, and with his senior status in the party, he did not have to keep looking over his shoulder while in office. IG had the support of the Syndicate, and these members of the Congress old guard expected her to be mindful of their views, particularly on economic issues.

Devaluation, Sharp Turn to the Left in Economic Policies and Rising Corruption

The US had suspended all aid to India and Pakistan at the time of the 1965 war. After IG took over as prime minister, she faced opposing pulls within the Congress party from the younger left and older right-oriented groups. Despite rumblings of discontent in the party's left, given the dependence on food-grain imports from the US and shortage of hard currency reserves, IG visited the US towards the end of March 1966. This was her first foreign visit and that too within two months of assuming office. IG's meetings with US President Lyndon Johnson went very well at a personal level. For instance, during IG's stay in Washington, President Johnson attended a reception at the Indian Ambassador B.K. Nehru's residence and stayed on for dinner to have more time for discussions with her in an informal setting. However, there are limitations to what can be achieved through personal diplomacy. Johnson was looking for India to soften its stance on Vietnam, and this did not happen. During this trip, the US administration, World Bank and IMF advised India in a coordinated manner that the rupee was substantially overvalued and that a correction was overdue.

On objective grounds, overvaluation of the rupee since the late 1950s was one of the causal factors which resulted in a chronic deficit in India's trade in goods balance. Hence, the more knowledgeable among Indian ministers and senior civil servants such as C. Subramaniam and L.K. Jha confirmed to IG that the rupee did need to be devalued. A couple of months after returning from the US, IG took the plunge, and on 5 June 1966 the rupee was devalued from Rupees 4.76 to Rupees 7.5 to a dollar. That is, the value of the US dollar in rupee terms increased by 57.6 per cent. Industrial licensing and trade regime controls were marginally relaxed along with the devaluation.

Domestic political circles and the lay public were inadequately informed about exchange rates, and for partisan reasons the rupee devaluation was portrayed as a self-inflicted disaster by opposition political parties. Commentators on both the right and left of the political spectrum were highly critical without either analysing or understanding the underlying economic compulsions which necessitated this devaluation. IG should have ensured that the economic logic for devaluation was explained in simple terms in all regional languages. Namely, that a country's prestige or honour is not linked to the strength of its currency, and an overvalued currency contributes towards trade deficits and can even lead to a balance of payments crisis. It was not IG's lack of understanding of the underlying economic issues which proved costly for the country. Heads of government are not expected to be subject specialists. IG failed to use impartial, well-respected experts to explain to wider audiences the reason for her decision. For instance, IG could have used Manmohan Singh's doctoral work which was published by Oxford University Press in 1964. Singh was cautiously optimistic about exports unlike his own thesis supervisor Professor I.M.D. Little, who was pessimistic about the prospects for raising India's exports in any substantial manner.[9]

Concurrently, there was rising resistance in the US to continued aid, in any form, to India. As a consequence of the anti-West rhetoric of Krishna Menon and others in the ruling Congress party, there was a caucus of US legislators which had bracketed India as a camp follower of the Soviet Union. Their influence contributed to the US administration stretching out the time taken to clear each food shipment. Additionally, bilateral US aid and multilateral financial assistance did not meet India's expectations. A US State Department official was reported to have remarked a few years later that it was satisfying to have India over a barrel on food shipments.[10] Even a junior foreign policy practitioner could have educated that US official that it is counterproductive to provide aid with bad grace.

I.G. Patel has provided details of the difficult discussions with the British, the US as also IMF and World Bank officials, and the offensive behaviour of some of them. According to Patel, 'Lyndon Johnson in fact had pursued a ship to mouth policy of food aid to compel India to introduce far reaching reforms in the agricultural sector.' Even though Johnson's pressure tactics must have been unwelcome he was right since India's subsequent use of high-yielding wheat seeds raised production considerably.

Patel also mentions that at a dinner in Paris, during the days that discussions were going on with the Aid India Consortium, he was asked how he felt the meetings were going, and he remarked, 'Not bad, we were lectured at for eight hours and we got a billion dollars. Not a bad exchange rate.' Hollis Chenery of the US happened to be present at that dinner and, according to Patel, gave negative feedback to the US government, saying that the Indians had behaved arrogantly at the consortium meetings.[11]

The issue of bank nationalization had been discussed often in Congress circles since the 1950s, but Nehru had ruled it out except for nationalization of the Imperial Bank (which became the State Bank of India). This issue now divided the Congress, and Morarji Desai, as the deputy prime minister and finance minister (1967–69), was firmly opposed to the growing demand within the Congress, tacitly supported by IG, for nationalization of banks.

In May 1967, IG replaced L.K. Jha, who was perceived as pro-West, with the left-oriented P.N. Haksar,[12] and Haksar became the principal secretary in the prime minister's office (PMO). L.K. Jha moved to Bombay and was the RBI governor[13] from July 1967 to May 1970. He was hesitant about IG's peremptory move to nationalize banks, while Morarji Desai favoured what was at that time called a 'social control' approach to managing private banks rather than taking over ownership.

The All India Congress Committee meeting in June 1967 adopted a resolution on the economic policies that the Congress party would henceforth promote. These policies included 'social' control of banking, further consolidation of 'state trading' in imports and exports, and even state control over trading in food-grains within the country.[14] The so-called Young Turks in the Congress party, including Chandra Shekhar, supported the resolution. Haksar did not support all aspects of this resolution, but he carefully orchestrated policies which can only be called populist to bolster IG's position within the party by appearing to be pro-poor to the electorate.

On 19 July 1969, IG had an ordinance issued to nationalize fourteen banks. V.V. Giri as the serving vice-president had earlier been elevated to acting President on 3 May 1969 after President Zakir Husain had passed away on that day. In his capacity as acting President, Giri approved the bank nationalization ordinance immediately.

The nationalization decision was popular, schadenfreude and all that, and there was dancing on the streets. Most private banks were owned by business houses, and a considerable proportion of their lending was to affiliate companies and they had little presence in rural areas. However, this populist decision has had damaging consequences for the Indian economy to this day. At most, a few banks which had persistently engaged in crony-lending should have been nationalized.[15] However, there was no economically sound reason to nationalize as many as fourteen banks. The cancer, if you will, of crony (capitalism) lending was treated by IG with the excessively aggressive treatment of gamma ray radiation of nationalization. The Supreme Court held this bank nationalization ordinance unlawful.

The confrontational manner in which IG chose to negate the Supreme Court's decisions sowed seeds of discord between her government and the higher judiciary. The Banking Companies (Acquisition and Transfer of Undertakings) legislation was approved by Parliament on 9 August 1969. This led to the Supreme Court vacating its stay order on the ordinance of 19 July. However, the Supreme Court passed another stay order on 8 September 1969 to prevent the government from issuing any directions in violation of the Banking Regulation Act of 1948. And, a judgment was issued by the Supreme Court in this case on 10 February 1970. The Supreme Court ruled by ten to one that bank nationalization was invalid since it did not provide for adequate compensation to private owners and hence violated a fundamental right under Article 31(2) of the Constitution. The lone dissenting voice in this ten-to-one verdict was that of Justice A.N. Ray.

The Banking Companies (Acquisition and Transfer of Undertaking) Act of 1970 was passed to override the Supreme Court judgment. Under this revised 1970 Act, compensation was specified. Further, the 1970 Act provided for the setting up of a tribunal if consensus on compensation could not be achieved.

That is, although the 1969 legislation was struck down, the 1970 Act allowed the nationalization of banks to prevail.[16]

An important development in Centre–state relations was the NDC's approval of the so-called Gadgil[17] formula in a meeting held in April 1969. It had been felt for some time that the Centre's financial assistance to the states during the first three Five Year Plans and the annual plans from 1966 to 1969 had been somewhat ad hoc. This was an attempt to provide an objective and relatively better framework.

In a separate move to tighten economic controls, in 1970 the Bureau of Industrial Costs and Prices (BICP) was established. The BICP's statutory powers were derived from the Industries Development and Regulation Act which had come into force in 1952. The BICP decided on the administered prices of steel, cement, copper and pharmaceuticals including inputs. Over time, these measures proved to be extremely costly for the economy. The controls gave far too much leeway to government officials to play favourites. Even with the best of intentions it is impossible for individuals, howsoever gifted and well qualified as economists or finance professionals, to figure what should be produced, in what quantities and at what prices. It should have been apparent from the evidence around the world that such controls would lead to mispricing and misallocation of scarce resources.

It appears that IG was oblivious or unconcerned about the longer-term negative economic consequences of several decisions that she took at the behest of her left-leaning senior-most adviser P.N. Haksar. IG's primary focus, to the exclusion of all other considerations, was on controlling domestic economic levers to buttress her political position.

Little attention was paid to implementation of genuine land reforms in rural areas or enforcement of minimum wages. The emphasis was on eye-catching populist moves, and the next such decision was abolition of privy purses. The continuation of such allowances to Indian princes, an arrangement agreed to since Independence, was clearly a distressingly unjustified anachronism by the late 1960s. However, moving abruptly to stop allowances for privileged princes did not mean that the poor received corresponding benefits. The legislation to abolish privy purses was passed by a two-thirds majority in the Lok Sabha on 2 September 1970 but failed to get the required number by just one vote in the Rajya Sabha. IG overcame this parliamentary impasse by getting a presidential order announced derecognizing princes. This was another example of IG's style of functioning, which was to bludgeon opposition and play to the gallery.

Through most of the 1960s, the government's emphasis in the agriculture sector had been on foodgrain self-sufficiency. Higher-yielding wheat seeds were increasingly used in northern India. However, it took time for the Green Revolution in wheat to raise yields, and India had to depend on (United States) Public Law 480 food-grain imports against rupee payments. In comparison, rice production stagnated and was one of the causal reasons for riots in south India where rice is the staple food. Food scarcity was also widespread in Bihar all through the second half of the 1960s. These scarcities led to higher food-grain prices, and in Delhi the first Super Bazar, intended to provide daily necessities at controlled prices, was set up in late 1966. Enough attention was not paid to the professed US desire to help India acquire higher-efficiency agricultural equipment. As India's population rose, surplus agricultural labour needed help to find alternative employment off land. This could have been an area for closer cooperation with the US and Europe.[18]

Since the mid-1950s, when the State Bank of India (SBI) was nationalized, it was expected to galvanize lending to the agriculture sector. However, till the late 1960s loans to this sector were extended mostly by rural cooperatives. The 1969 Rural Credit Review Committee suggested that commercial banks should increase their lending to rural borrowers. One of the justifications for the nationalization of fourteen banks was that this would raise lending to the agriculture sector through 'lead' (that is nationalized) banks. By 1972, this changed to so-called 'priority sector lending' under which banks were expected to ensure that prescribed proportions of lending had to be made to, for example, khadi, village industries and the agriculture sector.[19] Consistent with this objective of providing easier credit access to villagers, the setting up of regional rural banks was suggested in 1975. It was argued that depending only on nationalized scheduled commercial banks to meet priority sector lending targets would not suffice. Two years after IG came back as PM in 1980, the National Bank for Agriculture and Rural Development (NABARD) was set up under an Act passed by Parliament in 1982.

The setting up of financial institutions with the mandate to provide directed credit raised the fraction of formal credit to agriculture, thus somewhat reducing farmers' dependence on moneylenders. Table 1.6 in the Appendices shows that the loans from institutions rose three times from 1951 to 1971 and five times in 1981, while those from moneylenders dropped by more than half. To that extent, loans in the agriculture sector did not carry the usurious rates of interest charged by moneylenders.

Meanwhile, the overall objective of raising incomes sharply was not sufficiently met. For instance, per capita income rose from Rupees 247.5 in 1950–51 to Rupees 324.4 almost two decades later in 1967–68 (both numbers at 1948–49 prices).[20]

IG was convinced after the poor showing of the undivided Congress in the 1967 general elections that a sharper turn to the left was necessary to garner the support of the poorer sections of the electorate. The Dravida Munnetra Kazhagam (DMK),[21] then the dominant party in Tamil Nadu, and the communist parties, a significant force in West Bengal,[22] supported her left-oriented policies. Tamil Nadu and West Bengal have thirty-nine and forty-two seats in the Lok Sabha each and are among the states that have a large presence in Parliament. IG's strategy to beat back the challenge of the Congress (Organization) led by Nijalingappa was to outflank them from the left.

Subimal Dutt, an ICS officer, had been an Indian ambassador from 1947 onwards and also foreign secretary from 1955 till he retired in 1962. Prior to Independence, he had worked in the fields of education, health and agriculture. Surprisingly, in 1969, he was appointed chairman of a committee on industrial licensing. Knowledgeable economists may have been members of this committee, and experts must have been consulted. This is just one of so many examples of generalists heading committees or other bodies which were entrusted with making recommendations on matters that should have been left to specialists. Knowledgeable generalists do serve the useful purpose of demystifying the technical jargon of experts for the political executive. All aspects considered, far too much discretion was often left in the hands of generalists to finalise governmental decisions.

The report of this Subimal Dutt committee led to the adoption of the Monopolies and Restrictive Trade Practices (MRTP) Act in 1969. The MRTP Act was intended to prevent the concentration of economic power and leverage. In other words, to prevent companies from setting up monopolies in producing goods or services. Such monopolies invariably result in prices rising inordinately above cost of production plus profit.[23] In practice, the Act was often misused by government officials to exercise a stranglehold over industry and trade. Any company with assets of over Rupees 25 crore could be identified as an MRTP company, which would then need all manner of permissions for day-to-day operations and to grow. The definition of restrictive trade practices was sufficiently general, namely, any activity that could potentially impede the flow of capital to production. The cap was raised to Rupees 50 crore in 1980, and the Act was finally abolished as part of the wide-ranging economic reforms post 1991.[24]

In September 1970, the Communist Party of India (CPI) came to power in Kerala with Congress support. General elections were scheduled to take place in 1972, but IG wanted earlier elections and the Lok Sabha was dissolved on 27 December 1970. Unlike the elections in 1967 when the Syndicate had the dominant say in the choice of Congress candidates, this time IG was the sole selector and her slogan of 'Garibi Hatao' (abolish poverty) resonated with the electorate. IG was able to mobilize widespread popular support by portraying the Supreme Court judgment turning down the abolition of privy purses as the rich and the privileged hitting back at her.

Mohan Kumaramangalam, earlier with the CPI, had joined the Congress in 1969 and was appointed the steel and mines minister after winning the Pondicherry seat in the 1971 elections. He was a prime mover in the nationalization of coal and the setting up of the Steel Authority of India Ltd (SAIL) in 1973. SAIL became the holding company for all public-sector steel plants.

In a letter to Dorothy Norman dated 3 June 1973, IG lamented that Kumaramangalam had died a few days earlier in an air crash.[25] IG mentions in this letter that after the last parliamentary elections, she took Kumaramangalam into the cabinet 'to clean up steel production which was a mess' and that he did a 'marvelous job'. Private-sector companies do not provide products or services at fair prices if there is little competition. The setting up of public-sector near monopolies and behemoths such as Coal India and SAIL, respectively, reduced competition and impacted the overall efficiency of production in both these areas negatively.[26]

Russi Mody was the managing director from 1974 to 1984 and later chairman from 1984 to 1993 of the Tata Iron and Steel Company (TISCO). He was reported in the media as having said that as long as there was SAIL—presumably he meant as an inefficient producer of steel which was then sold at high prices to government-owned buyers—he could laugh his way to the bank.

Prior to Independence, a tariff board in the Ministry of Commerce advised on measures required to protect domestic industry. The tariff board was overtaken by a tariff commission, which was set up in 1951 to suggest duties on imports and on dumping of goods. This commission was abolished in 1976 and even stricter procedures were prescribed for restricting imports. At the same time, tighter conditions were stipulated under the Foreign Exchange Regulation Act, 1973, for all dealings in foreign exchange and the surrender of all hard currency earned on exports. The focus once again was mistakenly on preventing foreign exchange outflows rather than promotion of exports, which often depends on imports of inputs.

The monsoon was patchy and inadequate in 1972, and the following year the Organization of the Petroleum Exporting Countries (OPEC) raised oil prices fourfold (from US $3 to $12 a barrel) by stopping oil exports. As an immediate consequence of higher transportation costs to and within India, prices of food-grains and commodities of daily use went up sharply. This was reflected in the higher consumer price inflation numbers. The inefficiencies and patronage practices related to production and pricing of electricity, coal and food-grains rose substantially from 1969 onwards. This was accompanied by higher rent-seeking in government and public-sector circles. At around the same time, there were instances of individual wrongdoing which were not satisfactorily investigated by IG's government. The media carried the stories sketchily but the rumour mills worked overtime.

For instance, in May 1971, Rupees 6 million were handed over by an SBI cashier to Rustom Sohrab Nagarwala, allegedly on the basis of a phone call from the PMO.[27] Many questions about why basic banking norms were violated by the SBI cashier, and who Nagarwala was the front for, were left unanswered in that case. In 1986, the *Hindustan Times* reported that the CIA had used Nagarwala to sully IG's name at a time when the US was annoyed with India's policies on Bangladesh. This explanation, without any supporting evidence, does not explain why an SBI cashier handed over such a large sum of money, in cash, outside the bank's premises to Nagarwala.

In 1974, it was alleged that traders in Pondicherry had sought import licences supported by the forged signatures of twenty-one MPs. In an environment of scarcities and strict controls on imports, such licences were highly lucrative. Tulmohan Ram, an MP from Bihar, was perceived to be complicit, with the knowledge and perhaps instigation of then Commerce Minister L.N. Mishra. IG addressed the criticism not by dropping Mishra from the cabinet but by moving him to head the mammoth Ministry of Railways. Mishra, as the treasurer of the Congress party, was already widely perceived as a conduit for clandestine funds. He was mysteriously killed by a bomb attack while he was addressing a rally in Bihar in 1975. Again, there has been no satisfactory explanation to date about exactly who was responsible or why he was assassinated. During the Emergency, court hearings in the Tulmohan Ram case, the US Congressional hearings in the case of Boeing pay-offs in India, and the conviction of some of those accused in the Dalmia Jain Airways scam were censored and the media was not allowed to report on them.[28]

In the late 1960s and the 1970s, there were any number of accusations about the interference of the CIA and the KGB (Komitet Gosudarstvennoy Bezopasnosti) of the Soviet Union in Indian elections. IG would often refer to the threat to her life and the undermining of the Congress by foreign agencies, and her allegations were invariably directed against the CIA. Christopher Andrew and Vasili Mitrokhin have alleged that foreign intelligence agencies including the KGB wielded considerable influence with the Indian government when IG was PM.[29] It is impossible to confirm the numerous allegations made in their book. However, it is a fact that the ruling party led by IG and the opposition parties made numerous accusations against each other. These allegations included charges about acceptance of monetary assistance from foreign intelligence agencies. All this noise and fury distracted IG from sound economic policymaking or implementation.

By the early 1970s, P.N. Haksar was no longer in favour with IG because he did not support Sanjay Gandhi's plans to set up the Maruti automobile plant.[30] Haksar had objected because this car proposal smacked of state-supported nepotism. Sanjay was the only recipient of a licence to produce 50,000 cars out of many applicants, and Bansi Lal as Haryana chief minister provided 300 acres of prime land in Gurgaon for the project.

Vinod Mehta provides details and alleges that RBI officials were victimized because they objected to the demands for loans and overdrafts for Maruti. In addition to Maruti Limited, Sanjay Gandhi also set up an affiliated company called Maruti Technical Services (MTS). The partners in MTS included Sonia Gandhi, her two children and someone called Shroff. The Gandhi family owned 99 per cent of the equity in MTS which was paid handsomely for allegedly non-existent technical services. According to Mehta, by the end of 1976, Sanjay Gandhi was involved in building bus bodies, selling cement and steel, and became an agent for foreign multinationals.[31]

On the cover of his book, Vinod Mehta asks the rhetorical question, 'Why did a nation of over 600 million people bow to the whims and fancies of a Prime Minister's favoured son?' The answer is probably that just seven years after Nehru's passing, most of the values of honesty in public life had given way to a culture in political circles of abject subservience to executive power for personal gain. This shortcoming did not just affect ministers in government but also senior civil servants who were often rewarded with post-retirement positions. However, certain intrepid film-makers were not cowed by IG's government. For instance, a satirical film on the prevailing obfuscation and worse about Sanjay Gandhi's Maruti venture, which was titled *Kissa Kursi Ka* (The Case of the Executive's Chair), was released in 1977.

Multiple accounts have confirmed that as a fond mother, IG overlooked her younger son's high-handed behaviour with government functionaries. Haksar may have indicated his discomfort with Sanjay Gandhi's extra-constitutional clout within government. Instead of reining in Sanjay, IG moved Haksar out in 1973, and he was later appointed to an advisory position at arm's length from her as deputy chairman, Planning Commission. P.N. Dhar, an economist by training, was brought in as her principal secretary and served in that capacity till the general elections in 1977.

IG had poor personal relations with US President Nixon. This gave an added impetus to the downward slide in relations between India and the US. In the mid-1970s, even though the public manufacturing sector had grown and so had public-sector banking, well over 50 per cent of the Indian economy was still in the private sector. Although the share of agriculture was shrinking, it was and still is in May 2019 almost entirely private. It is ironic, therefore, that in stark contrast to this low point in India–US relations in 1971, in the same year communist China's leaders had their famous breakthrough meetings with US President Nixon and national security adviser Kissinger in Beijing. The US overlooked communism in China, and a decade later Deng Xiaoping opened up China for selective foreign investment from the US, thus promoting technology transfer and trade surpluses.

Even if for domestic political compulsions IG's government needed to be seen as distant from the US, there were no economic reasons to be hostile to FDI from that country. For instance, the US oil company ESSO,[32] which had set up a refinery in India in the mid-1950s, felt compelled to gradually wind up and was finally acquired by the Indian government in 1974. In the mid-1970s, the other foreign oil companies Exxon, Burmah Shell and Caltex were acquired by public-sector companies. For instance, the assets of Burmah Shell were bought by Bharat Petroleum (BPCL), and those of Exxon and Caltex by Hindustan Petroleum Corporation Limited (HPCL).[33]

Western oil companies were, and continue to be, involved in conspiracies. In 1953, they were involved in the overthrow of the democratically elected Iranian government of Mohammad Mosaddegh.[34] Western governments and multinational companies have usually sided with obscurantist, stuck-in-the-Middle Ages monarchies and sheikhdoms in the Middle East. It was logical, therefore, to be cautious about multinational oil giants. However, it would have been a demonstration of India's policymaking skills if it had attracted investments from international oil companies without allowing them to meddle in domestic politics.

Tables 3.1 and 3.2 in the Appendices show that the Central government's finances were steadily worsening during IG's tenure. For instance, the gross fiscal deficit[35] increased from 3.08 per cent of GDP in 1970–71 to 5.69 per cent during 1983–84, the last year of her second term in office. Capital outlays did rise but so did interest payments as a fraction of GDP. The steady increase in the gross fiscal deficit constrained the Central government's capacity to push development expenditure. The Central government's deficits were alarmingly high at over 5.5 per cent in the 1980s.

India's budget and related numbers are based on cash-based accounting and are not accrual based. Accrual-based accounting amortizes future and contingent liabilities of the government, and this provides a more accurate picture of government's finances. All companies in India have to follow accrual-based accounting norms. Of course, a number of assumptions would need to be made to follow accrual-based accounting for a country's finances, and several developed countries have chosen not to move to this norm. The larger point is that governments do tend to push out liabilities into the future to provide a sturdier picture of the country's economic health than would be warranted if bonds and guarantees issued by the government were to be taken into account.[36]

GDP growth rates fell and rose dramatically from one year to another in the 1970s. In the 1980s, GDP growth rates gradually rose to over 7 per cent. Growth was fuelled by higher fiscal deficits and was hence unsustainable.[37] Fiscal deficit numbers, which include all the state governments, provide a more comprehensive picture of the state of finances of the country. However, as PMs do not exercise direct control over state government budgets, the focus here is on the Central government's finances.

Consumer price inflation was also very volatile and often in double digits. Given high inflation and with no sign of higher productivity, the exchange rate did not depreciate adequately between 1970–71 and 1983–84. The high inflation in India during 1973–75 was driven by the sharp rise in oil import prices, as mentioned above.

The IG years were marked by extremely high rates of income tax. There were eleven different slabs for income tax from 10 to 85 per cent, and with a surcharge of 15 per cent, the highest rate touched an absurd 97.8 per cent. IG, presenting the Union government's budget for 1970–71 on 28 February 1970 (she was then holding concurrent charge as finance minister), remarked: 'If the requirements of growth are urgent, so is the need for some selective measures of social welfare. The fiscal system has also to serve the ends of greater equality of incomes, consumption and wealth, irrespective of any immediate need for resources.'[38]

Income tax collection remained mired around 1 per cent of GDP despite the high rates. Corporate tax rates were around 60 per cent and differed for widely and closely held companies. This was an era when import duties varied from zero to 200 per cent, and there were qualitative restrictions and import licensing. The discretion, high rates of taxation and duties led to widespread tax evasion and avoidance, and it was lucrative for the unscrupulous among tax administrators.[39]

The Janata governments of Morarji Desai and Charan Singh proved unstable, with competing egos and agendas, and midterm general elections had to be called within three years[40] of the first non-Congress government coming to power in Delhi in 1977. In January1980, IG was voted back to power with 362 seats in a Lok Sabha of 520 members. IG had not lost support in southern India even in 1977, and in 1980 she again won a huge absolute majority in the Lower House.

The antagonistic positions between the government and business were more symptomatic of the Indira Gandhi years from 1969–77. Post 1980, Indira Gandhi was somewhat chastened as it was starkly evident that excessively tight government controls had led to a scarcity-ridden economy without any compensatory semblance of distributive justice. At the same time, she was correct in her analysis of some Indian business houses who wanted to have their cake and eat it too. In an exclusive interview which was carried in the Sunday Review of the *Times of India* dated 14 August 1983, IG quipped to Fatma R. Zakaria that 'the industrialists who used to speak for a free market blame us and demand a sheltered market—just as bootleggers are said to favour prohibition'.

In fairness to IG, a few exploratory moves were evident even before Congress lost power in 1977. For instance, L.K. Jha, who was somewhat out of favour at that time, was asked to examine reforms of indirect taxes as far back as 1970. And, an income tax settlement commission was set up in 1976 based on the recommendations of the Justice K.N. Wanchoo Committee.[41]

After IG's return, L.K. Jha, who was considered pro-US compared to P.N. Haksar, was appointed chairman of the Economic Administration Reforms Commission (EARC) in 1981, and he held that position till 1988. The official resolution to set up this EARC said that it is 'an appropriate institutional arrangement for advising government on certain important areas of economic administration and on matters involving interaction between different sectors of government activity in this field'.[42] It is likely that IG was signalling a slight shift to the right in economic policies rather than expecting much from Jha in an advisory capacity. The EARC had a two-year term to begin with but continued for another four years after IG passed away in 1984. Rajiv Gandhi probably left the EARC undisturbed as a mark of respect to L.K. Jha, rather than expecting any substantive contributions from it. In comparison to China, India's communist neighbour, which was opening up steadily to trade and investment since 1979, even in her second innings IG's thinking was still too mired in state-directed economic growth.

The second oil price rise in 1979–80 was due to the revolution in Iran and the Iran–Iraq war. The Shah of Iran fled the country in 1979, and there were widespread disturbances there. As Ayatollah Khomeini took over, Iran's oil production plunged. The following year, the war with Iraq, which went on till 1988, meant that the upward bias to oil prices persisted for several years. In anticipation of pressures on India's balance of payments, IG's government concluded an IMF line of credit amounting to SDR 5 billion.[43] As there was no immediate or impending crisis, the IMF could not demand reforms. That is, IG's government did not consider any relaxation in industrial licensing policies, the excessively restrictive MRTP Act (which used to be applied subjectively) or cuts in government expenditure. About SDR 3.9 billion of this line of credit was drawn, and considerable virtue was claimed by the Indian government for not drawing the balance SDR 1.1 billion.

Break-up of the Congress Party and Centralization of Power

In the 1967 general elections, out of a total of 520 seats in the Lok Sabha, the Congress won 283 and lost power in eight north Indian states which had gone to polls at the same time. The individual results for the Congress were stunning since Kamaraj, S.K. Patil and Atulya Ghosh lost their seats. These three heavyweight Congress leaders were well known in the respective states of Tamil Nadu, Maharashtra and West Bengal. The fact that they lost demonstrated that they had come to be seen as somewhat distant from the pressing day-to-day concerns of voters. This was also the first sign of public disenchantment with senior Congress leaders. However, Indira Gandhi and Morarji Desai won with substantial majorities. The distrust between the two continued and came to a head over the choice for the next President of the country. Indira Gandhi prevailed in pushing the candidature of Zakir Husain who became President on 13 May 1967. The Young Turks of the Congress supported her. Nijalingappa replaced Kamaraj as Congress president in 1968, and almost from the start he had differences with IG.

The succession battle for the post of the next President started after Zakir Husain passed away on 3 May 1969. On 28 October 1969, Nijalingappa sent an open letter to IG in which he wrote 'you seem to have made personal loyalty to you the test of loyalty to Congress and the country'.[44] Would the worst detractors of Nehru have ever said that about him? A publicly acknowledged fact today about Indian politics is that many leaders expect junior politicians and officials to be personally loyal to them. This has to be unpalatable to self-respecting individuals since human beings can be expected to be loyal to ideas or causes, not individuals. An environment in which sycophancy is rewarded promotes mediocrity and worse in policy formulation and implementation in government.

IG and the Syndicate, which now included Congress president Nijalingappa, did not have a common candidate for the next President of India. While IG supported V.V. Giri for the President's post, the official Congress candidate was N. Sanjiva Reddy. The results were declared on 20 August 1969, and Giri won by a narrow margin. Matters came to a head between IG and the Congress party leadership in November 1969 when Nijalingappa expelled her from the Congress. The Congress had 429 members in the two houses at that time, and of these, 310, including 220 of the Lok Sabha, attended a meeting called by IG. From here on, the IG faction of the Congress in the Lok Sabha was reduced to a minority of 220 members in a house of 530. Consequently, IG had to depend on the CPI's support in Parliament, and CPI cadres were delighted with this tactical alliance.

IG centralized control over government incrementally and purged or cut down elements who were suspect. For instance, Y.B. Chavan, who had dithered in his support for IG, was stripped of the home portfolio and allotted finance in late 1969. IG had earlier split the IB, and allocated domestic intelligence to IB and foreign intelligence to a newly created Research and Analysis Wing (R&AW) in September 1968. These two agencies and Revenue Intelligence were made to report directly to the PMO instead of through the home or finance minister. This unprecedented concentration of administrative discretion in the PM's secretariat made it that much easier to silence doubters but also made timely course correction on economic and foreign policies less likely.

The fifth general elections took place in March 1971, and out of the 518 seats in the Lok Sabha, IG's Congress (R) won 352. Congress (O)[45] led by Morarji and others won just fifty-one seats. The Congress (O) made the cardinal mistake of being perceived as favouring big business and the richer classes since some of its members opposed bank nationalization and abolition of privy purses for princes. Populist economic policies and anti-West rhetoric had decidedly won, and IG was on the ascendant. In keeping with the rhetoric that government ownership was necessary to widen insurance coverage, General Insurance was nationalized in May 1971 (Life Insurance had already been nationalized in 1957).

IG now had a two-thirds majority in the Lok Sabha which enabled her to amend the Constitution. IG chose to whittle down state-level Congress leaders of long standing who were popular with local voters. For instance, she eased out the following well-known and popular chief ministers, M.L. Sukhadia of Rajasthan, Brahmananda Reddy of Andhra Pradesh, M.M. Chaudhuri of Assam and S.C. Shukla of Madhya Pradesh, over the course of 1971–72. This replacement of Congress stalwarts with those who were personally loyal to IG reduced reliable feedback from state capitals.

Foreign Policy—Ups and Downs

India's relationship with the Soviet Union changed after IG's return to power. According to Inder Malhotra,[46] this was partly because Soviet leaders had not remained in touch with IG while she was out of power between 1977 and 1980. In a reflection of the change in the relationship, in response to a question from the Soviet leadership at a bilateral meeting about what they should do next in Afghanistan, IG is said to have remarked dryly that the way out of that country was the same as the way in.

A more specific answer to what IG felt about India's relationship with the Soviet Union is evident from the following exchange between her and Ambassador Chandrashekhar Dasgupta.[47] Ambassador Dasgupta was posted to Singapore as the next Indian high commissioner in 1981. It was customary for Indian ambassadors and high commissioners to call on the prime minister before taking up their assignments in foreign capitals. In the course of Ambassador Dasgupta's call on IG, she asked a rhetorical question about why India had closer ties with the Soviet Union than with the United States. IG answered her own question and remarked that India did so because the Soviet Union was the weaker of the two superpowers; it had greater need for India's cooperation and was, therefore, prepared to accommodate India's interests to a much greater extent.

This characterization of India–Soviet Union ties by IG gives a sense that India was in the driver's seat in this relationship. The fact is that India had carried the burden of export pessimism and consequent import controls of its left-oriented economists and administrators for far too long. This made the rupee–rouble arrangement for defence equipment and other purchases from the USSR appear more attractive than was actually the case. If the long-term maintenance, replacement of parts and running costs of the equipment and armaments purchased had been taken into account, the cost of acquisitions from the Soviet Union would not necessarily be competitive. Although Western countries had restrictions on arms sales to India, transparent international bidding for defence imports should have been initiated post the 1965 war.

The following episode is symptomatic of the extent to which IG was oversensitive to leftist sentiments. This was a posture she had adopted since the late 1960s, and it had served her well in elections. In March 1983, India hosted the seventh Non-aligned Summit in Delhi. The chairmanship passed from Cuba to India, and Fidel gave that famous hug to IG in the main Vigyan Bhavan auditorium. Saddam Hussain was another 'non-aligned' leader who participated in that summit. There was a great deal of backslapping, and India as host had created this self-congratulatory atmosphere, somewhat defiant of the West.[48] In this environment any light-hearted remark about the left was not appreciated. Mani Shankar Aiyar, who was the joint secretary for external publicity in the Ministry of External Affairs, was the designated official to brief the media every evening. In one of the initial briefings, Mr Aiyar referred to communists as 'commies' and he did not mean any disrespect. However, stalwarts from Indian communist parties complained to IG, and Mr Aiyar was replaced, and for the remaining days of the summit then Secretary (East) K.S. Bajpai briefed the press.

As for China, Huang Hua, senior leader and involved with China's external relations over a long period, was sent to India by Deng Xiaoping in June 1981. This was a follow-up to Foreign Minister A.B. Vajpayee's visit to China in 1979.[49] An element of normalization of relations with China returned with the opening of Mount Kailash and Mansarovar lake in Tibet to Indian pilgrims in 1981. These sites had been closed to Indians since 1962. Deng Xiaoping is understood to have conveyed through Huang Hua that the India–China border could be formalized as per the existing Line of Actual Control (LAC). Effectively, acceptance of the border as it exists in Arunachal in the east for India, giving up its claim on Aksai Chin. G. Parthasarathy was a senior adviser to IG on foreign policy and is said to have counselled against it. The rumour is that he remarked to IG that no such deal should be concluded since the Chinese had killed her father. Narasimha Rao was the foreign minister at that time. However, as was the practice then, senior ministers would not speak their minds for fear of offending IG. Time was not necessarily on India's side in reaching a mutually satisfactory border agreement as the Chinese economy gradually became much larger than that of India.

China had a domineering presence in South East Asia in the past. The US had raised its profile with countries of this region by setting up SEATO and was supportive of the ASEAN grouping which was put together in 1967.[50] The India of the IG years was not sufficiently mindful of its historical relations with the ASEAN nations and of the potential for trade and investment. Surface transportation linkages between India and South East Asian countries were extremely limited during these years. Building of roads towards the ASEAN nations was difficult because of the pockets of insurgency in India's North-east, and Myanmar was more closed than now. In retrospect, India was too West oriented to even begin to 'look' East during the IG years.

By the late 1960s, India's trumpeting of non-alignment and a closer relationship with the Soviet Union was perceived as a more significant tilt away from the West than during the Nehru era. Tightening of economic controls and nationalization of banks contributed to this image domestically and in foreign capitals. Post the 1971 general elections, the rhetoric against the US and the so-called reactionary elements in the Congress was ratcheted up by pro-IG elements within the Congress, surely with her consent, and by the left parties.

Senior US politicians, officials and citizens from various walks of life in developed Western countries and even non-resident Indians (NRIs) often talk down to Indians. By definition, developed countries have high per capita incomes, and the unstated sentiment among those living in these countries is that they do not have the time or patience to figure out why India is poor in per capita terms. Residents of economically advanced countries also have a tendency to advise Indians on how to fix their problems. Officials from Japan and Germany, as defeated powers of the Second World War, are more careful and usually do not allow their condescension to show.

Some in the Indian government, civil servants and the political executive, are highly qualified and extremely well read. Invariably they are also thin-skinned about anyone talking down to them. Unfortunately, Indian leaders and senior officials allow their personal sense of outrage at being belittled during conversation to colour their judgement about government-to-government relations with developed nations. This was particularly true in the case of India's relations with the US during the IG years.

Bangladesh

In Pakistan, India's troubled neighbour to the west, there was continuing political instability after the 1965 war between the two countries. Field Marshal Ayub Khan had to finally go early in 1969, and General Yahya Khan, with little political acumen, came to power. Contrary to Yahya Khan's expectations, Pakistan's elections of December 1970 saw the Awami League win 160 out of 162 seats in East Pakistan, and Bhutto won eighty-one out of the 138 seats in West Pakistan.

Mujibur Rahman was the leader of the party which had won more than 50 per cent of the total 300 seats (for West and East Pakistan combined) and had the right to be invited to form the government. However, Yahya Khan and Bhutto had no intention of allowing Mujibur Rahman to take over as the PM of Pakistan. In the political impasse that followed, Yahya Khan declared martial law in Pakistan, and in March 1971, Mujibur Rahman declared East

Pakistan independent and was put behind bars. Yahya Khan ordered for the demonstrations in East Pakistan to be put down by Pakistani troops. In the Pakistani Army's violence against university students, professors and other protesters, casualties soon mounted from the hundreds to the thousands. Bangladesh has claimed that about 3 million people were killed by the Pakistani Army. Fleeing this genocide, a total of about 10 million refugees poured into India.

The Hindu refugees had inflammatory accounts about how they were singled out by Pakistani troops, and that a disproportionately high proportion of those killed or violated were from this minority community in East Pakistan.[51] As the burden of making living arrangements for the refugees and containing their resentment mounted, it became clear to IG that India would have no option but to intervene in East Pakistan. IG was prescient in recognizing that if there were to be a conflict with Pakistan, India would need a veto-wielding supporter in the UNSC.

Accordingly, on 9 August 1971, the Indo-Soviet Treaty of Peace, Friendship and Cooperation was signed in New Delhi. Six days later, at the Independence Day speech from the Red Fort on 15 August 1971, IG insisted that this treaty with the USSR did not mean that India had abandoned non-alignment. She referred to Bangladesh and to the risks ahead. US Senator Edward Kennedy was present at this function.[52]

It is to IG's credit and that of the Indian foreign policy establishment that an influential US senator was persuaded to visit the overflowing makeshift camps in West Bengal where Bangladeshi refugees were housed. Subsequently, Kennedy denounced the Pakistani Army's bloody suppression of dissent in Bangladesh as genocide. The *New York Times* of 17 August 1971 carried a report to this effect and that Senator Kennedy did not feel that the Indo-Soviet friendship treaty was 'in any way disadvantageous to US friendship with India'. The then Foreign Minister Sardar Swaran Singh had told him that India would be willing to sign a similar treaty with the US, although this did not happen.

The overall feedback from official Western circles, though, was that it was difficult to reconcile this level of 'friendship' between a democratic India and the communist Soviet Union. In September 1971, IG visited the Soviet Union and then went on a twenty-one-day tour of European capitals including France, the UK and the US. This was part of India's outreach to explain what was happening in East Pakistan to governments and the public in Western countries. The international community's and the UN's relative indifference must have come as a surprise even to the hard-boiled in Indian decision-making circles.

In another blunder on 3 December 1971, Yahya Khan ordered the Pakistani air force to attack western India, and war was declared between the countries on the following day, 4 December. Two days later, while the war was raging, India recognized Bangladesh on 6 December. The Mukti Bahini (Freedom Fighters) of Bangladesh provided invaluable information to the Indian side on the terrain, logistics and locations of Pakistani Army strongholds. As a consequence, the Pakistani troops in East Pakistan were easily and quickly outmanoeuvred by the Indian Army led by Lieutenant General J.S. Arora. On 16 December 1971, Pakistani Lieutenant General Niazi surrendered to a joint India–Bangladesh command. About 93,000 soldiers and officers of the Pakistani Army became prisoners of war.

Given the publicity about Pakistan's atrocities in Bangladesh, two permanent members of the UNSC, the UK and France, abstained from US-sponsored UNSC resolutions calling for an immediate end to hostilities between India and Pakistan during the two-week war. In any case, the Soviet Union repeatedly vetoed such resolutions. Within two months of the declaration of ceasefire, the UK, West Germany and France recognized Bangladesh in February 1972, even before Indian troops had fully withdrawn from this newly born country. China blocked the entry of Bangladesh into the UN using its veto till 1974.

Despite the almost intolerable pressures from various quarters for India to act earlier to stop the Pakistani Army's atrocities in East Pakistan, IG was tactically wise to wait and then wait some more. With the passage of time, there was wider dissemination of information about the violence perpetrated by the Pakistani Army against its own citizens, and NATO members were increasingly reluctant to give credence to Pakistan's claim that India was the clandestine aggressor in East Pakistan. IG's calculated patience in letting Pakistani genocide in East Pakistan get widespread media coverage in the West made it difficult for the US to provide material support to Pakistan. The genocide in East Pakistan is documented in detail in *The Blood Telegram* by Gary J. Bass.[53] It is speculated that Kissinger indicated to China that the US would not be averse to China opening a second front with India. In this context, the Indo-Soviet treaty may have contributed to keeping China at bay.

A retired senior official of the Ministry of External Affairs has hinted to the author that India received an assurance from China, through the good offices of Russia, that China would not intervene militarily in any way. Irrespective of the veracity of the multiple versions about how the end result was achieved, on this occasion China was outsmarted by India since it was not able to prevent the break-up of Pakistan, a state it had and continues to use to contain India.

At this stage, IG was at the height of her powers with an absolute majority in the Lok Sabha, the creation of Bangladesh and victory over Pakistan. She was hailed within and outside India as a decisive leader. India loomed too large in South Asia for China's comfort, and it is likely that it is since then that China decided to prop up Pakistan even more, including helping it to acquire nuclear weapon capability.

Sheikh Mujibur Rahman was released from captivity in Pakistan on 16 December 1971, and he returned to Dacca via Delhi and became the first prime minister of Bangladesh in January 1972. Indian troops needed to leave Bangladesh speedily to encourage international recognition of this new country, and they did so by March 1972. Publicly available records do not indicate that any discussions were ever held with Mujibur Rahman about leaving a small Indian Army contingent in Dacca for his personal protection. Of course, it was a broader failure of the Indian government that it could not protect Mujibur Rahman from assassination on 15 August 1975.

An armed Indian contingent may have saved Mujibur Rahman since it is unlikely that pro-Pakistan elements in the Bangladesh army would have confronted even a small Indian Army group directly. On the other hand, Mujibur Rahman was convinced that no Bangladeshi would ever harm him physically. His desire to be part of the Islamic world led him to allow elements of the Jamaat and others with similar views to come back from Pakistan. Perhaps it was difficult for him, taking domestic public opinion into account, to accept armed protection from a friendly yet non-Muslim-majority India. Mujibur Rahman alienated many in Bangladesh by banning all parties other than his own and declaring himself President for life in January 1975.

Mujibur Rahman's assassination resulted in huge opportunity costs for India's north-eastern states. By the end of the nineteenth century, the British had built a rail link from Sadiya in upper Assam to Chittagong port via tea estates and Lumding.[54] This railway line was used to transport oil from Digboi, and tea, bamboo and coal from sources all along the rail tracks. Assam and other states in the north-east became landlocked after relations soured with Pakistan. Indians in the rest of the country tend to forget that Kolkata was the dominant profit centre for the East India Company, and goods from the north-east were initially floated down on barges and later transported by rail to Chittagong port.

Sikkim

Sikkim had skirmishes with Bhutan and inimical relations with Nepal in the seventeenth century, and most of its territory was annexed by the latter in the eighteenth century. This relatively small state of Sikkim was of strategic importance for Britain because of trade routes via its territory to Tibet, and it regained its territorial integrity due to British intervention in the nineteenth century. In the early twentieth century, Sikkim obtained guarantees of independence and a protectorate status from Britain which were transferred to India in 1947. However, the Indian Constitution of 1950 made no explicit mention of Sikkim. At that time, Sikkim's population was about 100,000, and most senior positions in administration such as head of police were held by Indians. On balance, the chogyal (ruler) of Sikkim needed India more than vice versa.

In the early 1970s, as official Indian thinking about Sikkim was being revised, the then Foreign Secretary T.N. Kaul felt that Sikkim should be a part of India and could have an 'associated' state status. Kaul's overall judgement on the status of Sikkim was too sensitive to the concerns of Palden Thondup Namgyal, the chogyal, and his sister.[55] Over time, the number of people of Nepalese origin grew in Sikkim, and they, along with segments of the local population, wanted to be formally a part of India. Consequently, the chogyal's dalliance with the idea of striking out on his own was opposed by a majority of the by then multi-ethnic population of Sikkim.

As the law-and-order situation deteriorated in Gangtok, the chogyal finally agreed to a referendum. About 90 per cent of the vote in April 1975 was in favour of integrating with India. Kewal Singh had taken over as foreign secretary in 1972, and his wry comment on hearing this news was that this was 'too high' a vote of confidence in India. The Indian government skilfully took advantage of the diversity in local sentiments to hold elections to depose the chogyal and include Sikkim fully in India. The Indian Constitution was amended in 1975 to incorporate Sikkim. Given the strategic location of Sikkim, this was a significant success for Indira Gandhi's unhurried approach in this matter which blunted reservations in China and possibly the US.

Accord with Sheikh Abdullah

By February 1975, Sheikh Abdullah was again the chief minister of Kashmir, after a 1974[56] accord with the Indian government which was orchestrated by IG. This accord was negotiated over more than two years and the principal points were: (a) the definitive nature of the accession of Kashmir to India; and (b) the special status of the state under Article 370 of the Constitution. Subsequently, in 1977 Sheikh Abdullah won an overwhelming majority in the state assembly elections. Kashmir has had a troubled record of holding elections. The local population has on occasion rejected the verdict on the grounds that voting booths were captured or that counting, before automatic voting machines were introduced, was rigged. (For instance, a decade later, the 1987 elections which led to Sheikh Abdullah's son, Farooq Abdullah, becoming chief minister were widely perceived to have been rigged.)[57] In sharp contrast, the relatively high level of public trust in the results of the 1977 elections in Kashmir was a popular vindication of IG's judgement at having reached an understanding with Sheikh Abdullah. That accord and the peaceful and transparent elections in this sensitive state had a positive impact, at the margin, on India's image, particularly after the debacle of the Emergency.

Shimla Agreement—Missed Opportunities

IG did not display the same level of hard-headed clarity and risk-taking ability in the negotiations that led to the Shimla Agreement as she did prior to and during the Bangladesh war. Post the creation of Bangladesh, Yahya Khan had lost all credibility domestically, and Bhutto was named President of Pakistan on 20 December 1971. At that time, Sheikh Mujibur Rahman was still in prison in West Pakistan and was charged with treason which could have meant the death penalty. A combination of international opinion and Indian cajoling led to Mujibur Rahman's release in January 1972 and he returned to Dacca. There is no confirmation in publicly available official records but there are hints in writings about that period that Mujibur Rahman's release was perhaps secured by IG with a commitment to Bhutto for subsequent concessions to Pakistan.

Within two months of Mujibur Rahman's return to Bangladesh, he signed a bilateral Treaty of Friendship, Cooperation and Peace with IG in Dacca on 19 March 1972. The possible trial of senior officers among the Pakistani POWs was probably discussed at this time. Bangladesh initially wanted to try about 1,000 senior Pakistani officers for genocide but later agreed to reduce this list to about 195 officers. There was abundant evidence[58] of the numerous cases of torture, rape and mass murders committed by Pakistani troops. IG may have calculated that recognition of Bangladesh may be delayed indefinitely by Pakistan, Islamic countries and China, and did not press for an international tribunal to assess the nature and extent of the grave crimes committed against Bangladeshi nationals.

The official-level discussions with Pakistan on return of territory, POWs and related issues began in Murree, Pakistan in April 1972. The Indian side was led by Durga Prasad Dhar, and the Pakistani team was headed by Aziz Ahmed, a veteran civil servant.[59] Durga Prasad Dhar was active in Kashmir politics in the 1950s. Between 1969 and 1971, he was the Indian ambassador to Moscow and was closely involved in the deliberations leading to the friendship treaty with the USSR. After he returned to Delhi in 1971, he was associated with policy formulation during the war with Pakistan. Dhar fell seriously ill while the negotiations were on, and P.N. Haksar had to take his place.

The Ministry of External Affairs was conspicuous by its absence at these negotiations, possibly because the then Foreign Secretary T.N. Kaul did not have IG's confidence. P.N. Dhar's memoirs[60] of those times indicate that India was over-anxious to achieve a successful outcome to the negotiations. In this drive to conclude an agreement, India did not hold out for a definitive resolution of the Kashmir issue. Namely, that the ceasefire line would not just become the LoC but the international border.

According to various accounts of the period, Bhutto seems to have convinced IG that democracy in Pakistan would be in grave danger if he agreed to convert the ceasefire line in Kashmir into an international border. Even without the benefit of hindsight, it seems naive of IG and Haksar to have actually believed that Bhutto would build an open and plural democracy in Pakistan. Bhutto, as Pakistan's foreign minister in Ayub Khan's government, was high on virulent rhetoric against India from 1963 onwards. To an extent, Bhutto was responsible for the tense environment which led to Pakistan starting an armed confrontation in 1965—first in Kutch and then in Kashmir. Bhutto was also part of the army–politician nexus in West Pakistan that did not allow Mujibur Rahman to be PM of Pakistan after its 1970 general elections. It appears highly counterintuitive for the Indian side to expect such a man to be overly concerned about democracy taking root in Pakistan or to keep his word on resolving the border issue.

The Indian side could have hinted at the possibility of trials on the lines of Nuremberg. This would have got the attention of the Pakistani elite. According to P.N. Dhar, the chief official-level Pakistani negotiator Aziz Ahmed made 'some crude remarks in Punjabi about their wives not really missing their [Pakistani POWs in camps in India] husbands'.[61] It is not clear whether the possibility of publicly held trials was ever mentioned to Bhutto or his senior negotiator Aziz Ahmed.

P.N. Haksar was of the view that driving a hard bargain with Pakistan would have been similar to the onerous and hence counterproductive Versailles Treaty imposed on Germany after the First World War. This equivalence is misplaced. While Germany did commit genocide before and during the Second World War, it had not done so in the first. The knowledgeable Haksar must have been well aware of this. Obviously, there has to be some other explanation why India let Bhutto off the hook.

What may have worked was if India had insisted that in exchange for the LoC becoming the recognized border, it would no longer lay claim to what is called PoK, except a guaranteed trade and transit corridor through it to Afghanistan. However, P.N. Dhar says that 'Mrs Gandhi herself was worried that a formal withdrawal of the Indian claim on Pakistan-occupied Kashmir would create political trouble for her'.[62] From this statement, it appears that the future political fortunes of the Congress party were more important for IG than achieving a lasting solution to the Kashmir issue for the nation.

P.N. Dhar also mentions that 'Y.B. Chavan and Jagjivan Ram were unhappy about the return of POWs and territories to Pakistan without an adequate quid pro quo, but did not, as was their wont, articulate their misgivings clearly enough'. In R.K. Laxman's cartoon, below, Chavan and Jagjivan Ram can be identified on IG's left as mini-men in a cabinet so ludicrously dominated by her.

According to P.N. Dhar, in a briefing session when just Haksar and he were present with IG, Dhar suggested that India should not immediately give back captured Pakistani territory. IG flew into a rage, and Haksar indicated that Dhar should leave the room. Dhar says, 'My hunch is that she was under pressure—this could only have been from the Soviets—to return the occupied territories.'[63] There was similar speculation that Shastri had to give back the Haji Pir pass at the deliberations in Tashkent because of Soviet pressure. It is likely that there were back-room deals between the US and the Soviets for the latter to pressure India on both these occasions. The US wanted to maintain leverage in Pakistan which had provided military base facilities in the past and could be useful in the future. Pakistan did become particularly useful to the US from the late 1970s, and more so during the 1980s, as the logistical conduit through which mujahideen were armed by the US during the decade that Soviet forces were in Afghanistan.

The Soviet Union too wanted to gain influence with Pakistan. In a throwback to the nineteenth century 'Great Game' jousting between Russia and the UK, decision makers in Moscow may have harboured fond hopes of access to the Arabian Sea via Pakistan. Since that was an extremely low-probability outcome and hence an unlikely rationale for Soviet pressure on India, maybe the USSR had an interest in Pakistan's cooperation to keep extremist Islamic elements, in its soft underbelly, namely, the Central Asian republics, in check.

The Shimla Agreement was finally signed by the Indian and Pakistani heads of government, IG and Z.A. Bhutto, on 3 July 1972. The overarching guiding principles were that: all disputes in the future would be settled bilaterally, without conflict and hostile propaganda; territorial integrity of both countries would be respected; the LoC would replace the ceasefire line; and the heads of government would meet again for a final settlement of the Kashmir issue. All the POWs were gradually repatriated and the 5,000 square kilometres of territory captured in West Pakistan was returned.

Now, so much later, with the experience of the steady infiltration of extremists into Kashmir and Punjab, the Kargil war in 1999 and the November 2008 attack in Mumbai, it is obvious that the Shimla Agreement did not result in any measure of normality in India's relations with Pakistan. As a thought experiment, even if Pakistan had signed an agreement to convert the ceasefire line into a border, it could well have reneged on the grounds that the agreement was signed under duress. The bottom line is that Pakistan's military establishment self-servingly holds India responsible for losing East Pakistan. Hence, as long as the armed forces have a dominant say, the Pakistani state is likely to keep trying to wrest the Srinagar valley from India. However, all things considered, an opportunity was lost in India signing an agreement with Pakistan which did not convert the ceasefire line into an international border.

Nuclear Test and Technology Denial

Homi J. Bhabha died in a plane crash over the Swiss Alps on 26 January 1966, the same day that IG was sworn in as India's PM. Given Bhabha's stature as a scientist and able administrator, his untimely death slowed down all aspects of India's nuclear programme. However, IG did pay attention to the selection of respected replacements despite her preoccupation with the squabbling within Congress. The nuclear and space programmes were entrusted to eminent scientists such as Raja Ramanna, Vikram Sarabhai, Satish Dhawan and Brahm Prakash. In the field of agriculture, M.S. Swaminathan was put in charge of the Indian Council for Agricultural Research. IG accepted P.N. Haksar's recommendations and did not play favourites in technically demanding fields. Haksar was also successful in getting IG to continue with Nehru's approach to empower eminent specialists as secretaries to government and ensure minimal interference except for overall budget issues from generalist civil servants.

The 1968 Treaty on the Non-Proliferation of Nuclear Weapons (NPT) was agreed upon among existing nuclear weapon countries to let nations that had tested nuclear weapons before 1 January 1967 to retain such weapons, and prohibited all others from acquiring nuclear weapons or related technology. It is surprising that the then Foreign Secretary Rajeshwar Dayal and R. Jaipal, the joint secretary concerned in the Ministry of External Affairs, recommended that India become a party to this discriminatory treaty.[64] It is to IG's abiding credit that she overruled the foreign secretary and did not sign this treaty.

Subsequently, IG authorized India's first test of a fission device, which took place in Pokhran on 18 May 1974. Jairam Ramesh suggests in his book[65] that the decision to test a fission device must have been taken when P.N. Haksar was still at IG's side, and it was probably his influence that led her to go ahead with the test. This was a bold decision in a country beset with high inflation and underemployment, and the central and state governments were having to deal with frequent strikes and public demonstrations against perceived official apathy and connivance with corruption. There were clashes between agitators and the police in several states, all of which made the administration's tasks more difficult. Despite the criticism from several quarters that this was an attempt to distract the public's attention from everyday problems, the test raised IG's prestige domestically. Even the less technologically aware understood that this was quite a feat, and the scientists were applauded at a time when there was little else to cheer about.

Towards the end of the Second World War, the US scientist Robert Oppenheimer headed the Manhattan Project in a race to build nuclear weapons before any other country. Oppenheimer and his team orchestrated the first-ever successful test of a nuclear fission chain reaction in New Mexico, USA, on 16 July 1945. At a personal level, Oppenheimer was deeply conflicted about the destructive power of nuclear energy, and he was well aware of the teachings of the Bhagavad Gita. Oppenheimer is said to have rationalized to himself, on the lines of Krishna's advice to Arjuna that warriors have to carry out their duty (dharma) irrespective of the death and destruction caused in the process. In a press interview, Oppenheimer quoted[66] Krishna when He revealed Himself to Arjun with the brilliance of a thousand suns and said that the destruction of the Kaurava clan was inevitable, Arjun was merely the instrument and: 'Now I am become Death, the destroyer of Worlds.' Oppenheimer was comparing the imagery of Krishna's resplendent appearance and terrifying words with his own feeling of awe when he saw the blinding flash and sensed the overwhelming power from the concussion waves that were released by that first nuclear fission test.

China had conducted its first nuclear weapon test in October 1964 at its Lop Nur test site. The NPT was opened for signature in 1968 and the NPT came into force in 1970. Under this treaty's Article 1, China could retain its nuclear weapons. While IG was lauded at home, her decision to call the 1974 testing of a fission device a Peaceful Nuclear Explosion (PNE) was disingenuous and dented India's credibility internationally. The test did not meet India's strategic interests. To acquire strategic credibility, India needed to carry out more tests and declare itself as a nuclear weapon power. It is likely that in those domestically troubled times for IG, these issues were not discussed thoroughly within India's atomic energy and strategic establishments.

India could have reminded the West of the ambivalence with which the builders of their own nuclear devices viewed such weapons. IG should have remained noncommittal about end uses of nuclear fission. In any case, as an immediate result of India's so-called PNE the Nuclear Suppliers' Group (NSG)[67] was set up in 1974. Given the high probability of developed countries banding together to isolate India and ban transfer of nuclear technology or materials, the contingent next steps should have been thought through before the test.

The Soviet invasion of Afghanistan in late 1979 led to Pakistan becoming indispensable in the jihad against the Soviet Union for over ten years till about 1990. Consequently, the US was less inclined to clamp down on Pakistan's nuclear weapons programme. Taking this into account, at least by the early 1980s India should have pressed on towards nuclear weapons and corresponding delivery systems.[68] It is unlikely that such a decision would have led to additional economic sanctions and diplomatic isolation beyond what happened post India's nuclear tests in May 1998. A weakness in this line of reasoning is that the post-1991 economic reforms had not yet happened, and India was far more vulnerable to economic sanctions in the 1980s. That begs the question that if the Indian economy was indeed so vulnerable, why did IG not embark on systemic economic reforms in the 1970s?

Emergency—National Disaster

On 12 June 1975, the Allahabad High Court set aside IG's election to the Lok Sabha in 1971 and debarred her from contesting in elections for six years. The reasons for the court's decision were pathetically trivial and included the involvement of government officers in making arrangements for public meetings. It could not be anyone's case that IG would have lost that election. However, the popular mood had turned against IG in some parts of the country. For instance, in the Gujarat assembly election in that year, IG's Congress won less than an absolute majority—seventy-five out of 182 seats. Discontent was spilling over into the streets because annual consumer price inflation had shot up to 21.5 per cent in 1973–74 and even higher to 34.4 per cent in 1974. The fourfold rise in oil prices in 1973–74 fuelled inflation in India.

P.N. Dhar recounts[69] that there was wilful disregard of the law by those who had resorted to agitations starting from the drought year of 1972 and particularly from 1974.[70] Many of the state governments were headed by Congress chief ministers at that time. However, with the break-up of the Congress party those with political bases such as K. Kamaraj and others of the Congress (O) had been replaced by IG's appointees who were personally loyal to her. Hence, there were fewer early warnings, and local leadership had little ability to deal with the frustrations of limited job opportunities in the formal sector, higher inflation and reports of corruption in high places. The Navnirman student agitation in Gujarat caught the attention of average voters.

Veteran leaders such as Jayaprakash Narayan called for a mass movement against what they perceived was an unfeeling government. Public-sector workers and the average Indian were hurting badly. In this environment, George Fernandes called for an extensive railway strike that lasted three weeks in May 1974. Although the grievances were genuine, a line was crossed when Fernandes structured the railway strike to stop the movement of goods around the country and bring the economy to a grinding halt. All this fed into a strong anti-government sentiment and made IG extremely insecure about her position.

Nani Palkhivala argued IG's appeal in the Supreme Court, and Justice Krishna Iyer's judgment gave a conditional stay. This stay allowed IG to continue as PM but without the right to vote in Parliament. It is likely that the Allahabad High Court order's highly questionable stipulation that IG could not seek re-election for six years would have been reversed by the Supreme Court. However, Indira Gandhi was betrayed by her own cynicism and lack of faith in due process. Not enough of Nehru's understanding and patience in dealing with the Opposition in a democracy had rubbed off on her.

IG's self-perception that she was indispensable took precedence over all other considerations. Her government made the implausible allegation that the CIA was trying to topple her. Tragically for India, on 25 June 1975, IG decided to declare an Emergency[71] with the instantaneous approval of an unquestioning President Fakhruddin Ali Ahmed. The cabinet had not even been informed about the decision. Despite the provocations, internal and external, since the domestic agitations did not amount to an armed insurrection against the state, there was no reason for government to have imposed an Emergency. P.N. Dhar was surely wrong in his perception that Jayaprakash Narayan and IG were equally responsible for the Emergency.

Foreign Minister Sardar Swaran Singh was dropped, probably because IG anticipated that he would demur. Bansi Lal, who had helped IG's son Sanjay Gandhi set up the Maruti car plant in Gurgaon, was appointed defence minister. Opposition leaders, including Jayaprakash Narayan, Morarji Desai and Atal Bihari Vajpayee, were jailed. J.B. Kripalani (Acharya Kripalani), veteran freedom fighter, Congress president at the time of India's independence in 1946–47, was a trenchant critic of IG. Kripalani was in his nineties and was not arrested. Electricity was cut off to newspapers on Bahadur Shah Zafar Marg in New Delhi, and censorship was imposed on private media. One of the reasons was to first get the official side of the story out through government-owned All India Radio.[72] The then Congress president Dev Kant Barooah declared 'India is Indira and Indira is India'. As far as I can remember, IG did not ever publicly distance herself from this extreme level of sickening and hyperbolic sycophancy.

Inflation came down sharply in 1975, and there was deflation in 1976 with the imposition of tight controls and raids on hoarders of food-grains and other products. Sanjay Gandhi pushed for private-sector investment, but not in any systematic manner, to free it of the multiple controls which were in place. On the political front, due to Sanjay Gandhi, there was a distancing from the communists, and to that extent their influence on economic policymaking was diluted. However, there was no serious thought given to attracting FDI. In any case, the overall law-and-order situation was not conducive to attracting foreign investment, what with the allegations of forced sterilization and associated violence in northern India including the outskirts of Delhi.

Chapter V of the Industrial Disputes Act of 1947 titled 'Strikes and Lockouts' lays out in detail the conditions under which workers can be laid off.[73] In 1976, during the Emergency, the government amended this chapter, requiring firms to obtain government approval before any closure or dismissal of workers. Subsequently, in IG's second innings as PM, in 1982 this 1947 Act was amended again to further restrict the declaration of workers as redundant. On 15 August 1976, IG emphasized in her Independence Day speech from the Red Fort that 'there would be no deviation from the socialist path'.[74] Sanjay Gandhi's Maruti car venture was very much in the news at that time. It is likely that IG wanted to silence those who felt that she was shifting to the right.

An Urban Land (Ceiling & Regulation) Act was passed in 1976. This Act provided for government to acquire land above prescribed ceilings for nominal compensation and was meant to bring about 'an equitable distribution of land in urban agglomerations to sub-serve the common good'. Several state governments passed their own urban land ceiling legislation shortly thereafter. In theory, it does help urban development if individuals with excessively large landholdings use these for housing/commercial purposes or sell them. On the ground, this legislation did not result in a sharp upsurge in the development of urban land. Gujarat and Maharashtra have since repealed their Acts as these states felt that legislation of this nature did not serve any useful purpose.

IG's government had faced opposition from the Supreme Court on abolition of privy purses and bank nationalization. The narrative of some in the Congress was that the apex court was too rigid in the interpretation of the Constitution when it came to individual rights versus those meant for common good. The problem with this line of thinking was that the government's moves were less aimed at sustainable public welfare and were meant to engender popular support. Specifically, IG had the 38th Amendment to the Constitution passed on 22 July 1975 which disallowed any form of judicial review of the Emergency. The 39th Amendment, carried out a couple of weeks later, put the election of a PM outside the purview of any judicial scrutiny, effectively rendering the Allahabad High Court judgment irrelevant.

Separately, on the issue of the many who had been imprisoned under the Maintenance of Internal Security Act (MISA), the Supreme Court decided on 28 April 1976 that although there had been no trials, the government was within its rights to keep such individuals under detention.[75] This was a five-judge Supreme Court bench. Justice H.R. Khanna disagreed, but the four others, Chief Justice A.N. Ray and Justices M.H. Beg, Y.V. Chandrachud and P.N. Bhagwati, went along with the outrageous contention of the IG government that prisoners could be imprisoned indefinitely without trial. This pusillanimous judgment pandering to the wishes of the IG government was a pathetic commentary on the lack of a basic sense of justice among India's senior-most judges. Clearly, they did not want to antagonize the government of the day, and the motivation was probably to later be elevated to the position of chief justice.[76]

H.R. Khanna was next in line to become the chief justice. Instead, in January 1977, M.H. Beg, who was junior to Khanna, was appointed chief justice by Indira Gandhi, and H.R. Khanna resigned. Y.V Chandrachud rose to become the chief justice in 1978 when the Janata government was in power. Chandrachud has had the longest tenure of over seven years compared to all chief justices before or after him since Independence. The Janata government was short-sightedly too preoccupied with looking for a way to jail IG. Morarji Desai should have set aside seniority to deny Chandrachud the position of chief justice.

IG was banking on her hunch that the personal ambitions of the judges would prevail over fair application of the law. She was proved right, but the nation paid a heavy price with the highest levels in the Indian judiciary dropping to unprecedented lows in their judgments and setting a cynical precedent for those who followed. Late in his life, about thirty years too late, Justice P.N. Bhagwati was reported in the print media to have regretted his decision in the 'habeas corpus' case during the Emergency. Justice Bhagwati should have also regretted his letter, written while he was a sitting judge of the Supreme Court, praising IG excessively on her return as PM in 1980.[77]

The 42nd Amendment of the Constitution was approved during the Emergency by the Parliament in 1976. This amendment curtailed the powers of the Supreme Court and high courts to decide on the validity of laws passed by Parliament.[78] The MISA of 1971, the 42nd Amendment and the other changes in the law intended to give the government the power to overrule courts were inconsistent with any democratic construct.

During the Emergency, Sanjay Gandhi and his band of obstreperous supporters flouted rules and the law with impunity. This undermined security for the poor and minorities. Some among the elite, and particularly in government, were profuse in their praise for trains running on time and that public order had been restored. Privately, however, cynicism about the police, tax and administrative officials reached distressing proportions during the Emergency. It had done little to address the endemic patronage practices, for example, related to coal mining, production of power and foodgrain subsidies which stoked egregious wrongdoing by private individuals and government employees.

The consequences of the Emergency included the immense damage done to India's image, and the government's attention was drawn away from the country's multiple economic and social challenges. Inder Malhotra and Pranab Mukherjee[79] have suggested that IG need not have called for general elections in 1977. That is, she could have continued with an Emergency for at least another year and even indefinitely. Usually episodes of one-person rule end up in military dictatorships. Unlike in theocratic or communist countries, the Congress party did not have cadres of supporters in the army. An indefinite extension of the Emergency may eventually have led to the military taking over, along with calls for independence from some states supported by external powers.

Inder Malhotra's analysis of the years 1975–77 suggests that IG was not fully aware of what was going wrong during the Emergency, and it was others such as Siddhartha Shankar Ray who had advised her to impose an Emergency. This is ex-post rationalization. PMs are praised when things go well and have to take the blame if they take decisions with disastrous consequences.

Domestic Missteps

Since the mid-nineteenth century, the British had moved tribals and others from Bihar, Orissa and Bengal to Assam to work in tea gardens, coal mines and the oil industry which started with the first refinery in Digboi, upper Assam, in 1901. By the 1970s, feelings were running high in Assam about the continuous trickle of economic and political refugees from erstwhile East Pakistan and particularly at the time of the birth of Bangladesh in 1971. An agitation led by the All Assam Students' Union (AASU) and the All Assam Gana Sangram Parishad garnered considerable popular support of the local Assamese starting from about 1979. The agitation was directed at forcing the Central government to take legislative and administrative steps to stop and then roll back illegal migration into Assam, mostly from Bangladesh.

Under legislation going back to 1946 it is for the individual to prove residency and citizenship of India. Subsequently, in 1964 a tribunal issued an order which was consistent with the 1946 Act on the detection of foreigners. IG's government, for obvious partisan electoral benefit reasons, allowed illegal migrants to remain in Assam by passing the Illegal Migrants (Determination by Tribunal) IMDT Act in 1983. Ostensibly, the principal aim of the IMDT Act was to prevent harassment of migrants into Assam. However, unlike in the past, under the IMDT Act, it was for the government to prove that a suspected foreigner had entered and settled in Assam illegally.[80]

The cynicism with which this issue of 'foreigners' in the sensitive North-east was treated by IG and by subsequent Congress governments has had negative consequences for law and order in Assam and neighbouring states. It also led to a rise in widespread suspicion in Assam about the Central government's motivations. The difficult situation in Assam during 2018–19, due to the implementation of the National Register of Citizens in Assam, can be traced back to the IG years.

On 2 July 1984, the governor of the sensitive state of Jammu and Kashmir dismissed Farooq Abdullah's government. IG's second cousin B.K. Nehru, who was the governor of J&K, had to be replaced by the Sanjay Gandhi acolyte Jagmohan of the Emergency years since B.K. Nehru felt that dismissing Abdullah was unwarranted. Once the Abdullah government was sent packing by Jagmohan, Ghulam Mohammad Shah became chief minister. Unfortunately for Kashmir, Mohammad Shah was unable to increase private investment in storage facilities, fruit processing or related areas and thus increase formal sector employment opportunities outside the state government and affiliated agencies. There were public demonstrations, particularly in Srinagar, and again IG lost credibility and so did the Union government. In similar fashion as in Assam, the subsequent developments in Kashmir and loss of faith in the Central government among many in the Srinagar valley can be traced back to events in the early 1980s.

In August 1984, IG had N.T. Rama Rao's Telugu Desam Party (TDP) government (of undivided Andhra Pradesh) dismissed on the grounds that some TDP legislators had left that party. Rama Rao had come to power with a slogan of Telugu and Andhra pride ('Atma Gauravam'). According to media reports, Rajiv Gandhi, treated as heir apparent in Congress circles, had humiliated the then Andhra Chief Minister T. Anjaiah in 1982 at the Hyderabad airport. There were violent street incidents, and the army had to be called out to restore order. The TDP came back to power by September 1984 since TDP's breakaway faction plus Congress were outnumbered by Rama Rao's supporters. The Central government's image in another state and internationally was dented by these episodes of dismissal of state governments without reasonable cause.

Consistent with IG's practice of undermining state Congress leaders, she did not allow Giani Zail Singh, who was the CM in Punjab from 1972 to 1977, to return as CM in 1980. Instead she appointed Darbara Singh. Darbara Singh did not favour Zail Singh's policies of outdoing the Akali Dal in extolling the teachings of Sikh gurus and highlighting Sikh history. Darbara Singh felt that such partisan politics was not consistent with the Congress party's avowed support for secularism. Zail Singh was the home minister in IG's cabinet post 1980, and he encouraged his supporters in Punjab to maintain their lines of communication with radical Sikh elements.[81]

In April 1980, the head of a Nirankari sect was shot dead in Delhi, and in September 1981 Lala Jagat Narain, the owner of a number of newspapers published out of Jalandhar, was killed. In both cases, the finger of suspicion pointed at a Sikh preacher called Sant Jarnail Singh Bhindranwale. Jagat Narain's newspapers were critical of Bhindranwale. As per media reports of that time, Home Minister Zail Singh prevented the arrest of Bhindranwale.

About a year later, on 2 August 1982, IG wrote to her US-based friend Dorothy Norman[82] about the situation around her in the following terms, 'Is it because of age that one thinks things everywhere are deteriorating? . . . Yeats said things fall apart, the centre does not hold. What is the centre, and where?'[83] IG as PM was at the centre of all major decision making in India. And, the 'Centre' was not 'holding' because she had allowed the law-and-order situation in Punjab to steadily slip to crisis proportions.

IG's objective was for the Congress to appear more sympathetic to Sikh sentiments than the Akalis and thus prevent their return to power. Her decision not to take timely action against violent elements led by Bhindranwale, Zail Singh's dubious role and related details are well-documented in a 1985 book by Mark Tully and Satish Jacob.[84] Tully writes in compelling terms that the crisis in Punjab could not be blamed on 'external [to India] forces' alone.

Bhindranwale had stocked up a large cache of arms in Amritsar's Golden Temple, which is the most sacred of all places of worship for Sikhs. Why was this not nipped in the bud? By the summer of 1984, IG was left with no other option but to ask the army to take military action, called Operation Blue Star, to flush out extremists from the Golden Temple. The army had to use tanks and Bhindranwale was killed in the confrontation which took place in the first week of June 1984. As the title of the Tully–Jacob book says, this was literally IG's last battle. At the end of October 1984, she was shot dead at her

New Delhi residence by two Sikhs in her security detail. The damaging consequences for Punjab and the Indian state have been deep and long-lasting.

In another cynical misstep, IG countenanced the training of Liberation Tigers of Tamil Eelam (LTTE) guerrillas in Tamil Nadu, and this started around 1983. It is likely that the Tamil Nadu government headed by M.G. Ramachandran (MGR) had extensive contacts with all shades of opinion within the Tamil communities in Sri Lanka. Even if the state government had decided to look away from the setting up of training camps in Tamil Nadu, the Central government could and should have stopped such activities. In fact, as per articles in *India Today* magazine of that time, Central government agencies may have been involved in providing training in the use of arms and explosives. It is possible that to regain the electoral support which the Congress had lost to MGR's All India Anna Dravida Munnetra Kazhagam (AIADMK), IG decided to pander to pan-Tamil sentiments.

Legacy

If positives are netted out against negatives, on the foreign policy front IG's record is in positive territory. For instance, her calm and skilful handling of the crisis created by the influx of 10 million refugees from erstwhile East Pakistan. The strategic 'capital' created by the emergence of Bangladesh continues to pay dividends for India. The handling of relations with the US and communist USSR was coloured by the need to be seen as pro-poor in domestic politics. To an extent, she was pushed towards the Soviet corner by the US providing arms to Pakistan. On balance, the defence relationship with the Soviet Union needed a rethink post 1965 or at least after 1971.

IG's record on economic decision making is marked by an imposition of excessive controls with long-lasting negative consequences for the Indian economy. Among several other factors, two important preconditions to achieve high levels of sustained growth are low inflation and restrained fiscal and current account deficits. During IG's years as PM, inflation went over 10 per cent in seven out of her fifteen years in office. Inflation was over 34 per cent in 1974–75 before the imposition of the Emergency. In IG's defence, to an extent, this was due to the oil shock of the early 1970s, and in the following years, inflation did come down sharply. IG's government followed up on the Green Revolution by spreading the systematic use of high-yielding seeds which was initiated during the Shastri years.

Echoing the suggestion of Milton Friedman and others, Vijay Joshi[85] has pointed out that while government has to necessarily fund welfare programmes in education and healthcare for the poorer sections, the corresponding services can be more efficiently and effectively provided by the private sector. IG's twenty-point programme and Sanjay Gandhi's five-point programme during the Emergency relied not just on government for funding but also its rusty, inefficient and porous official machinery for implementation.

IG was able to assume the mantle of a progressive, egalitarian leader with Indian voters. This was ironic since her younger son Sanjay was high-handed in his behaviour with senior Central government ministers and chief ministers. Sanjay died in an air crash on 23 June 1980, within six months of IG taking charge as PM a second time. Thereafter, IG started grooming her older son Rajiv as her successor. Indira Gandhi's manoeuvrings to emasculate her own party and state-level leadership to lay the ground for one of her sons to succeed her as PM proved to be immensely damaging for Indian politics and the economy. The culture of dynastic succession was copied by regional parties as the popularity of the Congress party diminished in the states due to the local leadership being entrusted to those who were personally loyal to her. This was hugely negative and completely different from the Nehru years.

Despite the exposure to liberal thought at home and in her interactions with friends based in the West, IG was feudal in her mindset. Nehru and several of his eminent contemporaries sought to promote a sense of respect for each other as individuals. Nehru looked ahead to the future and tried to lead Indians out of their social and scientific backwardness. IG was reactive and backward-looking in domestic affairs. Unfortunately, IG did not give importance to building on the foundations of a forward-looking, pluralistic society that Nehru had laid. On the contrary, IG dealt Indian democracy a low blow with the imposition of an Emergency in 1975. The amendments to the Constitution carried out during the Emergency were self-serving. IG also curtailed press freedom and undermined the independence of the judiciary by favouring judges who gave judgments that were helpful to her.

The press has since regained some of its poise due to the democratic consciousness of the Indian people sensitized to such thinking during the Nehru years. Unfortunately, the same cannot be said for the judiciary. In recent years, judges have been accused by the media and social activists of financial corruption, and the finger of suspicion has been pointed towards those who have served at the highest levels of the Supreme Court.

Indira Gandhi's domestic decisions were often motivated by cynical self-interest. Nehru wrote to chief ministers almost every fortnight to explain the Central government policies and sought their feedback. When the combined strength of the opposition parties in the Lok Sabha was well below that of the

Congress, Nehru spent hours explaining his domestic and foreign policies in Parliament. IG by comparison had little patience for democratic niceties within the Congress, let alone in her interaction with opposition parties.

Although the country regained its balance, the Congress party did not recover from the body blows it received from IG's single-minded pursuit of complete domination of the party. Congress party leaders with popular followings in various states were either put out to pasture or cut to size. This undermining of Congress leaders resulted in a steady fall in popular support for the Congress in successive general elections. Over time the Congress came to depend on IG's heirs to lead the party. Ironically, IG's policy of centralization led to the growth of regional parties in several states, for example, UP, Bihar, Orissa, West Bengal and Andhra Pradesh.

One of the measures of mature leadership is the ability to accept constructive criticism. By all accounts, IG was not receptive to any form of criticism about the way in which she helped first one son and then pushed the second into politics. In national politics, IG did not alter her authoritarian ways after her return to power in 1980. In contrast to Crocker's description of the Nehru years as a status society, India became very much a money-nexus society with Indira Gandhi as PM.

In *Intertwined Lives*,[86] P.N. Haksar is quoted as having said in a letter to Bakul Patel[87] in September 1997 that he could hardly have been IG's conscience keeper since IG had no moral compass of what was right or wrong. *Intertwined Lives* rationalizes this devastating indictment of IG on the grounds that by 1997 Haksar was suffering from 'late life melancholy'. By all accounts, till his passing away, Haksar was known to be clinical and unsparing of himself and others in his assessments and not given to hyperbole. Another excuse given in *Intertwined Lives* is that Haksar was more balanced about IG in his feedback to Katherine Frank.[88] Well, that is not consistent with Frank's book on IG which is critical of the latter for being too much under the influence of her younger son who was allowed to exercise arbitrary power.

Commentators suggest that Haksar is to blame for the turn to the left that India's economy took in the late 1960s and early 1970s. India's PMs, including IG, cannot have it both ways. Just as the overall strategy and decision making regarding Bangladesh goes to her credit, she has to take the full blame for the long-lasting harm she did to the Indian economy. IG had no permanent advisers, only permanent personal-family interests. It is likely that she identified with Dev Kant Barooah's ill-advised praise that 'India is Indira and Indira is India'. By extension, what was not good for Indira was not good for India either.

All things considered, Haksar's comment that IG did not have a moral compass is justified. She did undermine the integrity of domestic political processes and institutions. A powerful magnet,[89] namely, her felt need to ensure dynastic succession, interfered with her moral compass and pointed her in the wrong direction. IG worked single-mindedly to ensure that one of her two sons, first Sanjay and later Rajiv, should succeed her as PM. IG muzzled the press during the Emergency. She also undermined the independence of the judiciary, from which it has still not entirely recovered.

At the same time, IG has to be credited with helping the socially and economically disadvantaged groups to band together to use the power of the ballot box to their advantage. Along with this success also came the immense failure of her inability to channel this electoral power of laggard groups to improve their educational and financial standing. Nayantara Sahgal (Indira Gandhi's cousin) claims[90] that India lost ten years of development thanks to IG's policies. Another way of evaluating the cost to the nation of IG's restrictive economic policies is to estimate what would have been the size of India's economy if the reforms of the early 1990s were carried out at the beginning of the 1970s. It is possible that Indian GDP may have grown at an additional 3 per cent every year over the last forty-eight years. If this assumption is realistic, the size of India's economy would have been close to US $10 trillion by 2018.

In the context of the cost for India of erroneous economic policies, I.G. Patel's criticism was both pointed and trenchant. In an article in the *Economic and Political Weekly*, he wrote that India had no option but to accept the conditionalities that came with an IMF line of credit in the early 1990s. Patel was of the opinion that 'the present [the balance of payments] crisis [in 1990–91] is because successive governments in the 1980s chose to abdicate their responsibility to the nation for the sake of short-term partisan political gains and indeed out of sheer cynicism'.[91] Patel was referring to the governments of IG, Rajiv Gandhi and V.P. Singh in the 1980s.

In the mythological epic Mahabharata, the Kuru clan was headed by the patriarch Dhritarashtra. Dhritarashtra's son Duryodhana was unfair to his cousins the Pandavas, and in the ensuing war between the two clans, all of Dhritarashtra's sons including Duryodhana were killed. In the words of the narrator, Sanjaya, Dhritarashtra's fatal mistake was excessive indulgence of his eldest son Duryodhana, that is, *'putra moh'*. Literally, those two words mean excessive attachment to one's children which prevents parents from accepting the shortcomings of their offspring. If parents happen to be heads of government, such infatuation can lead to national and personal tragedy as it did for India, IG and her sons.

In mythological tales around the world, even gods make errors of judgement, and at times their moral compass goes awry. This is a useful backdrop against which to reflect on IG's nearly sixteen years as PM. A fair summation probably is that her significant foreign policy achievements were overwhelmed by the long-lasting consequences of her domestic economic failures and undermining of democratic institutions. Many have pointed out that IG came back with a sizeable majority in the Lok Sabha in 1980. After she was assassinated in 1984, the sympathy around the country resulted in the Congress winning 404 out of 533 seats in the general elections to the Lower House of Parliament. Elections in Assam and Punjab had to be held in 1985 because of the serious ongoing security disturbances there.

IG's election victories, including the huge posthumous victory for her party in 1984, confirm that large numbers of Indian voters trusted her repeatedly. It does not mean that she lived up to their trust. IG is a representative example of the fallacy of composition. She displayed great courage and resilience in the creation of Bangladesh and by coming back to power in 1980. However, what was true about her in part was not true about her in totality. In totality, the balance is negative since IG countenanced brazen venality, and, starting with her own family, promoted blatant feudalism and nepotism in Indian politics. In fairness to all Indians, the Election Commission should not have just changed the election symbol of her party to a 'Hand' but also archived the name Indian National Congress as a political party forever.

IG was very particular about her dress and was exquisitely attired on foreign trips in the best Indian silk saris.[92] In India, IG invariably wore white or light-coloured saris, and on occasion she wore saris made out of khadi. Although IG did deliver speeches in Hindi, she was more comfortable in English. IG made do in English and Hindi, but she was not a proficient public speaker like her father or others who participated in the freedom struggle. On the India–Bharat divide, IG leaned more towards India than Bharat.

As for the 3 Cs (Character, Competence and Charisma), Indira Gandhi was highly Charismatic. She was Competent but only if it suited her domestic politics. Her high level of Competence in foreign relations was best illustrated in how she handled the birth of Bangladesh. As a direct consequence of her leadership, disillusionment with politicians and politics in general set in all over the country. To that extent, her Character was flawed to say the least.

IV

MORARJI DESAI

Sincere Yet Inflexible and Outmoded

For the obdurate people will not believe
What they do not see and distinctly feel

The Journey to the East, Hermann Hesse

Morarji Desai[1] was a deputy collector in Gujarat for over ten years after graduating from college. Later he joined the freedom movement and by the mid-1940s, he had been jailed several times by the British, including during the Quit India movement. Post the 1946 state assembly elections, Desai became the home and revenue minister in Bombay, and was chief minister of Bombay state from 1952 to 1956. Subsequently, after Gujarat and Maharashtra became separate states, he moved to Delhi and was finance minister in Nehru's cabinet from 1958 to 1963. Desai favoured less state intervention in the economy than Nehru and harboured the ambition of becoming PM after him. However, when Nehru passed away in 1964, he was overlooked by the Congress leadership, or the Syndicate, as it was then called. Lal Bahadur Shastri became PM and did not include Desai in his cabinet.

Later, when Shastri passed away in January 1966, Desai claimed that, given his contributions during the freedom struggle and experience in government, he should rightfully be the next PM. Unfortunately for Desai, senior Congress leaders were again not in his favour. It is apparent from these two failed bids for the prime ministership that while Desai was respected, he was not seen to have the conciliatory qualities that a fractious polity like India needs. Additionally, he had a strong political base in Gujarat and would have been too independent minded for the Syndicate's liking. As things turned out, Indira Gandhi was

115

elected decisively by the Congress parliamentary party members, and she gave Desai the finance portfolio.

Desai opposed the taking over of banks by government and resigned from IG's cabinet when she nationalized fourteen banks at one go in 1969. Desai would have felt considerable antipathy towards a much younger IG for having denied him the premiership after Shastri. This negative sentiment must have been aggravated by her jailing him and other opposition leaders during the Emergency.

In the 1977 general elections, IG and son Sanjay Gandhi lost from Raebareli and Amethi respectively. IG's Congress and its supporting parties were reduced to 189 members in the Lok Sabha. Opposition parties had fought the elections under a combination called the Janata Party, and this loose alliance won 345 seats. None of the major constituents of the Janata Party[2] could have formed government on their own. At that point of time, the other two contenders for the PM position were Jagjivan Ram and Charan Singh. Ram had resigned from IG's cabinet and had left the Congress party as late as 2 February 1977. By then, the immense public resentment against the Emergency must have become clear to a politically astute Jagjivan Ram. From the start, the Janata Party was riven with personality clashes as the head of each of the coalition members had differing views on how to govern and had ambitions to be PM. Acharya Kripalani was asked to decide who should be PM out of these three candidates, and his vote went in favour of Desai.

Desai was essentially a regional leader from Gujarat and he enjoyed recognition in Maharashtra. At eighty-one years of age, he was much older than Nehru or Shastri when they had become PM. All things considered, Desai made his mark in history as the first non-Congress party prime minister of India, and he was sworn in on 23 March 1977.

The Janata Party leaders had come together because of a common dislike for IG's high-handed and unjustified decisions during the Emergency years of 1975–77. The constituent parties did not have commonly agreed economic or social programmes. Desai was in favour of promoting the private sector in India. However, his government took the short-sighted decision of requiring foreign companies to compulsorily tie up with local companies. This led to the exit of IBM and Coca-Cola, which sent out a negative signal for inward FDI. In overall terms, instead of paying close attention to the economy and development, Desai and others in the Janata Party focused almost exclusively on bringing IG to book for excesses during the Emergency.

Given the sharp differences on government policies within the Janata Party government, Desai faced challenges from his two deputy

PMs Charan Singh and Jagjivan Ram. Charan Singh and his supporter Raj Narain felt that Desai was too focused on the well-being of urban India, and this needed to be corrected with pro-rural and farmer-friendly policies. Jagjivan Ram had no strong views which differentiated him from Desai or Charan Singh. For Ram, it was a question of how to seek out an opportune time for him to become PM. If Desai was convinced that Indira Gandhi's policies of excessive government controls had straitjacketed the economy, he needed to build a consensus for change across a wide cross section of business, social and political groupings.

Desai's lack of attention to the required changes in economic policies was apparent in his first Independence Day speech from the Red Fort on 15 August 1977. The newspaper report the next day focused mostly on Desai's promise to eradicate untouchability.[3] It takes time to address social prejudices, and Desai wisely reminded the nation that this was still work in progress. At the same time, Desai's first address from the Red Fort should have indicated, at least in broad terms, how he meant to raise growth and increase employment opportunities.

Desai appointed H.M. Patel, a former ICS officer, as the finance minister. During the years that Sardar Vallabhbhai Patel was home minister, H.M. Patel was cabinet secretary and was opposed to Nehru's left-of-centre economic policies. H.M. Patel's views were closer to those of C. Rajagopalachari and the Swatantra Party. Desai's other senior cabinet members consisted of farmer-friendly Charan Singh who was home minister and Jagjivan Ram who was defence minister. Trade unionist George Fernandes was industry minister, and agriculture was handled by Akali Dal leaders—first Parkash Singh Badal and then Surjit Singh Barnala. Madhu Dandavate, who was left-of-centre in his views about the economy, was minister for railways, and erstwhile Congress leader H.N. Bahuguna was minister for petroleum. The erratic Raj Narain was the minister of health and Mohan Dharia, who was perceived as a socialist, became the commerce minister. Desai also depended on socialists outside the government, such as Jayaprakash Narayan. H.M. Patel's budgets between 1977 and 1979 did not show any significant break with the past. There was no move to unshackle the Indian economy and this was understandable given the number of left-leaning ministers in the cabinet.

The profitability of railways and its complex, misleading accounting methodologies needed to be examined. However, given the contrarian pulls within Desai's government, it was too much to expect that Dandavate would be able to make significant changes in the working of railways. India was and remains highly dependent on oil imports. Bahuguna was perceived as a competent Congress chief minister of UP from November 1973 to November 1975. However, funding of oil exploration, empowerment of the petroleum-sector's publicly owned undertakings, and allowing the re-entry of the foreign private sector required a calmer political environment in Delhi. It was no surprise, given Dharia's left-leaning political views, that there were no bold moves to reduce import tariffs or promote exports and FDI under his stewardship of the commerce ministry. Desai had opposed bank nationalization, but he was unable to start a discussion on raising banking-sector efficiency by encouraging the entry of new private-sector banks.

Table 4.1 in the Appendices shows that gross fiscal deficits increased from 3.5 per cent to 5 per cent of GDP between 1977–78 and 1979–80, while capital outlays went down marginally from about 2 to 1.9 per cent of GDP. Consumer price inflation (CPI) was over 10 per cent in 1977–78. However, in 1978–79, inflation came down sharply to minus 0.2 per cent. The following year, CPI was again up to 9.4 per cent. It was a reflection of the performance of a Central government devoid of direction in Delhi that GDP growth went down from 7.3 per cent in 1977–78 to minus 5.2 per cent in 1979–80.

In January 1978, Desai's government wasted its limited political capital by demonetizing high-denomination notes. It should have been obvious that an effective demonetization exercise requires a number of follow-up steps which are best initiated in the first year of a five-year term. Desai, and later Charan Singh, did not have the time in office or the ability, given the shifting loyalties of the constituent parties, to bequeath a sound economy to the next government. The then RBI Governor I.G. Patel claims[4] that he had mentioned to Finance Minister H.M. Patel that demonetization would not have the desired effect of reducing 'black' money in the economy because unaccounted wealth is usually not stored in cash.

In what turned out to be a highly significant social, political and economic decision on 1 January 1979, Desai appointed B.P. Mandal as chairman of a commission to 'identify socially and educationally backward classes', and to examine the issue of reservations for this grouping. The terms of reference for the Mandal Commission did not include a review of the existing reservations of 15 per cent for Scheduled Castes (SCs) plus 7 per cent for Scheduled Tribes (STs) in government and public-sector institutions. The Mandal Commission submitted its report in December 1980 which recommended that 27 per cent of jobs in government undertakings should be reserved for OBCs. However, the Janata government collapsed before it could even consider implementing these recommendations.

Desai's views on foreign policy were far removed from ground realities. For instance, he favoured the elimination of nuclear weapons and was prepared to sign the NPT, provided all declared nuclear weapon countries were to denuclearize. Similarly, he had reservations about spying on other countries. It is rumoured that in a fit of openness about nuclear matters, Desai revealed to Pakistan that India was aware of the latter's uranium enrichment facilities at Kahuta. Desai is said to have written to Pakistani President Zia-ul-Haq expressing concern about Pakistan's nuclear weapons programme.[5] If true, Desai's openness may have hurt Indian intelligence-gathering efforts in Pakistan.

By July 1976, Indira Gandhi had restored diplomatic relations with China at the ambassador level. Desai had indicated his reservations in the past about the absorption of Sikkim into the Indian Union. This may have signalled to China that India was now less inclined, than during the Indira Gandhi years, to extend its influence in its neighbourhood.

Mao passed away on 9 September 1976, and the more pragmatic Deng Xiaoping took over. This was the setting in which Atal Bihari Vajpayee of the Bharatiya Jana Sangh (BJS), who was the external affairs minister in the Janata government, visited China in February 1979. Vajpayee's visit was significant as it restored a measure of normality to the bilateral relationship which had been in a comatose state since the 1962 war. There is continuing speculation about the extent to which China was serious about resolving the border issue at the time based on Deng raising it with Vajpayee at their meeting in the Great Hall. In any case, Vajpayee had to cut short his visit when China attacked Vietnam while he was on Chinese soil.

US President James (Jimmy) Carter visited India in January 1978. Carter chose not visit Pakistan on the same trip to signal that the US did not equate India with its troublesome neighbour. Earlier visits of US President Eisenhower and vice-president Nixon to the subcontinent had been to both countries. Carter indicated to Desai during his visit that if India decided to abandon nuclear weapons, the US would restart its supply of enriched uranium fuel to the nuclear power plants at Tarapur. The US had stopped supplying fuel for the Tarapur plants after India's nuclear test in 1974. Even without US tutoring, Desai did not want India to develop nuclear weapons. However, Desai was against the discrimination embedded in the 1968 NPT and he declined Carter's offer.

On this visit to India, Carter was said to have offered 'to develop the Brahmaputra basin on the lines of the Indus Waters Accord of 1960 between India and Pakistan'.[6] The US also offered to broker equitable water sharing between India, Nepal and Bangladesh. Desai did not respond to this offer since India preferred to resolve these issues with Nepal and Bangladesh on a bilateral basis.

In the forty years since Carter's visit in 1978, there have been floods in Assam annually during the monsoon season. Branches, leaves and leftover construction materials come down from the upper reaches of this major river in Assam, namely the Brahmaputra. Those who are in charge of urban regulatory bodies in Assam and its neighbouring states have allowed construction too close to the river. Over the decades the river has become shallower due to the accumulation of debris on its bed and because the river has not been dredged regularly. This makes the Brahmaputra prone to changing its course, causing loss of life and property.

Given the stakes involved, Desai's government should have found a way to avail of US expertise and financial assistance from multilateral institutions such as the World Bank to contain floods and improve the reach of assured irrigation. That is, without India having to surrender its right to conclude bilateral water-sharing agreements with Nepal or Bangladesh.

Towards the end of 1978, the cracks in Desai's government were clearly visible. Senior ministers, including Charan Singh, had serious differences with Desai, ostensibly on economic policies. The reality was that the parting of ways was driven by Charan Singh's ambition to be PM. While the Indian government was distracted by the sharp differences between Desai and his senior cabinet colleagues, clouds of war were gathering over Afghanistan with far-reaching consequences from then till now.

The left-leaning government of Afghanistan, with Babrak Karmal in charge as President after Hafizullah Amin was assassinated, was out of favour with the US. President Jimmy Carter's national security adviser Zbigniew Brzezinski has since said that the US started funding and sending shipments of arms to the Taliban to support them in their fight against the Afghan government. Brzezinski has commented that the US hoped that by doing this, they could draw the Soviet Union into a quagmire in Afghanistan. In response to a question from *Le Nouvel Observateur,* Brzezinski responded that he has no regrets at all, as a consequence, for having boosted extremist sentiment. According to him, the end, namely the demise of the Soviet Union, more than justified the growth of fundamentalism and terrorism since that time.[7]

Clearly, the Indian government was not in a position to act on this information even if it had any inkling of the situation on the ground in 1978–79. However, an earlier realization of the likely consequences in and around Afghanistan would have better informed Indian foreign policymaking.

Desai's time as PM of two years and four months was marked by incessant squabbling among the Janata Party coalition partners. The only point they all agreed on was that IG should be prosecuted. Desai set up a commission of inquiry headed by former Chief Justice of India J.C. Shah to look into ministerial and official misdoings during the Emergency. Instead of a patient, step-by-step approach to allow judicial processes to work unhindered, Desai's government made the cardinal mistake of arresting IG on flimsy charges on 3 October 1977 in Delhi. The charges were thrown out by a Delhi magistrate, and she was released the following day. IG gained the upper hand as the aggrieved party.

It also soon became clear to the electorate that it had fallen from the frying pan of the corruption, inflation, widespread unemployment plus excesses of the Emergency into the Janata government fire of appalling incompetence. In fairness to Desai, the wide divergence in the thinking and beliefs of the coalition partners made any kind of coherent governance next to impossible.

CHARAN SINGH
Short-sighted

Charan Singh (CS)[8] was a senior leader in Congress since before Independence and was imprisoned on more than one occasion during the struggle for freedom. CS was opposed to Nehru's planning policies for the agriculture sector and was successful in getting forward-looking land reforms legislation passed in UP. He left the Congress in 1967 and formed his own party called the Bharatiya Kranti Dal (BKD). With the support of socialists such as Ram Manohar Lohia and Raj Narain, he became the first non-Congress chief minister of UP—but for less than a year, from April 1967 to February 1968. Chaudhary Charan Singh, as he was called by his followers in western Uttar Pradesh, felt strongly about helping farmers, whose incomes were exposed to the vagaries of weather and manipulation of prices of their produce by intermediaries.

CS's party had been dissolved to form the Janata Party before the 1977 elections. In July 1979, abetted by Raj Narain, he pulled his party out of this coalition, and Morarji Desai resigned as PM. President Sanjiva Reddy invited Charan Singh, then seventy-seven years old, to form the government. At that point of time, Charan Singh had a letter of support from Indira Gandhi's Congress (I). On 28 July 1979, he became the fifth prime minister of India with the support of his sixty-four MPs and an assurance from Indira Gandhi that she would support him on the floor of the house. However, a day before the Lok Sabha was due to meet, Congress (I) withdrew its support, resulting in Charan Singh having to relinquish office on 14 January 1980 without ever having faced Parliament.

The Janata Party government had the numbers in the Lok Sabha to continue in power. Due to Charan Singh's ambition to be PM, which he was for a little over five months, general elections had to be held in January 1980, two years before the Janata Party's term would have been over.

Charan Singh must have known that the Congress would pull the rug from under him whenever elections suited Indira Gandhi. However, it appears he wanted to be PM, even if it were for a few months. His cynicism was reminiscent of Indira Gandhi's self-serving justification of the Emergency. To that extent, purely self-interest-driven politics started to become more common in India.

Legacy

The governments of Morarji Desai and Charan Singh were marked by sharp differences among the constituent parties and lasted about three years in all. While Desai's government went into overdrive to ensure a jail term for Indira Gandhi, it passed legislation to make the imposition of an unjustified Emergency more difficult in the future. Desai did the nation a disservice by appointing the Mandal Commission, which eventually led to additional reservations in government-owned institutions. Over the decades, reservations have often become a political ploy to appease the socially and economically downtrodden without pushing for effective policies to ensure equal opportunity for the underprivileged. A new low was reached in national politics in the formation and collapse of the Charan Singh government.

V

RAJIV GANDHI

Forward-looking Yet Catastrophically Error-prone

The brash unbridled tongue, the lawless folly of fools, will end in pain.

Euripides

Rajiv Gandhi (RG)[1] was the elder of Indira Gandhi's two sons. After the death of Sanjay Gandhi in a flying accident in June 1980, Indira Gandhi made it abundantly clear to the Congress party that she wanted Rajiv Gandhi to succeed her. RG was elected to the Lok Sabha from Amethi, Sanjay Gandhi's constituency, and was sworn in as an MP in August 1981. The first time RG had executive authority, albeit without a formal government position, was when he was authorized by IG to supervise the arrangements for the Asian Games which were held in Delhi in November–December 1982.

Indira Gandhi was assassinated on 31 October 1984, and President Zail Singh and Sardar Buta Singh pushed for RG to succeed her. Rajiv Gandhi was just forty years of age when he became India's youngest PM ever. A tidal wave of sympathy following IG's assassination swept the Congress to power with an overwhelming majority of 405 out of 543 Lok Sabha seats in the December 1984 general elections.

It was to prove counterproductive for the Congress party to have thrust this immense responsibility on RG who had limited formal education and administrative experience, or the political acumen to negotiate the complexities of governing a country as varied and poor as India. The reality was that the Congress had by now become overdependent on IG as the principal vote-getter, and obsequious sycophancy to IG's sons, first Sanjay and later Rajiv, was seen as a ticket to high political office.

RG took charge as PM in an environment of mass killings in Delhi, longstanding agitation against Bangladeshi settlers in Assam, and continued disturbances in Punjab. From the day RG took office and for the next few days, there were brutal revenge killings of several thousand Sikhs, mostly in Delhi but also in other parts of India. He and his government proved unequal to the task of dispersing the bands of roving murderers and the wanton massacre, particularly in less affluent east Delhi.

RG was reported to have commented on 19 November 1984 (Indira Gandhi's birth anniversary) that the earth shakes when a big tree falls.[2] It is not clear that RG meant to justify violence against Sikhs as an understandable expression of public anger caused by his mother's assassination. However, the substantive issue is that his government should have been able to stop the violence against the Sikhs within a couple of hours on 31 October. Others who held crucial positions at that time were Home Minister P.V. Narasimha Rao, Lieutenant Governor P.G. Gavai and Delhi police commissioner S.C. Tandon. Much after the event, I heard the former principal secretary to the prime minister, P.C. Alexander, say[3] on Indian television that he was unaware of the extent of violence after Indira Gandhi's assassination. Coming from a senior official in the then PMO, I found this statement crass beyond measure.

RG took office the same day his mother was killed. It is possible he was too grief-stricken to think of public order, and it was also the responsibility of the home minister and officials to take prompt action. Is the usual exemption from work for a person grieving over the unexpected and cruel death of a parent relevant in this case? RG could have asked one of the cabinet ministers to hold interim charge as PM for a fortnight or more to give himself time to grieve. By all accounts, including that of Pranab Mukherjee, those close to him such as Arun Nehru[4] pushed Rajiv Gandhi to take the oath of office administered by the vice-president and not even wait for President Zail Singh to return to Delhi. However, Zail Singh was able to return to Delhi in time to administer the oath.

On a personal note, on 31 October 1984, I happened to be in my ancestral home Tezpur (Assam) with my wife and infant daughter. I was on home leave from my posting as the first secretary in the Indian embassy in Havana. At around noon, one of my maternal uncles came over looking extremely agitated. He told us that the BBC had reported that IG had been shot dead by two of her guards in Delhi. My wife, daughter and I were scheduled to take an Indian Airlines flight from Guwahati the following day to return to Delhi. The three of us reached Delhi in the evening on 1 November. The taxi driver at Palam airport demanded an additional Rs 200 above the meter fare for the ride from the airport to Defence Colony. He expressed his fear about being stoned or attacked even though he was clean-shaven and not a Sikh. It is unbelievable that ministers and senior government officials claimed later that they were unaware of the violence against Sikhs in Delhi, which lasted at least three full days.[5]

The following day, on 2 November, the Ministry of External Affairs, realizing that I had not yet left for Havana, put me on 'special duty' in Delhi and I was told to help with the arrangements to be made for the foreign dignitaries who were to attend IG's funeral. I was directed to the temporary offices set up by the Ministry of External Affairs in the Ashok Hotel. In casual conversation in the hotel's control room, I expressed my anguish that while elaborate security arrangements were being made for visitors, Sikhs were being hunted down in several parts of Delhi. A colleague responded that the Sikhs had it coming. I was dumbfounded and saddened that it was not just the crazed mobs, lumpen or Congress elements—some among those around me in government also felt that the killing of innocent Sikhs was justified retribution.

Thirty-four years later, on 18 December 2018, the Delhi High Court sentenced Sajjan Kumar, a former Congress Lok Sabha MP from Delhi, to imprisonment for the rest of his natural life. Kumar was convicted for having personally instigated crowds to attack Sikhs. The court commented that 'criminals enjoyed political patronage'. Sajjan Kumar was imprisoned on 31 December 2018, and his appeal against the high court's judgment is pending with the Supreme Court.

The Rajiv Gandhi government appointed Judge Ranganath Misra to head an inquiry commission to look into the 1984 'riots'.[6] This commission's finding was that the government and the Congress party were not culpable in any way, and Justice Misra went on to become the chief justice of India. For the record, he was later chairman of the National Human Rights Commission and a Congress Rajya Sabha MP from 1998 to 2004.

Gyani Zail Singh had been elevated to the position of President of India in July 1982 by Indira Gandhi. She felt he could be useful in that position, and additionally she wanted to distance him from state-level politics in Punjab. Zail Singh remained President for five years till July 1987. By the time RG assumed office, Zail Singh had been the President of the country for about two and a half years. During the last year that Indira Gandhi was PM, her relations with Zail Singh deteriorated, possibly because Zail Singh continued to follow developments in Punjab and kept in touch with radical elements in that state.[7]

Traditionally, the Indian PM briefs the President on all significant issues. The periodicity of such briefings has varied depending on who was the PM. The relationship between RG and Zail Singh started off on the wrong foot because of media speculation that the President's phones were bugged by the IB. Additionally, RG's briefings of President Zail Singh were few and perfunctory. As the youngest PM since Independence, with no administrative experience of running a ministry, let alone the entire Central government, RG would have been well advised to keep his relations with the President on an even keel.

Pranab Mukherjee was the finance minister and a senior minister in IG's cabinet. When she was assassinated, Mukherjee was rumoured to have remarked that the next in seniority in the cabinet, implying himself, usually succeeds the Indian PM in the event of an untoward death. This alleged remark was perhaps perceived as excessive ambition by RG, and he dropped Pranab Mukherjee from the cabinet. Mukherjee was then removed from the Congress Working Committee, the principal decision-making body of the party. Subsequently, on 26 April 1986, Mukherjee was expelled from the Congress party, and he then formed his own party called Rashtriya Samajwadi Congress. This party merged with the Congress in 1989. Pranab Mukherjee's expulsion from the Congress was possibly due to a feeling within the party that none other than Rajiv Gandhi should have any chance of becoming PM. The prevailing culture of abject sycophancy in the Congress had no resemblance with the values of the party which had fought for India's Independence.

RG proceeded to be high-handed, not just with Pranab Mukherjee but also with other veterans such as Kamalapati Tripathi of Uttar Pradesh. Rajiv's disdain for some elders in the Congress was not entirely misplaced. Some of them had outlived any public welfare purpose they had at the start of their political careers, and had little concern for, or any sway with voters. Rajiv tried to make a break with the past in the same way that Indira Gandhi had distanced herself from Atulya Ghosh, K. Kamaraj, S.K. Patil and S. Nijalingappa when she became prime minister in 1966.

The coterie around RG included people who were roughly his age, and some were his contemporaries in Doon School. They were equally removed from the masses and did not have any experience of working in government. RG cut himself off from the Congress party faithfuls who were intensely loyal to his mother while gradually becoming cynical about the best interests of the people. He thus ended up neither hunting with the hound nor running with the hare. The corrosion of the party from within was due to IG's insistence on personal loyalty as the stepping stone for high positions, and RG took the party further down that path. As evident from Pranab Mukherjee's case, RG did not see the merit of picking his battles. Even if he was impatient to change the working of the Congress party and the government, he needed the support of those who knew how to avoid political pitfalls better than him.

Unrest in Border States

Assam had been on the boil[8] for nearly five years when RG took over as PM, and this had negative implications for India's relations with neighbouring countries to the east. RG's government deserves high praise for the 1985 Accord that his government concluded with the All Assam Students Union (AASU) and Asom Gana Parishad (AGP) to call off the Assam agitation. Under this Accord, the Indian Citizenship Act of 1955 was amended to include Section 6(A), which gives Indian citizenship to all Bangladeshis who came to Assam prior to 24 March 1971.[9] The logic for this cut-off date was that the Bangladesh government had given an undertaking that it would accept the return of all those who had moved from that country to India after March 1971. Although the Assam Accord did bring violent agitations and bandhs to a halt, greater attention needed to be paid to surface transportation linkages within the north-eastern states, with the rest of India and towards Myanmar and beyond.

As for Punjab, violent disturbances continued due to separatist sentiments in that state, exacerbated by Operation Blue Star. In retrospect, RG needed to reach out to pro-Khalistan elements in India and abroad. These elements were behind the bombing of the *Emperor Kanishka* (an Air India flight 182 from Canada to India) on 23 June 1984. All 329 passengers and crew aboard that flight were killed. Four troubled years later, in 1988, RG appointed K.P.S. Gill, an Assam cadre IPS officer known for his tough tactics in the North-east, director general of police in Punjab, while Siddhartha Shankar Ray was the governor. The last vestiges of separatism in Punjab were extinguished at considerable loss of life two years after RG's term was over by 1991.

Centenary Speech and Idealism

Despite the unrest around India, RG's initial phase as PM was marked by optimism. This sense of hope was underscored by RG's address as PM and Congress president at the party's centenary session in Bombay on 28 December 1985. RG's speech came as a breath of fresh air, and he loftily quoted Gandhi at this 100th anniversary of his party on how to choose between competing courses of action: 'Whenever you are in doubt or when the self becomes too much with you, apply the following test: Recall the face of the poorest and the weakest man whom you may have seen and ask yourself if the step you contemplate is going to be of any use to him.'

This was a high standard that RG had set for himself. On interfaith relations, RG recalled Nehru and said, 'to him [Nehru], secularism was the beacon light when waves of passion threatened to submerge us'. As for Indira Gandhi, RG said that she had 'analysed with clinical precision how the entire system had been weakened from within, how the party had once again been infiltrated by vested interests who would not allow us to move, how patronage and graft had affected the national institutional framework, how nationalism and patriotism had ebbed, how the pettiness and selfishness of persons in political positions had ruptured social fabric'.

In this speech, Rajiv Gandhi mentioned that India has 'government servants who do not serve but oppress the poor and the helpless, police who do not uphold the law but shield the guilty, tax collectors who do not collect taxes but connive with those who cheat the State and whole legions whose only concern is their private welfare at the cost of society. They have no work ethic, no feeling for the public cause, no involvement in the future of the nation, no comprehension of national goals, no commitment to the values of modern India. They have only a grasping, mercenary outlook, devoid of competence, integrity and commitment.'

As for the Congress party, RG mentioned that

> . . . we have distanced ourselves from the masses, basic issues of national unity and integrity, social change and economic development recede into the background. Instead, phoney issues, shrouded in medieval obscurantism, occupy the centre of the stage. Our Congress workers, who faced the bullets of British imperialism, run for shelter at the slightest manifestation of caste and communal tension . . . Corruption is not only tolerated but even regarded as the hallmark of leadership. Flagrant contradiction between what we say and what we do has become our way of life. At every step, our aims and actions conflict.

RG's speech in Bombay on 28 December 1985 has been quoted at length here since most of what he said on that day is relevant to the India of 2019. In his early days, RG was in a sweet spot—he was a young man, with a clean image, and he had an overwhelming majority in the Lok Sabha. RG had demonstrated in his Congress centenary speech that he was aware of the systemic shortcomings both within the political elite and among officials who needed to translate pious intentions into action. However, because of his lack of administrative experience or the iron will necessary to take on established interests, the country lost a golden opportunity for change.

The culture of courtiers had developed into a fine art form in the tamarind and laburnum tree-lined avenues of central (Lutyens's) Delhi during the IG years. Consequently, for RG, it was not clear who was sincere and who was pretending. This resulted in frequent changes in RG's inner circle. For instance, RG changed his finance minister (FM) three times in five years. RG first appointed V.P. Singh as FM in 1985 and then took charge of this portfolio himself in 1987. He then gave the finance ministry to N.D. Tiwari for less than two years, and finally S.B. Chavan for 1988–89 (see Table 3 after the prologue for the tenures of finance ministers since Independence). Towards the end of RG's tenure all crucial finance ministry meetings, including annual budget-related deliberations, were held in the PMO.

As was the case for finance ministers, there were four defence ministers between 1984 and 1989. To start with, P.V. Narasimha Rao was defence minister from December 1984 till September 1985. Then RG took over till end January 1987, and V.P. Singh was moved from finance to defence in January 1987. Singh resigned in less than three months in April 1987, and K.C. Pant was in charge of the defence ministry till the end of RG's term.

Arun Singh, born in 1944, the same year as RG, was his contemporary at Doon School and Cambridge, and they were close friends. Arun Singh was the minister of state for defence from the start of RG's term. Given the direct access that Arun Singh had to RG, he was more influential than the defence minister.[10] RG's cabinet was reshuffled too frequently, and this was not conducive to implementation of substantive reform.

Economic Context and Policies

RG inherited a sclerotic Indian economy gasping for breath because of the government's python-like grip on industrial licensing, foreign trade and investment. Consumer durables and electronics products were in short supply and import duties were exorbitantly high. India's trade in goods was perennially in deficit, and the manufacturing sector did not grow fast enough to raise employment in the formal and semi-formal sectors and draw workers away from subsistence, monsoon-dependent agriculture. Most of these shortcomings were plaguing the Indian economy since the mid-1960s and had grown to harmful proportions through IG's years as PM.

Turning to the environment for business, the prevailing view in government circles in the mid-1980s was that owners of businesses short-change workers by declaring lockouts. RG's remedy for this was worse than the ailment. Instead of loosening controls to allow companies to close businesses when there was no other option, the Sick Industrial Companies (Special Provisions) Act (SICA) was passed in 1985.[11] The infamous Board for

Industrial and Financial Reconstruction (BIFR) was established under SICA. In practice, BIFR and the corresponding Appellate Authority for Industrial and Financial Reconstruction (AAIFR) prevented struggling companies from ever folding up. BIFR's overriding logic was that workers needed protection from rapacious owners who stripped companies of assets and declared bankruptcy. It is likely that owners of some companies took such an approach. However, a blanket presumption on these lines resulted in the BIFR inordinately delaying disposal of appeals to shut down sick companies. Even without referring to Schumpeter's concept of 'creative destruction',[12] it should have been obvious that preventing terminally 'sick' companies from dying results in losses for the economy. Indian courts often took it upon themselves to rule against even the atrociously delayed decisions of BIFR to prevent closure of companies on the grounds that it would hurt workers.[13] Given the delays in a company being allowed to wind up, SICA and BIFR were effectively anti-worker since fresh investment and hence the creation of employment opportunities in the formal sector were inhibited.[14]

Readers who are old enough will remember the days when only those who had access to landline phones in offices or at home could book a 'trunk call' to another city or country, and talking times were restricted to three minutes which could be extended at extra cost. In 1984, during IG's last year as PM, forward-looking changes were adopted in government's telecommunication and information technology policies. Changes were also sought to be made in the regulations for production of two-wheelers. It is likely these initiatives were taken at RG's behest. Specifically, the Centre for Development of Telematics (C-DOT), which was set up in August 1984 by the Government of India, was actively supported by RG. Rural automatic exchanges came up and used electronic rather than electrical switching equipment which made subscriber trunk dialling booths ubiquitous even in rural India. C-DOT was able to connect remote parts of India with the rest of the country, triggering huge efficiency gains.[15]

The advances made in the 1980s helped to usher in the mobile phone revolution a decade later in the 1990s. The relative opening up to imported electronic products was a result of RG's understanding that the use of technology should be widened and deepened. However, not enough was done to drop the licensing requirements for manufacture of such items in India. At times, there was negative protection for local manufacturers of electronic equipment since finished products attracted lower rates of duty than intermediate parts. All said and done, in 2019 India is not that far behind developed countries in telecommunications, and RG was central to the start of it all in the mid-1980s.

Scooters and motorcycles were in short supply in the 1980s. Those who could obtain foreign exchange from relatives abroad or other sources could jump the queue. In January 1984, while IG was PM, the Hero Cycles group, with RG's support, concluded a collaboration agreement with Honda Corporation. This agreement enabled technology transfer and helped Hero Honda to produce two-wheelers in India which were fuel-efficient with less polluting emissions. By the beginning of the twenty-first century, Hero became the largest producer of two-wheelers in the world and had about 50 per cent share in the Indian market. In 2011, Honda exited from this partnership. Millennial Indians would have no memory of the frustration that earlier generations felt, because they can walk into a showroom and buy a two-wheeler outright or on an instalment payment plan.

It does not appear from publicly available records that the RG government was aware of the changes in economic policies in China. By the mid-1980s China must have started signing up FDI contracts with companies headquartered in the US or other Western countries to produce garments, furniture and other items of mass consumption. Consumer goods made in China started appearing in US retail outlets in the early 1990s, and by the late 1990s it was a deluge.

In the RG years, Indian businesses and the political-bureaucratic elite had too much invested in maintaining the status quo. India needed a campaign to persuade internationally competitive firms that investing in India would be profitable, and that the credit and market risks were manageable. According to a 2010 study,[16] China received about US $560 billion of FDI from 1980 to 2004. A World Bank report dated 16 July 2010 mentions that 'when market institutions were not fully in place in 1980s and 1990s, China experimented with opening up to foreign investment in selected coastal cities and in special economic zones/industrial parks with a focus on attracting export-oriented manufacturing'.[17] It is not clear why India, with a functioning private sector and a number of Indian-origin professionals working in the US, could not attract more FDI. During his term, RG did hire non-government economists. However, their recommendations to reduce government's chokehold on the Indian economy were factored into reforms only after P.V. Narasimha Rao took over as PM in 1991.

RG tried to reach out to the poor in rural areas through a series of so-called 'technology missions' which were started in 1987. These missions included: a) immunization; b) literacy; c) safe drinking water; d) oilseeds; e) telecommunications. The missions (a), (b) and (c) have been much discussed in Central and state government forums since the Nehru years. The success in implementing government programmes around the country has varied from state to state, and the southern and western states have done better than the Hindi heartland. To an extent, they had a head start since they were ahead in human development indicators at Independence. On (d), namely oilseeds, to reduce India's dependence on countries such as Malaysia for edible oil imports, this was a much-needed push and met with some success compared to the past since the RG government's efforts widened awareness and also improved access to seeds. On (e), telecommunications, Indira Gandhi's government had started improving the required infrastructure, and during RG's term, significant improvements were made in telecommunication connectivity around the country.

Returning to (b) and (c), to raise literacy levels and make safe drinking water available on a consistent basis to the poorest and those living in inaccessible regions, it is the steady extension efforts of fieldworkers which results in lasting improvements as compared to patchwork success. Obviously, heads of government just do not have the time to get involved with the implementation details of primary education and public health programmes. Thus it was crucial for India's PMs including RG to find ways to motivate the millions of field officials, primary schoolteachers and public health workers.

Fiscal Irresponsibility, High Defence Expenditure, Trade and Indirect Tax Reforms

The economic indicators during RG's term from 1984 to 1989 are detailed in Table 5.1 in the Appendices. Capital outlays as a percentage of GDP were at around the same level of about 2.5 per cent through these five years, but gross fiscal deficit was consistently high at around 7 per cent and was irresponsibly high at over 8 per cent in 1986–87. The automatic monetization of fiscal deficits through issuance of ad hoc short maturity treasury bills (T-bills), which started in the mid-1950s, was still in vogue during the 1980s. Consumer price inflation rose during RG's term and was at 12.7 per cent in 1988–89.

GDP growth rates, which were at 4–5 per cent from 1984 to 1988, shot up to 9.6 per cent in 1988–89 which was RG's last year in office. Some partisan commentators have suggested that this one year of high growth is evidence of reforms implemented by RG's government. It has also been suggested that economic reforms were not initiated in 1991 but were started by Indira Gandhi in the early 1980s and accelerated during the RG years. The boost to growth in 1988–89, in fact, came from fiscal profligacy. Montek Singh Ahluwalia, former finance secretary and deputy chairman, Planning Commission, has commented that 'some of this growth [in the 1980s] was fed by [high] fiscal deficits in the later years of the decade, which laid the foundations for the balance of payments crisis in 1991'.[18] Foreign exchange requirements were not financed by stable FDI inflows but by short-term hard currency debt which was a contributing factor to the 1991 crisis. These hard-currency borrowings were camouflaged since they were contracted by public-sector oil companies. The current account deficit rose to 2.7 per cent of GDP by 1988–89. In the foreign trade sector, no systematic effort was made to reform the anti-export bias of the past.

Prior to the 1980s, the highest annual defence expenditure was 3.76 per cent of GDP in the India–China war year of 1962. All through the five years that RG was PM, defence expenditure was consistently higher than 3 per cent of GDP. This number rose to 3.95 per cent of GDP in 1987–88, which was the highest ever for defence in the seventy-one years of independent India from August 1947 to May 2019. The rise in defence expenses was due to fresh acquisitions of weapons systems, from foreign sources, such as tanks, field guns, infantry fighting vehicles (IFVs), French Mirages and newer versions of Soviet MiG fighters. This sustained increase in defence expenditure was caused by RG's muscular approach to defence policies. For example, at the urging of Arun Singh and General Sundarji, the counterproductive Operation Brasstacks was mounted. This operation resulted in the massing of Indian troops on the border with Pakistan between November 1986 and March 1997. The Indian Peace Keeping Force (IPKF) at its maximum numbered about 100,000, and was in Sri Lanka from July 1987 to March 1990.[19]

During the Emergency, in 1976, the L.K. Jha Committee recommended use of value added tax (VAT) to make it easier to comply with and track indirect taxes. This committee suggested VAT at the manufacturing level and called it MAN VAT. Ten years later, in 1986, the then finance minister, V.P. Singh, introduced modified value added taxation (MODVAT). It was similar to the MAN VAT suggested by Jha and was an important reform for its time. V.P. Singh was finance minister for about two years, and a 'medium term strategy was outlined for the first time'.[20] During his tenure, the maximum income tax rate was reduced from 62 to 50 per cent and wealth tax from 5 to 2 per cent. The estate duty was abolished and corporate tax rate was brought below 50 per cent. In V.P. Singh's second budget, a significant number of reforms in indirect taxes were effected, including reducing the number of customs duty tiers. The Abid Hussain Committee on Trade Policies had started work in 1984 and the Foreign Exchange Regulation Act (FERA) was relaxed. However, there was no reduction in the reservations for small-scale industries.

In the last year or so of RG's term, the Prime Minister's Office did review the constraints that were binding the economy, including restrictions on industrial licensing, foreign investment and imports. This preparatory work came in handy later for P.V. Narasimha Rao's government to announce wide-ranging policy reforms almost from the day it took office.

Bofors Controversy

On 24 March 1986, fifteen months after RG became PM, the Government of India and the Swedish company Bofors signed an agreement worth about US $285 million for the supply of 155-mm Howitzer field guns. A little over a year later on 16 April 1987, Swedish radio reported that Bofors had bribed top Indian politicians and officials to win this contract. The alleged intermediaries included an arms dealer named Win Chadha and Ottavio Quattrocchi who was the Delhi representative of an Italian petrochemicals company Snamprogetti.

Three months later, on 15 July 1987, Arun Singh, who was minister of state for defence, resigned without giving any credible explanation for his decision to leave RG's government. It was reported by the media that after resigning, he went away to Almora and spent years there in seclusion. Separately, a Geneva-based journalist, Chitra Subramaniam reported that she had obtained documents from Swedish sources which confirmed payments to the Swiss bank accounts of Win Chadha and a front for Quattrocchi.[21] The then Comptroller and Auditor General T.N. Chaturvedi was critical of the way the contract had been concluded with Bofors.[22]

Given the adverse and intense media coverage, RG set up a joint parliamentary committee (JPC) to investigate the alleged pay-offs in the Bofors case. In May 1988, the JPC cleared the political executive and officials of having received any pay-offs.[23] Much later in 1992, Madhav Singh Solanki, the then Indian external affairs minister, was accused of having written to the Swedish foreign minister requesting that the ongoing Swedish investigations in collaboration with Swiss banks be stopped. Confronted with this accusation, Solanki resigned from the Indian cabinet.[24]

Both S.K. Bhatnagar, defence secretary at the time the Bofors deal was concluded, and Win Chadha passed away in 2001 without shedding any light on who if anyone had accepted bribes to get this deal done. In July 2013, Quattrocchi died in Milan, and there seem to be no leads left to prove guilt or innocence any more. To date, successive Indian governments have not been able to prove any wrongdoing on the part of those alleged to have benefited from this deal.

Although no one was legally held guilty, in public perception there was a cloud over RG's administration, and it was commonly believed that some who were close to RG had received kickbacks. Although it is unfair, in the court of public opinion those in high office can be deemed to be guilty unless they prove their innocence. RG's government had a huge absolute majority in the Lok Sabha and a fund of goodwill when he took office. The Bofors scandal muddied a substantial part of his image as Mr Clean.

Foreign Policy—Dangerous Posturing, Blunders and Successes

In line with RG's shuffling of his defence and finance ministers, he changed the foreign minister four times. First from 31 October 1984 to 24 September 1985, RG held concurrent charge as the external affairs minister (EAM), then Bali Ram Bhagat was EAM for seven months from 25 September 1985 till 12 May 1986, and P. Shiv Shankar held this portfolio for just five months. Shiv Shankar was followed by N.D. Tiwari from 22 October 1986 onwards for eight months and Rajiv Gandhi again from 25 July 1987 till 25 June 1988. Finally, P.V. Narasimha Rao held the external affairs charge till 2 December 1989. They were all seasoned politicians, and N.D. Tiwari and P.V. Narasimha Rao had been chief minister of Uttar Pradesh and Andhra Pradesh respectively. This cavalier treatment of regional leaders would not have gone down too well with voters in these states. The frequent changes would also not have allowed officials in this ministry to settle down and work as a team.

In this atmosphere of chopping and changing ministers, RG did manage to maintain the relationship with the Soviet Union. However, not enough attention was paid to the changes that were happening internally in that country. Two years after his government lost the elections in 1989, India was taken by surprise when the USSR broke up in 1991. There were limited numbers of intermediaries in the exchange of consumer goods and defence supplies between India and the Soviet Union. Those who benefited financially from this lack of transparency may have consciously injected a false sense of confidence that India's special economic–defence relationship with the USSR would not be disturbed.

RG and Gorbachev[25] had overlapping tenures as Gorbachev was at the helm of the Soviet government from 1985 to 1991. In the latter half of the 1980s, the Soviet Union had somewhat diluted its earlier politically solid communist moorings, but there were continuing discussions between India and the Soviet Union for collaboration on hydroelectric projects and manufacture of steel. However, the changes in the Soviet Union leading to its break-up presaged changes in India's economic and technological relationships with that country.

Gorbachev was convinced that the past policies of Russia dominating over the other republics within the USSR and its overweening influence in East Europe imposed too heavy a burden politically and economically. Hence he initiated the policies of perestroika (economic reforms) and glasnost (openness). Overcome by the needless loss of young Soviet soldiers in Afghanistan and military expenditures, which had been excessive for this uncompetitive commodity-exporting economy to bear, the Soviet Union broke up in 1991. Gorbachev's interactions with other world leaders included five meetings with President Ronald Reagan between 1985 and 1988, and seven meetings with President George W. Bush from 1988 to 1991 to discuss arms control and Afghanistan. Despite these preoccupations, Gorbachev met RG four times alternately in Delhi and Moscow. A highly significant agreement between the two countries was for India to lease a nuclear-powered missile-carrying submarine from 1988 to 1991 which was renamed INS *Chakra*. This experience helped India put together the Arihant class of indigenously built nuclear submarines, the first of which was commissioned in 2016. As of May 2019, about two-thirds, in value, of the stock of Indian military equipment has been sourced from the Soviet Union–Russia.

The joint statements issued by India and the USSR during the 1980s about global peace and disarmament were of little consequence bilaterally or internationally. For instance, the Delhi Declaration of 27 November 1986 includes platitudes about peaceful coexistence and includes the evangelistic goals of a 'nuclear weapons-free world' and 'complete disarmament'.

RG's attitude towards China was resolute but end objectives remained unclear. For instance, there was a stand-off between Indian and Chinese troops at Sumdorong Chu at the border north of Tawang in Arunachal Pradesh in July 1986. This wore off without any serious repercussions, but no understanding was reached at that time on how such border issues would be dealt with in the future.

The then Pakistani President (General) Zia-ul-Haq had attended Indira Gandhi's funeral and met Rajiv Gandhi in Delhi on 4 November 1984. They met again on the sidelines of another funeral, that of Soviet President Konstantin Chernenko, in Moscow on 13 March 1985. They met yet again in New York when they were both in that city to attend the UN General Assembly discussions in October 1985 and in Dhaka on 7 December 1985, when they attended the first South Asian Association for Regional Cooperation [SAARC] Summit. These meetings, and another one in India when Zia transited through Delhi on 17 December 1985, improved the atmosphere. Yet, just a year later, in November 1986, Operation Brasstacks made Pakistan suspicious about India's intentions.

Between November 1986 and March 1987, the Indian Army massed over half a million armed personnel on the India–Pakistan border in Rajasthan in an exercise called Operation Brasstacks. The Indian armed forces included infantry and mechanized and air assault divisions. The Indian troops were deployed slightly less than 100 miles from the border with Pakistan. An Indian amphibious naval force was also deployed not far from Karachi. In response, Pakistani troops went on a state of high alert.

Kuldip Nayar was in Pakistan in January 1987 in his capacity as a journalist and syndicated columnist. Nayar reported that A.Q. Khan had indicated to him on 28 January that Pakistan would not hesitate to use nuclear weapons to prevent Indian adventurism. The interview was published in London's *Observer* newspaper on 1 March 1987.[26] By this time, the ratcheting up of tension between India and Pakistan had been defused through diplomatic channels.

General Krishnaswamy Sundarji was the chief of army staff from 1986 to 1988, through the period during which the border skirmish took place with China and Operation Brasstacks was conducted. According to Natwar Singh, Arun Singh and General Sundarji had masterminded the massing of troops at the border between November 1986 and March 1987, and RG was unaware of this operation.[27] This is unlikely since the Indian PM receives daily briefings from the IB and R&AW, and any large deployment of Indian troops at the border with Pakistan could not have escaped the attention of both these agencies. My guess is that RG, the then de facto defence minister, Arun Singh and General Sundarji felt that a menacing approach towards Pakistan would make that country drop its support for Khalistan.

In April 1984, when Indira Gandhi was PM, the Indian and Pakistani armies confronted each other at the freezing heights of Siachen,[28] and the Indian Army was gradually able to gain control over this region. This was achieved at a considerable cost of the lives of young soldiers, and intermittent fighting continued with Pakistani forces till a ceasefire was declared in 2003. Even accepting the strategic value of an Indian military outpost at Siachen it was a failure of diplomacy on both sides.

All through RG's tenure, Pakistan encouraged anti-India sentiments in Kashmir and Punjab. In the mid-1980s, India–Pakistan discussions were complicated by Pakistan's growing confidence stemming from its perceived indispensability to the US in backing jihad in Afghanistan. All things considered, it should have been possible for the Indian government to find a solution for Siachen without giving any military advantage to Pakistan, while sparing Indian armed forces personnel the never-ending torture of defending this outpost.

Zia was blown to bits on 17 August 1988 in an air crash, possibly an internal conspiracy against him. After Zia's death, Benazir Bhutto came to power in Pakistan as an elected leader, and RG made his only visit to Pakistan on 15–16 July 1989 with more than the usual press publicity. The media in both countries was agog with unrealistic expectations, possibly because two young and photogenic leaders were heads of government of their respective countries. RG was forty-four, and Benazir Bhutto was just thirty-six years of age. However, the underlying reality, that Pakistan wanted India to make territorial concessions in Kashmir, meant that no substantive progress could be achieved. Nevertheless, there was an improvement in the climate for private visit visas.

Far away from India, I was the first secretary in the Indian embassy in Havana from September 1983 till September 1986. It was a small embassy with just two diplomatic officers, the ambassador and me. We were informed by the Ministry of External Affairs in early 1985 that RG had accepted Fidel Castro's invitation to visit Havana on his way to New York.

After one of many preparatory meetings, as we came out of the office of the Cuban foreign minister, Isidoro Malmierca Peoli, Fidel Castro was passing by. On hearing from Malmierca that we were tying up loose ends for RG's visit, Castro mentioned to his foreign minister that schoolchildren should be lined up on both sides of the road from the airport to RG's place of stay. Those were the days of government-orchestrated gestures for visiting dignitaries in several countries, including India. I remember wondering to myself whether this was a useful way for children to spend their time during school hours.

The then foreign secretary, A.P. Venkateswaran, arrived a week before RG reached Havana, probably because he felt that given the small size of the embassy, he needed to personally check that everything was in order. I received him at the airport, and as we drove to my residence to have lunch, he asked me who had written the briefs for the PM's forthcoming visit. I debated whether I should own up to writing them, as I was unsure whether he had found the briefs analytical enough. Deciding that honesty was the best policy, I confirmed that it was indeed I who had written the briefs. Hearing this, Venkateswaran had a hearty laugh. He said he knew that already, and was just checking whether I would try to pass the blame or the credit to someone else. Venkateswaran was a delightful conversationalist, with a never-ending repertoire of anecdotes and an irreverent sense of humour.

The US had imposed a trade embargo on Cuba and refused to have full diplomatic relations with that country. Consequently, for Cuba, this was an important visit of the head of government of a large democratic country. For India, the relations with Cuba were marked by a sense of companionship on the path of development, and independence from great power tutelage. In India's case, the desire not to be a camp follower of either the US or the USSR during the Cold War years manifested itself in 'non-alignment'. As for Cuba, given the hostility of the US, it became dependent economically and for security cover on the Soviet Union. However, Cuba under Fidel Castro's leadership also had a fiercely nationalistic streak which made the country an enthusiastic member of the non-aligned fraternity.

RG arrived in Havana on 21 October 1985 with more than a dozen senior officials in his delegation. Despite the best of efforts on both sides, there could be little substance to the visit beyond affirmations of friendship, economic cooperation and international solidarity. In material terms, this meant little for India. However, for the professedly left-leaning in RG's office, such as Principal Secretary Gopi Arora and those with similar views in the Ministry of External Affairs, this visit was probably intended to signal India's independence from the US in foreign policy matters. All things considered, the official delegation was excessively large, even taking into account the fact that RG was carrying on to New York to speak at the UN.

I returned to India from Cuba in September 1986 and heard informal reports that Foreign Secretary Venkateswaran was opposed to India's approach to the Tamil issue in Sri Lanka. It was reported by the Indian media in December 1986 that Venkateswaran had mentioned to his Pakistani counterpart during a visit to that country that the Indian PM would visit SAARC countries. It was also reported that Venkateswaran had mentioned, without prior authorization from the prime minister, that a visit by RG to Pakistan may be possible. The very next month, at a press conference in Delhi on 21 January 1987, RG, responding to a query about a possible visit to Pakistan, said that there would soon be a new foreign secretary. Venkateswaran happened to be in the front row at this press interaction and resigned the same day.

I remember the strong sense of solidarity that my colleagues in the Ministry of External Affairs felt with Venkateswaran. According to Natwar Singh, Venkateswaran had been guilty of 'irreverence' and of being 'openly and unwisely critical of the abilities and functioning of the Prime Minister'.[29] It is precisely such an official who can provide the political executive with objective feedback. However, given the feudal mindset among many in India's officialdom and political circles, it is obsequious acquiescence that is usually expected from those who are junior in the hierarchy. There is little sense of humour or the ability to take even a hint of criticism constructively. Soon after, Venkateswaran, who remained irrepressible, commented to a university audience in Madras that the students may have heard many distinguished diplomats but this would be the first time they would be listening to an 'extinguished' diplomat.

From mid-1987 onwards, the need to neutralize or at least soften negative public perception caused by the Bofors scandal seem to have impacted several of RG's foreign policy decisions. Specifically, the interventionist approach to

Sri Lanka was probably driven by the need to achieve a spectacular success in foreign relations.[30]

The training of LTTE guerrillas in India had started during IG's second innings as PM in the early 1980s.[31] I was the undersecretary for Sri Lanka and Maldives in the Ministry of External Affairs at that time. It was evident at my lowest level in the hierarchy that the Indian government was not sufficiently mindful of Sri Lankan concerns about Indian support for LTTE. For instance, the Sri Lankan equivalent of the Indian director, IB, would sit in my second-floor South Block room (which I shared with my fellow undersecretaries) for hours waiting to meet the joint secretary.

While this Sri Lankan official was cagey about what he had come to discuss, over several cups of coffee as he waited to meet my seniors, Sri Lanka's unease with India's actions became all too evident. Anita Pratap, the *Time* magazine correspondent in Delhi, had reported about the training camps for LTTE guerrillas in Sirumalai, Tamil Nadu. Karunanidhi of the DMK and other Tamil Nadu leaders competed with each other to show support for Sri Lankan Tamils and attended Eelam Tamil rights protection forums.[32]

Around the mid-1980s, Prabhakaran, the unreliable, egomaniacal LTTE leader, was in touch with Kuldip Sahdev, the joint secretary dealing with Sri Lanka in the Ministry of External Affairs, J.N. Dixit, Indian high commissioner in Colombo (1985–89), N. Ram of *The Hindu* newspaper and MGR, chief minister of Tamil Nadu.[33] Although for IG and later RG, it may have been about competitive pandering to pan-Tamil sentiments, given RG's overwhelming majority in the Lok Sabha, it is incomprehensible that Tamil Nadu politics was allowed to influence the Government of India's policies towards Sri Lanka to the extent that it did.

At the SAARC Summit in Bangalore in November 1986, Sri Lankan President Jayewardene was sharply critical of India's stance. This was unusual, since at multilateral meetings, heads of government do not usually bring up bilateral differences. Despite this tangible expression of Sri Lankan disquiet, on the instructions of RG, Natwar Singh, minister of state for external affairs, and P. Chidambaram, minister of state for personnel, met Velupillai Prabhakaran on the sidelines of this summit in Bangalore.[34]

Prabhakaran had come to Bangalore with MGR. It was absurd that an Indian chief minister was allowed to meddle in the internal affairs of a friendly neighbouring country, namely Sri Lanka, that was a member of SAARC, the non-aligned movement (NAM), the Commonwealth and the UN. It should have been evident even then that Prabhakaran was not interested in a negotiated settlement of any sort with the Sri Lanka government. For him, the ideal solution was a separate Tamil Eelam, one which would include the Indian state of Tamil Nadu, with him as the undisputed leader.

The Indian government was well aware that the Sri Lanka Sinhala leadership was a house divided and deeply conflicted about the extent to which India was seen to be meddling. While the personal agenda of certain leaders in Tamil Nadu was apparent, under no construct can it be convincingly argued that Indian national interest was served by helping separatist elements in Sri Lanka. This holds even if Sri Lankan Tamils were facing discrimination and worse in their homeland.

On the other side of the argument, it is likely that the international community would not have addressed the issue with any sense of urgency. However, there is little evidence that unilateral interventions of larger countries in the internal affairs of smaller neighbours is a better option. It was the narrow strip of water between India and Sri Lanka that eventually averted a repeat of the Bangladesh refugee crisis.

In its attempt to isolate and discredit the increasingly aggressive LTTE, the Sri Lankan government blockaded Jaffna from January 1987 onwards, leading to shortages of food and other supplies in this Tamil-majority region. In the first few days of June 1987, India sent nineteen fishing boats with food and medicine flying Indian Red Cross flags. These fishing vessels were accompanied by an Indian Coast Guard ship carrying journalists and Red Cross workers. The Sri Lankan navy turned these fishing boats back.

Given the strong sentiments in Tamil Nadu in favour of Jaffna Tamils, India tried to mediate but there was growing antipathy in Colombo to India's overtures. It is in this environment that the Indian government launched Operation Poolalai (Flower Garland). Also called Eagle Mission 4, this was to airdrop food and other supplies on 4 June 1987[35] to Tamil-majority regions, including Jaffna in Sri Lanka. As the internal situation had worsened in that country, there were appeals from various shades of political opinion in Tamil Nadu that the Indian government should do something. However, this was not a sufficient reason for India to violate Sri Lankan sovereignty.

Chinmaya R. Gharekhan was the Indian permanent representative (PR) to the UN from 1986 to 1989. According to Gharekhan,[36] he discussed the food dropping with Daya Perera, Sri Lankan PR, and persuaded him not to petition the UNSC on this matter. Gharekhan's reasoning with Daya Perera was that as neighbours, India and Sri Lanka had to live with each other, implying that they needed to understand the compulsions of each other's domestic politics.

Through the summer of 1987, the two governments had several rounds of discussions which culminated in the signing of an Indo-Lanka Accord on

29 July 1987. This accord was aimed at defusing tensions and bringing to an end the violence between separatist Tamils and the armed forces of the Sri Lankan government. The accord provided for an amendment of the Sri Lankan Constitution to delegate more powers to the Tamil-majority provinces and for the sending of an Indian Peace Keeping Force (IPKF) to Sri Lanka to whom the LTTE would surrender its arms. The LTTE was at best ambivalent about surrendering arms and against giving up their cause for an independent Tamil state. The situation on the ground soon degenerated into fighting between the IPKF and the LTTE, and about 1,700 Indian soldiers were killed. The last units of IPKF left Sri Lanka in March 1990.

It could be argued at a stretch that because of the embedded strategic risks, India had no option but to get closely involved in resolving the differences between minority Tamil and majority Sinhalese communities in Sri Lanka. According to this alarmist argument, prolonged hostilities between Sri Lankan armed forces and the LTTE may have drawn in Pakistan, China or the US, and one or the other of these countries may have established military bases in Sri Lanka. The costs, human and financial, for countries which set up military bases in foreign locations have often been higher than any long-term strategic or economic benefits. The many bases of the US, for example in the Philippines and Vietnam, proved to be unpopular with local populations and costly in the long run. Well, all things considered, it was well worth taking the chance that foreign powers setting up military bases, which would prove to be disastrous for India, was a low-probability event.

Some Delhi-based analysts rationalize the support for LTTE terrorists on the grounds that it was necessary to stem separatist sentiments in Tamil Nadu. Such an argument does not hold much water since the Indian Union had been able to successfully take a tough line against advocates of Khalistan and separatism in the North-east, and the same could have been done in Tamil Nadu.

On 30 July 1987, at the presidential residence, as RG was taking the guard of honour, a naval rating attacked him with the butt of his rifle. The images of this embarrassing attack were aired on television around the world. Another pointer about sullen Sinhala disaffection was the then Sri Lankan PM Ranasinghe Premadasa's refusal to be present at the signing of the accord or at the dinner hosted by President Jayewardene.

Chinmaya R. Gharekhan claims he had cautioned Rajiv Gandhi in the following terms about the accord, 'I am uneasy about the Accord because the very same people we have set out to help will turn against us.'[37] This cautionary advice proved prophetic. It was subsequently revealed by both Sri Lankan[38] and Indian Army generals that Premadasa, who took over as President at the beginning of January 1989, authorized the Sri Lankan army to provide LTTE with weapons to fight the IPKF.

Kuldip Sahdev,[39] the joint secretary dealing with Sri Lanka along with other responsibilities, felt that R&AW's daily briefings to RG received more attention from the PM than considered reports of the Ministry of External Affairs. Excuses were made later, by Congress acolytes, for RG's costly mistake to send in the IPKF on the grounds that the Indian generals were excessively confident, and R&AW did not have accurate information about where Prabhakaran and the separatist elements loyal to him were hiding.

J.N. Dixit was the Indian high commissioner to Sri Lanka from 1985 to 1989 and foreign secretary from 1991 to 1994. According to Dixit:[40] 'Rajiv Gandhi should not have sent in the Indian Peace-keeping Force [IPKF] to Sri Lanka. This was an unjustified military intervention into a neighbouring country. The alleged failure of the IPKF in neutralizing the LTTE and its subsequent withdrawal signified a major foreign policy failure for India, which Rajiv Gandhi could have avoided.' This foreign policy failure was second only to Nehru's missteps leading to the military defeat against China in 1962.

Dixit states a few pages later in the same book that: 'Whatever judgement may be passed about his [RG's] Sri Lanka policies, the logic of his objectives, his deep commitment to India's national interests and regional peace inherent in his policies at that point of time cannot be questioned.' Dixit's understanding about RG's motivations may well be true, but that does not detract from RG's deeply flawed understanding of the Sri Lankan situation and Indian national interest. Dixit must be respected though for making both statements in the same book and letting readers decide for themselves. Others who have held high positions in government and do not express themselves frankly do posterity a grave injustice.

RG espoused the cause of nuclear disarmament, taking the cue from his mother IG's 'Five-Continent, Six-Nation Initiative' (the other five countries were Sweden, Mexico, Argentina, Greece and Tanzania). After taking over as PM, he followed up with the leaders of these five countries and jointly called for a nuclear test ban in the Mexico Declaration of 7 August 1986. At a bilateral level, RG and Gorbachev signed a Joint Declaration on the Principles of a Nuclear-Weapons-Free and Non-Violent World on 27 November 1986. Subsequently, in June 1988, speaking at the UN in New York, RG called for an 'Action Plan for Ushering in a Nuclear-Weapons-Free and Non-Violent World Order'. This speech did not find even a single-line mention on the front page of the *New York Times* the following day. Nevertheless, Indian newspapers and television were agog at the seminal and historic significance of this speech.

A far-fetched rationalization of this Rajiv Gandhi speech was that he wanted to give one last opportunity to the five permanent members of the UNSC (P5) to give up their nuclear weapons before giving directions for India to go nuclear. An informed college student could have predicted that the P5 countries would not bother to engage with India or the others members of the Six Nation Initiative on this issue with any seriousness. This type of sycophantic ex-post rationalization made it difficult for officers of my vintage in government to take the public pronouncements of RG and his close circle of foreign policy advisers seriously. It was disconcerting to witness senior officers in the Ministry of External Affairs and the PMO vying with each other to claim credit for having drafted what they claimed was the most brilliant speech ever on disarmament. This harping on global nuclear disarmament sounded noble but also impossibly naive. Those in high office have to be mindful that credibility is difficult to acquire and even more difficult to retain.

From the mid-1980s onwards, while India was in this make-believe world of helping the world move towards universal nuclear disarmament, Pakistan was in the process of developing nuclear weapons. After Ronald Reagan became the US President in 1981, he wrote to Zia-ul-Haq questioning Pakistan about its uranium enrichment capabilities and a simulated nuclear fission test. On the face of it, the US was not satisfied with the stonewalling by Pakistan on this issue, and Senator Larry Pressler's amendment was passed in 1985. Under this Pressler Amendment, the US President was required to certify annually that Pakistan did not possess a nuclear explosive device and that US assistance would reduce the probability of Pakistan working towards acquiring such a device. Such a certification would then allow the US to provide economic and military assistance to Pakistan. The certification required under the Pressler Amendment met the concerns of US based non-proliferation lobbies, and the US government cynically ignored Pakistan's drive to acquire nuclear weapon capability.

All this while, within India there was mounting criticism about the country disavowing nuclear weapons. In May 1985, former finance minister in the Janata government, H.M. Patel, demanded in Parliament that India develop nuclear weapons. General Sundarji pushed for a focused nuclear weapons programme with the required delivery, command and control structures. Media reports and other references[41] suggest that by early 1989, RG had decided that India did need nuclear weapons. The Department of Atomic Energy (DAE) had continued to work on enhancing capabilities while waiting for such a political signal. Anecdotal evidence suggests that Naresh Chandra, the then defence secretary, was given the task to coordinate with the scientists and engineers of the BARC and the DAE to undertake the preparatory work to test nuclear weapons.

In 1986–87, I was based in Bombay as a deputy secretary in the DAE. While I was posted in Bombay, initially Dr Raja Ramanna was the chairman of the DAE and he was succeeded by Dr M.R. Srinivasan. My stint in DAE made me realize that the scientist–engineer community too is riven with personality differences and competing egos that at times prevent political executives and the civil services in Delhi from working as teams. This may also partly explain the stop-go nature of India's nuclear weapons programme. However, the tacit go-ahead given by RG at the beginning of 1989 did put India firmly on the track towards testing nuclear weapons.

In another highly significant initiative, Rajiv Gandhi was the first Indian PM to visit China after the 1962 war. The meetings during this visit in 1988, including with Deng Xiaoping, went well. The principal gain from this interaction was the setting up of a bilateral mechanism for talks between the foreign secretaries of the two sides to work towards resolving the border issue. Subsequently, the interlocutor was changed to the national security adviser on the Indian side.

Not much has been reported in the narratives of those who accompanied RG to indicate whether the economic policies of China to promote FDI and manufacturing were noted for adaptation or emulation back in India. China had changed not just its FDI policies to attract Western capital but also its stance on issues which had been irritants for the US. For instance, China dropped its support for left-leaning elements in ASEAN countries.

The following apocryphal story has done the rounds in the Ministry of External Affairs. That is, when RG met Deng Xiaoping and heard of all the changes that China had implemented, RG asked Deng, 'Don't you think these policies will result in rising inequalities?' Deng is said to have responded, 'I hope so, I sincerely hope so.'

After IG's return to power in 1980, she appears to have recognized that India's relationship with the Soviet Union had restricted India's options with the West. It seems that Soviet leadership was not sufficiently courteous to her when she transited through Moscow on the way to London at the end of 1978.[42] A recalibration of India–US relations followed. From 1982 onwards, RG was kept in the picture on external relations, and he did not carry the anti-US baggage of the Congress of the 1970s. RG felt that India needed technological upgradation and, in most fields, Western companies were better placed to provide the technical tie-ups. The US too was aware that with RG likely to step into IG's shoes, they had an opening to improve ties through closer technological cooperation.

It was in this atmosphere of high expectations of cementing closer Indo–US ties that RG visited the US as PM in June 1985. However, expectations on both sides were belied. The US did not deliver on the Cray XMP-24 supercomputer, disappointing the technology-minded RG. The US had reservations about the potential use of this computer for military and nuclear applications, and not just for meteorological studies as claimed by India. Instead, the US offered the XMP-14 computer with less sophisticated capabilities. Despite the new opening, the US continued to maintain some distance from India because of its tie-up with Pakistan on bleeding the USSR in Afghanistan.

The US was also suspicious that India had kept its lines of communication open with the leftist Sandinista government in Nicaragua and the Heng Samrin government in Cambodia which leant towards Vietnam. India has consistently maintained that it favours a multipolar world in which disputes are resolved through discussions at recognized international forums such as the United Nations. India was justified in maintaining its lines of communication with regimes which had difficult and even inimical relations with the US. At the same time, to dilute US strategic interaction with Pakistan and commercial ties with China, India could have pushed for eye-catching FDI tie-ups with large companies such as Boeing and closer classified interaction between research personnel in the two countries.

Domestic Missteps with Lasting Negative Consequences

The folklore is that the Babri Masjid located in Ayodhya, Uttar Pradesh, was built in the sixteenth century by a Mughal general over a temple dedicated to Lord Ram. In December 1949, Hindu devotees offered prayers at this site, broke into the mosque and placed idols of Lord Ram (avatar of Vishnu) and Sita inside. The government then locked up this space. On 1 February 1986, a Faizabad judge gave an order to unlock the mosque. Rajiv Gandhi, acting on the advice of Arun Nehru, was reported to have had the mosque opened within an hour of this court ruling.[43] This 'error of judgement' on the part of RG is referred to in the second volume of former President Pranab Mukherjee's memoirs titled *The Turbulent Years: 1980–1996*. RG's relationship with Arun Nehru soured after this, and subsequently, Arun Nehru left the Congress to join V.P. Singh's party.

Another issue on which RG showed poor judgement was the Shah Bano case. Shah Bano had been divorced in 1978 by her husband in Bhopal and offered inadequate alimony for which she went to court. In 1985, the Supreme Court ruled in favour of Shah Bano, whose case by then had become well-publicized. In order to appease conservative Muslim opinion, RG amended the Constitution to overturn the Supreme Court judgment. Arif Khan, a minister in RG's government, resigned in protest against this retrograde action taken by RG.

RG must have been briefed regularly by intelligence and regular sources about the ground-level situation in Jammu and Kashmir. It is surprising, therefore, that the 1987 Jammu and Kashmir assembly elections were perceived in that state and elsewhere in India as heavily rigged.[44] Farooq Abdullah became CM again, and his state government's performance in building trust and employment opportunities left much to be desired. Given the troubled history of this state since Independence, RG's government could have done better in ensuring free and fair elections in the 1987 J&K elections.

Legacy

Rajiv Gandhi began with a fund of goodwill around the country after the assassination of Indira Gandhi as her only surviving son. Since the death of Sanjay Gandhi in 1980, RG was groomed by his mother to step into her shoes. But the transition happened too suddenly when Indira Gandhi was assassinated, and RG became PM at age forty with no prior experience of any executive position within government or in the private sector.

RG's policies made significant positive changes in telecommunications, computing and in promoting a can-do attitude in the use of forward-looking technologies. Various committees had been formed by successive Central governments since the 1950s to devolve greater powers to local bodies. This was given a determined push by RG, and about two years after he had passed away in April 1993, the 73rd Amendment to the Constitution which gives legal status to Panchayati Raj[45] local bodies came into force.

RG's visit to China in 1988, the first by any Indian prime minister since the 1962 war, resulted in a thawing of some sort in the relations with that country. It also set up a forum for discussions about border incursions and disagreements. He raised the content of the strategic relationship with the Soviet Union by leasing a nuclear-powered submarine from that country. RG maintained the ties with the US but there were limitations to what he could have achieved with Pakistan, given the ground realities.

RG's major foreign policy misstep was the military intervention in Sri Lanka. It led to needless loss of Indian lives and made India look like a bully in dealing with a much smaller neighbour. It was tragic that a Sri Lankan LTTE suicide bomber caused his untimely death on 21 May 1991. The LTTE may have been concerned that if RG came back to power after the Lok Sabha elections in June 1991, he may have taken a hard line against them. RG was campaigning in Sriperumbudur in Tamil Nadu on that particular day. As he was no longer PM, he did not have the same level of security, and the suicide bomber was able to get close enough to bend down to touch his feet and then blow herself up. He was two months short of his forty-seventh birthday.

After the assassination of Indira Gandhi in the first week of November 1984, there were en-masse attacks on the Sikhs which traumatized them for a long time. It defies belief that the Central government, which is ultimately responsible for internal security around the country, took four days to bring the violence in Delhi to an end. As for inter-religious harmony, RG should not have allowed any form of worship at the disputed Babri Masjid–Ram Mandir site. The related issues have become a continuing source of inter-community tensions after the masjid was demolished in December 1992.

Kashmir suffers due to alienation from the rest of the country and insurgency. The lack of credibility of the state elections in March 1987 contributed towards a deep sense of estrangement of the average citizen there. The indifference at best, or complicity at worst, of RG's government has contributed to the continuing misery and violence in that state.[46]

The most telling difference RG could have made in the country was through economic reforms. He had an absolute majority in both houses of Parliament and complete control over his own party. There is no reason why the reforms after 1991 could not have started in 1984. Excessive government expenditures during his five years as PM, including for defence purchases, contributed directly towards India's balance of payments crisis of 1990–91. RG could have made himself aware by the mid-1980s of the wide-ranging economic reforms in China. Instead, he wasted his own time and diverted the focus of the Ministry of External Affairs by preaching universal nuclear disarmament.

RG could have tried to reform the Congress which was still the pre-eminent national party in the 1980s. It would have helped reinvigorate development efforts if workers of the Congress party had been empowered instead of letting the party continue on its downward slide to becoming a family-dominated fiefdom. There was an obvious contradiction between his trying to reform the party, as he had so eloquently outlined in his December 1985 address in Bombay, and the fact that he became PM only because he was Indira Gandhi's son.

Looking back, RG's tenure as PM was like watching a Greek tragedy unfold. There was a certain inevitability about the way events progressed. RG's sincere start was soon overtaken by brash decision making in which he mostly took the partisan advice of school friends, personal acquaintances and family retainers with disastrous results.

Based on his experience of attending meetings at high levels since the early 1980s and that the huge win for Congress was due to the assassination of his mother, RG would have known that he was unequal to the task of both heading the Union government and holding the post of Congress president. Accordingly, he could have promoted genuinely open and free elections within the Congress party and requested P.V. Narasimha Rao to take over as PM while he rebuilt the party as Congress president. This may be expecting too much of a person who did not see the contradiction between his inheriting the position of the prime minister of India and the requirements of inner democracy in a political party. The pity is that Rao's economic reforms may have started in 1984, and India may not have had short-lived coalition governments between 1989 and 1991. Of course, this is pure speculation.

On the India–Bharat divide, RG was way to the side of India. He was always dressed in the buttoned-up jacket called bandhgala in Indian diplomatic circles, and Western-style trousers. His preferred language for communication was English. RG could and did speak in Hindi but was less proficient in public speaking than his mother, Indira Gandhi. RG was probably not even conscious of the need to woo the average voter, and the latter's reaction to this distance was one of the reasons for the poor showing of the Congress party in the 1989 general election.

Moving on to the 3 Cs, RG was enormously Charismatic, and at the beginning of his tenure, he appeared to be compassionate and committed. Unfortunately for India, RG's Competence in formulating effective reforms was low. His lack of managerial competence also showed up in excessively frequent changes of his cabinet ministers. Given his lack of relevant experience it was unrealistic to expect him to skilfully manage the caste, community, regional and religious differences in India or the complex Sri Lankan Tamil issue. The entire Bofors episode and its aftermath was out of Character with the contents of his speech at the Congress centenary event in Bombay.

VI

V.P. SINGH

Downward Game Changer

V.P. Singh[1] was sworn in as PM on 2 December 1989.[2] All was not well with this Janata Dal coalition government right from the start. Devi Lal, the 'elder' statesman from Haryana, had cobbled together a weak consensus in favour of Singh. However, Chandra Shekhar[3] was resentful that this potpourri coalition of parties had not chosen him as PM.[4]

Early in his tenure, Singh moved to assuage Sikh sentiments. He visited the Golden Temple to seek forgiveness on behalf of the Central government and replaced S.S. Ray, then governor of Punjab, with civil servant N.K. Mukherjee. This was timely and much needed, given the declining yet continuing support for a separate state of Khalistan among some sections of the Sikh communities in the UK, Canada and the US. All shades of political opinion in Punjab, some more reluctantly than others, would have agreed that Operation Blue Star had become inevitable since heavily armed extremists had taken refuge in the Golden Temple. However, the question in the minds of many in Punjab was why Indira Gandhi's government had ignored the signs of a gathering storm till army action became the only option. Singh had correctly assessed that the Sikh community was looking for such a gesture, and it had been short-sighted of Rajiv Gandhi to not have sought visible reconciliation with Sikhs of all political persuasions during his five years as PM.

The gross fiscal deficit rose above 7 per cent in the two years between 1989 and 1991, and the current account deficit went up from 2.3 per cent to 3 per cent of GDP. Since Singh failed to sound the alarm on these mounting deficits, he was partly responsible for the full-blown balance of payments crisis by around January 1991. Given the gravity of the situation,

Singh should have initiated discussions with the IMF as soon as he assumed office. He probably did not want to be seen taking the help of an institution which would have imposed conditionalities. Any tightening of the fiscal belt and other austerity measures, plus the much-required devaluation, may have been perceived as anti-poor. According to I.G. Patel, '. . . this was obviously politically inconvenient in 1988 and 1989 when winning elections was the only concern. The government of V.P. Singh (must have) been aware of the writing on the wall. But it preferred to add its own (brand of) fuel to the fire, a la loan waivers and the red herring of reservations. It was left to the feckless Chandra Shekhar government to start serious negotiations with the Fund when it was almost too late.'[5]

Over the decades, much has been said or done by successive Indian governments in the name of the 'common man', whose bemusement used to be caricatured in R.K. Laxman's cartoons.

The quotas in government-owned/affiliated educational institutions, companies and banks are the same as for jobs in government. Namely, 15 per cent of available vacancies for SCs and 7.5 per cent for STs. To consider further reservations the First Backward Classes Commission, headed by

Kaka Saheb Kalelkar, was set up by a Central government order dated 29 January 1953.[6] The Kalelkar report's recommendations were rejected by Nehru's government in 1955[7] on the grounds that the tests used to assess 'Backward Classes' were not objective or adequate. It is possible that the decision makers of that era were apprehensive that this would open up a 'Pandora's Box' of further demands for reservations and consequent controversies.

The Second Backward Classes Commission, headed by B.P. Mandal, had submitted its report in 1980.[8] Indira Gandhi and Rajiv Gandhi, with large majorities in the Lok Sabha, were the prime ministers between 1980 and 1989 and chose to not act on the recommendations of the Mandal Commission. However, they both did not formally reject this report either. After he was out of power, Rajiv Gandhi explained in Parliament on 6 September 1990 in a speech lasting over two hours why he felt that the Mandal Commission's report needed more discussion, and that the 'creamy layer' needed to be removed.[9] That leaves us with the inevitable conclusion that IG and RG chose to postpone the electorally difficult decision related to reservations for OBCs while in power. In their defence caste-based parties found it politically paying to demand further reservations.

For example, the Samajwadi Party of Mulayam Singh Yadav and the Rashtriya Janata Dal of Lalu Prasad Yadav had come to power in their respective states of UP and Bihar on the slogans of empowerment for the socially and economically backward, and had supported Singh in his quest to become PM. Accordingly, on 6 August 1990, the V.P. Singh government accepted the Mandal Commission's recommendations for OBC reservations. This decision led to widespread protests and self-immolations by upper-caste students. However, the acceptance of the Mandal Commission report by Singh was aimed at obtaining the electoral support of the OBCs, who were estimated to add up to about 41 per cent of India's population in 2007.[10] The implementation of this reservation of an additional 27 per cent of vacancies for OBCs started in 1993.[11]

The subsequent demands from other communities around India who feel that they face social and economic discrimination are an indication that the decision not to accept the recommendations of Kalelkar's First Backward Classes Commission was perhaps correct. The agitations for additional groups to be included among OBCs has led to confrontations within and across political parties[12] and with the police, accompanied by loss of life as happened in May 2008.[13] This was when relatively well-off Gujjars of Rajasthan demanded OBC status and 5 per cent reservation for themselves. This would have raised the total reservations to 54.5 per cent, which would be above the ceiling of 50 per cent stipulated by the Supreme Court.[14]

The way forward is to build a meritocratic India with economic and social protection for the poorest and the weakest. Merely adding more reservations undermines the objective of building a socially caring system where the underprivileged are enabled to compete on par. A number of communities who are currently demanding OBC status are not among the poorest or the most socially disadvantaged.

The situation in India was and is that an adequate number of formal-sector jobs are not being created in the private sector. Singh was not PM long enough to raise formal-sector employment. Hence, he cannot be blamed for the jobs situation which was and continues to be difficult. However, he does share the responsibility for further raising the clamour for reservations for jobs in government and public-sector institutions. The irony is that even if all requests for OBC reservations are granted, government and parastatals can absorb only a miniscule fraction of those seeking salaried employment.

In 1989, Singh decided to help the poor in rural areas and announced a waiver of all loans below Rs 10,000 for farmers, artisans and weavers. Although the stated motivation for this loan waiver was laudable, this step created another unsustainable precedent. A culture of responsible borrowing needs to grow in India to create the climate for private firms to invest in the manufacture of consumer durables. Such an environment cannot be engendered in an atmosphere of loan write-offs. Government needed to find other ways to help the poor rather than weaken credit practices in the country.

V.P. Singh had appointed Ajit Singh as the industry minister, and progress was made in that ministry in thinking of ways to relax government's overweening control over industrial licensing and the attendant cornucopia of restrictions. However, left-leaning Madhu Dandavate, as the deputy chairman of the Planning Commission, was opposed to reducing licensing controls over industry. Additionally, Singh's precarious position as the head of an unstable coalition meant that he probably did not want any single minister to be given credit for implementing much-needed reforms.

Mufti M. Sayeed, home minister in the Singh cabinet, was a prominent political leader from Jammu and Kashmir. On 8 December 1989, the home minister's daughter Rubaiya Sayeed was abducted by Jammu and Kashmir Liberation Front (JKLF) operatives. The kidnappers sought the release of five persons who were in jail in Srinagar at that point of time on a range of serious charges. Farooq Abdullah, the chief minister of J&K, counselled against yielding to the blackmail of the JKLF but he was overruled.[15] The five prisoners were released in exchange for Rubaiya Sayeed.

The Singh government, and particularly the home minister, could have been more alert given that he was from the sensitive state of Jammu and Kashmir. This is not to imply that the events would necessarily have unfolded any differently if the home minister had taken precautionary steps. The considerable alienation of many in the Kashmir Valley was the result of decades of flawed state and Central government policies. The unfortunate implication for India's image among those who would take hostages or commit acts of terrorism on Indian soil was that India was a 'soft' state and an easy target.

An urgent decision Singh had to take on a foreign policy issue was about the IPKF in Sri Lanka. The Sri Lankan government headed by Premadasa was urging India to withdraw its armed forces. Singh and his external affairs minister I.K. Gujral agreed, and the Indian armed contingent was withdrawn in March 1990. J.N. Dixit has argued[16] that this premature withdrawal was used by LTTE to re-establish its hold over the northern and eastern provinces of Sri Lanka. Dixit's logic is at variance with India's consistent position that there should be no armed presence of foreign powers in any country without the express consent of the local government.

Saddam Hussein's Iraq invaded Kuwait in August 1990, and there was widespread condemnation of this aggression. It would have been naive to think that the West, led by the US, would allow Saddam to retain possession of the Kuwaiti territory that Iraq had occupied. The then minister of external affairs I.K. Gujral visited Iraq and was photographed hugging Saddam. This image, interpreted by some in the media as an expression of India's support for Iraq, did its damaging rounds around the world. On a positive note, the Singh government did successfully carry out a major airlift operation to bring back Indians who were in distress in Iraq. In this context, it was claimed by the then government's supporters that Gujral's visit to Iraq and apparent bonhomie with Saddam Hussein was to buy time to evacuate Indian workers from there.

In September 1990, BJP leaders L.K. Advani and Pramod Mahajan embarked on a 'Rath Yatra' to garner support for their proposal to build a temple in Ayodhya dedicated to Lord Ram. This move was aimed at boosting the BJP's image with the majority Hindu community around the country and was opposed by the CMs Mulayam Singh Yadav and Lalu Prasad Yadav. The Bihar government arrested Advani on 23 October 1990 in Samastipur and thus prevented kar seva at the Ayodhya temple site which was planned for 30 October 1990. The BJP withdrew support from the Singh Central government on the grounds that it had not been supportive of kar seva in Ayodhya, and V.P. Singh's coalition government fell on 10 November 1990, less than a year after it was formed.

CHANDRA SHEKHAR
Harmful Interlude

Chandra Shekhar[17] had parted company with the Congress party at the time of the Emergency and was respected for preferring to go to jail. By contrast, V.P. Singh had continued as a junior minister in IG's cabinet and was promoted to cabinet rank during the Emergency. Chandra Shekhar probably felt that he deserved to be the leader of an anti-Congress coalition in 1989, and was aggrieved when Singh became PM. He left the Janata Dal coalition that Singh had forged when the BJP dropped its outside support after differences with Singh on the rebuilding of a Ram temple in Ayodhya. Inexplicably, Chandra Shekhar, with just sixty-four Lok Sabha members who called themselves Janata Dal (Socialist), accepted the cynical support of Rajiv Gandhi's Congress which had 211 members in the Lok Sabha to form government. Chandra Shekhar was sworn in as PM on 10 November 1990 but had too short a time as PM to address the looming balance of payments crisis, let alone to take any major policy decisions. For Chandra Shekhar and several parties which were either part of or supporters of the Janata Party, the catchwords were socialism and social engineering.

By mid-1990, six months before Chandra Shekhar had taken over as PM, it was abundantly clear that there was no option but to seek assistance from the IMF. By then it had become difficult for India to finance its current account deficit, and international banks which provided short-term credit were reluctant to continue doing so. Consequently, the Chandra Shekhar government sent RBI and Ministry of Finance officials to Washington DC at the end of 1990 for discussions with the IMF. As a result, the Indian government was able to negotiate an IMF line of credit of about US $1.8 billion. By January 1991, India's foreign exchange reserves had come down to a mere US $1.1 billion. Shortly thereafter, India had barely enough hard currency left for about three weeks of imports. It is in this environment of economic crisis that Chandra Shekhar asked Dr Manmohan Singh to be his economic adviser.

As the situation continued to worsen, the Chandra Shekhar government decided to move gold out of the country as collateral for hard currency loans. In mid-1991, about 47 tonnes of gold were moved to the vaults of the Bank of England and the Union Bank of Switzerland. The loans received for the gold, which included an option to repurchase the gold, amounted to US $405 million. These loans were repaid by November 1991, but the gold was left where it had been sent as Indian property. Unfortunately for Chandra Shekhar, the most remembered event of his short tenure as PM is the airlifting of gold from India.

In March 1991, the Chandra Shekhar government agreed to refuelling facilities for US military aircraft in Bombay and Madras.[18] The Congress protested against this and also alleged governmental spying on Rajiv Gandhi. All this occurred while India's foreign exchange reserves continued to erode to precipitously low levels as NRIs made net withdrawals out of their hard currency deposit accounts in Indian banks. It is in this environment of extreme difficulties in India honouring its external debt obligations that the Congress party withdrew its support to Chandra Shekhar's government. And this was within four months of the Congress helping him to become PM. The Congress was merely waiting for an excuse to precipitate midterm elections, and this must have been obvious to Chandra Shekhar from the outset. Chandra Shekhar continued as caretaker PM till 21 June 1991.

Legacy

V.P. Singh plumbed to low depths of self-interest-driven politics to become prime minister of a manifestly unstable coalition. He had made a name for himself as a crusader against the corruption of big business houses as finance minister in Rajiv Gandhi's government for which he was moved from that position. He was also seen as principled for resigning from the position of defence minister because of his discomfort about the allegations of bribe-taking in the purchase of the Bofors guns. Singh was projected as a social reformer with the implementation of the Mandal Commission's recommendations, but he overlooked the long-term negative fallout for the country.

Singh needed to have discussions with the BJP before matters reached a flashpoint with Advani's arrest in Samastipur. That is, well before Advani's announcement that kar seva would be carried out at the site of the proposed Ram Mandir (temple) in Ayodhya. Singh could have taken the initiative to have frank discussions with all shades of political and social opinion to arrive at an understanding that an impartial body, or the courts, would be asked to deliberate on what would be acceptable all around. Either Singh did not understand the danger of communal conflict embedded in the Ram Mandir issue, or he looked away and hoped that it would blow over on its own.

V.P. Singh, Lalu Yadav, Mulayam Singh and the BJP had papered over their differences on economic issues at the time of the formation of the Singh government. Singh chose to focus more on keeping his rickety coalition together rather than the immediate danger of default on India's external debt. In any case, given the competing interests and egos, it was only a matter of time that differences would resurface leading to the collapse of the Singh government.

Chandra Shekhar had built a formidable reputation for himself as a committed socialist in the 1960s and 1970s, and had defied Indira Gandhi during the Emergency. It is a sad commentary on how much he was prepared to compromise on his past beliefs that he accepted the support of Rajiv Gandhi's Congress to be PM from November 1990 till March 1991.

VII

P.V. NARASIMHA RAO

Economic Reforms—Better Late than Never

A person should not be too honest, straight trees are cut first;
Never share your secrets with anybody;
A man is great by deeds not by birth

Chanakya also known as Kautilya, 320 BC

In Hindu belief, Narasimha is one of the divine avatars of Vishnu who assumed the form of part-man and part-lion to destroy evil and restore dharma. Two well-documented biographies of P.V. Narasimha Rao[1] have been published in recent years.[2]

Rao was a member of the Andhra legislative assembly from 1956 onwards and a minister in the Andhra Pradesh (AP) government for nine years by the time he became the chief minister in September 1971. Rao was selected for the post of AP CM by Indira Gandhi because of his deference to her and his years of experience in state-level politics. One of Rao's major initiatives after becoming CM was land reforms. This became an important objective for him, and legislation was enacted to limit landownership which inevitably angered large landowners.

The average Andhra voter too turned against Rao for accepting a Supreme Court judgment which provided for reservations in government jobs for people from the Telangana region of Andhra Pradesh. Consequently, support for Rao within the AP Congress eroded, and Indira Gandhi asked him to step down from the position of CM in January 1973. President's rule was imposed thereafter, and this happened even though the Congress party had an absolute majority in the state legislature. Clearly, IG viewed land reforms as secondary to retaining the support of the politically influential large landowners. She also probably did not want Rao to develop too large a following among the landless in AP.

In keeping with his prudent nature, Rao hid his disappointment and stayed out of Andhra politics, doing his reading and visiting his daughter in the US for the next few years. Rao never returned to state-level politics post-1973, although he was a veteran of state government administrations. Another Congress leader, Vengala Rao, was appointed CM by IG. In October 1974, in a signal that he was being rehabilitated, Rao was appointed a general secretary in the Congress party. However, Rao was not part of IG's inner circle. Like the average Indian, he too learnt about the Emergency on the morning of 26 June 1975 from an announcement on All India Radio.[3]

Unlike in the north, the Congress party did extremely well in Andhra Pradesh, even in the post-Emergency general elections of 1977, and Rao was elected from Hanamkonda in Andhra Pradesh. Rao won again from this constituency in the midterm general elections in 1980. Rao was quietly and consistently loyal to IG in her wilderness years between 1977 and 1980. For this, and for keeping quiet after losing his CM position in 1973, he was appointed foreign minister after she came back as PM in 1980.

Despite Rao's win in 1989, he was disappointed with his low profile within the Congress. He packed up his belongings and was all set to leave Delhi when Rajiv Gandhi was assassinated on 21 May 1991. Despite the consequent wave of sympathy, Congress fell well short of an absolute majority, winning 226 out of 545 Lok Sabha seats in the 1991 general election.

Meanwhile, the BJP increased its share of seats from two in 1984 to eighty-five in 1989 and to 120 in 1991. The Janata Dal's seats fell sharply from 143 in 1989 to sixty-nine in 1991. The changes in the political fortunes of the various parties in the 1991 general elections provides a sense of the uncertain environment which prevailed prior to formation of the Central government in mid-1991.

Although there were other contenders in the Congress party such as Arjun Singh for the post of PM, a set of fortuitous circumstances led to their elimination. Rumour has it that it was on P.N. Haksar's advice that Rao was chosen. He was sworn in on 21 June 1991 to become India's first 'accidental prime minister'. Rao was acutely aware that he was a compromise candidate and that many in the Congress party were waiting for an opportunity to unseat him. For instance, Arjun Singh left in protest after the demolition of the Babri Masjid.

Rao looked for an economist of standing to take charge of the Ministry of Finance, and he first requested I.G. Patel who declined for personal reasons.

This position was then offered to Manmohan Singh. Rao understood that the country needed an economist with experience in government as the finance minister. At the same time, Rao appointed seasoned civil servants Amarnath Verma and Naresh Chandra as principal secretary to the PM and cabinet secretary respectively. He gave them the required authority within government to push through decisions taken on economic reforms.[4] The various ministries of the Central government tend to work in silos. Hence this delegation of authority to proven administrators was a shrewd move on Rao's part.

In another calculated move, Rao rehabilitated Pranab Mukherjee who was in political wilderness during the Rajiv Gandhi years. Rao appointed Mukherjee as the deputy chairman of the Planning Commission (June 1991 to May 1996). The Gadgil formula was revised by the National Development Council (NDC) after Mukherjee took over. The revised construct for assistance to states stood the test of time and was used till 2014–15.

Rao gave political cover to Manmohan Singh and his team[5] while they implemented reforms which hurt established private-sector interests and went against the grain of the political left. For instance, when Manmohan Singh offered to resign following the Harshad Mehta stock market scam, Rao did not accept his resignation. Rao was aware that for economic reforms to gain ground, he needed continuity in crucial positions.

The principal message in Rao's first Independence Day speech on 15 August 1991, less than two months after taking over as PM, was that the 'country had been brought back from the brink of economic disaster'. Despite his expertise in the area of foreign policy, for the most part Rao stayed away from this topic in his speech.[6] His strategy on the Kashmir and Ram Mandir–Babri Masjid fronts was to address these issues quietly and through procrastination. In the first two years of his government, Rao stayed away from controversial issues to fight the battles on the economic front where he faced entrenched interests. With his experience of the aborted land reforms in Andhra Pradesh, Rao did not want economic reforms to be sidetracked by outcries that foreign companies were being favoured over domestic Indian industry.

Economic Reforms

India and China started out at about the same per capita income around the mid-twentieth century. Even in 1990, the per capita incomes in these two countries were not that different. India was at US $385 and China at US $349. In the subsequent decades, the Chinese economy grew faster and consistently as compared to India. Deng Xiaoping had started on economic reforms in

China by the late 1970s. By the early 1990s, China was starting to become a source for exports of competitively priced garments and consumer goods to the developed West. It took more than a decade for the reforms to yield results in China. By 2016, the per capita numbers for India and China were at $1749 and $8116 respectively.[7] As Rao was probably more widely read than IG or Rajiv Gandhi, he had a better grasp of the changes in China and the desperate need for economic reforms at home.

The stifling controls on industrial and import licensing in India go back to the late 1950s of the Nehru era. However, it was through the first phase of the years, when Indira Gandhi was PM from 1966–77, that a combination of licensing and bureaucratic controls reached their zenith. After she came back to power in 1980, she did try to open up the country to better communications technology, but no systemic reforms were undertaken, and the complex web of bureaucratic permissions continued.

Rajiv Gandhi did want change, but his thinking was inchoate, and he was soon overwhelmed by Bofors and the unnecessary involvement in Sri Lanka. Despite these distractions, Central government committees during the Rajiv Gandhi years did examine how to dilute the inefficient stranglehold government had on every aspect of industry, foreign trade and investment.[8] In the early 1980s, relaxations were granted on the capital account for NRIs to invest in Indian stock markets which also became a route for round-tripping of unaccounted income of resident Indians, who were able to thus evade tax.

Unlike Indira Gandhi in 1980 or Rajiv Gandhi post-1984, Rao did not have an absolute majority in the Lok Sabha. However, he did have the help of two significant events which concentrated the minds of the influential in India's political and bureaucratic circles. One was the airlifting of Indian gold to the UK and Switzerland in exchange for hard currency credit lines to avert a default on India's hard currency debt repayments. The other was the collapse of the Soviet Union. Since Independence, the political elite in India has worried about a break-up of India along communal, ethnic or regional lines. It was clear that the Soviet Union had struggled to meet the aspirations of its people for easier availability of consumer goods. Despite some diehard opposition from the left,[9] the middle-of-the-road Indian was convinced about the need to open up the economy and free it of controls—at least on industrial production.

As mentioned earlier, by mid-1991, India was on the brink of defaulting on its hard currency debt. Overvaluation of the rupee during the 1980s had contributed to making exports uncompetitive and imports attractive, leading to sustained trade and current account deficits. Therefore, the first and immediate action needed was a devaluation of the rupee which was done in two steps. Till

Rao took over in 1991, the RBI used to arrive at the rupee exchange rate by pegging its value to a basket of currencies. Given the various Indian lobbies which favoured a 'strong' rupee for jingoistic, financial or private consumption reasons, the rupee's trade-weighted REER[10] was substantially overvalued against hard currencies by 1991.

Consequently, on 1 July 1991, RBI announced a 9 per cent reduction in the value of the rupee. And on 3 July 1991, the rupee was devalued by a further 11 per cent. This two-step devaluation of the rupee was consistent with an overall strategy to bring the rupee down to realistic levels. It is worth noting that the devaluation of the rupee was effected within ten days of Rao taking office as PM and before Dr Manmohan Singh's budget speech on 24 July 1991. In subsequent years, the RBI started monitoring the REER of the rupee on a systematic basis, and its value was also targeted.

In 1989–90, the department of industry headed by A.N. Verma had examined ways to abolish industrial licensing, excluding those areas covered by specific legislation for strategic reasons or reserved for the small-scale sector. This preparatory work proved extremely useful, and Rao was convinced that the prevailing stringent controls on industrial licensing had to go. Accordingly, he chose to retain the Ministry of Industries portfolio himself, and sweeping changes in industrial policy were quietly announced by P.J. Kurien, the minister of state for industries, in Parliament on the morning of 24 July 1991. To tactically divert attention from the momentous changes announced by Kurien, the budget speech was delivered the same day in the evening.

As Rao had anticipated, there were howls of protest from the old guard in the Congress. However, once the reforms were described as a logical sequel to what the party had embarked on during the 1980s, the discordant notes were quietened. Rao was at his best in managing the political-economy aspects of containing opposition to the reforms within the Congress-led coalition government of that time and with the public at large. Despite the hard currency shortage crisis and the need to mortgage the country's gold, it is quite possible that if one of the other Congress contenders had become PM, the government may have resorted to patchwork interim solutions. That is what previous governments had done.

In the evening of 24 July 1991, Finance Minister Manmohan Singh presented the Central government's budget announcing several reforms. The norms for FDI were liberalized, technology tie-ups with foreign firms were made easier, and the list of industries reserved for the public sector was reduced from eighteen to eight.[11] Rao did not try to introduce reforms in labour law or change policies on reservations for small-scale industries.[12] Another less talked about yet important reform was in indirect taxes. The MODVAT introduced during the years that Rajiv Gandhi was PM was extended to nearly all commodities. At the same time, excise duty rates were reduced.

Overall, the emphasis was on reducing internal and external imbalances that included fiscal and current account deficits. Although foreign trade was liberalized, imports of consumer goods was not. The explosion in the exports of IT services starting in the late 1990s would not have been possible without the trade liberalization initiated during the RG years and accelerated in the Rao years.

A tax reforms committee (TRC) headed by Raja Chelliah submitted its interim report in December 1991 and two final reports in August 1992 and January 1993. The recommendations included reducing personal income tax down to 20 to 40 per cent and corporate tax to 40 per cent. The Chelliah recommendations also included doing away with the needless distinction between closely and widely held companies. For indirect taxes, Chelliah's sound suggestions included reduction in import duties, restructuring of excise rates and elimination of end-use exemptions.[13] These TRC recommendations were gradually implemented through the 1990s by the Congress-led government headed by Rao, then Deve Gowda's United Front and the National Democratic Alliance (NDA) of Atal Bihari Vajpayee. With P. Chidambaram as finance minister in 1997–98, personal tax rates were brought down to three slabs of 10, 20 and 30 per cent. As a result, direct tax collection went up to about 2.7 per cent of GDP by the late 1990s. Taxation at 5 per cent was levied on three services in 1994.[14]

The civil aviation and telecommunications sectors were opened to the private sector during 1991–95. For instance, Jet Airways started its air-taxi operations on 1 April 1992, and regular operations began in 1995. The first signs of loosening of government controls in the telecommunications sector had begun in 1981 when Indira Gandhi was PM. Further steps were taken under Rajiv Gandhi, such as the setting up of C-DOT. There was a demand for additional loosening of government controls in the early 1990s. The Rao government responded by deciding on a National Telecommunications Policy which set out the road map for introducing private ownership, the services to be provided and the regulatory structure. The first mobile and Internet services started in India on Independence Day, 15 August 1995. The Telecom Regulatory Authority of India (TRAI) was set up two years later in 1997.

Rao was pilloried on the grounds that the reforms were introduced at the prodding of the IMF and the World Bank. These two Bretton Woods institutions were supportive of the reforms undertaken by the Indian government. However, it would be unfair to those who had worked in the PMO, the Ministry of Industry and the Ministry of Finance from 1989 to 1992, if pressure from the Bretton Woods institutions were to be interpreted as the sole reason for economic reforms undertaken by Rao's government. The winds of change and relaxation of controls had been blowing, but very gently, since the early 1980s.

After the Soviet Union broke up in 1991, the US was the sole remaining superpower. Francis Fukuyama's 'The End of History' essay, written in 1989 and converted into a book titled *The End of History and the Last Man* in 1992, was widely read at the time. In the early 1990s, the US economy, with few domestic economic controls, open capital account and a low-tariff trade regime was held up as the model for developing economies. It is likely that the failure of the Soviet economic model helped decision makers in the Indian government to make the case for a less regimented economy.

In comparison to the attention paid to industrial policy, exchange rate, foreign trade and investment reforms, the changes effected in the Indian financial sector did not attract comparable levels of attention. This was probably because these changes were less widely understood and also because there were no immediate losers. The first M. Narasimham[15] Committee (Committee on the Financial System) was set up by the finance ministry on 14 August 1991 with broad terms of reference to identify ways to improve the functioning of the financial sector. This committee's recommendations were tabled promptly in Parliament within four months by December 1991.

The Union government and the RBI had agreed in 1955 to the issuance of ad hoc ninety-one-day maturity T-bills. Over the decades, such issuance of T-bills became a way for the government to monetize its deficits. The RBI would necessarily purchase whatever volumes of T-bills were issued by government to meet its financing requirements, and RBI's credit to government would increase accordingly. Around 1982, treasury bills added up to 19 per cent of reserve money, and this number had risen to an unhealthy 77.3 per cent by 1991. This steep rise in the T-bill component of reserve money was an indication of the high dependence of the successive governments of Indira Gandhi and Rajiv Gandhi on RBI for credit. On 9 September 1994, the Ministry of Finance concluded an agreement between the government and RBI to phase out this self-serving government practice by 1996–97.[16]

The Cash Reserve Ratio (CRR)[17] and Statutory Liquidity Ratio (SLR)[18] were high at 15 and 38.5 per cent respectively in the early 1990s.[19] These ratios were gradually reduced to enable banks to raise lending. In 1994 the bank nationalization law was amended to allow government ownership to come down to 51 per cent from 100 per cent. Public-sector banks continued to be majority owned by government but that ownership did not any longer need to be above 51 per cent. In 1995 the RBI introduced primary dealers[20] and got them to participate in the auctioning of government securities.

RBI's bank oversight function was also strengthened. Rao had no appetite to make PSU (public sector undertaking) banks fully board driven. However, he could have done more to reduce the unbridled discretion of the Appointments Committee of the Cabinet (ACC) headed by the PM, in appointing heads of PSU banks, and also in segregating government from their lending decisions. Successive RBI governors too did not push enough for greater transparency in the lending decisions of public sector banks.

Substantive changes were effected in the capital markets sub-sector with far-reaching positive consequences for the economy. For instance, the National Stock Exchange (NSE) was set up in 1992 with automatic order matching rather than open outcry. And the National Security Depository Limited (NSDL) was up and running by August 1996 and hard-copy share certificates became a thing of the past.

The finance ministry should have reviewed the loopholes that the policies of the Indira Gandhi government, with Pranab Mukherjee as finance minister, had created for round-tripping of unaccounted Indian income via tax havens. The 24 August 1982 India–Mauritius Double Taxation Avoidance Treaty was ostensibly meant for attracting foreign capital. Such capital from external sources could be invested in Indian stock markets or as FDI and was taxed at the minuscule rates of taxation in Mauritius. A dead giveaway of the round-tripping game was that a number of Indian companies which received fund transfers via Mauritius had little or no visible business activities in India. Conversely, it could be argued that but for such treaties with Mauritius, Singapore and Cyprus, the volumes of foreign investment would have been much lower.[21]

Reverting to the first few years of the 1990s, approval for FDI proposals up to 51 per cent equity was made automatic. For higher than 51 per cent cases, a Foreign Investment Promotion Board (FIPB) was set up. The hitherto restrictive Foreign Exchange Regulation Act (FERA) was amended to make the business environment easier for firms which had received foreign equity. The investment norms for equity investments by foreign institutional investors (FIIs) were designed to attract higher inflows.[22]

Within a year of the advent of widespread economic reforms in 1991, Indian stock markets were hit in mid-1992 by the Harshad Mehta scam.[23] Mehta's methodology was to borrow from public, private and foreign banks, and from financial institutions such as the Unit Trust of India (UTI) by depositing bankers' receipts (BRs) as collateral. Mehta used BRs issued by the Bank of Karad (BoK) and the Metropolitan Cooperative Bank (MCB), which had issued them without the support of adequate government securities, as per normal practice. These large volumes of borrowed funds were then invested in stocks. As the prices of specific stocks, and to that extent stock indices, went up sharply, retail investors were lulled into thinking that a bull run was on and they too could jump in and book quick profits. The SENSEX went up from 1200 to 4500, that is 275 per cent appreciation in one year, between April 1991 and April 1992.

Harshad Mehta was initially lionized as a discerning investor by the doyens of Indian private and public-sector financial institutions, and his access to capital increased accordingly. However, it soon became apparent that some of the BRs against which Mehta was borrowing were not secure. Estimates vary about the volumes of profits that Mehta made. With the unveiling of Mehta's methods and the fact that nothing magical was happening to justify the sharp rise in stock prices, the markets took a steep tumble in the first week of August 1992. The stock market came down sharply by over 50 per cent in one day (there were no circuit breakers at that time to limit stock price movements), and the bearish sentiment lasted till about 1994–95.

Given the clamour from the Opposition, Rao's government had to agree to the setting up of a JPC to look into the Harshad Mehta episode. This JPC was headed by Congress MP Ram Niwas Mirdha who was not known to have any knowledge about financial markets. The JPC glossed over the shortcomings in the practices of Indian and foreign banks, including of the State Bank of India, accepting BRs issued by little-known banks.

The Harshad Mehta episode showed up the seamy, collusive nature of wrongdoing which involved working and senior-level personnel employed in Indian banks, stock exchanges, the UTI and other financial institutions. It should not have been so easy for Mehta to run the racket that he did. Mehta was jailed in 1992 on charges of fraud, and remained in prison till he died nine years later, on 31 December 2001, of a heart attack.

It was surprising that more was not done by Finance Minister Manmohan Singh and his officials of that time to reduce the risk of future financial-sector scams of a similar nature. In retrospect, it appears that at senior levels in the finance ministry, RBI and even SEBI, there was limited understanding about stock markets in particular and financial markets in general. In this context, it is important for the Ministry of Finance to employ a chief financial adviser (CFA) in addition to the chief economic adviser (CEA). Financial markets have become too complicated with the use of derivatives and accounting dodges for even highly qualified economists to unravel. This may not have been so obvious prior to 1992 but it should have been, following the Harshad Mehta episode. It was because of an absence of systemic reforms in the regulatory oversight of cooperative banks that the next stock market scam took place about eight years later in 2000.

Reverting to 1992, a dubious practice in Indian stock markets called *badla* was also used by Harshad Mehta. Under the badla system, stocks could be traded on payment of margins agreed upon between individual brokers without the oversight of stock exchanges, and settlement could be deferred indefinitely. Badla trades created counterparty risks and defaults leading to cascading problems in the settlement of regular trades in stocks. Following the Harshad Mehta episode, badla trading was banned in 1993. However, the finance ministry succumbed to lobbying pressure from brokers and allowed badla trading to restart in 1996. The suspension of badla trading should have been maintained till derivatives such as futures and options were introduced. These derivatives transactions are traded on stock exchanges which stand as guarantors of transactions, thus eliminating credit risk exposure to individuals.

In the 1990s the Ministry of Finance did not pay sufficient attention to sound accounting as a check on the health of the financial sector. The financial sector cannot function efficiently if there are widespread accounting malpractices, just as a car will stall if the lubricant for the engine is not replaced at prescribed intervals. As the world discovered to its cost in 2008, a lack of understanding about what is happening at a micro-level in the financial sector can prove very costly for the macro-economy. Financial-sector breakdowns take a long time to heal and for the corresponding economies to recover.

Specifically, the Institute of Chartered Accountants of India (ICAI) regulates the accounting profession in the country. Although ICAI is a statute-based body, this is the equivalent to bankers setting up their own institution to regulate banks. After 1992, a separate regulator should have been set up for accounting. The Ministry of Finance did not take full advantage of the public outcry about Harshad Mehta episode to set up a separate regulator at arm's length from practising accountants.

During Rao's tenure, the Ministry of Finance did not move towards reforming India's insurance and pension sub-sectors. At that time, the insurance space was dominated by fully government-owned companies such as Life Insurance Corporation (LIC). The required changes to enable private-sector entry would have brought faster growth to this important part of the financial sector. This would have fostered competition with attendant benefits of lower insurance premiums and better service. Separate legislation to set up regulators for these segments of the financial sector could have been enacted. The development of these sub-sectors was and continues, even in May 2019, to be crucial to developing deeper long-term debt markets. Funds accumulated by these sub-sectors are usually invested in long-term debt to reduce asset-liability mismatches. Allowing FDI in the insurance and pension sub-sectors could have been initiated during Rao's term.

Almost all the spadework for the amendments to the Indian Constitution to empower panchayats in villages and municipalities in urban areas by making them 'institutions of self-government' was done during the years Rajiv Gandhi was in power. PM Rao's government dug out the work done and got the necessary legislation passed in December 1992. The 73rd Amendment added a section titled 'The Panchayats', and the 74th Amendment added 'The Municipalities'.

The panchayats amendment provides for elections to these village-level bodies, and a significant feature is that one-third of the seats are reserved for women. The municipalities law envisages the setting up of district planning committees. Each state was enjoined to set up state finance commissions for allocation of funds to panchayats and municipalities. Although such commissions have been set up, state governments have been tardy and wilfully negligent in making these professional and competent enough. As a result, local bodies in villages and urban areas have not received the required amounts of funds, nor have they been helped to build capacity to meet their financing needs on a sustainable basis.[24]

On a separate note, the availability of power in Maharashtra and most other parts of India was patchy and inadequate in the 1990s. In this context, in 1992, the Dabhol Power Company was established to put up a power plant in Maharashtra, with US companies GE and Bechtel responsible for supplying equipment and getting the construction done, and Enron as the project manager. The project was under implementation from 1992 to 2001 and was mired in charges of corruption. In 2001 Enron was charged in the US for breaking the law on issues unrelated to Dabhol. The Maharashtra State Electricity Board (MSEB) finally refused to purchase power from this plant on the grounds that the tariff charged by Enron was too high. This plant was taken over by Ratnagiri Gas and Power Private Limited (RGPPL) in 2005.

The Dabhol power project is an example of precisely how not to increase power production capacity. The emphasis was on guaranteeing a high US dollar return for Enron which managed the project. The MSEB initially guaranteed an assured tariff for the power project which was counter-guaranteed by the Maharashtra government. A further Central government guarantee was approved by the finance ministry. With the benefit of hindsight, work should have started on cost-plus pricing and a national power grid during Rao's term.

As Table 7.1 in the Appendices shows, Rao's government was able to contain and reduce gross fiscal deficit and the net primary deficit while steadily raising the economy's rate of growth. The current account deficit was kept below 2 per cent of GDP, foreign exchange reserves grew and so did exports. However, there was double-digit inflation in four out of the five years of Rao's term. Inflation impacts the average Indian directly and would have contributed to the inability of the Congress party to come back to power in 1996.[25]

The economic reforms were essentially about reducing discretionary decision making by government, and some progress was made towards this goal. All PMs after Narasimha Rao have continued to reduce controls and the direction, although halting at times, has been towards further economic liberalization.[26] Among the missing elements in the reforms, nothing substantive and sustained was initiated in the agriculture sector. Further, labour and land-acquisition reforms were not contemplated. No serious attempt was made to address the fact that the cost of Indian labour, factoring in its low productivity, was relatively high, even though India is a labour-surplus country. The Rao government made no serious attempt to address this problem by turning the spotlight on the efficacy of vocational and skill development centres around the country. There was abundant anecdotal evidence that competent electricians, carpenters, plumbers and skilled masons were in short supply.

The reforms in the first half of the 1990s were not followed up vigorously enough in the second half of the decade. However, the steps taken during the years Rao was PM combined with those implemented post-1998 have pushed India's GDP growth rate above the global average from the 1990s till 2019. Availability of televisions, phones, cars and two-wheelers has increased. Telecom too has been a hugely successful story since the late 1990s. India is now much more of a consumers' market. This is a substantial positive change from the pre-1990s era when products and services were rationed to applicants waiting in interminable queues for a scooter or a telephone connection. The wider and easier availability of consumer items has made the sense of deprivation higher among the poor.[27]

By 1993 the important change for the Indian economy was that it had shifted from industrial licensing and tight controls on imports and FDI to one in which decisions which impacted domestic and foreign investments and foreign trade were more determined by market signals. Within two years of Rao taking over, India's crisis in servicing its hard currency debt abated and the pace of reforms also slowed down in tandem. Another factor which reduced Rao's appetite for reforms was that state-level electoral results were negative for Rao. For instance, in the 1993 UP elections, the Congress party was marginalized by a combination of the Samajwadi Party and the Bahujan Samaj Party, and it lost in Delhi in the same year to the BJP (see about Delhi's special status act below). This reduced Rao's writ, which was limited to begin with, within the Congress and may have contributed to his reluctance to continue with economic reforms.

Babri Masjid

The agitation for a temple dedicated to Ram in Ayodhya, Uttar Pradesh, was supported by many in that state and around the country. Extreme elements within Hindu communities did their bit to inflame passions. They felt that the

Ram temple should be built at the site of the Babri Masjid since this mosque had allegedly been built over a temple site.[28] The contrary view that the mosque was not built over a temple is detailed in an article titled 'Archaeologist Who Observed Dig Says No Evidence of Temple under Babri Masjid'.[29]

The BJP had withdrawn its support to the Janata Dal government headed by V.P. Singh when its demand that a Ram temple be built at Ayodhya was not met. The Uttar Pradesh government headed by then BJP chief minister Kalyan Singh too did not take any decisive action for the construction of the temple. As large numbers of kar sevaks had gathered in Ayodhya in December 1992 Rao must have been aware of the imminent danger of the Babri Masjid being damaged or destroyed.

Under the Indian Constitution, law and order is a state subject. In order for the Central government to take action, Rao would have had to convince the then President Shankar Dayal Sharma (also from Congress) to declare a threat to national security and then use the army or paramilitary forces. In retrospect, it may be that UP authorities and the Central government felt that the prudent course of action was to allow extremist sentiments to prevail and plead later that they were unaware of the ground-level situation. Rao probably weighed the political benefits and downside of siding with either Hindu or Muslim sentiments. He is alleged to have retired to his bedroom so that he could not be contacted as the masjid was being brought down on 6 December 1992.[30] This resulted in the Muslim community feeling a sense of betrayal towards the Congress.

About three months after this depressing moment in India's communal and political history, on 12 March 1993, the Bombay Stock Exchange and other locations in Mumbai were bombed. About 300 persons lost their lives and the Indian mujahideen and other groups claimed responsibility.[31] In the communal riots that followed around the country, several thousand were killed or seriously injured, and property worth up to Rs 90 billion was damaged.[32] As a consummate politician with over four decades of experience in senior positions in government, Rao chose inaction which led to the avoidable loss of so many lives.

Special Status for Delhi, Supreme Court and No-confidence Motion

The genesis of the current problems in administering Delhi can be traced back to a Rao decision of 1992. Going back to the early post-Independence years, Delhi became a part C state under the States Act of 1951. Land, police and public order were placed outside the purview of part C states. Subsequently,

Jawaharlal Nehru felt that the Central government should be fully responsible for Delhi, and accordingly, Delhi's C state status was revoked under the 1956 States Reorganisation Act. Thereafter, Delhi did not have a CM, and the lieutenant governor was the senior-most authority in the Delhi administration.

Supporters of statehood for Delhi felt the local citizens should have their own legislature and mobilized for it over the next three decades. Finally, it was on 2 January 1992, just six months after Rao had taken over as PM, that the Government of National Capital Territory of Delhi (NCTD) Act was passed. While full statehood was not granted to Delhi under this legislation, a Delhi chief minister was then onwards empowered to share in administering the national capital with the Central government. The BJP won forty-nine out of seventy seats in the Delhi elections, and Madan Lal Khurana became CM in 1993, thirty-seven years after Delhi's statehood was withdrawn in 1956.

Despite having an elected CM, Delhi continues to have a complex administrative structure. An April 1958 Act of Parliament had set up the Municipal Corporation of Delhi (MCD). This Act was amended in 1993 during Rao's tenure to create three municipal corporations for north, south and east Delhi, and elections are held for these three corporations. Central Delhi (Lutyens's Delhi) is administered by the New Delhi Municipal Committee which is headed by a Central government appointee.

Other parts of Delhi are administered by the Cantonment Board under the Directorate General of Defence Estates and the Delhi Development Authority (DDA) which reports to the lieutenant governor. The 1992 NCTD Act compounded the problem of multiple authorities in Delhi, leading to each blaming the other for the city's shortcomings. Official records in the public domain do not provide any statement by Rao on this issue. Rao could have gone to the court of public opinion and explained that, given that this Union territory had been administered reasonably well by the Central government since 1956, no change was warranted. He could have pointed out that several major capitals around the world, such as Washington DC, Beijing, Mexico City and Brasilia, are essentially under the administrative control of the Central governments of those countries.

The collegium system of selecting judges for high courts and the Supreme Court was instituted while Rao was PM. The senior judiciary was probably concerned ever since the arbitrary action of the Indira Gandhi government in 1977 overlooking H.R. Khanna, the senior-most judge at that time, for the position of chief justice. The Advocates-on-Record Association had filed a case against the Union of India about then existing procedures which gave primacy to the Central government in approving the names proposed as judges by the

Supreme Court.[33] Perhaps Justice J.S. Verma's recollection of the weakening of the judiciary during the Emergency resulted in his 1993 judgment in favour of a collegium system for appointments of judges to high courts and the Supreme Court.[34]

Under this collegium system, a panel of judges headed by the chief justice of the Supreme Court is responsible for the selection of judges instead of the Central government. It is likely that this change happened because of the perceived weakness of Rao's coalition government. To assuage concerns in judicial circles about past government high-handedness in the appointments of judges, Rao could have suggested that the selection of judges be effected by a PM-headed committee out of names suggested by a body consisting of Supreme Court judges and a few other prominent personalities.

The Indian legal system is based on practices in the UK. In the UK, judges are selected by a Judicial Appointments Commission (JAC). These choices have to be approved by the Lord Chancellor and the PM, and they have the right to accept or reject the nominations made by the JAC. In the US, the President nominates Supreme Court judges who then have to be approved by the Senate. By contrast, India has moved to a system in which judges appoint judges. The larger point here is that the current Indian practice of judges selecting judges is not followed in two developed countries from where India has borrowed most of its legal system and practices.

All through Rao's term as PM, the Congress was irrelevant in UP, India's largest state. Rao's inability to be a vote getter for the Congress party in assembly elections around the country, combined with the challenges to his leadership from within the Congress, encouraged the Opposition to table a no-confidence motion against Rao's government in mid-1993. The vote on this motion was taken on 28 July 1993, and four Jharkhand Mukti Morcha (JMM) MPs supported Rao's government to defeat this no-confidence motion. Allegedly, a sum of about Rupees 16 million was deposited in the bank accounts of each of these MPs during 1–2 August 1993.[35] Another new low was reached in national politics. Although there were coalition governments between 1977 and 1980 and from 1989 to 1991, the PMs of those governments were not accused of trying to win votes of confidence by bribing MPs.

Two years after Rao demitted office, on 17 April 1998, the Supreme Court ruled that MPs who took bribes for voting in favour of one party or the other were immune from prosecution since there is constitutional immunity for voting in Parliament.[36] Shailendra Mahato was one of the ten accused in the JMM bribery case. On 29 September 2000, Rao was convicted by a CBI judge in this same case. He was acquitted of all charges before he passed away in 2004. The CBI's investigations into corruption at high political levels and inconclusive court cases added to cynicism about Indian politicians. Rao bears some of the responsibility for this further slide in the credibility of those in public life.

Kashmir, Neighbourhood and the Major Powers

The 1991 elections to the Lok Sabha could not be held in J&K due to the state of unrest in this state. The dissatisfaction at a popular level can be traced back to the alleged rigged state assembly elections in 1987. By the early 1990s, the Soviet Union had crumbled, and the US had less reason to supply weapons to the mujahideen in Afghanistan. In this confused situation, Pakistan saw an opportunity to engineer infiltration of extremists into Kashmir.

In 1990 Seymour Hersh wrote in the *New Yorker*[37] that there was a possibility of the use of nuclear weapons due to differences between India and Pakistan over Kashmir. Twenty-eight years later, in June 2018, Penguin Random House US published *Reporter: A Memoir* by Hersh. Hersh says that he can now reveal that in 1990, based on confirmed CIA information, Pakistan feared an Indian invasion and was preparing to retaliate with nuclear weapons. The tone of this Hersh account describing India–Pakistan relations in 1990 to be more 'frightening than the Cuban missile crisis' was unconvincingly alarmist.

Relations between the two neighbours had deteriorated due to the Pakistani government's promotion of extremism in Kashmir. The Pakistani assessment that the people of Kashmir were ready to side with infiltrators was a throwback to Operation Gibraltar[38] of 1965. At one stage in 1990 the Indian High Commission in Islamabad had to stock food and other provisions in the mission's office building in case Indian personnel needed to be moved into these premises prior to repatriation.

Rao had inherited a difficult situation in J&K, but he had to focus on the balance of payments crisis after he took over and the challenges his government faced later. Whatever may be the reasons, Rao was not able to focus on longer-term solutions for Kashmir, including creation of employment opportunities to give the local population a greater stake in peace and order. However, despite his relative neglect of development in Kashmir, Rao accorded high priority to relations with Pakistan. Ignoring Pakistan's role in fomenting extremism in Kashmir, he met Pakistani PM Nawaz Sharif six times between 1991 and 1993. These meetings took place in the two countries or on the sidelines of the UN in New York. It is likely that due to Rao maintaining a steady dialogue with Pakistan, the latter's instigation of terrorist violence in India was less than what it might have been otherwise.

Rao's government looked for a closer relationship with the ASEAN nations and coined the phrase 'Look East Policy' and India became a dialogue partner with the ASEAN grouping in 1992. Later in 1996 India became a full member of the ASEAN Regional Forum (ARF). Rao understood that while India's economic relationships with the West would continue to be important, there was considerable potential for increasing trade and investment ties with countries to its east.

To make headway in India's relations with Bangladesh, Rao needed to work out mechanisms for sharing of river waters between India and Bangladesh. Shortage of water for farming is a controversial and often emotive issue in most Indian states, including West Bengal. By 1991, Chief Minister Jyoti Basu and the Communist Party of India (Marxist) (CPI[M]) were well entrenched in West Bengal.[39] Rao did not have the political ballast to arrive at a practical accommodation with Bangladesh and Jyoti Basu's West Bengal on sharing of Ganga water, particularly since the CPI(M) was strongly opposed to Rao's economic reforms.

To the discomfiture of Rao's government, Alexander Rutskoy, a Russian vice-president, referred to the use of the United Nations to resolve the Kashmir issue during his December 1991 visit to Pakistan. Following the break-up of the Soviet Union, with Boris Yeltsin in charge, there was a shift in the Russian attitude on Kashmir. India had to be careful as it needed continuity in the defence relationship with Russia. India and Russia agreed that the latter would take on the responsibilities of intergovernmental agreements that India had concluded with the erstwhile Soviet Union. However, the defence equipment that India had bought from the USSR was put together from parts made in separate Soviet republics. To maintain continuity of access to spare parts and servicing over the remaining life of Soviet equipment, India reached out to the former republics of the USSR. For example, Ukraine as a centre of metallurgical excellence; Kazakhstan, with its launching sites for space vehicles; and Kyrgyzstan's Lake Issyk-Kul for testing torpedoes, had linkages with their counterpart institutions in India. India has historical ties with the Central Asian republics, and they are rich in minerals and fossil fuels. Rao was presciently quick to establish relationships with the former Soviet republics.

Payments for trade in goods and services between India and the Soviet Union, and for India's purchase of defence equipment, was under a rupee–rouble arrangement at an exchange rate that was administratively determined by the governments of the two sides. India paid for its imports in rupees, and the USSR paid in roubles. With the break-up of the Soviet Union, the rupee–rouble exchange rate needed to be modified since the Russian rouble's value fell sharply against convertible currencies. Russia had substantial net balances of rupees because of India's high-value defence imports.

A rupee–rouble agreement was signed between the two countries during Boris Yeltsin's visit to India in February 1993. It was agreed that the cut-off date for the exchange rate for all past debt, as of 1 January 1990, owed by India to Russia (as successor state of the Soviet Union), would be Rs 19.9 to 1 rouble. For transactions from 1 April 1992, the new exchange rate became Rs 31.57 to 1 rouble. This agreement, which specified the rupee–rouble exchange rates for past Indian debt and for future transactions, was heavily criticized on the grounds that several Indian business houses came to know of the exchange rates in advance and made huge windfall gains. It is not clear from publicly available records whether Russia got an unduly favourable deal in the setting of these exchange rates. Irrespective of criticisms about the government-mandated revisions in the rupee–rouble exchange rates, the Rao government has to be complimented for closing this issue which had become an irritant in bilateral relations. Going forward, bilateral trade and purchases of military equipment and spares were based on exchange rates which were transparent. To that extent, both sides could henceforth compare prices of products and services with those of third-party providers.

Rao reached out to the US despite the latter leaning towards Pakistan on Kashmir during President George W. Bush's tenure from 1989 to 1993. Post-1993, there was pressure on India on non-proliferation when President Bill Clinton was in office. With an eye to US sensitivities, and also because pandering to anti-Israel sentiments in Arab quarters had run its course, Rao gave the go-ahead for India to establish diplomatic relations with Israel in January 1992. This was a much-needed injection of reality into India's foreign policy towards countries in West Asia and the Gulf region.

India had been a staunch supporter of the African National Congress (ANC) through the long struggle against apartheid in South Africa. Nelson Mandela was finally released after twenty-seven years in prison in 1990, and he led the ANC to victory in the elections in South Africa in 1994. Rao was quick to react to these momentous developments in a country with which India had had a long association, and he established diplomatic relations with South Africa in 1993.

On China, Rao took a practical step-by-step approach. One of the complications about the India–China border issue is that McMahon's explanatory note describing the line named after him in the eastern sector of the

India–China border is not fully consistent with the depiction on corresponding maps. There were several rounds of negotiations between India and China during the Rao years, and an agreement was reached to maintain peace at the frontier while the border issue was being resolved. With this end objective, 'A Border Peace and Tranquility Agreement' to 'maintain the status quo'[40] was signed by Rao during his visit to Beijing on 7 September 1993.

Earlier, on 4 June 1989, Chinese troops had faced off with student demonstrators in Tiananmen Square in Beijing. China's economic reforms over a decade since 1979 had created losers too. The protesters were upset about inflation and changes in the economy, and sought greater freedom of press and democracy. The protesters were put down with force and perhaps thousands were jailed.[41] It does not appear that in India's exchanges with the US government in the 1990s, there were any discussions about coordinating efforts to contain China by slowing its accession to the World Trade Organization. It may have been impossible anyway since those were the years that US multinationals were profiting enormously by shifting the production of consumer goods and garments to China.

To sum up, given the vulnerabilities of Rao's coalition government, his foreign policy performance was remarkable. According to Ambassador K.S. Bajpai, Rao was the shrewdest PM ever. He did not have Nehru's global name recognition or Indira Gandhi's charisma but played the international relations game adroitly with a limited political hand at home and a sputtering economy to start with in 1991.

Legacy

India was on the brink of defaulting on its external debt when Rao took over as PM in July 1991. The economy needed life support because of the high levels of government expenditure in the 1980s which ended with two short-lived coalition governments focused only on their own survival. Some analysts advance the argument that Rao had no option but to do what he did. Similar arguments could be made for why India should have effected economic course corrections in the early 1980s and definitely by the second half of Rajiv Gandhi's term as PM. However, it was Rao who took the bit in his mouth and went ahead with sweeping economic reforms.

Rao's tenure as PM was constantly under threat from within his own party and from coalition partner parties. It was almost magical that he managed the difficult political act of undertaking much-needed reforms and remained PM for five years. At the same time, Rao's reforms were circumscribed by the extent of political consensus Rao could achieve within his party and the coalition government.

An oft-repeated argument is that India goes close to the brink of disaster and then somehow inevitably claws its way back, just before hurtling down to its doom. There was nothing inevitable about India climbing its way out of the economic pit it had dug for itself by 1991. The Soviet Union had made many mistakes in how it had run its economy, and it was not just the invasion of Afghanistan—expensive as it was in terms of lives lost and the economic cost—that broke up the USSR. It was more the refusal to be practical about its economic choices and the inability to empathize with the discontent of its average citizens who craved for consumer goods and a better standard of living.

It is conceivable that if the USSR had embarked on systemic economic reforms, even by the early 1980s, it would still be one country. This is to emphasize that there was nothing predestined about the reforms which were implemented by Rao's government. The tendency of subsequent governments, particularly those led by the Congress party, has been to downplay Rao's contributions. Perhaps because that would be consistent with the implicit Congress party stance that it was only Indira Gandhi and subsequent generations of her family members who have the ability to lead the country successfully.

Rao's singular contribution was to seize the window of opportunity created by the balance of payments crisis and the all too visible break-up of the USSR to authorize far-reaching reforms. He was an able manager since he delegated the formulation of policies to informed experts who had decades of experience in government, RBI or the World Bank. Rao could not have got the reforms done without the team around him and Manmohan Singh as finance minister, who in turn was supported by knowledgeable experts in the Ministries of Finance and Commerce and the RBI. The same or other highly trained and motivated officials had worked with earlier PMs but they could not initiate a break with the past.

India had gone through trying economic difficulties in the 1970s and 1980s. Systemic reforms did not happen because Indira Gandhi and later Rajiv Gandhi did not have the understanding or the inclination to do so. In Indira Gandhi's understanding, less government control over the economy meant she would be less in charge of the political processes at the Centre and in interactions with state governments.

Rao was better than most Indian PMs in dealing with administrative crises. For instance, in 1993 there was a severe earthquake in Latur, Maharashtra, which measured 8.2 on the moment magnitude scale.[42] This earthquake was estimated to have killed about 10,000 people and displaced hundreds of thousands. Rao supported the Maharashtra state government to provide immediate relief and also set up schemes to help in the economic rehabilitation of the Latur region.

On foreign policy issues, Rao was perceptive about the short-term and long-term requirements. An example of a near crisis was Pakistan's attempt to incite riots and create disaffection in Kashmir. Rao was regularly in touch with his Pakistani counterpart and initiated steps which came to be called confidence-building measures.

He responded with sound measures to the break-up of the Soviet Union. And, although there are reservations in some quarters, Rao resolved the rupee-rouble exchange rate issue and quickly established relations with the former republics of the USSR. The opening up to China occasioned by Rajiv Gandhi's visit was followed up by the setting up of a mechanism to work towards settling of border differences. Rao was mindful about keeping relations with the US controversy-free. However, Rao did blink when asked pointedly by the US if India was preparing to test nuclear weapons and he chose not to do so in the face of possible US economic sanctions.

Rao was slow in reacting to issues which could have negative implications for his tenure as a minister or PM. For instance, Rao did not lift a finger to stop the killing of Sikhs in Delhi after the assassination of Indira Gandhi when he was the Union home minister. The demolition of Babri Masjid and subsequent violence will also remain a black mark against his record. In this context, the recurrent Congress claim that if an Indira Gandhi family member had been PM, the masjid would not have been demolished sounds hollow.

A number of communal riots happened under the watch of Indira Gandhi and Rajiv Gandhi. For instance, the Nellie massacre in Assam,[43] in which about 3000 were killed, took place on 18 February 1983 when Indira Gandhi was PM and Assam was under President's rule, that is, the Central government was in charge.[44] Rajiv Gandhi was PM when thousands of Sikhs were killed in the nation's capital. The Babri Masjid issue, in fact, came to the fore because RG allowed the locks of the Ram Mandir at this site to be opened. From December 1949 till 1986 the gates had been locked. In 1986 a local judge ruled that Hindu worship would be allowed. RG's government should have sought a stay order on the grounds that allowing access to worshippers of any religion could lead to clashes in the future.

Rao was said to be close to a 'god-man' called Chandraswami and used to seek his advice.[45] This proximity to a so-called tantric is the type of weakness that many Indian politicians in high office have exhibited. Notwithstanding this quirk, Rao had an inquisitive mind and kept himself briefed about latest events and advances around the world. Another inconsistency in Rao's mental make-up was that the people he admired behaved very differently from how he did when it came to making difficult choices. For instance, in Rao's thinly veiled autobiography called *The Insider*,[46] he expresses deep admiration for Swami Ramananda Tirtha. Rao uses the following words to describe the Swami's attitude towards the rich and powerful: 'This Sanyasi stood for the people and for Democracy, and declared to the mighty and oppressive Nizam—I shall break, but not bend!' Time and again, Rao chose to bend rather than break to further his own career. Rao's deliberate and exaggerated humility towards Indira Gandhi and later Rajiv Gandhi was inconsistent with the quality of self-respect he admired in Swami Ramananda Tirtha. It is likely though that in the prevailing culture of the Congress party, he would not have progressed to become PM if he did not have this element of self-effacement.

Unfortunately, Rao was not accorded the dignity of a state funeral in Delhi after he passed away on 23 December 2004, even though he had held the senior-most positions in Andhra Pradesh and the Central government. He was a minister and chief minister of Andhra Pradesh, and in the Central government had held the positions of foreign, defence, home, human resource development minister, and finally prime minister.

Rao's origins in a village in Andhra Pradesh, and his personal life which was way to the side of Bharat on the India–Bharat scale, are well-documented.[47] Rao was comfortable speaking not just in Telugu and Marathi, but also in Hindi and English. Although Rao did put on a bandhgala coat and trousers on occasion, he was more often dressed in the traditional dhoti and kurta.

Rao was extremely well read as political leaders go in India, or for that matter, anywhere in the world. His wide reading and personal experience of politics at the local level in Andhra Pradesh made him sensitive to the needs and aspirations of Bharat as well as India. However, on the public cynicism index, Rao did little to change the average voter's considerable scepticism about those who seek political office in India.

On the 3 Cs, Rao was high on Competence as he demonstrated through the handling of the 1991 balance of payments and economic crisis. His managerial excellence too was evident in his selection of PMO officers. Rao's compassion for the landless cost him the chief minister's position in Andhra Pradesh. However, he was low on Charisma, and despite his multiple language skills, he was not an effective public speaker. As for overall Character, this could vary for Rao depending on the occasion. He did not show enough courage of conviction to stop the demolition of the Babri Masjid. Rao was influenced by so-called god-men, and that too was not a stirring example of Character.

All things considered, Rao deserves the nation's gratitude for steering the Indian economy out of grave trouble. His lasting legacy is that he left behind an economically stronger and more stable India than the one he inherited. He had the perspicacity and tenacity to set in motion an irreversible reform process which has led India on to a path of sustained higher economic growth.

VIII

DEVE GOWDA AND I.K. GUJRAL

Prime Ministers of Wobbly, Short-lived Coalitions

In the general elections in 1996, P.V. Narasimha Rao–led Congress won 140 seats, and the BJP's tally rose to 161. As the single largest party, the BJP formed the government on 15 May 1996. This effort, with Atal Bihari Vajpayee as PM, collapsed when the BJP could not cobble together the required majority in the Lok Sabha and Vajpayee resigned just thirteen days later on 28 May 1996.

The Janata Dal, with just forty-six seats, formed the United Front (UF) or National Front government with the support of Congress. The UF consisted of the Janata Dal, the Left Front and the Telugu Desam Party (TDP). A combination of the Janata, regional and state parties supported by the Congress came to power, and H.D. Deve Gowda,[1] a long-standing Karnataka leader, was sworn in as PM on 1 June 1996. Given the experience of the Congress-supported governments of Charan Singh and Chandra Shekhar, it should have been obvious to Deve Gowda even before he took office that his government would not last long.

The media described the Gowda government's budget of 1997 as a 'dream' budget because the highest income tax rate was brought down to 30 per cent from 40 per cent, and tax on dividends in the hands of shareholders was dropped. The ceilings on FII investments in stock and debt markets were raised, and a few import duties were lowered marginally.[2]

The reforms effected by Narasimha Rao's government were path-breaking, yet much remained to be done. After the Rao-led government was voted out, there was concern whether Deve Gowda, with an unstable coalition, would be able to stay the course. The chief ministers of the two states with the most seats in the Lok Sabha were Mulayam Singh Yadav of the Samajwadi Party in UP

183

and Lalu Yadav of the Rashtriya Janata Dal in Bihar. Harkishan Singh Surjeet of CPI(M) played the kingmaker in the background.

The political backgrounds of the parties supporting Deve Gowda's government were incompatible, and hence this coalition was unstable. However, it is to Deve Gowda's credit that though he was only steeped in Karnataka politics, he was able to maintain continuity and took small incremental steps towards rational economic policies. Although gross fiscal deficits continued to be elevated at around the same levels as during the Narasimha Rao years, the current account deficit was contained, and the rupee exchange rate was wisely allowed to adjust downwards. This despite the constraints of coalition politics with CPI (M) supporting the government without participating in it.

Deve Gowda had no experience of dealing with foreign policy issues. Consequently, Foreign Minister I.K. Gujral had a relatively free hand to manage India's external relations. The so-called Gujral doctrine of that time was not to insist on reciprocity with neighbours. Gujral felt that India, as the largest South Asian country, should not insist on concessions in equal measure, e.g., from Bangladesh on sharing of river waters or from Nepal for granting its citizens free access to India.

The Congress claimed that Deve Gowda's government was not keeping it adequately informed. That was just a pretext to withdraw support. After the Deve Gowda government was disbanded on 21 April 1997, the Congress felt that it was not in a position to do better if general elections were to be held immediately and decided to support a government led by I.K. Gujral[3] again without participating in it. The Congress was not in a position to form government with the help of coalition partners. This is because Narasimha Rao had distanced himself from the Congress by this time, and Sitaram Kesri, who was earlier the treasurer, was the Congress president from 1996 to 1998. Kesri was not known for his leadership qualities.

Most regional parties in the south were ideologically opposed to the BJP. Consequently, it was a gloomy period in national politics since no coalition could form a stable Central government. Finally, a group of parties with a wide range of views somehow banded together and I.K. Gujral was sworn in as PM on 21 April 1997. Prior to becoming PM, Gujral had been the information and broadcasting minister in Indira Gandhi's government when the Emergency was declared in 1975. He was seen as incompetent in administering the sweeping curbs that Indira Gandhi had imposed on the print media and was replaced by V.C. Shukla. Gujral was packed off to Moscow as India's ambassador to the Soviet Union and was based there from 1976 to 1980. Gujral resigned from the Congress in the mid-1980s and contested the 1989 Lok Sabha election as a Janata Dal candidate and was elected from Jalandhar. He was the foreign minister in the V.P. Singh government.

Gujral remained PM of a coalition government till 19 March 1998. Deve Gowda was PM for less than eleven months, and Gujral too was PM for a little short of eleven months. In Gujral's case, his government lost the support of the Congress party in November 1997. Effectively, Gujral was PM for seven months and caretaker PM for another four months.

The short-term considerations of the leaders in the Gowda and Gujral governments led to a loss of valuable years in India's quest to raise growth and reduce poverty. The coalitions that supported Deve Gowda and Gujral were avowedly motivated by the need to make India socially and economically a more equal society. It is comically tragic that the two principal leaders of UP and Bihar, Mulayam Singh Yadav and Lalu Prasad Yadav, have ended up creating feudal legacies. The sons of these two leaders have been CM in UP and ministers in Bihar respectively.

The politics of appeasement of caste-based groupings and subgroups was further strengthened by the cynical politics during 1997–98. This had already become glaringly apparent during the years that V.P. Singh and Chandra Shekhar were PM, and this negative trend came even more to the surface as self-serving arguments were made to justify the coalitions that allowed Deve Gowda and Gujral to be PM for less than a year each.

IX

ATAL BIHARI VAJPAYEE

Decisive, Balanced Yet Susceptible

Hone, na hone ka kram,
Issi tarah chalta rahega,
Hum hain, hum rahenge,
Yeh bhram bhi sada
Palta rahega

The cycle of being and not
Being shall continue as ever,
We are and shall remain
—this illusion too will be nurtured forever[1]

From the poem 'Yaksha Prashna' by Atal Bihari Vajpayee

Atal Bihari Vajpayee[2] was an eloquent and fiery speaker in Hindi, whether in public meetings or in Parliament. His powers of persuasion and oratory are evident from the ten times that he was elected to the Lok Sabha. His first victory was in 1957 and last in 2004, a span of nearly half a century. He was said to have impressed Jawaharlal Nehru even though he was critical of the government's performance before and during the 1962 war with China. Given his organizational skills, Vajpayee became the national president of the Bharatiya Jana Sangh (BJS)in 1968. Since he was prominent in national politics at that time, he was arrested by Indira Gandhi's government during the Emergency and put in jail along with a number of well-known Opposition leaders from 1975 to 1977.

Following the Emergency, the Janata Party came to power in 1977 with Morarji Desai as PM. Vajpayee joined Desai's government as the foreign minister. Earlier, Vajpayee was often a member of the all-party delegation of MPs that visited New York annually to attend UN General Assembly meetings. Vajpayee was therefore well informed about foreign affairs by the time he took over the external affairs portfolio. Vajpayee's principal achievement during the short tenure of the Janata Party government was his visit to China in February 1979. This was the first high-level visit to China since the 1962 war. While Vajpayee was in Hangzhou, the Chinese attacked Vietnam, and Vajpayee cut short his visit and returned to India. Although Vajpayee's visit to China ended abruptly, it served to facilitate a return visit by Huang Hua (Chinese FM) to Delhi in 1981. These exchanges created the favourable atmosphere for Rajiv Gandhi's visit to China in 1988. Vajpayee continued border talks with China during his tenure as PM which had been institutionalized by PM Narasimha Rao.

In 1977, the BJS contested under the combined banner of the Janata Party, including Janata Dal, Congress (O) and others. The BJS separated from other Janata Party constituents in the 1980 general elections and won only thirteen seats in the Lok Sabha that year under the new name of Bharatiya Janata Party (BJP). In 1984, at the height of Congress party strength in the Lok Sabha, the BJP was down to just two seats. Vajpayee was the acceptable public face of BJP leadership, and this enabled it to steadily increase its share of seats from eighty-five in 1989 to 120 in 1991, and 161 in 1996. In May 1996, a Vajpayee-led coalition government was formed, but it lasted for just thirteen days. Thereafter, Deve Gowda and later I.K. Gujral were PMs of two short-lived coalitions.

The BJP's efforts, combined with those of its National Democratic Alliance (NDA) partners, finally brought this coalition to power for an extended period after the 1998 general elections. Vajpayee was sworn in as PM on 19 March 1998 at age seventy-four. The NDA's coalition partners included the Shiv Sena from Maharashtra, Telugu Desam Party from Andhra Pradesh and Akali Dal from Punjab. Vajpayee's NDA government fell in April 1999 after losing a no-confidence motion by just one vote because Jayalalithaa's AIADMK party withdrew support. Fresh elections were held in October 1999, and the next NDA coalition government with Vajpayee at its head lasted a full term till the general elections of May 2004.

One of the significant strategic achievements of Vajpayee's government was that India became a declared nuclear weapon power after it tested nuclear devices in May 1998, within a few months of his assuming the office of PM. By comparison, Indira Gandhi was ambivalent about the purpose of the 1974 test, calling it peaceful, and she did not authorize further testing even after she came back to power in 1980.

In the 1980s, the public posture of first Indira Gandhi and then Rajiv Gandhi was that India's first preference was to seek international consensus on nuclear disarmament. It is in this context of drift about India's nuclear weapons policies that General K. Sundarji, chief of army staff of the Indian Army from 1986 to 1988, made the following scathing comment, '. . . between the mid-Seventies and mid-Eighties India's (nuclear) decision making . . . appears to have enjoyed something between a drugged sleep and post-prandial siesta . . . the really big secret is that India has no coherent nuclear weapon policy and worse still, she does not even have an institutionalized system for analyzing and throwing up policy options in this regard.'[3]

In 1989, Rajiv Gandhi had finally given the signal to the scientific community that they could go ahead with plans for testing nuclear weapons. Though P.V. Narasimha Rao was preoccupied with domestic economic and political issues, he provided the required support to the scientists and engineers who were preparing for further testing of nuclear devices. It is rumoured that Rao almost gave the go-ahead for testing in 1995 but backed down in the face of US pressure.[4] In the two subsequent short-lived governments of Deve Gowda and I.K. Gujral, Mulayam Singh Yadav was the defence minister. Despite Yadav's bravado about how he was ready to authorize testing, these two governments did not have the coherence or appetite to bite the nuclear bullet.

The developed countries were sharply negative about India's first nuclear test in 1974. Immediately thereafter, the Western countries led by the US set up the London Club, which later became the NSG, to deny India access to nuclear technology, fuel and equipment. Consequently, it must have been abundantly clear to Vajpayee that the West could react to further nuclear testing by India with economic sanctions, including imposing a moratorium on loans to India from multilateral institutions such as the World Bank. In 1998 the Indian economy was much more dependent than in 2019 on below market cost and long maturity loans from multilateral development banks.

At the same time, India was not a signatory to the nuclear NPT of 1968. Further, India had consistently maintained that this treaty is discriminatory since it allows the declared five nuclear weapon powers to retain such weapons while ignoring the security concerns of non-signatory countries. Almost immediately after Vajpayee took charge as PM in March 1998, Vajpayee and Principal Secretary Brajesh Mishra were briefed about the country's preparedness to test nuclear weapons by the relevant experts. It was reasonably certain that the USA and other nuclear weapon powers including China and

Russia would react adversely to India going ahead with the tests. Nevertheless, three successful nuclear tests were conducted on 11 May 1998—one fission, another fusion and one low yield. Two low-yield tests were again conducted on 13 May 1998. The Vajpayee government was able to conduct these tests within two months of coming to power, indicating that the scientific community was ready and waiting for the political green signal.

The US was caught unawares, and President Bill Clinton was reported to have learnt about the first test from the media. Irrespective of the arguments for and against nuclear weapons, it was quite an achievement for the fledgling Vajpayee government to have kept the final decision and preparations for these tests secret from prying foreign eyes. India explained its decision to test on the grounds of national security.

Vajpayee set up the first National Security Advisory Board with defence expert K. Subrahmanyam as the convener. This group developed the doctrine of no first use of nuclear weapons, and the Indian government announced that it would abjure first use in any future conflict. India's nuclear weapons would act only as a deterrent, and if deterrence against a nuclear attack failed, these weapons would be used for a retaliatory strike. This was another example of a holier than thou sentiment which tends to creep into India's foreign and security policy pronouncements. To date, the US and Russia have not relinquished the first-use option. Vajpayee need not have announced no first use of nuclear weapons, and it was up to subsequent Indian governments to revise this position.

In situations of extremely tense relations with any country which is actively pursuing, say, a policy of 'a thousand cuts' to hold India back, it could be useful to leave the adversary guessing at what point India would use nuclear weapons. Clearly, it has to be an existential threat for India to use nuclear weapons first since the 'enemy' would counter-attack with nuclear weapons. In practice, India could follow the principle of no first use yet not affirm that it is India's inflexible position, no matter what the threat or provocation.

Pakistan conducted its nuclear weapon tests within a fortnight on 28 and 30 May 1998. Clearly, they were well prepared too and waiting for an appropriate moment. The subsequent commentary in some Indian and foreign quarters was that India had gained little since Pakistan had now overtly demonstrated that it had nuclear weapons, which neutralized India's conventional superiority. But by the same logic, India had demonstrated that it had a force equalizer vis-à-vis China.

The larger the number of countries which possess nuclear weapons, the higher the risk that nuclear weapons may be used intentionally or through human error. However, the responsibility for nuclear proliferation rests with the five declared nuclear weapon powers which are also the five permanent members of the UNSC. Although the NPT enjoins them to move towards nuclear disarmament, there has been no perceptible movement towards this desirable goal on their part. This is also because in a world full of mutual suspicion, it is currently impossible to set up transparent mechanisms to verify universal nuclear disarmament.

The US and other developed nations, particularly Australia and Ireland, criticized India's nuclear tests sharply. Bilateral aid from developed countries to India had already shrunk to small numbers by 1998, and ongoing discussions on future aid froze. The US, using its largest shareholder status in the World Bank, pushed through a board decision for this multilateral bank to not make any fresh loans to India except for 'humanitarian' purposes. According to the Articles of Agreement of the World Bank, political issues cannot determine any of its lending decisions. India's nuclear weapons tests were driven by political-strategic considerations, and hence should not have influenced the World Bank's lending decisions. It was not a surprise for the Indian government that the US used its status as founder and dominant shareholder to wilfully violate the principles on which the World Bank was set up.

Pakistan and India, two undeclared nuclear weapon powers in South Asia, became known nuclear weapon powers. Did this enhance or reduce India's security? This is not a question that can be answered only in the context of India–Pakistan relations. In Vajpayee's letter to the US President, the threat from a militarily powerful China was cited as one of the reasons for India going nuclear.

India's policies about deployment of nuclear weapons took some time to think through after the May 1998 tests. India's nuclear doctrine was that it would aim at acquiring the capability to launch nuclear weapons from land, air and sea. The sea-based platform included nuclear-powered submarines carrying nuclear-tipped ballistic missiles, namely SSBN (ship, submersible, ballistic, nuclear) capability. These submarines can be underwater for months at a time. Out of the public eye, Vajpayee's government worked on setting up nuclear weapons command and control structures.[5]

Rapprochement with the US and Others

The US took the lead to isolate and punish India after the nuclear tests. The first three paragraphs of the UNSC resolution 1172, which was unanimously adopted on 8 June 1998 were worded as follows:

The Security Council this morning condemned the nuclear tests conducted by India and by Pakistan in May, demanded that those countries refrain from further nuclear tests and urged them to become parties to the Treaty on the Non-Proliferation of Nuclear Weapons (NPT) and to the Comprehensive Nuclear-Test-Ban Treaty (CTBT) without delay and without conditions.

Endorsing the Joint Communique issued by the Foreign Ministers of China, France, Russian Federation, the United Kingdom and the United States at their meeting in Geneva on 4 June, the Council, by adopting unanimously resolution 1172 (1998), expressed its firm conviction that the international regime on the non-proliferation of nuclear weapons should be maintained and consolidated. It recalled that in accordance with the NPT India and Pakistan cannot have the status of a nuclear-weapon State.

Expressing grave concern at the negative effect of those nuclear tests on peace and stability in South Asia and beyond, the Council urged India and Pakistan to exercise maximum restraint and to avoid threatening military movements. They were also urged to resume their dialogue on all outstanding issues, particularly on all matters pertaining to peace and security, in order to remove the tensions between them. They were encouraged to find mutually acceptable solutions that address the root causes of those tensions, including Kashmir.

Boris Yeltsin was the Russian President at that point of time. Russia, and earlier the Soviet Union, had sided with the other four members of the UNSC on matters related to nuclear proliferation. Hence it was no surprise that Russia did not veto this UNSC resolution number 1172. However, the hyphenation with Pakistan and reference to Kashmir was unwelcome and disturbing.

Vajpayee sent a small delegation led by Brajesh Mishra[6] including Rakesh Sood[7] to Moscow in June 1998 to reason with the Russians. The two-member team was joined by Ronen Sen, the Indian ambassador to Russia. The atmosphere at the meeting with Yevgeny Primakov, the Russian foreign minister and later prime minister, was icy even though it was summer in Moscow. Primakov was frank which is 'diplomatese' for rude. After listening to Mishra explain the compulsions that had led to India's decision, Primakov brushed all of that aside and remarked bluntly that India had achieved nothing by carrying out the tests. Mishra was taken aback and asked what Russia wanted India to do at that stage. Primakov responded that they expected India to sign the NPT. India has consistently maintained since the NPT came into force in March 1970 that it was discriminatory and India could not be a signatory. Given India's long and well-known opposition to the NPT, Mishra was puzzled and asked Primakov how exactly India could sign the treaty now. Primakov pulled out a pen and signed on a piece of paper with a flourish and said 'like this'. Mishra got up abruptly and led the Indian side out of Primakov's office, remarking as he left that he had taken too much of Foreign Minister Primakov's valuable time.

Since it was clear that Russia was not going to be of any help to reduce India's isolation, Vajpayee entrusted the task of starting a dialogue with the then unchallenged superpower US to Jaswant Singh. Singh was first appointed deputy chairman of the Planning Commission and later minister for external affairs. Jaswant Singh enjoyed a relationship of trust with Vajpayee and thus engaged with confidence with Strobe Talbott,[8] the US deputy secretary of state, over many rounds of talks. These discussions were crucial to the two governments' understanding of each other's concerns.

Following Pakistan's armed incursion in Kargil in June 1999, the US had delivered a stern message to that country. This did not go unnoticed in Delhi. Unlike Indira Gandhi's left-leaning posture, Vajpayee's government did not have any such background to overcome with the US. Given the security preoccupations about China and Pakistan, and that the US was the pre-eminent economic and military power at that time, India needed to mend fences with the US.

The official US position moved gradually, and finally accepted the fait accompli of nuclear India and Pakistan. The lesson, if there was one, was that India should have declared itself a nuclear weapon power after its test of 1974, instead of waiting for twenty-four years till 1998. Of course, in 1974 India's economic situation was far more fragile and dependent on bilateral and multilateral hard currency loans and grants. However, this was due to the short-sighted, populist economic policies of Indira Gandhi and crowd-pleasing anti-West postures. A cautious approach to Western sensitivities and gradual opening up of the economy would probably have precluded sustained Western economic sanctions if India had declared itself a nuclear weapon power in 1974. A first-past-the-post approach may have also shut the nuclear door in Pakistan's face. The fact is that Indira Gandhi was too busy countering the challenges posed by the agitation led by Jayaprakash Narayan; she chose to allow her personal political priorities to distract her from declaring India a nuclear weapon power. Of course, it would have been a slow and difficult grind out of the isolation India would have faced, and the USSR too may have withheld military technology and spares. Well, all things considered, this was one of the important inflection points in India's nuclear and strategic history.

Pakistan

Given Vajpayee's long-standing interest in foreign affairs, he retained this portfolio when he became PM in March 1998, and his government pushed hard for better relations with Pakistan from the time it took office. As a result of Vajpayee's efforts, on 23 September 1998 the two governments agreed to resolve bilateral differences through negotiations. By the end of 1998, the two countries had agreed to start a bus service between Delhi and Lahore via the border check post at Wagah. It was officially announced that the first such bus would reach Lahore on 21 February 1999. Vajpayee's schedule included a function in Amritsar on 19 February. On learning that Vajpayee was to visit Amritsar just two days prior to the bus arriving in Lahore, Nawaz Sharif was reported to have said to Vajpayee that since he 'was coming to his doorstep he could not let him go back without visiting his home in Lahore'.

Vajpayee accepted the invitation and was accompanied by a large Indian delegation which included business leaders, Kuldip Nayar, Dev Anand, Mallika Sarabhai, Javed Akhtar, Kapil Dev, Satish Gujral and Shatrughan Sinha. Nawaz Sharif received Vajpayee and his delegation at the Wagah border with an open display of warmth. Subsequently, Vajpayee spoke at a public function, and his message of peace and a desire for a fresh start is recalled by many as having touched their hearts.[9]

Officials on both sides worked overtime to put a bilateral agreement together which came to be known as the Lahore Declaration. The two leaders signed this joint declaration on 21 February 1999. A memorandum of understanding pertaining to confidence-building measures (CBMs) on nuclear and conventional weapons was signed by the two foreign secretaries. The joint declaration included precautions for the two sides to not use nuclear weapons against each other accidentally.[10] There was a televised news conference which was relayed in both countries, and the atmosphere of warmth augured well for the future.

Since 1989, no Indian PM had visited Pakistan, and Vajpayee appeared to have broken fresh ground. Narasimha Rao had tried to mend relations with Pakistan. However, right through Rao's term from 1991 to 1996 Pakistan was fomenting trouble in Kashmir, believing that the time was ripe to help separatist elements in that state. If Pakistan had not been perceived to be actively fomenting terrorism in Kashmir, Rao may have visited Pakistan.

A negative element during Vajpayee's visit to Lahore was the attitude of the top brass of the Pakistani armed forces. The Pakistani chief of army staff General Pervez Musharraf and the Pakistani air and naval chiefs P.Q. Mehdi and Fasih Bokhari were not present at some important functions at this summit. It was evident that the Pakistani military leadership was not on the same page as Prime Minister Nawaz Sharif. The inimical intentions of the Pakistani military leadership became evident just three months later in May 1999 when the Pakistani Army moved across the LoC into Kargil in Kashmir.

The two-month Kargil conflict claimed the lives of hundreds of soldiers on both sides.

Five months later, in October 1999, army chief Pervez Musharraf seized control of Pakistan's government, deposing Nawaz Sharif, and he was formally declared President on 20 June 2001. The Western nations ignored yet another overthrow of an elected leader in Pakistan by an army general. Strobe Talbott of the US was in regular touch with Jaswant Singh, then Indian foreign minister, and this contributed to the Clinton administration's attitude of mild, even hypocritical, censure towards Pakistan in the last three months of 1999. The US was more concerned that Musharraf should not execute Nawaz Sharif on the lines of Zia-ul-Haq having Zulfikar Ali Bhutto hanged in 1978.[11] By January 2000, a Republican administration with George Bush Jr as President and Dick Cheney as vice-president took over in the US, and Pakistan's instigation of the Kargil conflict was downplayed.

On 24 December 1999, Indian Airlines flight 814 with 176 passengers and fifteen crew was hijacked by five masked gunmen while it was flying from Kathmandu to Delhi. The aircraft was first made to land in Amritsar to refuel and stood on the tarmac for as long as forty-five minutes. The terrorists on board the aircraft indicated that they would kill all passengers and crew members if Indian security forces tried to board the aircraft. Indian counterterrorist agencies did not act in time, and the aircraft left without refuelling. The hijacked plane next landed in Lahore, was refuelled there and flew on to Dubai. In Dubai, the hijackers released twenty-eight passengers, and among them was one who had been stabbed and had succumbed to his injuries.[12]

India first sought the help of the Pakistani and then UAE authorities while the aircraft was on the ground in Lahore and subsequently in Dubai but were refused permission to access the aircraft. The aircraft finally landed in Kandahar, Afghanistan, which was under the control of the Taliban. India had no diplomatic relations with the Taliban regime, and the Indian Embassy had been shut down in September 1996 when the Taliban reached the outskirts of Kabul. In exchange for the hostages, the terrorists demanded the release from Srinagar jail of: (i) Maulana Masood Azhar (who later founded the terrorist group Jaish-e-Mohammed); (ii) Mushtaq Ahmed Zargar (militant belonging to the Jammu Kashmir Liberation Front [JKLF]); and (iii) Ahmed Omar Saeed Sheikh (linked to several Islamic terrorist organizations such as Jaish-e-Mohammed, Al-Qaeda, Harkat-ul-Mujahideen and the Taliban). The three extremists whose release was sought were flown to Kandahar by the Indian government, and Jaswant Singh was in that flight along with senior Indian foreign office and intelligence officials. The same plane brought back the remaining hostages to Delhi on 31 December 1999.

Vajpayee's government was perceived in several quarters as weak-kneed because it surrendered to the demands of the terrorists. The counter to that accusation was that, of the hostages, only one person was killed and the others came back to India safely. However, the three who were released from jail in Srinagar were later involved in the attack on the Indian Parliament in December 2001, the killing of the US journalist Daniel Pearl in Pakistan in 2002, and probably the terrorist attack on Mumbai in November 2008 as well. The subsequent cost in lives lost was higher due to this decision, but at the time this hostage dilemma took place that was difficult to anticipate.

Indian governments have to pick their way carefully through a range of domestic and international media pressures to engage or break with Pakistan. At times, Indian media's prima donnas try to get directly involved in making foreign policy. They engage in ostensibly secret confabulations with senior Indian ministers and the Pakistani High Commission in Delhi to mediate an understanding on Kashmir. The Western media, on its part, often unhelpfully points to Kashmir as a potential nuclear flashpoint, and does not have the time to educate itself about the long and difficult history of this Indian state. The BJP-led NDA government of A.B. Vajpayee did manage with a combination of firmness and discussion to keep hope and optimism up in those quarters in Kashmir who view the relationship with the rest of India with a measure of realism and hope. Vajpayee's call for '*Insaniyat, Kashmiriyat and Jamhooriyat*' (humanity, Kashmiri-ness and democracy) was welcomed by a broad spectrum of political opinion in Kashmir.[13]

Despite Musharraf's role in the Kargil conflict which took place soon after Vajpayee had visited Pakistan in 1999, Vajpayee suspended disbelief to meet President Musharraf in New Delhi in July 2001. Vajpayee spoke of conciliation, and wisely called for the views of all peace-loving Kashmiris to be taken into account. However, as could have been anticipated, the talks broke down after Musharraf gave a hard-hitting press conference in Agra.

CNN reported on 17 July 2001 that 'Musharraf again and again held forth on his favourite theme—Kashmir—squarely blaming the Indians for their intransigence on the issue'.[14] Of course, there were hardliners in the Indian foreign office as well, and the then home minister L.K. Advani was reported to be sceptical about Pakistani assurances. In press and other interactions after he was out of power, Musharraf has blamed 'hardliners' on the Indian side for sabotaging the talks. This is not credible coming from a general who was responsible for the hostilities in Kargil, and that too just a few months after Vajpayee had visited Lahore.

A couple of months later, on 13 December 2001,[15] extremists entered the compound of the Indian Parliament in Delhi. The five terrorists, allegedly belonging to Lashkar-e-Taiba (LeT) and Jaish-e-Mohammed (JeM), were shot dead by Indian security forces. In the crossfire, eight Indian security personnel and a gardener were also killed. Two months earlier, on 1 October 2001, in a similar incident, about thirty-one persons had lost their lives in a terrorist attack on the state assembly in Srinagar, Kashmir.[16]

Vajpayee's government was under pressure from several quarters, including Opposition political parties, for not taking pre-emptive action to prevent these recurring acts of terror against the Indian state. The finger of suspicion for high-profile acts of terrorism, including the hijacking of the Indian Airlines plane and the attack on the Indian Parliament, pointed to elements in Pakistan. In retaliation, the Indian government mounted the ill-advised Operation Parakram to mass half a million Indian troops along the LoC with Pakistan from December 2001 to June 2002. There were reports that India was also considering strikes against training camps for extremists in Pakistan.

Vajpayee should have known better than to have allowed the ferrying of such a large number of Indian troops to the border with Pakistan. Nothing was achieved except that the government had to pick up a big fat bill. Vajpayee could have explained to everyone with his customary flair that mindless muscle flexing would achieve little for Indian security. It was clear to all thinking people that when two neighbouring countries possess nuclear weapons, conventional military build-ups are counterproductive.

The US decided to categorize JeM and LeT as terrorist organizations, and Musharraf too described the attack against the Indian Parliament as an act of terrorism. US public opinion was highly inflamed about Islamic extremism following the 11 September 2001 terrorist attacks on the World Trade Center in New York and the Pentagon in Washington DC. For the last few years of Musharraf's tenure, even though he was probably the principal force behind Pakistan's misadventure in Kargil, there was less shelling on the border and there were signs of reduced Pakistani encouragement of extremist violence in Kashmir. Unfortunately, some constituencies in Pakistan's army and intelligence circles continue to hope that if India were to be racked by terrorist violence, it may be pushed into giving up Kashmir. The hard-boiled in Pakistan's 'deep state' need fellow Pakistanis to perceive India as an existential threat to justify high military expenditures.

Vajpayee, as a perennial seeker of consensus and accommodation with Pakistan, visited that country again in 2004. It is not clear why Vajpayee continued to hope for a significant breakthrough in Pakistan's attitude on issues related to Kashmir or towards India even after the two grievous experiences of 1999 and 2001. It is logical for India to persist with discussions at the level of officials and through unofficial channels to keep jingoistic elements on both sides in check. However, interactions at the level of heads of government need to be preceded by sufficient groundwork for lasting agreements to be reached. The reality was and is that there is no option but to wait for at least a few more decades or even more to pass so that memories of past conflicts fade with the passage of time. In the interim, the best that India can do is to ring-fence contentious issues, and prevent or at least significantly reduce border conflicts with Pakistan and violence in Kashmir.

Afghanistan

Vajpayee's government was able to reopen the Indian Embassy in Kabul after the US-led forces had driven the Taliban regime leaders Mullah Omar and Osama bin Laden into hiding by about mid-November 2001. India contributed human resources and funding to help build roads and subsequently over several years the local parliament building. These gestures of support from India were welcomed by most ethnic and political groups in Afghanistan. During the Taliban years extremist elements in Afghanistan had supported the infiltration of terrorist elements into Kashmir.

Afghanistan continues to be riven even in 2019 with competing jealousies across rival clans and the machinations of great powers.[17] Vajpayee and his successors have been careful not to be identified with any one faction and to be seen as helping to improve living conditions across all communities in that war-ravaged country.

Iraq and Weapons of Mass Destruction (WMDs)

The consensus in India was that the bombing of Iraq, which started in March 2003 without UN approval, was unjustified. Further, there was no tangible evidence that Iraq had any so-called weapons of mass destruction. Later in the same year, the US wanted India to send troops to Iraq, and given US pre-eminence at that time, this request could not be rejected offhand. As per whispers in South Block, when Vajpayee was pushed hard from within the BJP to agree to the US request, he asked the following question: Will Indian troops retaliate with deadly force when they are sniped at by poorly armed Iraqis who are against US occupation? This question is said to have silenced the supporters of Indian armed involvement in Iraq.

Over a decade later in July 2016, John Chilcot's report[18] titled 'The Iraq Inquiry' stated that Tony Blair's government had exaggerated the threat from

Saddam Hussein, and any plans that the UK had for the aftermath of the war were 'wholly inadequate'. Vajpayee was thus prescient; he was able to pull off the balancing act of not rushing Indian troops to Iraq without antagonizing the US.

Revival of Economic Reforms

Improvements in Macro Indicators

The Vajpayee government had inherited a difficult fiscal situation from the shaky, short-lived coalition governments of Deve Gowda and I.K. Gujral. The gross fiscal deficit as a fraction of GDP was gradually brought down from 6.3 per cent to 4.3 per cent over the six years that Vajpayee was PM. The net primary deficit also decreased, and gross capital formation went up from 23.5 per cent in 1998–99 to 26.1 per cent in 2003–04. To the extent that fiscal deficits were reduced, government freed up capital for private investment.

Table 9.1 in the Appendices indicates that GDP growth rates were initially up and then down for the three years between 2000 and 2003. It is only in 2003–04 that growth rose to almost 8 per cent in Vajpayee's last year in office. Consumer price inflation was tamed significantly and went down from 11 per cent at the start to 3.9 per cent at the end of his term. The higher growth would have enhanced employment opportunities, and lower inflation provided a measure of relief to the poor. The exchange rate was allowed to depreciate gradually, and exports were actively promoted which went up from 8 per cent of GDP in 1998–99 to about 12 per cent by 2003–04. The current account deficits in the first two years of Vajpayee's term changed to surpluses in the last three years, and this number was a positive 2.3 per cent of GDP in 2003–04. Coupled with portfolio capital inflows, this resulted in foreign exchange reserves going up sharply to almost 19 per cent of GDP by 2003–04.

Vajpayee's government passed the Fiscal Responsibility and Budget Management (FRBM) Act in August 2003. Under this Act, legally mandated fiscal deficit targets and ceilings were established for the first time. The FRBM Act also prohibited the RBI from purchasing government debt securities in the primary market. The objectives included elimination of revenue deficits and bringing overall fiscal deficit down to 3 per cent of GDP by 2008.[19] Through the six years that Vajpayee's government was in power, it had to overcome the consequences of the lower risk appetite among developed country investors following the 1998–99 Asian financial crisis.[20]

The relatively low number of personal income tax returns filed has been a matter of concern for successive Indian governments. To enable better direct tax compliance and bring greater transparency and ease in filing of tax returns, the Ministry of Finance set up a task force on direct taxes chaired by former finance secretary Vijay Kelkar. Dr Kelkar's task force submitted its report in December 2002, and its recommendations led to enhanced use of individual specific PAN cards and easier filing of tax returns online.[21]

Financial Sector Reforms, World Bank Loans, Scams and Appointments Made by MoF

A number of far-reaching financial-sector reforms were implemented during the Vajpayee years. The banking sector was plagued with cases of default which were languishing in the BIFR or in courts for decades. After considerable discussion and examination within government, the Securitisation and Reconstruction of Financial Assets and Enforcement of Securities Interest (SARFAESI) Act was approved by Parliament in 2002. This Act provides for the setting up of Debt Recovery Tribunals (DRTs). However, over time, defaulting borrowers were again able to postpone accountability by clogging DRTs and courts with numerous cases.

In the late 1990s, the Indian insurance sector's life, accident and old-age-related coverage was limited to a small fraction of the population compared to even moderately developed countries.[22] Vajpayee's government took the initiative to open up the sector to domestic private entities and to foreign investment. The NDA government's initial proposal was for foreign investors to own up to 74 per cent of equity in Indian insurance companies. That proposal was vehemently opposed in Parliament as a sell-out, and it was finally decided that foreign investors could hold up to 26 per cent. The Insurance Regulatory and Development Authority (IRDA) was set up in 1999 and the Pension Fund Regulatory and Development Authority (PFRDA) in 2003. In the decade after Vajpayee left office in 2004, the coverage of the insurance sub-sector has grown, and now offers a richer menu of options to policyholders.

Separately, the then finance minister Yashwant Sinha brought in a fuller version of a value added tax, and in 1999 it was called central value added tax (CENVAT). This was another step forward in the long journey since the 1970s to rationalize indirect taxes. The following year, in 2000, the Vajpayee government started discussions with state governments on this topic. This gradually led to the adoption of VAT by several states for their sales taxes.

In 2004, towards the end of Vajpayee's tenure, Dr Vijay Kelkar proposed a comprehensive Goods and Services Tax (GST) for the entire country.[23]

Since Independence, India has taken substantial loans from multilateral institutions, such as the World Bank (IBRD). The importance of these long-maturity hard currency borrowings has diminished with time as the size of the Indian economy has grown and so have foreign trade and direct and portfolio investments. Prior to the mid-1990s, all IBRD loans were offered as currency pool loans (CPLs).[24] India's foreign exchange earnings from its exports were and are principally denominated in US $—the globally dominant reserve currency.[25]

Thus, there was a significant currency mismatch between India's reserves and the CPLs from the IBRD and SDR-denominated IDA loans. This was a huge disadvantage for India since the yen, Deutschmark and Swiss franc components of CPLs and IDA loans increased in US $ terms as these currencies steadily appreciated against the dollar. For India the principal amounts due on CPL loans kept increasing in US $ terms, and that was the currency in which India's exports and other hard currency inflows were and are invariably invoiced. The Ministry of Finance and the RBI needed to coordinate their efforts to hedge against currency risk by contracting currency swaps out of the non-US $ debt components of the CPLs.

For the same reasons of sharp, hard currency appreciation against the rupee, India needed to better manage its Japanese yen official development assistance (ODA) loans. The benefit from low yen interest rates was overwhelmed by the appreciation of the yen. Prepayment of such loans in the early 2000s and replacing these even with loans from commercial sources would have resulted in considerable savings.

Following the nuclear weapons tests of May 1998, there was concern within government circles in India that there might be a shortage of foreign exchange going forward. This was because Western donor governments and multilateral banks such as the World Bank and Asian Development Bank were reluctant to provide fresh loans except for so-called humanitarian purposes. Consequently, in 1998 the Indian government raised US $4.8 billion through Resurgent India Bonds (RIBs) marketed to NRIs at higher interest rates than those offered on government bonds of developed countries. The same stratagem was adopted to raise US $5.5 billion in 2000. The second time the bonds were called India Millennium Deposits (IMDs), to overcome any shortage in foreign exchange inflows because of the so-called Year 2000 problem for systems to migrate to the new millennium. These hard currency bond issues were prudent anticipatory steps to avoid a situation similar to what India went through during the balance of payments crisis of 1990–91.

During the Vajpayee years there were substantial reforms in India's capital markets.[26] Badla had been reintroduced in the second half of the 1990s. The stockbrokers in Mumbai were strongly in favour of continuing with the non-transparent practices of badla. However, they could not logically oppose the proposal to introduce derivatives,[27] namely futures and options, since these instruments can provide the same elements of speculation as badla but without counterparty credit risk. This is because these two forms of derivatives are traded on stock exchanges, effectively ensuring that contracts are honoured.

At that time, I was working in the Ministry of Finance and pushed for an amendment of the Securities Contracts (Regulation) Act (SCRA) 1956. The proposal was to expand the definition of securities in the SCRA to include derivatives. The CCEA gave the go-ahead for this change after the secretary (economic affairs) and the finance minister (FM)[28] approved the proposal.

During those years, Dr Vijay Kelkar and then Dr E.A.S. Sarma in that sequence held the charge of finance secretary/secretary, economic affairs. It was a privilege to report to them. I was also fortunate that in my years in the MoF, first Dr Shankar Acharya and then Dr Rakesh Mohan were CEA. The persons named above were highly knowledgeable in their respective areas of specialization and men of unimpeachable integrity. Several Indians who have excelled in the private sector, academia, the medical profession or other areas of work have a tendency to generalize and tar those who work in government as financially corrupt or incompetent. While this may be true of some, I can assert without any hesitation that the professionals named above were among the best examples of sound judgement and probity.

Reverting to the day the amendment was to be approved by Parliament, I received a call that I should rush to FM Sinha's office. When I reached there, he asked me to explain what derivatives were and exactly what had led to the collapse of Barings in 1995. Nick Leeson had bankrupted the venerable British bank by taking highly leveraged and unhedged positions in derivative transactions. I explained the errant conduct of Leeson and the refusal of Barings senior management to rein in this rogue trader. Since Leeson had initially recorded large profits, the bank allowed him to trade and also do the settlement of his own trades, contrary to established practice. As I was warming up to get into further details, the FM put up a hand to tell me to stop. He smiled and said that he did not need to know as much about derivatives as me, and he was convinced that he now already knew more than any other MP.

Badla was banned and the amendment to the SCRA was passed, and futures and later options were introduced on Indian stock exchanges by 2002. The NSE was quick off the block to corner overwhelming fractions in the markets of these new instruments. The introduction of derivatives trading overcoming the resistance of badla operatives was another feather in the cap of the MoF led by Yashwant Sinha and the government headed by Vajpayee. Another major stock market reform, namely the separation of ownership of Indian stock exchanges from broking services through demutualization was also effected by 2002.

In 1999 pensions were under the purview of the Ministry of Labour as the Employees' Provident Fund Organization (EPFO) fell under its administrative jurisdiction. I put up a note to then secretary (economic affairs) Dr E.A.S. Sarma suggesting that pensions should logically be dealt with by the MoF since decisions related to pensions of government personnel had implications for government's finances. After MoF took on this responsibility, Dr Sarma remarked with a laugh that no good idea goes without being punished, and 'pension reforms' was added to my charge. Thus began the struggle to convert government pensions from a fully defined pay-as-you-go benefit system to defined contributions.

If benefits are defined, pensioners receive retirement benefits which are known in advance. The norm at that time for government pensioners was 50 per cent of last pay drawn with periodic revisions for increases in the cost of living. By contrast, for pensions based on defined contributions, each month a government or parastatal employee puts in a specific proportion of his/her pay into a fund that is topped up by the government or public-sector employer up to a prescribed proportion of the salary of the employee. These contributions can then be invested in schemes pre-approved by the regulatory authority concerned in government bonds, other AAA-rated debt securities or stocks, depending on the risk appetite of the employee. Over thirty to forty years, which is usually the longest possible period of employment in government, such defined contribution investments in government debt plus other debt and equity market securities should result in annuities for retiring employees which would be higher than 50 per cent of last pay drawn. Vajpayee's government has to be credited for starting this process of reforms in government pensions.

On 1 November 2000, Dr E.A.S. Sarma, the secretary (economic affairs), was informed that he had been moved from the Ministry of Finance to the Ministry of Coal. Dr Sarma had done only about a year in the department of economic affairs. When I met Dr Sarma on 2 November, he said that he had been moved five times in the last few years, and this latest transfer out of the MoF was the last straw for him. It is because our political leadership finds it difficult to accommodate upright and qualified officers such as Dr Sarma that projects in the infrastructure space or in human resource development involving long gestation periods do not get implemented honestly. Vajpayee's government was not fair to Dr Sarma.

In 1999 the SEBI Act prescribed a minuscule amount of a few thousand rupees as penalty for market transgressions. Such a low penalty was no deterrent for brokers and others engaging in fraudulent transactions in Indian capital markets. Consequently, I obtained approval of the FM to amend the SEBI Act to raise the penalty to at least three times the profits the guilty were estimated to have made. The Ministry of Finance also proposed to the Cabinet Committee on Economic Affairs (CCEA) that government should not follow the Appointments Committee of the Cabinet (ACC) approach to select the SEBI chairman, and that a five-member jury headed by eminent retired or serving professionals from the government, regulatory bodies and the private sector should shortlist three candidates. If for any reason none of these candidates was acceptable to the government, it could ask this group to go back to the drawing board and suggest fresh names. However, government would not come up with new names on its own.

The then secretary (economic affairs) happened to be on tour when this cabinet note came up for discussion in the CCEA, and the FM asked me to attend in his place.

The discussions in the CCEA are still vivid in my memory. Only one minister supported the amendment of the SEBI Act to revise the way future chairpersons for this regulator would be appointed. Another cabinet minister commented that this was a devious way for officials to take away the power that the electorate had given to the political executive to make crucial appointments. Despite a lone minister's exhortation that government should not only do the right thing but also be seen to be doing so, the majority of ministers objected to this proposal. FM Yashwant Sinha gave up when his colleagues would not listen. However, he did so only after challenging his cabinet colleagues to confirm that they had never rung him up to recommend names even for junior positions such as executive directors of public-sector banks.

Unfortunately, Vajpayee seemed to be asleep most of the time through this cabinet meeting. It is likely that he was listening attentively but did not want to intervene. The fact is that this particular part of the amendment to revise the way the chairman of the SEBI would be selected did not go through. It could have been copied for appointments to the heads of other regulatory, investigation and constitutional bodies and PSUs. Nevertheless, I was relieved that CCEA did approve the hiking of fines for fraud.

In the 1990s, external commercial borrowings (ECBs) were rationed out to individual borrowers within an overall annual ceiling. Reliance Industries Limited (RIL) had borrowed over US $1 billion in instalments in the first half of the 1990s, and a substantial portion of the proceeds had not been brought back to India. This violated the provisions of the relevant legislation and MoF rules that governed ECBs. When I joined the MoF, one of the outstanding issues that needed to be resolved was whether the withholding of tax exemption benefit to bond-holders, on interest paid by RIL on its ECBs, should be withdrawn. It was obvious in the Ministry of Finance that a deputy governor in RBI was strongly inclined to excuse RIL and he had proposed that no action be taken except for a reprimand. Finally, in 2001 MoF took the view that RIL had denied other potential borrowers the opportunity to access funding from external commercial sources since there was an annual ceiling on the total volume of ECBs that could be contracted by all borrowers. Consequently, the withholding of tax exemption benefit was withdrawn and RIL was asked to pay this sizeable tax to government.

RIL contested the government's stand, and the case went to court. I was surprised that former finance minister P. Chidambaram and former Chief Justice of India Y.V. Chandrachud represented RIL. It seemed incongruous that, having worked in the public space, they chose to represent a company which was clearly in the wrong. Attorney General Soli Sorabjee represented MoF, and I remember briefing him repeatedly about the details. The government won the case in Delhi High Court.[29]

The finance ministry under Yashwant Sinha took the initiative to propose the setting up of a public debt office independent of RBI. The logic was that both government and the central bank should not be involved in the issuance of government debt or its management. And over time this would help establish a market-based government yield curve. RBI resisted this initiative, and was able to convince the Ministry of Finance that as long as government ran large fiscal deficits, it was not in the interest of the country to set up a separate public debt office. This was a counterproductive argument. One of the ways of making government wary of running large deficits is for interest rates on its debt securities to be based on investor appetite.

Unit Trust of India

The Vajpayee government was compelled to agree to a Joint Parliamentary Committee (JPC) investigation into allegations about wrongdoing in the Unit Trust of India (UTI) in 2001. Set up under a 1964 Act of Parliament, UTI was a public-sector mutual fund whose seed capital came from RBI, LIC and SBI. The heads of major public-sector financial institutions such as the Industrial Development Bank of India (IDBI), LIC, SBI and an RBI deputy governor were on its Board. While the chairman was appointed by the government, the

Ministry of Finance had decided that it was an independent mutual fund to be run by professional asset managers. It appeared though from media reports and questions in Parliament that average investors felt that UTI had some form of government backing. The MoF tried to dispel this notion, and as far back as May 1997, MoF withdrew its only board member from UTI.

After the general elections in 1998, Vajpayee needed the support of Jayalalithaa's AIADMK to form the first NDA coalition government. It was rumoured in North Block that P.S. Subramanyam had to be appointed chairman UTI[30] as this was one of the nine conditions for AIADMK's support. Other deserving candidates, including Dr P.J. Nayak, an IAS officer, an executive director in UTI at that time, and who was a joint secretary in MoF earlier, were passed over.

In 1999–2000, UTI was the market leader by far among Indian mutual funds. It had the largest volume of assets under management and offered several investment schemes targeted at different groups of investors. UTI got into liquidity and near-insolvency problems in the 1990s because it offered assured return schemes while a disproportionately high percentage of its assets were invested in stocks. About 70 per cent of UTI's assets were invested in equity, while its assured return schemes were similar to debt liabilities. This was a classic asset–liability mismatch, and a government-appointed committee headed by Deepak Parekh[31] had recommended that UTI should replace its investments in equity with highly rated debt to achieve a better balance between assets and liabilities.

P.S. Subramanyam procrastinated in moving UTI to a sound financial footing despite being prodded to do so by expert committees and by MoF. It was increasingly evident from end 2000 onwards that Subramanyam had ignored the MoF's suggestions on vital issues of UTI's liquidity and solvency and instead raised peripheral issues in his letters to MoF, e.g., pay increase for UTI staff.

US-64 was UTI's flagship scheme mutual fund, and Subramanyam ignored written suggestions from MoF when the stock market was doing well in mid-2000 to convert US-64 to a net asset value (NAV) basis. The NAV of each US-64 unit was at Rs 17, that is, 70 per cent above the par value of Rs 10 at that time. If UTI had done so, US-64 assets would have marked to market daily, and investors would have known how this scheme was faring. By June 2001, assets under US-64 amounted to about Rs 128 billion. And, Subramanyam continued to keep US-64's asset–liability mismatches secret from unitholders.

On Friday, 29 June 2001, at about 5 p.m., Subramanyam came to my office in the Ministry of Finance without an appointment or prior information.

He informed me that at the UTI board meeting which was going to take place on Monday, 2 July 2001, in Delhi, he was going to recommend that redemption of US-64 units be temporarily stopped or that it be moved to a NAV, which was by then below the par value of Rs 10. I told him that I had no authority to tell him what UTI should do, and also that MoF considered UTI to be a board-driven institution. It was, therefore, to the UTI's board members that he should turn. I did tell him though that my own sense was our stock markets would react adversely to such an announcement. I also requested him to immediately write to Finance Secretary Ajit Kumar with copies to the FM's office and adviser to FM Dr Rakesh Mohan with full details of our discussion.

After Subramanyam left, I went up from my ground-floor room to Finance Secretary Ajit Kumar's room on the first floor and briefed him about Subramanyam's irresponsible proposals. Subramanyam had an explanatory letter delivered to the residences of the finance secretary and adviser to the finance minister two days later on Sunday, 1 July. This letter said that UTI management would propose at the board meeting which was scheduled to take place at noon on 2 July 2001 that UTI felt compelled to stop redemption of US-64 units. Ajit Kumar explained the situation fully to FM Yashwant Sinha by the morning of 2 July 2001.

At about noon on 2 July 2001, the UTI board went ahead with its meeting, and, surprisingly, the board members approved Subramanyam's proposals. Once the news spread that UTI needed to stop redemption of US-64 units, the stock markets took a beating. MoF was concerned about systemic risk and reassured market participants that government would do whatever was required to protect the legitimate interests of investors and maintain market stability.

Going back in time, from June 2000 to June 2001 UTI's board members[32] chose not to insist that UTI urgently implement the Deepak Parekh Committee's recommendations and take cognizance of the multiple communications from MoF to the same effect. Additionally, the UTI board failed to get UTI management to keep financial-sector regulators, SEBI and RBI, informed about the extent of the incomprehensibly high market risks embedded in several of its investment schemes.

The blame game began in earnest by 2 July 2001 evening. Opposition parties found it convenient to pillory the government for not having averted the sense of crisis which understandably gripped US-64 unitholders. The insinuation was that members of one or the other political party in the NDA coalition were secretly in touch with the chairman UTI to further their personal financial interests.

Taking the irresponsible and motivated conduct of Subramanyam into account, MoF decided by 3 July morning that he and another senior UTI manager M.M. Kapoor who was an executive director, had to be immediately relieved of their responsibilities. It helped that Jayalalithaa was no longer part of the NDA coalition. MoF felt that the sacking of Subramanyam needed to be done when markets were shut, and with speed and confidentiality. For this formal approval of the Appointments Committee of the Cabinet (ACC) was required.[33] A cabinet meeting was to be held at the residence of Vajpayee at 7, Race Course Road (now called Lok Kalyan Marg) on 3 July, and both finance minister and home minister (L.K. Advani) were to attend. Ajit Kumar also needed to be present. I requested Ajit Kumar to personally carry the file for Subramanyam's dismissal—in case he chose not to resign—to the FM first, the home minister (HM) next, and finally to Vajpayee for their signatures. This was to prevent any information about the decision to sack Subramanyam leaking to the press. To keep the matter confidential, I wrote the note in my own hand for Ajit Kumar, who obtained the approval of the ACC.

At about 10 p.m. the same evening, Ajit Kumar came to my residence, located off Satya Marg in New Delhi, and handed me the file with the signatures of FM, HM and PM. I called up Subramanyam and told him that he could resign or the government would have no option but to dismiss him. Subramanyam's first reaction was that he could not send a resignation letter since he was at home in Mumbai and his office was closed. I informed him that the office of chairman IDBI had been kept open for him to send a fax to my office. My own office was also kept open without explaining the nature of the emergency. At about 11:30 p.m., I received a fax in my office from Subramanyam saying he was resigning from the post of chairman UTI with immediate effect. Within the next five minutes, I sent back a fax to him stating that the government had accepted his resignation. I called up Ajit Kumar at that late hour to inform him that Subramanyam had chosen to resign.

The next day, 4 July 2001, G. Vassal, the senior-most among UTI's executive directors, became acting chairman of UTI. I have always been surprised when the government procrastinates on personnel decisions related to appointments or dismissals. This particular dismissal demonstrates that if the government takes a firm line, immediate action can be taken against those who game the system.

LIC and SBI were under the jurisdiction of the banking and insurance division within MoF. Inexplicably, the role of the high-powered UTI board in the disappointing and possibly criminal behaviour of some in UTI's senior management was not investigated by MoF. In fact, the LIC chairman, G.N. Bajpai, was appointed chairman SEBI in February 2002. Subsequently, when he visited me in North Block, I asked him bluntly about his role in the UTI board meeting on 2 July 2001. My specific question was why the board did not stop Subramanyam. Bajpai's hesitant reply was that he was under the impression that the MoF had approved this course of action. I asked him whether he had received this information from the finance secretary or from someone else since it was not from me. Bajpai mumbled something to the effect that Subramanyam had led the board members to understand that his proposals had been approved by MoF. Effectively, what Bajpai was saying was that he, as LIC chairman and a UTI board member, did not consider himself competent enough to assess the proposals submitted by UTI management with professional independence. All he needed was a nod from someone he thought was close to political power centres to agree to UTI's proposals, even if they made little financial sense.[34]

At that critical board meeting on 2 July 2001, the members should have asked for some time to consider the matter. If they felt MoF needed to be consulted urgently, they could have done so since they were all in Delhi. Later, when the FM was asked by the media about UTI's decisions, he was reported as having said that he was not aware of the details. This may well have been true, but the FM could have explained that MoF does not get involved in UTI's day-to-day administration. And that, in the first instance, UTI's board members needed to explain why they did not heed MoF's advice for over a year. Unfortunately for FM Yashwant Sinha, the impression after that first press interaction was that MoF did not know what was going on and was asleep at the wheel. Subsequently, Yashwant Sinha was moved to the Ministry of External Affairs, and Mr Jaswant Singh became FM.

Incidentally, on page 214 of Yashwant Sinha's book titled *My Years as Finance Minister*, Penguin-Viking, 2007, he mentions that he did not know if I had informed the then finance secretary Ajit Kumar of my informal conversation with Subramanyam on the evening of 29 June 2001.[35] On the same page of his book, Yashwant Sinha mentions that after his discussion with Finance Secretary Ajit Kumar on the morning of 3 July, he left for a meeting with the prime minister. According to Mr Sinha, he 'was certain that the UTI Board would not accept such an outrageous suggestion [about the US-64 units]'. Mr Sinha adds, 'In retrospect, it appears to me that I committed a mistake by not cancelling my meeting with the Prime Minister and calling an emergency meeting of my officials in order to act before the UTI Board took its final decision.'

Former finance minister Yashwant Sinha is correct in his ex-post assessment that he should have called a meeting of MoF officials and UTI board members. Subramanyam and UTI officials should have been excluded from that meeting. UTI could have been advised to push back the board meeting to a later date at which measures could have been announced to anticipate concern about UTI's financial health.

In the wake of the UTI crisis, a number of meetings took place in MoF chaired by the FM to consider ways of government providing financial support for UTI to meet its obligations to its unitholders. A so-called 'cash-neutral' suggestion was for government to provide UTI with government bonds. UTI would use the government bonds as collateral to raise capital from private sources. Senior officials in MoF who suggested this mechanism reasoned that no fresh cash would need to be allocated, and government would need to 'merely' service the bonds. The obvious question here was that at some point in the future, the government would need to return the principal to bondholders.[36] I made so bold as to suggest in the presence of the FM, RBI governor and others that if cash outflow was government's concern, it could issue zero-coupon bonds, and it would be for future governments to service such bonds. This was to point out the absurdity of this cash-neutral mechanism which the Indian government often tends to turn to in distress situations.

At its root though, the problem was that the government had been imprudent in giving Subramanyam the charge of India's largest mutual fund at that time. This was definitely not one of Vajpayee's better decisions. Over the decades after Nehru and Shastri passed away, India's political leadership has often taken blatantly politically motivated decisions in appointments of heads of public-sector financial institutions and regulatory bodies. Upright officials are then expected to somehow 'manage' the situation so that none of the mud from financial scams sticks to ministers and other political leaders. This has been a growing trend at state government and Central government levels since Indira Gandhi's prime ministership.[37]

Infrastructure—Roads, Electricity, Railways, Telecommunications, and Disinvestment

Vajpayee launched important programmes in the infrastructure sector which were designed and funded innovatively. Transportation infrastructure was given a boost through the National Highway Development Project's (NHDP) work on the Golden Quadrilateral Highway which started in 1999. The objective was to connect the four major Indian cities—Delhi, Kolkata,

Chennai and Mumbai. The underlying rationale, in addition to the benefits of surface connectivity, was to raise economic activity on both sides of the arterial roads. Another major road initiative, the Pradhan Mantri Gram Sadak Yojana (PMGSY or the Prime Minister's Village Roads Project) was launched by the Central government in December 2000.[38] Funding for these projects was raised by levying a fuel cess of Re 1 per litre of petrol/diesel. This road initiative has been continued by successor governments and has raised rural incomes through improved connectivity to sales centres. PMGSY has also led to easier access for villagers to nearby semi-urban areas with better educational and health facilities. See Table 9.2 in the Appendices for PMGSY road length completed since 2000–01

Turning to the power sector, India's consumption of electrical power in per capita terms at 0.9 megawatt-hours[40] in 2016 was very low compared to major economies. The same number for China is 4.3 megawatt-hours, and for the US it is 12.8 megawatt-hours. This is to be expected, given that China and the US have much higher per capita incomes. The numbers illustrate the considerable distance India will eventually have to cover in per capita energy consumption levels to reach those of countries such as China.

The Indian Central and state governments tend to subsidize power consumption for targeted groups depending on their electoral weight. This is natural in India's 'one person, one vote' multiparty democracy. Assured availability of power is not just conditional on adequate power generation but also on a national grid which delivers power in a cost-efficient manner to every corner of the country. These issues have been well-understood within the Indian government and the relevant public sector bodies such as Power Grid Corporation of India for decades.

It is to the Vajpayee government's credit that a systematic review of the power sector was conducted and a new Electricity Act adopted in 2003. Electricity regulation under existing state and Central government legislation was subsumed under this new Act. Prior to this, the power sector was governed by three separate Electricity Acts—of 1910, 1948 and 1998. The State Electricity Boards were responsible for generation, transmission and distribution of power. The new 2003 Act was aimed at separating generation from transmission and distribution, along with arm's-length determination of tariffs. It was well known by the beginning of the twenty-first century that a substantial fraction of what was categorized as transmission losses was actually theft of power. Since power producers were invariably publicly owned, the loses due to theft of power were often ignored or even connived with. Separating production from distribution did not make state-owned power producers more efficient. However, having private companies bid for distribution licences meant that greater care was taken to reduce so-called transmission losses and ensure that consumers paid what was due from them promptly and regularly. Tariffs for power were invariably subsidized heavily and varied depending on consumer category. The rates for power consumption needed to be raised to a cost-plus basis to make power production economically viable, and that again was done to an extent for urban consumers.

Similarly, it was known for long that Indian Railways, the largest public-sector body in the country, needed to be reformed. The accounts of this giant organization do not correctly estimate profits/losses as they do not fully take into account the depreciation of fixed assets. Further, not enough investment has been made to increase track length and to make transportation by rail easier to schedule, safe from theft, and cost-effective compared to road transportation.

Nitish Kumar was the railway minister during 2001–04. During those years, a measure of transparency was brought about when the Rakesh Mohan Committee report on railway reforms was released in August 2001. The report recommended corporatization of Railways, rebalancing of passenger fares, and making accounting in Indian Railways similar to that of any registered company.[41] Although several expert groups were set up subsequently to focus on implementing the Rakesh Mohan Committee recommendations, Vajpayee's government did not move towards corporatizing Indian Railways.[42]

The Vajpayee government made an impressive start in divesting public-sector assets. Even before economic reforms were initiated by Narasimha Rao, past governments had recognized that there would be efficiency gains from government divesting its equity stakes in public-sector companies that are not critically important or central to national security. Despite the many naysayers, Vajpayee's government was able to reduce to minority status, or bring to zero, government equity in several public-sector undertakings including Modern Foods, Bharat Aluminium Company Ltd, Hindustan Zinc, Indian Petrochemicals and Centaur Hotels. The most significant of the government's divestment decisions was to reduce its equity share in Maruti Udyog Ltd.

In May 2002, the government allotted its share in a rights issue to Suzuki, giving this Japanese company majority control. At the same time, the government also sold its existing Maruti shares through a public issue which was underwritten by Suzuki. Gaining of majority holding in the Maruti company encouraged Suzuki to bring in technology and capital, and this has resulted in

Maruti Suzuki becoming the largest car producer in the country today. The disinvestments effected during Vajpayee's tenure were effective privatizations, unlike the variants which have been attempted by successor governments.

By the mid-1990s, the mobile phone revolution was under way in developed countries. Earlier, during Rajiv Gandhi's tenure, the network efficiency of landlines in smaller towns was improved. This process continued through the 1990s, and it became easier to make calls to and from remote parts of India. A telecom regulator was set up in 1997, and Vajpayee's government gave this sector a boost by the corporatization of the public-sector telecom company Bharat Sanchar Nigam Limited (BSNL) which offered its services at low fees. This enabled the government and TRAI to pressure private players into reducing user charges, which led to a snowballing rise in the number of mobile phone owners. Telecom licences were issued on a profit-sharing model rather than upfront licence fees, and there were no major allegations of corruption in the allocation of licences.[43] By 2016, it was estimated that there were close to a billion mobile phone numbers in India.[44] This has to be one of the notable success stories of independent India since mobile phone connectivity has led to instantaneous diffusion of news to all corners of the country and economy-wide efficiency gains.

Tax and Trade Reforms

A significant reform process initiated during the Vajpayee years was the setting up of a three-tiered structure for excise taxes. Excise taxes were simplified to just three rates of 8, 16 and 24 per cent, with an overwhelming percentage of the excise revenue collected from items that were taxed at the 16 per cent rate. This simplification was accompanied by the setting up of an empowered group of state finance ministers. This move to involve state governments was a throwback to the Nehru era when meetings of the NDC, which included chief ministers and the ministers in Delhi, were taken seriously. The Vajpayee government's initiative to set up this empowered committee led to a state VAT system, which was subsequently implemented by the government of Dr Manmohan Singh. This was an important step towards GST since it was incrementally easier for indirect taxes due to be assessed and collected.

On the trade front, the Vajpayee government reduced quantitative restrictions on most imports by 2004. Customs duties were steadily reduced, although this was resisted by elements in the Indian private sector which continued to have apprehensions about their ability to cope with foreign competition. It is a measure of Vajpayee's political acumen that he was able to build allies across a broad spectrum of political opinion to improve India's competitive abilities by selectively opening up the economy to the rest of the world. The consequences were positive since software exports and exports of goods rose steadily between 1998 and 2004. Specifically, software exports went up five times, and exports of goods as a percentage of GDP went up from 8 to 11.9 per cent of GDP. (See Tables 9.3 and 9.4 in the Appendices.)[45]

Legacy

Vajpayee has left a lasting impact on Indian politics. He and L.K. Advani built up the BJP and made it the national party that it is today. It is natural for a country of India's size, with its many languages and differences, to have regional parties which represent state-level interests. At the same time, India needs national parties which can combine regional with national interests. For a long time till 1996, the Congress—although Indira Gandhi converted the party into a personal/family fiefdom—was the only party which could call itself national. It is to Vajpayee's credit that he was able to widen the

BJP's appeal from the Hindi heartland to become more of a national party. Unfortunately for the country, the Congress party has lost most of its cadre base around the country, and the BJP has not been able to widen its appeal in south India.

On the economic front, the Vajpayee government had to deal with the fallout of the East Asian crisis of the late 1990s and the sanctions imposed by the US after the nuclear tests. Despite the dot-com bust of 2001–02, India's software exports increased steadily. In overall terms, the economic performance of Vajpayee's government was a substantial improvement over that in the preceding three decades, except for the Narasimha Rao years from 1991 to 1996. Vajpayee's economic policies were designed to learn from the experiences of the Rao period, build on those gains by opening up the economy and enhance competition. Rao and Vajpayee, both headed coalition governments and found ways to push systemic economic reforms.

On the downside, just as Rao had done, Vajpayee shied away from the politically difficult yet vital task of reforming land and labour markets. Some Vajpayee appointments of regulators and heads of financial-sector institutions were questionable. However, Vajpayee was by no means unique in this respect. Progressively, since the sloganeering about committed bureaucracy during the Indira Gandhi years, the Central and state governments often appoint pliant officials to positions which have constitutional, administrative, regulatory or financial clout.

The hijacking of Indian Airlines flight IC 814 could have been handled better by Vajpayee's government. All the passengers and crew of that flight except one returned safely to India. However, three terrorists were released, and they were subsequently responsible for a number of deaths in India and elsewhere. Additionally, India came to be seen as a 'soft' state that capitulates to terrorist blackmail.

A significant Vajpayee failure was the Central government's inability to contain the 2002 communal riots in Gujarat in which about a thousand people—mostly Muslims—were killed. It is likely that following the 27 February 2002 Godhra train burning tragedy in which fifty-nine kar sevaks were killed, there were IB reports that trouble was brewing in Gujarat. As the senior-most BJP leader and prime minister, Vajpayee should have acted in coordination with the Gujarat government to contain the violence. As was true of the 1984 riots in which Sikhs were killed in Delhi, and the Babri Masjid demolition in Ayodhya, the Central government has the final responsibility to maintain not just external but also internal security in every part of the country.

Vajpayee was the first non-Congress party leader to complete a full term as PM. He was PM for six years, including the short-lived coalition government which collapsed in April 1999. Just two months after coming to power in March 1998, Vajpayee went ahead with the nuclear tests in May 1998. This was one of the boldest decisions taken by any Indian PM. The negative economic and other repercussions were contained, and Vajpayee's government engaged shrewdly with the US to bring relations gradually back to normal. Patching up with the US yet keeping India out of the Iraq war was also a significant foreign policy success.

Vajpayee was mindful of the sensitivities of India's neighbours, and with Pakistan, he was remarkably patient. In the border state of Kashmir, Vajpayee was ever the statesman, willing to walk that extra step if it helped to calm tensions and bring those who were alienated from the Indian state back to believing in a peaceful resolution of differences.

Vajpayee was invariably dressed in the common dress of Bharat, namely dhoti, kurta and sandals. At times, on foreign visits, Vajpayee wore a bandhgala and trousers, but he looked uncomfortable in this dress. Vajpayee was the most outstanding public speaker in Hindi at the level of PM since Independence. He had an uncanny ability to relate to the audience, and his sympathy for the average Indian was evident from his personal simplicity. Although Vajpayee was not that comfortable in English, those who belong more to India, as distinct from vernacular-speaking Bharat, were comfortable with his leadership. This was because Vajpayee was inclusive by nature.

Turning to the 3 Cs, Vajpayee's sterling quality of Character was evident from the fact that for the most part, he selected officers with high levels of integrity for his own office. His Charisma was widely acknowledged as he was always amiable, good-natured and accommodating. Although Vajpayee gradually spoke less and less and looked sleepy in official meetings, he was cleverly Competent since he delegated responsibility to those with proven abilities. Vajpayee's strength of Character was called into question at the time of the hijacking of the Indian Airlines flight and during the killings in Gujarat.

Vajpayee's ability to empathize with an opponent's point of view made him widely acceptable across India's fractious political spectrum, and as PM, he led an unwieldy and politically disparate coalition of parties. He was always prepared for dialogue, even if the probability of a breakthrough or thawing of relations was negligible. Vajpayee's wide appeal across party lines was evident for a final time from the outpouring of grief and praise when he passed away on 16 August 2018.

The BJP-led NDA coalition did not come back to power in 2004. The Congress and others commented that the BJP had overdone the 'India Shining' slogan during the election campaign for the 2004 general election. Be that as it may, Vajpayee did raise optimism levels in and about India.

X

MANMOHAN SINGH

Long-lasting Achievements Yet PM in Name

No! I am not Prince Hamlet, nor was meant to be;
Am an attendant lord, one that will do
To swell a progress, to start a scene or two,
Advise the prince; no doubt, an easy tool,
Deferential, glad to be of use,
Politic, cautious and meticulous
Full of high sentence, but a bit obtuse;
At times, indeed, almost ridiculous—
Almost, at times, the Fool

The Love Song of J. Alfred Prufrock—T.S. Eliot

Dr Manmohan Singh is the only prime minister to date with a doctoral degree.[1] He had a long list of achievements before he was sworn in as PM on 22 May 2004. At various stages of his career, he has worked as economic adviser in the Ministry of Commerce, chief economic adviser in the Ministry of Finance, governor RBI, deputy chairman of the Planning Commission and finance minister. As the finance minister from 1991 to 1996, Dr Singh had the full support of Prime Minister P.V. Narasimha Rao to launch reforms which unshackled India's economy.

The Congress and BJP won 145 and 138 Lok Sabha seats respectively in the 2004 general elections.[2] The Congress was able to cobble together a United Progressive Alliance (UPA) which included M. Karunanidhi's DMK and Lalu Prasad Yadav's Rashtriya Janata Dal among others. The left parties chose to support the UPA government without participating in it.

After it was clear that the Congress-led UPA coalition would be able to form a government, there was high drama about who would be the prime minister. The family loyalists in the Congress party wanted their party president, the Italy-born Sonia Gandhi (SG), to be the next Indian PM. Although the Indian Constitution does not bar a naturalized Indian from becoming the PM,[3] there were adverse commentaries against her candidature for the post in the Indian media. Sushma Swaraj, a senior BJP leader, announced that she would shave her head in protest, if SG became PM. In stark contrast, some Congress leaders demonstrated their loyalty by literally weeping on live television and worshipfully demanding that she be PM.

For practical political reasons, and to avoid giving the Opposition a rallying point, SG chose not to be PM and anointed Dr Singh for the post. Since 1947, Dr Singh was the first person with little political capital, even within his own party, to become the PM. PMs who were in office for short terms, including Charan Singh, V.P. Singh, Chandra Shekhar, I.K. Gujral and Deve Gowda, had all won Lok Sabha or state assembly elections, and (barring Gujral) had political bases of their own. Cabinet ministers of the Central government have often been Rajya Sabha members. However, all Indian PMs with political stature have been repeat members of the Lok Sabha. From SG's point of view,

Dr Singh was the ideal candidate for PM since as a former academic with a retiring nature, he would never challenge her politically or stand in the way of Rahul Gandhi emerging as a future PM.

Dr Singh had contested only one Lok Sabha election in 1999 from the South Delhi constituency which he lost by a huge margin. He has been a Rajya Sabha member from Assam continuously since 1991. As required by the prevailing law in 1991, Dr Singh established his resident status in Assam by renting housing space in Guwahati. The in-state residency requirement for membership of the Rajya Sabha was dropped in 2003. The change in the law was challenged in the Supreme Court by prominent journalist Kuldip Nayar because it negated the objective of providing representation from the states in Parliament embedded in the Representation of the People Act for the Rajya Sabha. However, the Supreme Court upheld the amendment.

In the thirty years from 1947 to 1977, during which period the Congress party was continuously in power at the Centre, the country had a Congress PM but the president of the Congress party was someone other than the PM. It was only after Indira Gandhi returned as PM in 1980 that she also assumed the role of the Congress party president. In the years that Dr Singh was PM, several cabinet ministers used their closeness to the Congress president Sonia Gandhi to take decisions independently of him.[4] A National Advisory Council (NAC) with SG as its president was set up to counsel and even restrain the PM. The NAC was, on occasion,[5] more crucial to decision making than the PM or the cabinet committees. This was an aberration, and the de facto position was that the Congress party president and the NAC reserved the right to overrule the government if and when it felt it was politically necessary to do so.

I.G. Patel commented after the UPA came to power in 2004: 'I do not think there is much difference between Sonia Gandhi being the Prime Minister or Manmohan Singh occupying the post. Either way, Gandhi will take care of the larger political picture. It hardly makes a difference in terms of division of labour and nature of work . . . So, do not judge Singh too severely on the macro-economic front. And do not underestimate his savviness on the political front.'[6]

Foreign Policy

Dr Singh was given a freer hand on foreign policy issues by SG than on the domestic economy or political issues. The finance, defence, home and commerce ministers in Dr Singh's cabinet were power centres on their own and reported to the Congress president rather than to the PM.[7] It follows that Dr Singh preferred to spend time on India's external relations.

India was a nuclear weapon country by the time Dr Singh became PM. He continued with Atal Bihari Vajpayee's policies of repairing India's relations with the developed West. In this context, the most significant foreign policy achievement of Dr Singh's government was the breakthrough that India achieved through the India–US Civil Nuclear Agreement.[8] Under Dr Singh's overall guidance, India took careful steps to appease the non-proliferation lobbies in the West without compromising core Indian interests. The relationship with the US had been somewhat restored by the Vajpayee government, and Dr Singh built on this inheritance. He took the initiative to visit the US early in his first term in July 2005 and established a close working relationship with the then US President George W. Bush.[9] Dr Singh's efforts were greatly helped by the US administration's view that India needed to be supported as a potential counterweight to China. Condoleezza Rice, who was the US national security adviser (NSA) from 2001 to 2005 and later Secretary of State in the second term of Bush Junior, was a consistent proponent of this line of thinking. Brajesh Mishra, principal secretary in Prime Minister Vajpayee's office and the first Indian NSA, had established close working relations with Rice. J.N. Dixit took over as the NSA in Dr Singh's government, but he passed away abruptly in January 2005 and was replaced by M.K. Narayanan. Given Narayanan's lack of exposure to foreign affairs,[10] the foreign secretary in the Ministry of External Affairs took the lead in negotiations with US interlocutors to get India out of its nuclear isolation.

Dr Singh and his government worked cautiously to persuade the US to relax the NSG's rules for India. The NSG works on consensus, and several NSG members persisted with their objections. India was patient in its diplomacy to get the US to wear down the objections of difficult NSG members. The US had to finally use the full weight of its economic and military stature to get China, Austria and Ireland to drop their objections.

The proponents of the India–US Civil Nuclear Agreement also had to get around suspicions within India. The fear in several circles in India was that the country would compromise on the independence of its strategic nuclear capabilities by agreeing to intrusive inspections. The solution agreed to with the US, after prolonged and difficult negotiations, was for India to separate its military nuclear installations and activities from civilian nuclear power facilities. It was also agreed that only India's civilian nuclear facilities would be under International Atomic Energy Agency (IAEA) safeguards. As part of this arrangement, India was exempted from the earlier NSG prohibition of the supply of any nuclear materials including fuel to India.

The CPI (M), led by General Secretary Prakash Karat, made it clear from the outset that they were totally against the 123 Agreement. For the CPI (M), the potential benefits for India's atomic energy programme were subordinate to the political significance of India leaning towards the West by collaborating with the US. It was fortunate that the Ministry of External Affairs (MEA) had two successive foreign secretaries, first Shyam Saran and then Shivshankar Menon, who were highly knowledgeable, superbly gifted in the art of diplomacy and masterful in their drafting skills. The other secretaries in the MEA, Nalin Surie and N. Ravi, played their supporting roles to perfection. They were deputed by Dr Singh to convince counterparts in the five countries which are permanent members of the UNSC and officials of NSG member countries.

The Congress party was apprehensive about losing CPI (M)'s support in Parliament. As I watched from within South Block,[11] it appeared preposterous that knowledgeable individuals could be so ideologically coloured in their thinking that they could not separate their personal political preferences from national interest. The BJP opposed this agreement due to political differences with the Congress rather than any significant shortcomings in the proposed agreement.

It is to Dr Singh's credit that he did not change course, and in July 2008, he sought a vote of confidence in the Lok Sabha on the 123 Agreement. Dr Singh was probably able to convince SG once the Samajwadi Party led by Mulayam Singh had confirmed that they would support the government. The final tally in the vote of confidence was 275 votes for UPA and 256 for the Opposition. The Samajwadi Party's thirty-seven votes were crucial to the UPA winning this vote. The Left Front, with fifty-nine members, all voted against the government. After the Opposition lost this vote, the Left Front withdrew support for the UPA government.

The 123 Agreement was finally signed between India and the US in Washington DC in the last week of September 2008. At about that time, in an awkward interaction between Dr Singh and Bush Junior which was covered on US television, Dr Singh observed, 'India loves you, Mr. President.' These gushing expressions of friendship are common in the US but it was grating when it was replayed on Indian television. Well, if that is what it took for the US to push NSG members to agree to a waiver for India, so be it.[12]

In the mid-1980s, when I was deputed to the Department of Atomic Energy (DAE) in Bombay, the target for nuclear power production was 10,000 MW to be achieved by the year 2000. In May 2019, India's nuclear power plants produce about 6000 MW. India has fallen far short of its targets, and currently the slogan is for the country to produce 20,000 MW of nuclear power by 2020. It is unrealistic, to say the least, to expect that this objective will be achieved.

If the extent of financial and other liabilities in the case of accidents had been clarified well, the India–US Civil Nuclear Agreement would have motivated international companies to bid aggressively for setting up nuclear power plants in India. Foreign companies need a measure of certainty about potential liabilities to obtain adequate insurance cover. It was under the watch of Dr Singh's government that the Indian Parliament passed the Civil Liability for Nuclear Damage Act (CLNDA) in 2010. This Act was consistent with relevant International Atomic Energy Agency (IAEA) precedents. However, it also brought in the concept of vendor liability, based on amendments introduced by Opposition parties, led by the BJP. These amendments are ambiguous and have created uncertainties for foreign vendors such as Areva, Westinghouse and General Electric (GE).

Under CLNDA, the potential financial liabilities for companies which set up nuclear power plants in India have been deemed by insurance companies to be unquantifiable and hence unacceptable. Comparatively, local operators of plants are less exposed to potentially huge financial liabilities in the event of an accident. The discussion in the Indian Parliament when this Act was passed was coloured by the fact that Union Carbide's foreign owners had not paid adequate compensation to the victims of the December 1984 Bhopal gas tragedy.[13] Dr Singh's government should have better explained the distinction between the Bhopal case and the reasonable levels of compensation for potential accidents in nuclear power plants included in CLNDA. In the Bhopal gas tragedy case, there was no international comparator provision for compensation when the initial permission was granted to Union Carbide to set up this plant. The facility had come up under Indian domestic law which did not envisage an accident in which over 3000 people could be killed and over half a million affected by the poisonous methyl isocyanate that was released into the atmosphere. Hence compensation was woefully inadequate in what has come to be regarded as the worst industrial accident anywhere in the world.

Currently, Russia is the only country which is collaborating with Nuclear Power Corporation of India Limited (NPCIL) to set up nuclear power plants in India. This cooperation with Russia has been feasible because of a bilateral agreement with the Soviet Union dating back to 1988,[14] under which liabilities will be borne by the Indian public-sector companies involved and ultimately the Central government. As of May 2019, no other foreign or Indian private-sector company has concluded an agreement with NPCIL to produce nuclear power in India. Dr Singh's government did not take timely steps to counter the negative implications of the CLNDA for private suppliers of nuclear power equipment and technology.

Russia and Eurasia

In April 2005, I returned to India from the World Bank and joined the Ministry of External Affairs as joint secretary (Eurasia division). At that time, the Eurasia division in MEA was responsible for Russia and other CIS (Commonwealth of Independent States made up of the former republics of the USSR) countries, the Shanghai Cooperation Organisation (SCO) and the BRIC (Brazil, Russia, India and China)[15] grouping. India and Russia have annual summit meetings at the level of heads of government alternately in the two countries. This practice was followed scrupulously by Dr Singh, and I attended three such summits during 2005–07 as a member of the Indian delegation. I was the MEA officer responsible for coordination within the government in preparing the background papers and notes for these summits. The briefing sessions took place at Dr Singh's residence at 7, Race Course Road (now called Lok Kalyan Marg). I often found the inputs from the various ministries to be fairly indifferent. However, Dr Singh was always alert, read all the briefs sent to him and was detail oriented. My assessment from these briefing sessions was that Dr Singh wanted us to be thorough but did not favour any out-of-the-box thinking.

As of 2006, about 70 per cent of the stock of India's military equipment by value had come from Russia or the erstwhile Soviet Union, and this high fraction underlines India's strategic dependence on Russia. Since then, India has been diversifying its arms purchases and has been buying more from the West, particularly the US and France. In my meetings with India's uniformed services during 2005–07, I would often hear about their dissatisfaction with the increasing costs and delays in the deliveries of spares from Russia. The Russian explanation was that some of the equipment still in use in India had long since been discarded in Russia, and Russia had to incur high costs to restart old facilities to produce spares. The acrimony over this and time delays for spares underscores the need for India to be self-reliant for its military hardware. However, all things considered, Russia continues to sell or lend to India highly sophisticated military equipment and technology which would not be available from the developed West. For instance, Russia has leased nuclear-energy-powered submarines to India. Dr Singh was acutely conscious of the need to maintain close relations with Russia even as India improved ties with the US.

In June 2005, Congress president Sonia Gandhi travelled to Russia for a four-day private visit at the invitation of President Vladimir Putin. The then external affairs minister Natwar Singh joined her in Moscow even though it was billed as a private visit. SG travelled to Russia in a Reliance India Limited (RIL) aircraft.[16] A little after that visit, during a briefing session in South Block, Natwar Singh turned to me and in an aside remarked that the Congress party had paid for the use of the RIL plane. I figured Natwar Singh wanted the word put out that the Congress president had not taken any favour by using the RIL plane.

During 2005–07 India was an observer in the SCO,[17] and Natwar Singh as external affairs minister and then Murli Deora as the petroleum minister represented the Indian PM at SCO summit meetings in Astana (Kazakhstan) and Bishkek (Kyrgyzstan) in July 2005 and August 2007 respectively. China linked India's upgrade to SCO member status to Pakistan's membership of SCO. Both countries became full members a decade later in June 2017. This was another instance of China equating India with Pakistan.

Even as an observer, India would have benefited by cosying up somewhat more to the four Central Asian members of the SCO. Central Asian countries feel hemmed in between the Russian 'bear' to the west and the Chinese 'dragon' to the east and see India to the south as non-threatening. However, because of a lack of cost-efficient transportation linkages between India and Central Asian countries, trade ties have remained muted. Central Asian countries are oil and gas rich, but trade between them and India has to be through third countries as they are landlocked. Ironically, surface connectivity was not an issue in the early sixteenth century when Babur came to India probably on horseback from the Fergana Valley in Uzbekistan. With today's heavy machinery and engineering technologies, road and rail routes could be built between India and Central Asian countries if it were not for the troubled regions of Afghanistan and Pakistan that are literally in the way. The opportunity cost for India of not insisting, in Shimla in 1971, on a trade and transit corridor to Afghanistan through what is called Pakistan Occupied Kashmir has been enormous.

Pakistan, China and Other Neighbouring Countries

During his years as PM, Atal Bihari Vajpayee had reached out repeatedly and unsuccessfully to Pakistan. And, during the first term of Dr Singh between 2004 and 2008, there was talk about a PM-level visit to that country. Dr Singh was born in what is Pakistan today, and his mother tongue is the same as that of the dominant Punjabi community there. However, during those first four years, Dr Singh's government was focused mostly on concluding the 123 Agreement with the US, maintaining relations with Russia, the EU and China, at least at the same level as in the past, and in raising the level of economic interaction with Japan.

At the end of October 2008, I called on the then king of Belgium in Brussels to present my credentials.[18] I was allowed to jump the queue of other ambassadors who had been waiting longer than me as the Belgian king was to visit India in early November 2008. On 26 November 2008, barely two weeks after that royal visit, the Oberoi hotel in which they had stayed, the Taj hotel and other prominent locations including the Chhatrapati Shivaji Terminus in Mumbai came under attack by ten terrorists who had been trained in Pakistan. About 166 people were killed and another 300 injured in south Mumbai. Only one among the ten terrorists, Ajmal Kasab, was captured alive. Kasab confirmed later that he was a Pakistani national and that the organization behind the attack was Pakistan-based Lashkar-e-Taiba. This terrorist attack became a highly negative game changer in India's relationship with Pakistan.

Although several US and European nationals were killed, there was little sympathy expressed for India by the developed West. If any persuasion was at all needed, this attack made it abundantly clear that when it comes to matters of national security, each country is on its own. In this case, the less said the better about the European Union (EU). As the Indian ambassador in Brussels, I met with European Commission, Belgian and other officials. There was next to no mention in any EU official statement about this monstrous act of terrorism, but the Belgian government was somewhat more forthcoming. Europe and the rest of the developed world was too preoccupied with the global financial crisis and climate change to take any substantive notice of the terrorist attack on India.

Soon after this attack, the MEA sent out circular messages to Indian ambassadors around the world. These multiple messages directed us ambassadors to meet with local government officials to get them to understand the gravity of what had happened and to stress that the terrorists were Pakistani nationals who were trained in that country. Accordingly, I briefed the ambassadors to the EU from the five permanent members of the UNSC and other politically and economically significant nations. It was soon obvious to me that local officials and ambassadors accredited to the EU and Belgium felt that India, as a large country aspiring to be a permanent member of the UNSC, should be able to look after its own security. There was a weary look on the face of Kim Darroch, the UK's ambassador to the EU,[19] as I briefed him, that conveyed all too clearly we have heard India complaining about Pakistan and vice versa much too often. In fact, the Dutch ambassador to the EU laughed in my face when I explained that this particular terrorist attack could not have happened without the full support of the Pakistani establishment.

The United States–India Nuclear Cooperation Approval and Non-Proliferation Enhancement Act was signed into law on 8 October 2008 by the then US President George W. Bush. This agreement was preceded by a consensus approval of the NSG to allow its members to collaborate with India in using nuclear energy for peaceful purposes. The Pakistani nationals who attacked Mumbai in November 2008 must have been trained by the Pakistani Army for several months. However, it is possible that the India–US agreement for nuclear cooperation may have been the proverbial last straw for the Pakistani Army. The visible improvement of relations between India and the US may have persuaded the deep-state elements in the Pakistani Army to launch a terrorist attack on Indian soil, even though it could be traced back to them.

Former NSA Shivshankar Menon writes that 'I myself pressed at that time for immediate visible retaliation of some sort'.[20] Menon goes on to say that on 'sober reflection the decision not to retaliate militarily and to concentrate on diplomatic, covert and other means was the right one'. The emphasis was on getting Pakistan's government to accept the overwhelming evidence made available to them by Indian authorities that this terrorist attack originated from Pakistan.

Given the tortured history of India's relationship with Pakistan, it should have been obvious that Pakistan would keep stalling and not take any tangible action. The danger was that absence of an effective and sustained reaction from India would embolden Pakistan to persist in initiating and supporting terrorist atrocities in India. The next Indian general election was in May 2009; it is possible that Dr Singh's government was reluctant to take explicit action against Pakistan because of the unpredictable fallout on the electoral fortunes of the Congress party.

India could have started supporting Baloch autonomy openly at international forums by end 2008. Further, Pathans who inhabit eastern Afghanistan have family, language and societal links with Pathans across the Durand Line[21] in western Pakistan. Some among the Pathans in Afghanistan have never accepted the Durand Line as the border. This is despite landlocked Afghanistan's dependence on access to Pakistani ports for transit trade. India could have explored the possibility of supporting those Pathans who want Pathan-majority regions in western Pakistan to be ceded to Afghanistan. Although Pakistan has close government, people-to-people and religious ties with the West Asian and Gulf countries, India could have worked actively from November 2008 onwards with these and Western countries to stem financial support for terrorist groups based in Pakistan.

India also needed to examine other ways to pressure Pakistan. For instance, India is not using its full share of waters of the eastern rivers Ravi, Beas and Sutlej, under the 1960 Indus Water Treaty. To do that, India needs to build irrigation canals which take years to construct. Dr Singh's government could have shown its seriousness of intent by starting to build these canals. India needs to tread carefully in this matter though, since the sources of the Indus and Brahmaputra rivers are in Tibet which is under Chinese occupation.

In 2012, during a visit of the then foreign secretary Ranjan Mathai to London where I was based as the Indian high commissioner, I hosted a dinner at the Athenaeum Club to which Mark Sedwill,[22] Kim Darroch and others were invited. During the course of this dinner, the topic of Osama bin Laden and how he was killed in Abbottabad came up. Mr Sedwill quipped that if Pakistan knew that Osama was in Abbottabad, 'then it is a rogue state'. If, however, Pakistan did not know that Osama was hiding in Abbottabad, a kilometre from the Pakistani Army's main training centre, 'then Pakistan is a failed state'. Discounting the obvious element of pandering to Indian sentiments in Mr Sedwill's comment, I found that in private conversation, other UK Foreign and Commonwealth Office professionals agreed with the substance of what Mr Sedwill had said.

The issue then is why UK policy downplays and ignores the promotion of terrorism in India and Afghanistan by the Pakistani 'establishment'? The answer lies in the fact that the UK's economic—including that of investment advisory services—and military engagement with the Middle East and Persian Gulf Arab countries (Pakistan has close relations with these countries) outweighs that with India. For example, the GDP per capita in purchasing power parity terms in 2018 for the Gulf Cooperation Council (GCC) countries was US $68,194 while that of India was US $7873.[23] The GCC defence budget is expected to be above US $100 billion in 2019[24] and the same number for India in 2019–20 is budgeted at US $61 billion. Unlike India which spends a significant fraction of its defence budget on salaries and pensions, a much higher proportion of the GCC's defence budget goes towards purchase of defence equipment from the West.

Globally, Islamic banking assets amounted to about US $1.5 trillion in 2018. The sovereign wealth funds of Saudi Arabia and the United Arab Emirates were around US $700 billion and $800 billion respectively at the end of 2018. Substantial proportions of these funds are invested via financial intermediaries based in London and New York.

Ambassadors of some European countries based in Delhi suggest privately that India should show greater understanding in its dealings with Pakistan since the latter is smaller. This is factually true, and India needs to show not just understanding but also generosity towards Pakistan and other smaller neighbours. In this context, it is useful to compare Pakistan's size with that of major European countries. Pakistan is larger in surface area than France, Germany or the UK, and its population is about the same as that of these three countries combined. Pakistan's standing army and reserves, at 1.1 million men, is 2.6 times that of these European countries put together.[25] The UK and France are nuclear weapon powers but so is Pakistan. Thus, it grates a bit to hear gratuitous advice about patience with India's smaller neighbour, Pakistan. Pakistan is much smaller than India but definitely not a small country.

Dr Singh paid a bilateral visit to China in January 2008 and again to attend the Asia–Europe (ASEM) Summit meeting in October 2008. Congress president Sonia Gandhi attended the 2008 Summer Olympics in Beijing with her family. Border talks continued, and the agreement forged for this purpose during the tenure of P.V. Narasimha Rao was the template. India did not progress much on the border talks with China during Dr Singh's tenure, and it would have been unrealistic to expect any significant forward movement. China would like to keep India confined to South Asia even as it chips away at India's natural predominance in this region.

In overall terms, which are just as relevant in 2019 as they were when Dr Singh was PM, China is wary of India's example as a functioning multiparty democracy and the acceptability this brings with affluent Western democracies. However, as China's labour costs rise along with its per capita income, it could be persuaded to invest in India in mutually acceptable sectors. This is particularly pertinent in the context of its large surplus in trade of goods with India. The exports of Indian information technology services to China have not gone up to the extent expected, but that is also because China has remarkable capabilities of its own in this sector.

India has a long history of close relations with landlocked Nepal. There are strong bonds of kinship through marriage between the people living close to the border on either side, and the linguistic, social, cultural, religious and economic linkages between the two countries are many and varied. The two countries have an open border, and Nepal depends on India for supplies of fuel and medicine. In recent years, and particularly after K.P. Sharma Oli became the prime minister in February 2018, Nepal has tried to reduce this dependence on India by reaching out to China.

In the overall context of India–Nepal relations and in India's own interest, as the much larger country, it needs to be generous and flexible in its dealings. It is of particular importance to give a sense to the Nepalese people and its ruling elites that India does not take Nepal's concerns lightly. Given its proximity, it is mind-boggling[26] that Dr Singh did not visit Nepal even once during his entire tenure of ten years.

Over the ten years 2004–14 that Dr Singh was PM, Nepal was going through political difficulties as the communists and left extremists gradually came around to participating in elections. At the same time, diehard monarchists made a last-ditch effort to carve out political space for themselves. The Nepalese army was affected by the cleavages in domestic politics and was sceptical of the Maoists. The Nepalese army felt that the leftist cadres needed to be fully disarmed before they could be welcomed to participate in Nepal's electoral process. Notwithstanding the difficulties in India–Nepal relations due to these developments, it was important for Dr Singh to have visited Nepal to underline India's support for the pro-democracy elements in that country and to promote closer cooperation in the irrigation and hydropower sectors.

On the eastern flank, India's relations with Bangladesh were on an upswing since Sheikh Hasina became PM because she is less tolerant of India-baiters in her country. Assam and the other states in the North-east were denied access to Chittagong port shortly after Partition, and India's north-eastern states became progressively landlocked as India's relations with Pakistan deteriorated. It was an opportune time for Dr Singh while he was PM to further improve surface linkages between north-eastern India and the rest of the country via Bangladesh.

On a positive note, Dr Singh did resolve the long-standing 'Tin Bigha' Corridor issue by signing an agreement to this effect with Bangladesh PM Sheikh Hasina in September 2011. The two countries conceded small pieces of land to each other and India leased a tiny strip of land in perpetuity to Bangladesh to allow free movement of its nationals between the two enclaves that belong to Bangladesh. This concession by India was welcomed in Bangladesh and improved the environment for discussions on closer economic, trade and transit ties between the two countries.

At the same time, Dr Singh could have handled the sharing of the Teesta waters with Bangladesh better by first working out an understanding with Mamata Banerjee, the chief minister of West Bengal. Water is an emotive issue in India, and it would not have been easy to placate Banerjee. One possible way to get West Bengal's cooperation was reduce its debt burden which had grown to unsustainable proportions during the thirty-four years that CPI (M) was in power. The problem perhaps was that Dr Singh did not have Sonia Gandhi's permission to make financial concessions to Banerjee-ruled West Bengal.

The Indian and Sri Lankan governments have a history of having to periodically resolve issues related to fishing rights in the waters between the two countries. Indian and Sri Lankan fishermen are frequently apprehended by coastguards for straying into each other's waters and are released after mediation between the two governments. Over centuries, Tamils of Indian origin have migrated to the northern and eastern regions of Sri Lanka. Some Tamils went as bonded labour in the nineteenth century to work in the tea gardens in the Nuwara Eliya region. The Anuradhapura area is a world heritage site and was the centre of Theravada Buddhism. It is also famous for Buddhist carvings and works of art.

Given the civilizational linkages and strategic interests, the history of India's involvement in the Sri Lankan civil war, and that India has permanent interests in securing its southern coastlines, it is surprising that Dr Singh chose to not pay an exclusively bilateral visit to Sri Lanka during his tenure. He did visit Sri Lanka in the first week of August 2008 to attend the fifteenth SAARC Summit. However, Dr Singh did not attend the Commonwealth Summit in that country in November 2013. While the Canadian PM chose not to attend this Summit, the British PM David Cameron was present.

The two major Tamil Nadu parties, DMK and AIADMK, compete with each other to show their concern for Sri Lankans of Tamil origin. Mahinda Rajapaksa, the Sri Lankan President from 2005 to 2015, was perceived in Tamil Nadu as too harsh on Sri Lankan Tamils in his drive to crush the LTTE.[27] The DMK party's support for the UPA coalition government was crucial, and that probably explains Dr Singh's decision not to visit Sri Lanka on a bilateral basis while Rajapaksa was the President in that country.

Developed Countries in Asia and Europe

In his ten years in office, Dr Singh injected considerable energy into India's economic relations with Japan. He successfully sought Japan's technical and financial assistance to complete high-visibility Indian infrastructure projects. The Delhi Metro, Nizamuddin bridge over the Yamuna and the Delhi–Mumbai Industrial Corridor (DMIC) are examples of projects that were either completed or started with Japan as a partner during these years. Given the combination of technical support provided by Japanese companies and long-maturity financing at lower than market cost that Japan's official agencies have provided, it is easily India's most valuable partner in conceiving and completing long-gestation development projects. During Dr Singh's tenure, the two countries scrupulously held annual bilateral summit meetings alternately in India and Japan. Given Japan's troubled history with China, it is seeking to counter China's widespread influence in Asia by bolstering India. Be that as it may, Dr Singh's government nurtured the relationship and gave it the time and attention it deserved.

Over the decades, India–UK economic relationship has steadily atrophied. In anticipation of the visit of the UK PM David Cameron to India from 18 to 20 February 2013, I worked with Oliver Letwin, a junior minister of state in the cabinet office, on a proposal for an industrial plus information corridor. The suggestion was for this corridor to be built between Mumbai and Bengaluru with British technical and financial support. Mr Letwin was enthusiastic and convinced all concerned; the British government was ready to provide about £2 billion per annum for up to three years for the project. The proposal was for British private firms to work with Indian agencies to crowd in funding and technology from private and public-sector companies around the world. The expectation was that about £1 billion each year would be the British government's equity investment in the project, and another £1 billion would come from a reserve pool which was dedicated to promoting clean energy solutions. The Indian High Commission in London and British government agencies did a detailed study on the locations through which the freight corridor would be built and how real estate development along the route would pay for the development of 'smart' cities along this corridor. The thinking was that as the corridor was built freight and transport connectivity would improve and the real estate on both sides would become more valuable. Chunks of real estate could then be auctioned to fund development of townships along the corridor to which surplus low-skilled agricultural labour could migrate for employment, for example, in the construction sector.

The proposal was discussed with the foreign secretary in MEA and was brought to the attention of Dr Singh and the commerce minister. I took care to explain that the project would develop rural areas along the route of this Mumbai–Bengaluru corridor and increase formal-sector employment opportunities. However, the proposal was vetoed by the department of industrial policy and promotion (DIPP) without providing any convincing reason. A secretary-level officer in DIPP was negative on the grounds that other projects like the Delhi–Mumbai industrial corridor needed to be completed first. DIPP did not have to choose between projects because the sources of funding for this corridor were different from those for other projects. Unfortunately, Dr Singh was too distracted by the end of 2012 by the need to counter several allegations of corruption against his government to be able to focus on long-term projects and intervene in the matter.

India and several EU countries have a history of close relations from well before Independence. Post-1971, the EU allowed imports of Indian textiles at lower than prevailing import tariffs under its Generalized System of Preferences (GSP). The two sides coordinated their interaction and cooperation on a range of economic and political issues, including climate change, through regular exchanges of visits at the highest levels of government. One of the central themes of discussions between the EU and India has been how best to promote trade in goods and services. In this context, a Broad-based Trade and Investment Agreement (BTIA) has been under negotiation between the two sides since 2007. The discussions were suspended in 2013 and restarted in 2017–18. However, despite high-level meetings, this agreement is nowhere near finalization.[28]

During my tenure as the Indian ambassador to the EU, the ninth summit between India and the EU took place in Marseille, France, on 29 September 2008. The then President of France Nicolas Sarkozy was the head of the EU delegation, and Dr Singh led the Indian government team.

Dr Singh arrived in Marseille from New York on 28 September 2008, on an Air India Boeing 747 as per the norm. When an Indian PM arrives at a foreign destination, the Indian ambassador receives her/him at the airport. In this case, both Ranjan Mathai, as the Indian ambassador to France, and I were present. Immediately after we met Dr Singh in the holding area in the front part of the aircraft, Ranjan Mathai blurted that in addition to the India–EU meetings, Nicolas Sarkozy had requested a one-on-one meeting with Dr Singh. Apparently, Sarkozy wanted to seek the Indian PM's views about the ongoing financial-sector meltdown. This was just thirteen days after the New York–headquartered investment bank Lehman Brothers had folded up.[29]

Dr Singh smiled and replied, 'Sarkozy should speak to Jaimini as he would be better able to explain what is happening in international financial markets.' Ranjan looked startled as he was not sure whether Dr Singh was serious or not. It was apparent to me that Dr Singh had made that remark in a lighter vein.

In the many meetings I have attended either in a group or individually with Dr Singh, I do not remember him ever smiling as broadly as on that day. It was clear he was more relaxed than usual. By the time Dr Singh was in his car and we took our positions in the convoy of cars, I received a phone call that Dr Singh had decided to have a meeting in his suite in the hotel immediately on arrival and that I was required to attend.

Others at this meeting included Foreign Secretary Shivshankar Menon, National Security Adviser M.K. Narayanan and Secretary (West) Nalin Surie from MEA. The meeting began with Dr Singh asking me for a note, within the hour, on the ongoing financial-sector meltdown and the implications for India and for international financial markets. To keep the contents of the note confidential, I went to Nalin Surie's hotel room and worked with an India-based typist and finalized the write-up.

Subsequently, after I was back in Brussels, I received requests for follow-up notes on developments in the international financial sector and related topics and their possible impact on India. It was surprising and gratifying that Dr Singh asked me for these notes when he had the finance ministry and the RBI at his disposal. Sometime later, on a visit to India, during a one-on-one meeting with Dr Singh, I requested that perhaps government could transfer me back from Brussels to any position in the Indian financial sector. Dr Singh responded that there were no vacancies. I almost fell off my chair in surprise. It became evident that for all financial-sector positions at a senior level, the final call was made by those close to the Congress president and not by the PM.

Reverting to the India–EU Summit of 2008, Sarkozy was peremptory in his dealings with senior French and EU officials around him, even when the Indian delegation was in the room. For instance, at the delegation-level talks, Peter Mandelson, European commissioner for trade, and Kamal Nath, commerce minister, got into an argument about the proposed BTIA. It was embarrassing for us on the Indian side to hear Sarkozy cutting off the EU commissioner for trade so abruptly. The tenth India–EU Summit in Delhi in 2009 was far too focused on climate change issues, and there was no progress on the BTIA.

Dr Singh pushed for trade and investment agreements between India and major trading partners, and he let the negative lists (items excluded from tariff reductions) be long, if necessary, to conclude an agreement, as was the case with the India–ASEAN free trade agreement. The unstated logic was to get Indian industry to be competitive by lowering India's high import tariffs. Indian industry understood this tactic of Dr Singh well and invariably fought back for continued protection. The same could have been done with EU BTIA, but the EU side refused to agree to a long negative list.

Dr Singh visited Brussels for the eleventh India–EU Summit on 10 December 2010. The EU delegation was headed by Mr Herman Van Rompuy (former PM of Belgium) as the president of the European Council, and Mr José Manuel Durão Barroso, as president of the European Commission.

The two sides were on the same page on issues such as working towards eliminating terrorism and agreed on the principles to mitigate climate change. However, on the topic which could change India–EU relations qualitatively, namely the BTIA, again there was no forward movement. From 2013, even the pretence of BTIA negotiations was abandoned.

Jairam Ramesh, as the minister for environment, was the head of the Indian delegation to the United Nations Climate Change Conference held in Cancun, Mexico, from 29 November to 11 December 2010. At a briefing session for Dr Singh in Brussels on 9 December 2010, Dr Singh looked preoccupied and asked me to get in touch with Jairam Ramesh immediately and seek a report on the ongoing climate change conference. Dr Singh was concerned that Jairam Ramesh was straying from the Indian government's point of view and getting too close to that of the US. This episode demonstrated the lack of coordination within the Indian government and of ministers striking out on their own, at times at variance with the position of the Indian PM.

Looking back, the Indian government seemed to spend more time than warranted in parsing every word and comma in international climate change documents. Perhaps this was because environment was an issue on which Dr Singh enjoyed full autonomy from his party president. The bottom line for India is that it needs to better conserve the environment within the country. Dr Singh's government did a competent job of spreading the word that India needs to be mindful of environmental issues, not because of international pressure but in its own long-term interest.

Dr Singh made a few errors in handling matters related to the setting up of new multilateral development banks (MDBs) and the United Nations. In the context of MDBs, in January 2008, I was based in Delhi as the additional secretary (economic relations) in MEA. I was struck by the fact that capital-deficient developing countries such as India had little option but to accumulate foreign exchange (FX) reserves denominated in hard currencies, particularly in US dollars. By then, China was no longer a capital-deficient country, and had invested a substantial fraction of its huge current account surpluses in US government bonds and bills since these securities are among the most liquid in secondary debt markets.

I proposed in a note to the then foreign secretary Shivshankar Menon that India should consider consulting with like-minded countries in Asia including China about setting up an Asian Investment Bank (AIB). The proposal was for Asian countries to use some of the capital which was being invested in debt instruments of developed countries to fund long-term infrastructure and other projects in Asia. Menon felt that this was an idea worth exploring and offered to bring it to the attention of the PM.

As there was no reaction from the PMO about this suggestion, I published the proposal in my monthly column in the *Business Standard* in January 2008.[30] In April 2009 a Chinese think tank suggested that such a bank needed to be set up. Another four and a half years later, in October 2013, Chinese President Xi Jinping proposed the setting up of an Asian Infrastructure Investment Bank (AIIB) during a state visit to Indonesia. AIIB became operational from January 2016 and is headquartered in Beijing. China holds about 30 per cent of the equity, and India holds 8.4 per cent.

India would have had a greater say in shaping the priorities of the AIIB if it had taken the lead, and perhaps this institution would have had its headquarters in Delhi. While it can be argued that the location of the AIIB headquarters does not matter, the learning in setting up a multilateral financial institution would have been considerable.[31]

The BRICS bank[32] is headquartered in Shanghai and has an Indian national as its first president. India should have requested for the AIIB or the BRICS bank to be headquartered in India, even though the possibility of that coming to pass was limited.

My suggestion for India to take the initiative to set up an AIB was drawn on the experience of the European Investment Bank (EIB) headquartered in Luxembourg. EIB's bond borrowings which are marketed to private investors are guaranteed by member European governments, and according to its charter, almost all of its lending is to private European companies. I urged Philippe Maystadt, EIB president, when I met him in Brussels in 2009, that EIB should lend to Indian private-sector companies. He responded that as a rule, EIB only lends within Europe, and it had disbursed a few loans in the poorest African and Asian countries at the specific request of member countries. My prodding led to discussions within EIB, and within 2009 this multilateral bank loaned €100 million to Volkswagen to set up a car manufacturing plant in Pune. Since then, EIB has supported renewable energy projects in India. Specifically, it has disbursed loans via the SBI for wind energy projects. As of end 2018, the total EIB portfolio of loans in India amounted to about €2 billion, half each in renewables and urban transport.

Towards the end of 2005, a former UN official, Shashi Tharoor, was proposed as India's candidate for the United Nations Secretary General (UNSG) position. Before this decision was taken by Dr Singh, he had directed the then foreign secretary Shyam Saran to check if the five permanent members of the UNSC would support Tharoor's candidature. Saran's British counterpart

Michael Jay informed him that the UK, the US and France, three among the five permanent members of the UNSC, had decided to back the candidature of Ban Ki-moon, the former foreign minister of South Korea, and hence could not support Tharoor. China and Russia, who were contacted separately by Saran, were non-committal. Shyam Saran conveyed this information to Dr Singh. Despite the obvious impossibility of Tharoor becoming the next UNSG, Prime Minister Manmohan Singh's office directed India's permanent mission to the UN in New York to announce that Shashi Tharoor would be India's candidate for the UNSG position. Shyam Saran was not informed about these instructions. This episode shows Dr Singh in an extremely poor light. It is possible that, left to himself, Dr Singh may have gone by the foreign secretary's information, but possibly he had instructions from the highest level of the Congress.

Thereafter, the Government of India spent a considerable amount of money and time in sending officials and Tharoor jetting around the world to convince countries to support this stillborn candidature. The five permanent members of the UNSC have never sought the position of Secretary General for one of their nationals. The convention since the UN was founded in 1945 has been for a national from a smaller country to be appointed to the UNSG position. As the joint secretary in charge of the Eurasia division in MEA, I was asked, as were other joint secretaries, to speak to the ambassadors of the countries under their charge. I spoke to the Russian and Central Asian representatives in Delhi. It was apparent from the half-smiles on the faces of the ambassadors that they found the whole exercise amusing as it was common knowledge that Tharoor did not stand any chance of winning enough support to be the next UNSG. It was an awkward contradiction for India since it was simultaneously also trying to become a permanent member of the UNSC along with Germany, Japan and Brazil. Predictably, the most active opponents to the candidature of these four countries were Pakistan for India, China for Japan, Argentina for Brazil and Italy for Germany.

In 2005, I had come back from the World Bank, and it seemed that several of my colleagues kept their disbelief about India's negligible chances of becoming a permanent member of the UNSC well hidden. The then external affairs minister Natwar Singh exhorted us in the MEA to work hard at convincing countries within our charge to support India. When Natwar Singh asked for feedback, I mentioned that the permanent members were unlikely to support India in the near future. My esteem for Natwar Singh went up a notch that day as he must have been annoyed with my observation but did not express any irritation and smiled indulgently. This was a prime example of MEA frittering away the valuable time of its limited Indian foreign service personnel on highly premature pursuits. Although Dr Singh took a close interest in foreign policy matters, he did not suggest course correction on this issue to his cabinet colleague Natwar Singh.

Macroeconomic Management

Table 10.1 in the Appendices shows that from 2004–05 till 2010–11 India's GDP growth rates[33] were high and touched 10.3 per cent in 2010–11. The fallout of the global financial crisis of 2008–09 impacted India adversely, and the growth rate came down to 3.9 per cent in that year. Growth was over 6 per cent in two out of the remaining three years from 2011 to 2014 but did not bounce back to the levels achieved in the pre-financial-crisis years. The high GDP growth rates of 8 per cent or more in seven of the first eight years of Dr Singh's government was unprecedented.

The Ministry of Statistics and Programme Implementation (MOSPI) has since announced a new series on national income data with 2011–12 as the base year instead of the earlier base year of 2004–05. The change of the base year to 2011–12 has been used by the Central Statistical Office (CSO) to go back in time and recalculate GDP growth rates. According to the revised numbers which were made public on 28 November 2018, GDP growth rates during 2004–14 were significantly lower than those estimated earlier.

One of the suggested causal reasons for the downgrading of growth rates during the Dr Singh years is that growth in services was overestimated. For instance, growth in telecommunications was based on the rise in mobile numbers and was recalculated using minutes of usage. It would be more accurate to estimate the value added in the telecom sector by adding up revenues earned rather than minutes of usage. In November 2018, the NITI Aayog[34] created a controversy by taking the lead in providing revised GDP numbers. This responsibility had earlier been shifted to the CSO by the Planning Commission which was later replaced by the NITI Aayog. It is unclear as of May 2019 whether the revised growth numbers announced by NITI Aayog are accurate. Hence Table 10.1 lists the growth numbers as reported earlier by RBI.

Irrespective of the technical and political arguments about India's GDP growth numbers in the twenty-first century, it is reasonable to conclude that growth rates during the first ten years of this century were high. The high growth rates were driven by reforms carried out during the six Vajpayee years, the impetus received from the upswing in the global economy including the US, Europe and China, and Dr Singh's government's efforts to raise investment. Over the ten years of Dr Singh's government, exports went up from 11.8 per cent of GDP to 17.2 per cent. This was achieved despite the real effective exchange rate (REER) of the rupee going up by 13 per cent between 2004 and 2014.

At the same time, the current account deficit was volatile and reached a dangerously elevated level of 4.8 per cent of GDP in 2012–13. India has a perennial adverse balance in its trade in goods; it was exports of IT services and remittances from NRIs which prevented the current account from going even deeper into the red. As has usually been the case, the rate at which FX reserves were accumulated depended on net foreign portfolio investments in Indian equity and debt securities.

Consequently, India became more vulnerable to changes in foreign investor sentiment about India's growth prospects during Dr Singh's second term between 2009 and 2014.[35] In the summer of 2013, the US Federal Reserve (central bank) announced that it would gradually 'taper' off its purchases of government and mortgage-backed securities issued by private financial institutions.[36] This announcement meant that US interest rates could rise, and the hitherto higher interest rates on Indian government debt securities became less attractive for foreign investors. Large volumes of what are called 'carry' trades to convert US dollar into Indian rupees to take advantage of higher rupee interest rates were reversed in August–September 2008. Foreign portfolio investors sold their holdings of Government of India debt securities and Indian stocks, resulting in a sharp net outflow of FX amounting to nearly US $30 billion.

By July 2013, Dr Singh's government had been in power for over nine years. Dr Singh and RBI were complacent that the unusually low interest rates in developed countries would persist and were not prepared for FX outflows. This was surprising since Dr Singh, as the finance minister in 1991, had to deal with a full-blown balance of payments crisis. Ironically, given that this has never worked anywhere in the world, RBI governor Subbarao tried to stem the outflow of foreign exchange by raising rupee interest rates.

With the change of the RBI governor in September 2013, about US $35 billion was raised in the last quarter of calendar year 2013 through deposits from NRIs. The country had to pay higher hard-currency interest costs because RBI had to guarantee these returns on fresh inflows. The RBI and the Ministry of Finance were remiss in not ensuring adequacy of the country's FX reserves. In 2007–08, India's FX reserves to GDP ratio was 25.8 per cent, and this number came down to 16 per cent by 2012–13. Following the global financial crisis of 2008 RBI should have purchased hard currency at every opportunity. If necessary, RBI could have sold rupee debt securities to soak up liquidity to contain inflation. Since 2007, China's foreign currency reserves have hovered around 30 per cent of GDP. RBI should have maintained India's FX reserves to GDP ratio at least at about 25–26 per cent.

The overall fiscal deficit number, which was between 3 and 4 per cent of GDP for the first few years of Dr Singh's government, rose irresponsibly to between 5 and 6.6 per cent of GDP for the last six years from 2008 to 2014. Towards the end of Dr Singh's first term, the fiscal deficit went up to 6 per cent even before the global financial crisis in 2008. This was because the government pushed up spending with an eye on the general elections of 2009. The fiscal deficit number remained high, between about 5 and 6 per cent, till the end of Dr Manmohan Singh's premiership. The net primary deficit also went up between 2008 and 2013. These official finance ministry numbers do not tell the full story. If off-budget liabilities such as petroleum and fertilizer bonds are taken into account, the Central government's fiscal deficit went over 8 per cent.[37] It is possible though that Dr Singh had little say in deficit-related decisions taken by Finance Ministers Pranab Mukherjee and P. Chidambaram.

On a positive note, Dr Singh's government pushed the Goods and Services Tax (GST) proposal to consolidate indirect taxes for the country. State governments were unwilling to cede their right to revenues from taxes on fuel, alcohol and real estate. Despite such exceptions, the empowered group of state finance ministers made considerable progress towards a unified GST under the leadership of Union finance minister P. Chidambaram. Unfortunately for the country, the BJP, for partisan, short-sighted political reasons, did not cooperate to have the required GST legislation passed in Parliament. The concept of a countrywide GST had been launched earlier by the BJP-led government of Atal Bihari Vajpayee.

Systemic Achievements and Missteps

During Dr Singh's premiership, several forward-looking systemic policy changes were aimed at ensuring minimum levels of employment, improvements in governance and for benefits to reach the economically marginalized. Under the Right to Information Act, which came into force in October 2005 replacing the Freedom of Information Act of 2002, individuals can seek information from government and public-sector bodies. This legislation has introduced higher levels of transparency and improved governance. All governments prefer to maintain a discreet silence about decisions driven by political considerations. It is creditable that Dr Singh's government went ahead with this law. Although the Central and state governments can seek exemption from the purview of this Act on grounds of national security, it has made the functioning of officials more transparent.

Another forward-looking legislation adopted by Dr Singh's government was the National Rural Employment Guarantee Act, 2005, now known as the Mahatma Gandhi National Rural Employment Guarantee Act (MGNREGA), which came into effect in February 2006. MGNREGA has been criticized for its inadequacy since it guarantees just 100 days of work per annum at prescribed wage rates, and the implementation has been patchy in several states. However, given the abundant evidence of misery in several rural areas around the country, this was an important step towards alleviating poverty.

Some economists have suggested that India should provide a universal basic income (UBI) to all Indian citizens. An important difference between UBI and MGNREGA is that the latter is paid for work done rather than as a dole which could create a dependency syndrome among able-bodied workers. It is debatable whether UBI can be implemented any time soon in India, even if exceptions are made based on ownership of cars and tax returns to exclude higher-income earners. The potentially high cost of making UBI a reality means the government has to take the politically difficult step of reducing fertilizer, electricity, tax and other non-merit subsidies.

The personal identity card Aadhar, with biometrics registration as a precondition, was conceptualized by Nandan Nilekani, the former CEO of one of India's largest information technology companies. Despite obstacles created by the Ministry of Home Affairs, the project was undertaken by Dr Singh's government. Nilekani mentioned to me during a conversation at his residence in Delhi that he had sought Dr Singh's intervention to resolve turf issues between ministries. It soon became clear to him that Dr Singh had limited authority with his cabinet colleagues, and it was up to Nilekani to convince all concerned. It is fortunate that he persisted, and with the support of the subsequent NDA government, Aadhaar is an extremely useful reality today. Aadhaar's data integrity is not perfect, but it is a step forward in helping government to get its cash assistance to intended beneficiaries in a reliable manner. Of course, India has some distance to cover in providing uninterrupted Internet connectivity in rural and remote parts of the country.

The Right of Children to Free and Compulsory Education Act was passed by Parliament in August 2009. On paper, this Act is a belated step in the right direction. However, it is in the sincere and steady implementation of the numerous schemes for primary and secondary education that state and Central governments have been found wanting. One of the consequences of this Act has been the promotion of children up to grade eight irrespective of their performance in basic tests of literacy and numeracy. The proximity of this legislation to the general elections of 2009 gives the impression that this was another of the several steps that Dr Singh's government took with a view to garnering support during the impending elections.

Prior to the general elections of May 2014, the National Food Security Act was passed in September 2013. The implementation of numerous Central and state government laws and schemes to subsidize foodgrains and ensure their availability needs to be consistent across the country. Dr Singh made the right to food justiciable without the means for government to make standardized implementation possible in a cost-efficient manner.

An institution which was and continues to be in desperate need for reform was the Food Corporation of India (FCI). FCI does not have adequate storage space for the grains it acquires at minimum support prices (MSPs). Dr Singh's government did not have time to set up the mechanisms for consistent implementation of the Food Security Act since it was voted out of power seven months later. However, it did little in the ten years it was in power to reduce the alleged corruption associated with FCI or to overhaul it.

High MSPs are usually politically determined and cannot be fiscally sustained by several states. Dr Singh's government would have done better to examine MSP programmes for foodgrains which has resulted in unsustainable budget deficits in states such as Punjab. Dr Singh's government also did little to push for honest implementation of assured irrigation schemes around the country and particularly in states in which the UPA was in power. It is painfully evident that Indian farmers, and hence the economy, were and continue to be overdependent on fickle monsoons.

Funding for Infrastructure

The Indian Central and state governments are invariably short of funds to finance large, long-term infrastructure projects and seek funding from multilateral financial institutions such as the World Bank and ADB (Asian Development Bank) to complement government spending for such projects. Significant volumes of bilateral financing are difficult to source except for specific projects such as those supported by Japan. West Asian and Gulf countries exporting oil and gas have large trade surpluses parked in their sovereign wealth funds, and Dr Singh's government felt that these could be tapped to fund projects in India.

Accordingly, around mid-2007, Dr Singh authorized a four-member delegation led by Montek Singh Ahluwalia to visit Saudi Arabia. The other three members of the team were Amit Mitra (then Secretary General of the Federation of Indian Chambers of Commerce and Industry and now the finance minister of West Bengal), Rajiv Lall, then managing director of the Infrastructure Development Finance Company (IDFC), and me. I was the additional secretary (economic relations) in the MEA at the time. During our visit to Riyadh, we first met the chairman of the Saudi Arabian Monetary Authority, Hamad Ibn Saud Al Sayari. Al Sayari's response was that the Saudi side could consider funding infrastructure projects in India, but the Government of India would have to provide a sovereign guarantee, and the return on Saudi capital, in hard currency terms, would need to be considerably higher than on the yields on US government debt securities. Indian public-sector banks accept hard currency term deposits from NRIs at interest rates which are higher than the rates of return available in countries such as the US or Germany. Effectively, the Saudi central bank governor asked for even higher interest rates than on NRI deposits and with an explicit guarantee from the Indian Central government. The Indian government was unwilling to provide such a guarantee since the volumes involved would have been high and the execution of projects would necessarily involve the private sector.

Our next port of call was Prince Al-Waleed bin Talal bin Abdulaziz al Saud, one of the wealthiest individuals in Saudi Arabia with a private business empire which extends to most developed countries. A similar pitch was made to Al-Waleed to interest him in investing in India. His response was direct and succinct. He said that he employed investment managers based in London and New York, and the Government of India had to convince them.

Our final major meeting was a farce. We went to the residence of a Saudi royal. He was about eighty-two years old and was seventh in the line of succession to the Saudi king. He was the Saudi defence minister at one point of time and was stripped of this responsibility because he had shot one of his aides in a fit of anger. However, he had the important responsibility of keeping track of the line of succession. The Indian ambassador to Saudi Arabia, M.O.H. Farook,[38] accompanied us for this meeting. At the beginning of the meeting, the Saudi royal thanked Ambassador Farook for sending him Ayurvedic oil. He added, with a lascivious smile, that his twenty-four-year-old Bedouin doctor wife did the massaging and this had reduced his knee-joint pains. The Saudi royal went on to embarrass Mr Farook by suggesting that since the ambassador was a widower for several years, he could find him a young Bedouin wife. He then subjected us to a long lecture about the huge investments the Saudi government was going to make in its own country. All in all, this was a waste of time for our delegation but an interesting glimpse into the lifestyle and thinking of a high-ranking Saudi royal family member.

Given the limited interest from foreign investors in funding infrastructure in India, Dr Singh's government had to rely more on the Indian private sector to part-finance and execute these projects. Financing raised by Indian private-sector companies on their own was limited, and in the power and transmission, road and steel sectors, funding support came mostly from Indian public-sector banks (PSBs). Over time, the large volumes of lending by PSBs resulted in what was described as the 'Twin Balance Sheet Problem' in the Economic Survey of 2015–16. PSBs and private companies ended up with huge amounts of impaired assets and unserviceable liabilities (debts) on their balance sheets.

We have a loan scheme. I assure you it is equally good. Why can't you try that instead?

It now seems that PSBs received signals from government that speed in disbursement of funds was of the essence, and they did not need to carry out rigorous scrutiny for financial viability to extend credit. Irrespective of whether this allegation is correct or not, Dr Singh's government was not proactive enough in pushing the required concomitant government approvals through, including for environmental protection and land acquisition. On the contrary, between 2005 and 2006, the Planning Commission prevented executors of projects, even public-sector ones such as the National Highways Authority of India (NHAI), from issuing new contracts on the grounds that a new Model Concession Agreement was required.[39]

Due to higher government spending combined with MGNREGA and more than usual spending on subsidies by the Central government, the deadlines for the implementation of the targets of the Fiscal Responsibility and Budget Management Act (FRBMA), 2003, were first postponed and subsequently suspended in 2009. In 2011, the prime minister's Economic Advisory Council was compelled to advise Dr Singh's government to reduce fiscal deficits as required by the FRBMA.[40] It is surprising that Dr Manmohan Singh as PM and Montek Ahluwalia as deputy chairman of the Planning Commission did not pay sufficient attention to keeping fiscal deficits within safe upper bounds. After all, they were the finance minister and finance secretary respectively during the reform years of 1991–96. The only logical explanation is that they had less than the required influence on decisions taken by the finance ministry.

Land and Labour (Factor) Markets

Although it may have been politically unrealistic, more was expected from an economist PM in reforming India's factor markets—in land acquisition and labour rights. In October 2008, four years into Dr Singh's first term, the Tata group had to move the Nano small car project out from Singur in West Bengal due to the agitation of farmers against acquisition of their land. Even the Left Front government led by CPI(M), which was in power for over three decades by then, could not convince farmers that setting up a car manufacturing plant would lead to jobs and development of Singur.

Later, the Tata group announced that the Nano project had been moved to Sanand in Gujarat. The then chief minister of Gujarat, Narendra Modi, saw an opportunity and moved with alacrity to meet the requirements for the Tata Nano car project. As was evident from the sharp confrontation between the Tata group and farmers, land acquisition was and remains a highly charged issue.

This confrontation should have convinced Dr Singh's government that the 1894 Land Acquisition Act needed to be amended so that land purchases to set up industries was made easier while remaining fair to those who sell their land. Unfortunately, the ground reality in many states is that the politically well-connected have acquired farmland and changed land-use norms to make windfall profits. The Robert Vadra[41] episode in the acquisition of land in Haryana is such an example. When Dr Singh's government passed a revised Land Acquisition Act in September 2013, it abjectly surrendered its responsibility to make land acquisition easier. This legislation was piloted by Jairam Ramesh, the minister for rural development, and the new law, called the Land Acquisition, Rehabilitation and Resettlement (LARR) Act, 2013, made purchase of land for industrial or other purposes even more difficult than in the past. Along with other requirements, a 'social impact assessment' was stipulated in the LARR Act. The objectives of preventing acquisition of multi-crop land or more land than is required for stated end purposes are laudable. However, the balance shifted further away from a reasonable compromise between farmers with landholdings and those who need land for industry. The situation became worse for the latter. Instead, a more practical piece of legislation should have been adopted for land acquisition. It follows that Dr Singh needed to do a better job in convincing farmers and left-wing activists that while government has the eminent domain[42] right to acquire land, it would ensure that such acquisition would be done transparently, quickly and fairly.

As is said often, India has way too much legislation and limited implementation of its laws. This is particularly true about labour laws in India. Labour markets in India are governed by numerous rigid and onerous regulations with the objective of protecting the interests of organized workers. An illustrative list of the many pieces of legislation includes the Workmen's Compensation Act, 1923; Industrial Employment (Standing Orders) Act, 1946; Employees' State Insurance Act, 1948; Factories Act, 1948; Minimum Wages Act, 1948; Maternity Benefits Act, 1961; and the Payment of Gratuity Act, 1972. The Contract Labour Regulation and Abolition Act of 1970 is applicable to all firms with more than twenty workers. Under India's multiple labour laws, the numbers of workers which trigger one condition or the other for firms to comply with are: seven, ten, twenty, fifty and 100. In practice, these many laws work against the interests of workers as employers try to limit the number of employees they hire below threshold numbers in order to avoid the application of one or other of the Acts mentioned above.

About 84 per cent of workers in India's manufacturing sector work in firms with forty-nine or less employees, and only 10.5 per cent of the manufacturing workforce is employed in firms with 200 or more workers. Comparatively, in China 25 per cent of the workforce is employed in small companies while 52 per cent work in larger firms. In labour-intensive firms such as those that produce garments, 92.4 per cent of Indian workers are employed in firms with forty-nine or less workers, whereas in China about 87.7 per cent of apparel workers are employed in large firms. Labour costs account for about 80 per cent of the cost of producing garments in India, and the relatively small production units do not achieve economies of scale.[43]

India is a labour-surplus country, and about 80 per cent of its workforce is self-employed in low-productivity farming and related activities. For landless farmers or those with landholdings below an acre, life is hard and uncertain. Given a choice, many among the landless would readily move to salaried jobs, even in locations far from their place of birth. Employment opportunities in the formal sector could rise if the dozens of Central and state government laws and corresponding regulations were to be reduced and simplified. Dr Singh's government could have paid greater attention to simplifying and unifying labour-related legislation. This, coupled with honestly supervised investments in the construction of infrastructure could have started systematic, as distinct from episodic and unfair, processes of weaning away surplus agricultural labour towards formal-sector employment.

The Sick Industrial Companies (Special Provisions) Repeal Act was passed by Parliament in 2003 which was to do away with the Sick Industrial Companies Act (SICA) of 1985. SICA harmed rather than helped workers as company owners shied away from making investments in new businesses because it made closing down any loss-making company virtually impossible. The Repeal Act empowered the Central government to also dissolve the Board for Industrial and Financial Reconstruction (BIFR) which had been set up under SICA. BIFR had become an obstructionist body which endlessly debated the consequences of shutting debt-laden companies. Despite the obvious merits of proceeding with the abolition of BIFR, Dr Singh's government did not notify the Repeal Act to make it easier for creditors to seek resolution in pending cases of insolvencies.[44]

Agriculture

At its core, the solution to the woes of the agriculture sector is to move the hundreds of millions currently engaged in subsistence agriculture to the production of value-added farm products or manufacturing.[45] The efforts being made to improve delivery of primary education and imparting of skills to families of farmers need to be more than doubled. Instead, Dr Singh's government used the same tired and half-baked solutions of interest rate subsidies and loan waivers for the agriculture sector.

The productivity and profitability of the agriculture sector vary widely around the country. Each Indian state has its own specific difficulties. Crop patterns have changed over the decades based on availability of assured irrigation and MSPs for grains. A National Commission on Farmers was set up by the Central government in November 2004. This commission, headed by Professor M.S. Swaminathan, mentions in its report submitted in October 2006[46] that the size of landholdings for about 40 per cent of farmers is less than 1 acre. Clearly, this is way below an economically viable size.

An agricultural debt waiver and debt relief scheme (ADWDRS) was announced in June 2008, eleven months before the 2009 general elections. In this scheme, a complete waiver of debt was provided to small and marginal farmers (those with landholdings of up to 2 hectares) and a one-time relief of 25 per cent was envisaged for other farmers (with more than 2 hectares), provided they paid the balance 75 per cent of the 'eligible amount', which included interest and principal components. According to a World Bank study, the ADWDRS 'waived Rupees 71,500 crores of agricultural debt issued by commercial and cooperative banks between 1997 and 2007. The programme covered all agricultural loans in India that were overdue at the end of 2007 and remained in default until February 28, 2008.' The target was to cover over 36.9 million small and marginal farmers and around 6 million other farmers.[47] According to this cross-country World Bank study, this was 'one of the largest household debt relief programs in history. The volume of debt relief granted under the program corresponded to 1.6% of India's GDP.'

This policy of waivers for agricultural debt was not unique to Dr Singh's government. Over the last few decades, several state and Central governments have agreed to farm loan waivers. This measure provides relief to farmers with larger landholdings since it is mostly that category of farmers which has access to loans from public-sector financial institutions. Farmers with little or no land have to depend on informal moneylenders for credit. A more sustainable course of action would have been for Dr Singh's government to increase opportunities for subsistence farmers to work for salaried incomes in activities other than basic farming.

India's experience in using genetically modified (GM) BT (*Bacillus thuringeinsis*) cotton seeds which are pest resistant has been hugely beneficial. Production of cotton has soared and so have exports. Yet during Dr Singh's time, India chose not to move forward with other genetically modified seeds. The debate was overtaken by those concerned about the longer-term consequences of using GM seeds for cereals and edible products. A Tata Energy Research Institute (TERI) study provides details about the nature of GM seeds and the extent to which these are used and for what crops in several countries including India, China, Brazil and the United States.[48] Unfortunately, GM seeds became an issue in turf battles within the Indian government which involved the departments of biotechnology, agriculture, veterinary science and health, and the Ministry of Environment, Forests and Climate Change. If not for food products, such seeds could have been cleared for cultivation of cash crops. This issue of using GM seeds became more about the extent to which Monsanto[49] would profit from the sales of its seeds than development of profitable agriculture which would benefit Indian farmers.

When the CPI (M) withdrew its support in 2008 over a disagreement about the 123 Agreement, it was a potential boon for Dr Singh's government as it could have from then on pushed for economic liberalization. Unfortunately, Dr Singh's government stuck to populist policies with an eye to winning enough seats to form government again after the next general election of 2009.

Corruption Scandals

Irrespective of the wisdom of the decision for India to host the Commonwealth Games in Delhi in October 2010, the ground reality was that preparations had to be completed in time. Although the amounts involved were relatively small, allegations of corruption against Dr Singh's government started with accusations about blatant violations of norms in buying of equipment and awarding of contracts for the Games. Congress Lok Sabha MP Suresh Kalmadi, chairman of the Commonwealth organizing committee, was accused of wrongdoing and finally arrested in April 2011.[50]

During Dr Singh's government's first term from 2004 to 2009, there were other allegations of wrongdoing, for example, about the allocation of coal mines by the Central government in return for kickbacks. Dr Singh was the coal minister when the controversial coal block allocations were made.[51] In March 2014 the office of the Comptroller and Auditor General (CAG) suggested that the coal ministry's allocations of mines were inefficient and by implication suspect. On 1 December 2018, a special CBI court held that H.C. Gupta, former coal secretary, and other senior officials were arbitrary in coal block allocation decisions.[52] The following day, on 2 December 2018, it was reported that the IAS Officers Association had put out a statement which categorized the 'conviction of honest IAS officers in the coal scam' as most unfortunate.[53] At some stage in this lengthy process, I had expected Dr Singh to make a statement that even if the decisions made by the officers were subsequently determined to be suboptimal, they had acted in good faith under his charge.

In January 2008, in another case which led to accusations of corruption, A. Raja, the then telecommunications minister, allotted 2G spectrum on a first come, first served basis. In November 2010, Vinod Rai, who was the CAG, submitted his findings in this matter to Parliament.[54] The CAG estimated that the government had lost about Rs 1.76 trillion because the licences were issued at way below market value. Dr Singh's government's ministers and spokespersons insisted that the shortfall estimated by the CAG was hugely overstated. Even if the estimated loss of revenue was incorrect, it was apparent that the allocation of spectrum was unfair and non-transparent.[55]

Taped conversations between A. Raja, the telecom minister, and Niira Radia, the head of a public relations firm, which became public in May 2010, confirmed that bribes were paid for 2G telecom spectrum allocations. In February 2011, A. Raja was sent to judicial custody in Delhi's Tihar jail for twenty months, and he was later released on bail. The Delhi High Court set up a special court to hear 2G cases. A month after Raja, Ms Kanimozhi, a DMK MP, and the then telecommunications secretary, Siddharth Behuria were jailed under similar charges.[56]

Dr Singh offered no explanation or comment about the alleged wrongdoing of A. Raja—one of the cabinet ministers in his government. At a press conference on 16 February 2011, Dr Singh used the expression 'coalition dharma'[57] to explain the continued presence of A. Raja in his cabinet. According to Dr Singh, the DMK, which was part of the UPA, had insisted that Raja was the party's choice for a ministerial position in Delhi. On 22 February 2011, the late Ms Jayalalithaa, who was the AIADMK head in Tamil Nadu, characterized Dr Singh's comment as 'weak-kneed'.[58]

On 21 December 2017, almost nine years after former telecom minister A. Raja and others were implicated, a special CBI judge acquitted all nineteen accused in the 2G telecom case, including A. Raja and Ms Kanimozhi. The CBI judge ruled that the prosecution had failed to prove its case. The CBI's credibility was tarnished yet again. All things considered, it was an interminable and unedifying spectacle in which Dr Singh was perceived to be soft about the wrongdoing of his ministers and coalition partners, because their support was needed in Parliament. According to multiple media reports, CBI officials appear to be politicized and partisan in their investigations and they try to further the interests of the party in power in Delhi.

The perception that Rajiv Gandhi's government was involved in the Bofors bribery case had hurt the Congress party in the 1989 general elections. It is a sad commentary on the performance of India's investigating agencies that nearly two decades later, Bofors-related cases were still meandering through Indian courts. After Dr Singh's government took over in 2004, the CBI was criticized for not opposing the de-freezing of O. Quattrocchi's bank accounts in London, and for informing the Crown Prosecutor in the UK that there was no case against Quattrocchi. The chief metropolitan magistrate in Delhi, Vinod Yadav, was reported to have said on 6 January 2011 that 'I agree that there are certain mala fide intentions in the case' when Supreme Court lawyer Ajay Agrawal submitted that the probe agency and the Central government had tried to protect this Italian businessman.[59]

Vodafone is a London-headquartered mega telecommunications company which provides mobile phone, data and other services in India. Along with Airtel and Jio, it is one of a few private telecom companies which has name recognition internationally. In 2007, Vodafone's Dutch subsidiary acquired the India operating licence of Hutchison Whampoa's wholly owned subsidiary in the Cayman Islands for US $11 billion. At that time, Indian tax authorities estimated that Vodafone was required to pay about Rupees 80 billion[60] as capital gains tax since it had not withheld that amount while paying Hutchison. The Indian government claimed that it had informed Vodafone about this. Vodafone went ahead with the purchase on the grounds that the transaction was between two entities which were non-resident and hence not liable to pay any taxes in India.

Subsequently, Vodafone contested the Indian government's tax claim and finally won the case in the Supreme Court of India in 2012. The Ministry of Finance, with Pranab Mukherjee as FM, had fresh legislation passed to overturn the Supreme Court judgment and pressed tax claims on Vodafone. This came to be later described as a case of 'retrospective taxation'. As of May 2019, the case is under consideration with an international arbitration tribunal under the provisions of the India–Netherlands Bilateral Investment Treaty.

I was the Indian high commissioner to the UK when the Indian government decided to enact legislation to overturn the Supreme Court judgment in the Vodafone case. It was abundantly clear from my conversations with a number of chief executive officers of globally significant companies headquartered in London that India was literally being 'penny wise and pound foolish' in changing the relevant tax law with retrospective effect. Although a lower court had agreed with the government's tax claim, the Supreme Court had ruled in favour of Vodafone. Therefore, irrespective of the soundness of the Indian government's original tax claim, the MoF action to change the law retroactively detracted from the country's efforts to project India as a destination friendly to foreign investments. This was a counterproductive initiative of Pranab Mukherjee as finance minister, and Dr Singh was either indifferent or helpless to do anything about it.

At the end of May 2017, the CBI filed first information reports (FIRs) on cases related to the purchase of aircraft for Air India. The allegation was that the number of aircraft bought was far in excess of what was necessary, and that Air India's profit-making routes had been surrendered to foreign airlines for less than adequate compensation. These cases pertain to the years that Dr Singh's government was in power and Praful Patel was the civil aviation minister. The CAG questioned the decisions taken by the civil aviation ministry in 2011 and so did the Parliament's Public Accounts Committee in 2014.[61]

The central vigilance commissioner (CVC) is appointed by a three-member committee consisting of the PM, the home minister and the leader of the Opposition. In 2011, the members of the appointment committee were Dr Singh, P. Chidambaram and Sushma Swaraj of the BJP when P.J. Thomas, an IAS officer of the Kerala cadre, was selected as the CVC. This appointment was opposed by Sushma Swaraj and also through writ petitions which were filed by the Centre for Public Interest Litigation with the Supreme Court. On 2 March 2011, the Supreme Court struck down the appointment of P.J. Thomas.[62] It was not clear why Dr Singh's government persisted with the appointment of Thomas in the face of objections from the Opposition. Dr Singh should have changed their proposed appointee because the subsequent Supreme Court verdict brought unnecessary controversy to the appointment of the CVC.

In December 2012, the conduct of Ranjit Sinha as the director of the CBI became controversial. CBI was investigating the so-called coal block scam. Law Minister Ashwani Kumar asking the CBI Director Sinha to come to his office on 5 March 2013 was seen as an attempt to influence the investigation.[63] As a consequence, the Supreme Court was constrained to call the CBI a 'caged parrot speaking his master's voice' during hearings in the first week of May 2010.[64] The criticism led to Ashwani Kumar's resignation on 10 May 2013. Ranjit Sinha was also alleged to have met those who had been accused in several cases of financial wrongdoing, which were under investigation by the CBI, at his official residence. It is surprising, to put it extremely mildly, that Dr Singh's government chose Ranjit Sinha for the crucial position of director CBI.

Yet another case of alleged corruption at high levels of Dr Singh's government was that of the Railway Minister Pawan Kumar Bansal.[65] Mr Bansal resigned on 10 May 2013 after his nephew Vijay Singla was arrested for trying to interfere in the promotion of a railway board member.[66] There were also rumours about a bribery scandal involving Bansal's private secretary.

The Lokpal and Lokayuktas Act, 2013

The high-profile nature of the many corruption cases which came to light by 2011 led to an anti-corruption movement which mounted huge demonstrations in Delhi. These eruptions of public anger against blatant corruption were covered extensively by the visual and print media. Initially, Baba Ramdev was in the news for demanding that money which had been illicitly siphoned away from India should be brought back. This was a vague and generalized accusation. The pressure tactic used most effectively by Baba Ramdev and later Anna Hazare to press for their demands was to go on fast. The followers of Anna Hazare such as Arvind Kejriwal made broad accusations of corruption against government officials and ministers. They demanded fresh legislation to set up a national Lokpal, an ombudsman, who would be empowered to investigate charges of corruption against the highest in the land including the PM.

Dr Singh's government capitulated in the face of these threats of fasting unto death. It would have undoubtedly been politically damaging for the UPA government if any of those fasting had passed away. However, the spectacle of Dr Singh's government struggling incoherently to appease agitators did not make it popular with voters. The cardinal mistake made by Dr Singh was to allow the agitation to reach the proportions it did right in the heart of Delhi. The problem for the Congress party was that the Anna Hazare 'movement', which was mostly confined to Delhi, received extensive television coverage and was watched around the country.

After melodramatic moments inside and outside Parliament, Dr Singh's government had the Lokpal and Lokayuktas legislation passed in the Lok Sabha on 27 December 2011. The Lokpal is meant for the Central government and Lokayuktas for the state governments. The bill was passed by the Upper House two years later on 13 December 2013 and came into force on 1 January 2014 with the approval of the President.[67]

There is no guarantee that the Lokpal and others in and around this office would be inflexibly non-partisan and honest, particularly when the political and financial stakes are high. The Central Vigilance Commission has watchdog representatives in all public-sector organizations. The CBI has wide powers to investigate and prosecute those engaging in corrupt practices. The Serious Fraud Investigation Office (SFIO) is a statutory body meant to investigate wrongdoing by corporates. The Directorate of Revenue Intelligence is meant to keep an eye out for smuggling of gold, firearms or narcotics. Dr Singh's government should have explained to the country that having yet another oversight body would not necessarily reduce corruption.

Legacy

Dr Singh had greatness thrust upon him when he became finance minister and again when he was elevated to the position of PM. He rose to the occasion as FM but could not as PM. After Narasimha Rao's term as PM and that of Dr Singh as finance minister ended in 1996, Dr Singh did not seek to be a leader in the Congress party with a political base of his own. Consequently, as an appointee PM in 2004, with no pressing economic crisis, Dr Singh needed the Congress president's approval for almost all decisions.

The expectation after the Congress-led UPA coalition came back to power with more seats in the Lok Sabha[68] in 2009 was that Dr Singh would exercise greater authority within the cabinet and on economic policies. However, Dr Singh had limited freedom of action on issues related to the economy, internal security, defence purchases and selection of ministerial colleagues and senior officials. By contrast, he had considerably more autonomy in foreign policy matters. Although the Congress party had traditionally taken a wary attitude towards the US, Dr Singh's government carried forward the considerable work done during the Atal Bihari Vajpayee years to normalize relations with that country. Dr Singh was able to convince Sonia Gandhi to go against the CPI (M)'s wishes in pushing for the 123 Agreement. This was the most significant achievement of Dr Singh's ten years in office because the agreement ended the denial of nuclear materials and technology to India since the 1974 nuclear test. Dr Singh also recognized the importance of India's economic cooperation with Japan and pushed it to a higher level of engagement.

In the neighbourhood, the Pakistani establishment keeps pointing to India as an ever-present existential threat. This, combined with the November 2008 terrorist attack on Mumbai, ensured that no progress could be made on relations with this western neighbour. In Afghanistan, Dr Singh was successful in convincing the local leadership of that time that India could be a counter to Pakistan's harmful pro-Taliban influence in that country. Dr Singh was successful in his efforts in discouraging the setting up of training camps on Afghan soil for attacks in Kashmir or elsewhere in the Indian heartland.

On the domestic front, Dr Singh and his government provided a lifeline to the landless poor by passing the MGNREGA. The setting up of biometrics recording centres for Aadhaar numbers was also an extremely useful achievement. Over time, a more widespread use of Aadhaar will stem leakages in the government's financial assistance programmes by ensuring that cash benefits reach intended beneficiaries.

The RBI did not accumulate an adequate volume of FX reserves during Dr Singh's two terms. Consequently, when there was a sharp rise in net FX outflows in July–August 2013, there was a run on the Indian rupee, and the exchange rate slipped from around Rupees 63–64 to Rupees 68 to a US dollar within a month. Although this was a necessary downward correction since the rupee's REER was overvalued, the sharp depreciation eroded foreign investor confidence. Dr Singh's much graver error of judgement was that of encouraging PSBs to raise lending volumes without adequate checks on the viability of the long-term projects that were being funded. This was the genesis of the non-performing assets (NPAs) problem that the country is grappling with even as of May 2019.

The Group of Ministers (GoM) mechanism was overused during the Dr Singh years and became a way to delay decisions on issues which had huge financial implications or were politically contentious.[69] 'In the Dr Singh Government 68 GoMs and 14 Empowered GoMs or EGoMs were constituted to consider issues ranging from gas prices to selling shares in Public Sector Undertakings and mega power projects. The then Defence, External Affairs and later Finance Minister Pranab Mukherjee used to (head most) EGoMs and GoMs. At one particular time he was heading more than two dozen such committees.'[70] These GoMs and EGoMs (empowered group of ministers) gave an appearance that the ministers concerned were working faster towards solutions which would be acceptable to all without necessarily achieving much.

Dr Singh undertook several systemic reforms but failed to make even minor progress in reforming the two important factor markets of labour and land. The existing rules and regulations applicable to these crucial areas are major impediments in the way of promoting private investment necessary for job creation.

Dr Singh began his first term in 2004 with an image of personal probity. Sanjaya Baru was Manmohan Singh's media adviser from 2004 to 2009, and he calls Dr Singh an 'Accidental Prime Minister' although 'appointee PM' may be a more apt description.[71] This book suggests that Dr Singh may have been an unwilling victim of the multiple intrigues of Ahmed Patel, a close confidant of Sonia Gandhi. Irrespective of what was the truth about these portrayals in Baru's book, the fact is that Dr Singh chose to remain PM till May 2014. In his second term, a rash of corruption scandals became public, and then the huge public agitations in Delhi for a Lokpal immobilized him and compromised the reputation he had started out with. For average voters, the buck stops with the head of government (PM), even if she/he is an appointee, if there are scandals about financial or other wrongdoing.

In September 2013, Rahul Gandhi publicly tore up a copy of the proposed ordinance that Dr Singh's government was in the process of issuing.[72] This ordinance may have enabled Lalu Prasad Yadav to contest elections even though he had been convicted in several corruption cases.[73] The ordinance had been approved by the cabinet, and Dr Singh happened to be in the United States on an official visit when this incident took place. Dr Singh does not appear to hold anything against Rahul Gandhi for symbolically tearing up a Union cabinet-approved ordinance. During December 2018–March 2019, Dr Singh accompanied Rahul Gandhi to boost the electoral prospects of the Congress party in the 2019 general elections. Consequently, the conclusion has to be that Dr Singh does not hold Sonia Gandhi or the Congress party responsible for forcing him to look the other way on politically charged issues or allegations of corruption.

Narasimha Rao and even Indira Gandhi, due to the sudden death of Lal Bahadur Shastri in Tashkent, were accidental PMs. However, both of them were elected to the Lok Sabha several times. The division of work between Dr Singh heading the government and Sonia Gandhi as the Congress party president, presented as a virtue at the start in 2004, became a liability later on. The Congress party's strength in the Lok Sabha came down from 206 in 2009 to just forty-five seats in the 2014 general election. This was probably because the electorate was displeased with Dr Singh's lack of accountability and the extent of behind the scenes executive power enjoyed by Sonia Gandhi.

Towards the end of Dr Singh's second term, the focus to get a third term for a Congress-led government reached absurd levels. For instance, Dr Singh took the decision of awarding the Bharat Ratna to Sachin Tendulkar. This to me appeared to be a cynical ploy to get the votes of India's teeming young cricket lovers in the 2014 general election. In Dr Singh's defence, it could be argued that given the multiple problems which afflict India, the benefits of having one coalition government for an uninterrupted ten years overwhelmed all the ills stemming from corruption in high places and distorted/delayed decision making. Effectively, the country was spared the uncertainties and consequent lack of direction that prevailed during the short-lived governments headed by V.P. Singh, Chandra Shekhar, Deve Gowda or I.K. Gujral.

In his public persona, Dr Singh was more comfortable with the English-speaking, Western-educated elite even though he came from a humble background. His education and long years as a senior national and international bureaucrat, and his subsequent political career made him part of the 'India' elite. Dr Singh usually spoke in English from prepared texts, rather than spontaneously, which created a distance between him and his audiences. He was often dressed in a bandhgala suit; even when he wore a starched white kurta, he was not seen as part of the 'Bharat' of the common man. He spoke in stilted Hindi only when he had to and appeared to be more comfortable with specialists and government officers rather than fellow politicians.

Assessing Dr Singh on the 3Cs compared to other PMs, his personal integrity was never in doubt. However, even though integrity is a necessary prerequisite, it is not sufficient to qualify a person as being of high Character. Dr Singh showed character only when he chose not to bend in the 123 Agreement with the US. In most other cases, if he sensed any conflict with the political interests of the Congress party, he took the line of least resistance, showing weakness of character. Dr Singh's Competence was evident during the years he held positions as an economist, governor of the RBI and finance minister. However, Dr Singh chose to make his peace with political as opposed to national-interest-driven objectives too often as PM, and that reduced his competence. His score was extremely low on the Charisma index, and he was not an effective public speaker. Dr Singh showed little ability to make personal connections which made it difficult for ministers, officers and others to relate to him.

Cynicism levels among Indian voters about government and those in public life have been on the rise for the last several decades. All things considered, there was a sharp upward spike in public cynicism over the years that Dr Singh was PM. This was negative for the country and has probably tarred Dr Singh's overall reputation beyond redemption.

XI

NARENDRA MODI

Result Oriented, Charismatic Orator and Controversial

Nirmamo nirahaṁkārah sa śāntimadhigacchati

It is only those without a sense of (personal) Ownership (over worldly
possessions) and (excessive) Ego who attain Peace

Bhagavadgita

Narendra Damodardas Modi[1] was sworn in as prime minister on 26 May
2014 after a historic win for his party, the BJP. Since Independence, only
the Congress governments of Jawaharlal Nehru, Lal Bahadur Shastri, Indira
Gandhi[2] and Rajiv Gandhi had an absolute majority in the Lok Sabha. With
the general election of 2014, the BJP became the first non-Congress party to
win an absolute majority in the Lok Sabha.

Gujarat has a long history of fractured mandates in the state assembly
elections going back to the 1970s. Modi changed that and led the BJP to
form government in Gujarat thrice consecutively with decisive victories in the
state assembly elections of 2002, 2007 and 2012. In the thirteen years that
Modi was the chief minister of Gujarat, the state benefited from an increase in
infrastructure, power generation and irrigation. According to a study titled the
'Economic Freedom of the States of India', Gujarat's average state domestic
product (SDP) growth rate was consistently high during the years Modi was
CM.[3] Other analysts hold the view that there is no 'evidence in favour of the
claim that Modi's leadership had any significant additional effect on Gujarat's
growth rate in the 2000s'.[4] Irrespective of the arguments about whether Modi's
leadership raised Gujarat's growth rates above trend levels or not, Gujarat did

make impressive progress in building roads and providing electrical power reliably to farmers. Modi pushed to make Gujarat business-friendly and an attractive investment destination for both domestic and foreign private-sector firms. He orchestrated the annual Vibrant Gujarat conferences which were attended by CEOs (chief executive officers) of large multinational corporations as well as domestic companies.

CEOs of Indian firms have confirmed on record that during the years Modi was CM, his government responded speedily to their requests for purchase of land and regulatory clearances.[5] In short, Modi built an impressive track record in administering Gujarat. This gave him a larger-than-life image in Gujarat, and gradually through migrant workers in the neighbouring predominantly Hindi-speaking states as well.

However, he assumed charge as PM with a blemished record on the law and order front. On 27 February 2002, a train in which Gujarati kar sevaks[6] were returning from Ayodhya was burnt at the Godhra station in Gujarat. It was reported that fifty-nine kar sevaks were burnt to death when their compartment was set alight.[7] This incident was followed by retaliatory riots in Ahmedabad and other parts of Gujarat. According to media reports, over 1100 people were killed in the post-Godhra riots, out of which about 880 were Muslims and 250 Hindus. In some quarters in India, the feeling was that Modi had consciously prevented the police from stemming the violence. And if the Gujarat government did not have the will or the means to stem the retaliatory violence, the NDA-led Central government of Atal Bihari Vajpayee should have stepped in to do so.

By end December 2018, the Gujarat High Court had sentenced those held responsible in the Naroda Patiya, Sardarpura, Gulbarg Society, Ode Village and Dipda Darwaja cases to life imprisonment.[8] In May 2019, seventeen years after the riots of 2002, in the horrific Bilkis Bano case of rape and murder, the Supreme Court has directed the Gujarat government to provide financial relief.[9] The allegations against Modi's state government were examined by a special investigation team (SIT) appointed by the Supreme Court. This SIT had reported in February 2012 that there was no evidence to implicate Modi or the several other accused. The SIT's findings were challenged, and at the end of May 2019, the Supreme Court had scheduled further hearings.

According to British author Andy Marino, there is 'little chance that a charge will ever be brought against Modi, but even if there is, it would probably be thrown out. That is why, after twelve years, the Supreme Court monitored investigation has so far found nothing tangible against him—not even dereliction of duty.'[10] By contrast, a 2018 book by K.S. Komireddi is sharply critical of many aspects of the Modi government's conduct during the 2002 riots. Komireddi says that 'a special investigative team constituted by the Supreme Court did not find adequate evidence of Modi's complicity in the [2002] violence. But of incompetence there could be no question: Modi failed in every respect.'[11]

Indian public opinion remains divided about the state government's inability to prevent communal violence in Gujarat in February–March 2002. Some continue to feel that Modi, as the chief minister, could and should have saved lives, while others have accepted the SIT's report. Till such time as the Supreme Court rules otherwise, everyone has to accept that the state government of Gujarat, Central government agencies and judiciary have done their best to punish the guilty.

Prior to the 2014 general election, the BJP went through an internal power struggle in which Modi emerged as the undisputed leader, displacing veteran L.K. Advani.[12] Thereafter, Modi carried out a presidential-style campaign in the lead-up to the voting. Modi's skills as an orator were on full display, and the other parties did not have a comparable leader who could match him in content or delivery in reaching out to the electorate. In the sixteenth Lok Sabha election of 2014 the BJP won 282 seats, and the Congress was a distant second with forty-four seats.[13] The image of the Congress party was severely dented due to several high-profile corruption cases and the Anna Hazare movement.

It is worth noting that although the BJP won an absolute majority in the Lok Sabha with an all-India average of 31 per cent of the vote, this was less than the 41 per cent of the vote won by the Congress(I) after the Emergency in 1977. However, since regional parties were not as significant in 1977, there was little splintering of votes across parties in that general election. Further, the BJP vote share was much higher in states such as Rajasthan, Gujarat, UP and Madhya Pradesh, but the party had little support in Kerala, Tamil Nadu, West Bengal and Orissa. While the Congress vote share reduced from 28 per cent in 2009 to 18 per cent in 2014, the BJP's went up from 19 per cent to 31 per cent between 2009 and 2014. Even as some states remained unmoved by Modi's magic, there was a palpable feeling around the country that Modi's government would shake things up in Delhi and get matters which were stuck or not moving at all in the Central government from 2010 to 2014 to move faster.

Modi chose not to include senior BJP leaders such as L.K. Advani, Murli Manohar Joshi, Yashwant Sinha or Arun Shourie (all ministers in Vajpayee's government) in his cabinet. Their experience and collective memory would have been an asset as leaders to whom the government could turn to for advice. Further, they are valuable repositories of information about how to work with regional parties and non-NDA state governments since the BJP did not have an absolute majority during the Vajpayee years, 1998–2004.

The non-inclusion of these experienced leaders in Modi's cabinet led to difficulties in government formation in Delhi. It was impractical to entrust defence and finance, two of the heaviest ministries in the Central government, to Arun Jaitley. These two ministries cannot be run by one person, even if the PMO is keeping a watchful eye on both. If the ministers of the Vajpayee era were not acceptable to Modi, he could have selected non-politically affiliated experts with domain knowledge to head one of these two ministries. The choices of Radha Mohan Singh, a veteran Lok Sabha member from Bihar, and Smriti Irani, a thirty-eight-year-old former television actress, as cabinet ministers for agriculture and human resource development respectively left many scratching their heads. The general reaction was that Modi would have been better served if he had selected from among those who are knowledgeable about these two important arms of government.

Modi has allowed a perception to gather ground that he prefers officers who worked with him when he was chief minister in Gujarat. Any tendency towards keeping decision making confined to a like-minded group is usually not successful in a large corporation, let alone a country as large and diverse as India. Despite the BJP's absolute majority in the Lower House of Parliament, Modi needed friends in the Rajya Sabha to help his government pass non-money bills.

Modi made his first speech from the ramparts of the Red Fort on 15 August 2014 and struck a chord with the masses by speaking about empowering the ordinary Indian who lives from hope to hope. Modi also spoke with conviction about promoting cleanliness, creating employment and rooting out corruption. An earthy remark about gender sensitivity was that parents should not just question their daughters but also their sons when they come home late. By all accounts, he was able to connect with listeners. Modi's once-a-fortnight 'Mann ki Baat' messages to the nation on radio was also a welcome initiative for many. Radio as a medium is available to practically everyone, even the poorest in rural and urban areas. In barber shops and roadside tea stalls, people listened to Modi the narrator and orator. It was an innovation and a way for the head of government to talk directly to the people on a regular basis. A cynical interpretation is that these radio talks were motivated by Modi's desire for self-promotion, but it cannot be faulted in principle.

This chapter assesses Modi's five years as PM right up to May 2019. The consequences of the Central government's foreign and economic policies take time to unfold and become apparent. Hence the analysis and conclusions in this chapter are tentative.

Foreign Relations and National Security

Modi's incredibly high and sustained energy levels in reaching out to the rest of the world began right from the start of his tenure. He visited countries that no Indian PM had visited in a long time, such as Fiji, Nepal, Mauritius and Australia. The negative perception about Modi after the 2002 communal riots and the de facto travel ban to the developed West was set aside by these countries post-2014. Consequently, Modi was able to have frequent high-visibility interactions with the heads of government of the US, Germany, France, the UK and Japan in addition to China and Russia bilaterally and in multilateral forums such as the G20, SCO and BRICS. Modi amply demonstrated that he could easily handle the pressures of relentless intercontinental travel and having to deliver high-octane speeches in foreign locations. Overall, the defining characteristic of much of his diplomacy was the personal touch and the effort he put in to develop a one-to-one connection with the heads of government he met.

Modi's tenure was off to a flying start with his invitation to the SAARC heads of government to participate in his swearing-in ceremony in Delhi. It was attended by the heads of government of Afghanistan, Sri Lanka, Bhutan, Mauritius, Pakistan, Nepal and the Maldives. Bangladesh was represented by the Speaker of their Parliament. Given the history of conflict with Pakistan, this early visit by then Pakistani PM Nawaz Sharif augured well for bilateral relations. Modi was perceived as a statesman who understood the primacy of good relations with neighbours.

At the end of the following year, Modi arrived in Lahore on Christmas Day, 25 December 2015. The public announcement of this visit was made just hours before Modi's arrival in Pakistan while he was still in the air after having visited Russia and Afghanistan. It appeared at that stage that Modi's personal diplomacy could turn out to be more effective than the cautious confidence-building steps taken by successive governments of the two countries in the past. Dashing any such hopes, on 2 January 2016, within a week of Modi's visit to Pakistan, there was a terrorist attack on the Pathankot[14] air force station of the Indian Western Air Command. The five attackers and seven Indian security personnel were killed in that incident. The infiltrators wore Indian Army fatigues, and the media reported that the terrorist organization JeM was behind this attack.[15] All through the next eight months of 2016, there were incidents of shelling across the India–Pakistan border, often with fatalities on both sides. This was in sharp contrast with the second half of Pervez Musharraf's years as Pakistan's President from 2004 to 2008, when the shelling from the Pakistani side first reduced and then almost completely stopped.

The next armed infiltration was on 18 September 2016 when an Indian Army brigade headquarters at Uri was attacked by four terrorists, and seventeen Dogra Regiment personnel were killed in the exchange of fire.[16] Again, the militant outfit JeM was blamed for this outrage. These attacks led to jingoistic calls on some Indian television channels for retaliation. Eleven days later, on 29 September 2016, the Indian Army claimed that it had conducted 'surgical strikes' against terrorist training camps across the LoC in PoK. The Pakistani side denied that the Indian Army had crossed the LoC. These incidents of terrorism on Indian soil were accompanied by unrest and violence in the Indian state of Jammu and Kashmir.[17] It is possible that among the reasons for these repeated attacks on the Indian armed forces was the discomfort of the Pakistani Army, a dominant part of the deep state in that country, with any improvement in the atmospherics between India and Pakistan.

Seventeen years earlier, PM Nawaz Sharif was Vajpayee's host during the latter's visit to Pakistan in February 1999. Vajpayee's speech in Lahore and the positive media commentaries in both countries probably rang alarm bells in the Pakistani establishment. Soon thereafter, in October 1999, Sharif was deposed, and the Pakistani Army chief Pervez Musharraf took over as head of government. Reverting to recent events, in July 2017, Nawaz Sharif was removed from office on corruption charges and sentenced to ten years imprisonment a year later. The Pakistani establishment replaced him with a lightweight non-Punjabi politician, and hence more pliable, Imran Khan, who became PM on 18 August 2018.

After the incidents of terrorism in Punjab and J&K in 2016, the Modi government decided that there could be no discussions with Pakistan on any topic. Thereafter, border clashes and infiltrations became less frequent. The chauvinistic explanation on Indian TV channels was that Pakistan had learnt its lesson. A more likely reason was that the Pakistani deep state was now comfortable with the prevailing atmosphere of unfriendliness, and that saner minds in Pakistan would find it difficult to assert that India is not an existential threat. Modi's initial tactics of giving primacy to personal diplomacy with Pakistan did not take into account the long history of India's troubled relations with that country. On a more substantive note, the Modi government announced in September 2016 that it would increase the use of waters of the eastern rivers, Ravi, Beas and Sutlej, within the framework of the Indus Water Treaty. To that end, a dam is to be constructed on the Ravi river at Shahpurkandi.[18]

On a per capita basis, J&K received a disproportionate share of all Central government grants to states during the years 2000–16.[19] Over time, such financial assistance has come to be taken for granted and has created a dependency syndrome. The parlous state of the J&K government's finances was evident before and during the 2014–19 period. For example, the gross fiscal deficit for this state as a fraction of its SDP varied from a high of 6.8 per cent to 4 per cent for the four years from 2015–16 to 2018–19.[20] The BJP was a coalition partner with the PDP (Peoples Democratic Party) in J&K from 1 March 2015 to 19 June 2018, except for a few months from January to April 2016 when Governor's rule prevailed. It was a welcome surprise that such a government could be formed at all. The sources of the state's revenue need to be widened and deepened. Although it was difficult, the Modi government should have made the coalition work since it has implications for law and order in that state and relations with Pakistan.

A calmer situation in the Kashmir Valley is in the interest of J&K and the rest of the country. The BJP and Modi's government did not measure up to this task during its tenure. Governor's rule was reimposed in December 2018 after the BJP decided to leave the alliance in June 2018. As the much larger party compared to PDP, with a national presence and in power at the Centre, the BJP could have focused more on the need for J&K to raise revenues and push employment-generating investment. Modi could have tried to bring all parties together to form another interim coalition government in time to have fresh assembly elections.

The BJP also needed to find ways for the state and Central government representatives to talk to all segments of the Kashmiri population. As of end May 2019, it appears that Modi was not able to engender a sense of confidence in the Central government among all sections of the people of Kashmir. Kashmir experts may well feel that this is too simplistic a statement given the years of mistrust and the violence which has claimed both innocent civilian lives and those of the armed forces. The ground situation in J&K and the use of force by Indian security forces is recounted very differently by domestic and foreign observers. Domestic commentators tend to take the official point of view in their reporting.[21] International observers such as the Office of the United Nations High Commissioner for Human Rights[22] was critical about the use of force by security forces in its report dated 14 June 2018. External commentators could be misinformed or deliberately biased. Nevertheless, the Central government has the responsibility to improve the security situation in Kashmir. And the law and order situation in the state should be consistent with India's self-image as a liberal and tolerant democracy which allows for the holding of local elections with high percentages of voter participation.

In continuation of past practice, within a month of assuming office, Modi visited Bhutan on 15–16 June 2014. Over the past several decades, well before the Modi government came to power in 2014, the content of the relationship has included India's economic and technical support to develop the hydroelectricity potential of Bhutan. India and Bhutan have also agreed to provide surplus power from Bhutan's hydroelectric projects to Bangladesh.

Modi's initial outreach to India's other Himalayan neighbour, namely Nepal, was well received. Modi's first bilateral visit to Kathmandu was in August 2014 and again in the same year in November to attend the eighteenth SAARC Summit. A massive earthquake in Nepal in April 2015 killed about 9000 people, injured several times that number and rendered many homeless. The Modi government's quick response to provide substantive support in material and medical assistance was well appreciated and made for a good start for Modi's engagement with Nepal.

The following year, in 2016, the constitutional amendments introduced by the Nepalese government were perceived in the terai region of India, in UP and Bihar bordering Nepal, to be against the interests of the plains people of Nepal called 'Madhesis'.[23] Relations between the two countries took a downward turn due to resentment in Nepal that India was slowing the movement of fuel and even medicine to the mountainous regions. Nepal has always had concerns about its landlocked geography and its dependence for items of daily necessity on India. Modi needed to take a longer-term view of the relationship rather than allowing the perception that India was indifferent to Nepal's requirements to gain ground through 2017.

Nepal's left-leaning parties and others formed a coalition government in February 2018 after the general election, with K.P. Sharma Oli as PM. It was to be expected that the newly formed government would reach out to China to reduce dependence on India. The Kosi and Gandak rivers flow from Nepal into Bihar and UP, and finally merge with the Ganga. Bihar and parts of Uttar Pradesh are exposed to floods caused by these two rivers during monsoon. If Nepalese political parties stopped working at cross-purposes, Nepal and India could benefit from hydroelectric and irrigation projects. There was a rethink in India's Nepal policy following China's positive reaction to Nepal's overtures. Modi changed course and received PM Oli in Delhi in April 2018. Unlike his predecessor Dr Manmohan Singh who neglected Nepal, Modi had visited that country four times till the end of May 2019. These exchanges of visits at the level of PMs led to an improvement in bilateral relations.

By any metric, economic or strategic, China is a highly important neighbour for India. Modi was quick off the mark on India–China relations. He had visited that country four times while he was the chief minister of Gujarat during the years he was not welcome in Western countries. Since becoming PM, Modi has visited China five times, and the only other country he has visited this often after assuming office was the US. These visits to China were on a bilateral basis and also to attend multilateral meetings of the G20, BRICS and SCO.

Chinese President Xi Jinping came to India on a bilateral visit early in Modi's tenure in September 2014. Symbolically, the visit started in Modi's home state of Gujarat, and through Xi Jinping's stay in India, there were several photo-opportunity occasions, including the two leaders sitting on a swing next to the Sabarmati river. At that time, there was talk of large Chinese investments in Indian infrastructure projects. Modi paid a return bilateral visit to China in May 2015 and went to Xian, Xi Jinping's home town.

After these warm and friendly interactions between Modi and Xi Jinping, the two countries had the Doklam confrontation in mid-2017.[24] In this eyeball-to-eyeball situation, it was not clear who would back down. The Chinese side claimed that a piece of territory located strategically on a tri-junction of India, Bhutan and China belonged to them. It became public on 17 June 2017 that China had started constructing a road southward on the Doklam Plateau, and the Indian Army stopped the Chinese workers from progressing farther south. China tried to pressure Bhutan into accepting their claim but Bhutan remained tacitly in India's corner, and finally, on 28 August 2017, India and China announced that they had withdrawn their troops and were back to the status quo ante.

After the tense confrontation in Doklam, the two leaders met bilaterally in Wuhan in April 2018. Considerable significance was attributed to this meeting by Indian and international media, and China was seen to be a bit more accommodating. This was probably because China was feeling pressured by President Trump's accusations about China following unfair trade and investment policies.[25] Additionally, Chinese firms such as Huawei were accused of stealing proprietary technology from Western companies.

India has decided not to be associated with what is now called China's Belt and Road Initiative (BRI). In a significant eye-catching move Modi's government did not participate in the first summit-level meeting of the Belt and Road Forum for International Cooperation which took place in Beijing during 14–15 May 2017.[26] One of India's main objections is that BRI includes a so called China-Pakistan Economic Corridor (CPEC) which will pass through Pakistan Occupied Kashmir and give China access to Gwadar port. More broadly, as the Modi government has presciently concluded, there is no convincing reason for India to climb on to this BRI bandwagon which is to push China's foreign policy and economic objectives as far and widely as possible. The longer-term Chinese objective is to have a dominant say in setting the terms for international trade and investment and to push Chinese hegemony to levels that the US has enjoyed around the world since the end of the Second World War.

The difficulties in India–China relations are embedded in the latter's long-term goal to contain India such that China is accepted as the unquestioned power in Asia and beyond. This is evident from a number of Chinese postures such as its claim on Arunachal Pradesh, that the Dalai Lama curtail alleged anti-China activities, and the propping up of Pakistan ignoring its direct involvement in acts of terrorism in India. The differences about the border came to the surface during the Doklam confrontation. It is to the credit of successive Indian governments' efforts to maintain close relations with Bhutan that this small country decided not to capitulate to China. As mentioned elsewhere in this book, Bhutan has more to fear from an embrace from China, with its large Buddhist population in Tibet, than from India. On a lighter note, at times it pays off in relations with smaller neighbours to be a bumbling well-meaning country like India rather than one which is militarily powerful and focused exclusively on self-interest, such as China.

It is abundantly clear that Modi and Xi Jinping had a number of opportunities to push ties between the two countries to higher levels of cooperation. However, there are limits to high-visibility personal diplomacy translating into real benefits. In the past five years of the Modi government (May 2014 – May 2019), relations with China ostensibly improved and then took a turn for the worse. As the Indian economy and its international footprint grow, it can expect more opposition from China. The open-ended squabbles that President Trump has started with China, including the demand for US tourists to visit Tibet, probably mean that China would be hesitant to embark on another Doklam type of confrontation with India any time soon.

Modi did go beyond the platitudinous references to 'Act East' as a signal of India's intent to pay more attention to countries to the east. The ASEAN heads of government were invited as the principal guests at the Republic Day function on 26 January 2018. Although the warm welcome, including the references to age-old ties, was pleasing to watch and hear, the ASEAN countries were focused on tangible next steps and suggested that India should move faster on the negotiations of the Regional Comprehensive Economic Partnership (RCEP). As in the past, there was nervousness in the Indian private sector about another free trade agreement, and the Modi government's position on trade agreements, regional or global in scope, has not been articulated clearly— to all appearances it was hesitant to negative.

Modi built on the achievements of previous Indian governments in engendering the feeling of a common destiny with Bangladesh. Cross-border sales of power rose, there were improvements in the bus linkages between Guwahati and Kolkata via Dhaka and transportation of goods and passengers by river waterways, coastal shipping and trains. The two countries chipped away at the trade and transportation barriers created post-Partition and particularly after the 1965 India–Pakistan war.

Modi visited Bangladesh in June 2015, and the Bangladesh PM Sheikh Hasina paid a return visit in April 2017. Although Teesta water-sharing arrangements could not be concluded, much has changed in India's relations with Bangladesh. Sheikh Hasina, Mujibur Rahman's daughter, has been the Bangladesh PM for the last ten years, and she took recourse to legal action prior to jailing and executing those responsible for genocide in East Pakistan in 1970–71. She won another huge victory, by seemingly impossible proportions, in the election of December 2018. It is likely that in time, the Indian North-east would again have unfettered access to the sea via Bangladeshi ports as it did during the colonial era. It is strategically and economically important for India's north-eastern states to be linked to mainland India by high-speed motorways, waterways and rail connectivity via Bangladesh. This has not yet been followed up vigorously enough.

Among developed countries, Modi focused most on the US. He visited the US and the UN in the first few months of his tenure in September 2014 and was able to establish an equation with President Barack Obama. The US government responded positively to Modi's overtures, and President Obama attended the Republic Day event in January 2015 as the chief guest.

In Modi's visits to the US in 2015, 2016 and 2017, he made it a point to meet with business leaders and heads of technology giants such as Facebook, Google and Microsoft. This was a welcome departure from the past. These interactions with technology giants should in time make for greater interest among such companies to invest more proactively in India. The reach of US products and services can be significantly expanded by catering to India's young population—41.6 per cent of whom were below twenty-five years of age, and 69.2 per cent below forty-four in 2011.[27]

At the same time, there are limitations to how much well-orchestrated sales pitches can achieve unless the providers of capital are convinced that the returns on their investments in India would be high enough to compensate for the risks of investing in an emerging economy. Further, high-technology companies are mostly engaged in dispensing services that need higher educational skill levels and provide fewer job opportunities than those in manufacturing. The Indian services sector just cannot provide employment to meet the requirements of the millions of underemployed who want to enter the formal job market.

After Donald Trump took over as the US President, Modi went on a bilateral visit to that country in June 2017. Since then, India's relationship with the US has been somewhat rocky, primarily because President Trump takes a transactional approach to foreign relations. He expects all US trading partners, even India with whom the US has a marginal trade deficit, to make trade concessions. Trump's decision to withdraw US troops from Afghanistan will raise the risks for Indian personnel working in that country. In all of this, Modi was more of a spectator, like the other heads of government of the G20 grouping of nations, as a less assured US kept taking decisions unilaterally.

Modi followed up energetically on the concerted efforts of his predecessor Dr Manmohan Singh to strengthen India–Japan economic and technical ties. The Indian PM's work in bolstering collaborative efforts is helped by Japan's need to promote India vis-à-vis China. Since Modi's first visit to Japan, in August 2014, he and the Japanese PM have had several annual summit meetings.

Given its own horrific experience of atomic bombs being dropped on Hiroshima and Nagasaki on 6 and 9 August 1945 respectively at the end of the Second World War, Japan had reacted negatively to India's nuclear tests in May 1998. However, as India's relations with the US improved in the first decade of the twenty-first century, Japan's attitude reverted to one of supporting economic development in India. In the past fifteen years, Japan's financial and technical support has been crucial in the building of bridges, underground metro railways and industrial corridors. The proposed bullet train between Mumbai and Ahmedabad with Japanese technology and financing is not an optimal use of India's money or time. There are so many other priorities, including improving safety in Indian railway networks. However, one saving grace could be the transfer of engineering technology to India in such a collaboration.

Modi visited France and Germany in April 2015, and the French President François Hollande was chief guest at the Republic Day function in 2016. German Chancellor Angela Merkel visited India in October 2015, and French President Emmanuel Macron was in Delhi in March 2018. In the last several decades, the bilateral relationship with France has been particularly important because of collaboration in the defence sector. Specifically, India has bought fighter aircraft in the past and has now contracted to purchase Rafale warplanes.[28] However, at the margin, the relationship with France has also been coloured by allegations of corruption in this Rafale deal. At the outset of the negotiations, India was to buy 126 Rafale fighters. This number was reduced to thirty-six ready-to-fly planes during Modi's visit to France in April 2015 on the grounds that the fighters are required urgently.[29]

The agreement for the supply of these fighters includes an 'offset' clause under which the French companies involved (Dassault, Thales, Safran and MBDA) will need to source 50 per cent of the value of the deal, estimated to total about €4 billion, in goods and services from Indian defence equipment suppliers. In October 2016, it was announced that the Anil Ambani Reliance Group would be a 51 per cent partner with Dassault Aviation to manufacture components of the Rafale fighter in India.

Opposition parties including the Congress have been shouting themselves hoarse that the Anil Ambani Group, with no experience in the manufacture of defence equipment, was shown this favour by Dassault at the behest of Modi's government. France is also a leader in superfast trains and nuclear power. Unfortunately for India's bilateral relationship with France, the Rafale deal has cast a shadow over the possibility of closer cooperation in other high-technology fields.

Germany has a tradition of students learning trade skills through programmes in vocational schools called Berufsschule. Such trainees are absorbed into the workforce, and it reduces the need for all students to seek higher educational qualifications. India is trying to learn from this German practice of trade-specific vocational training, often with the support of industry giants. India's two-way trade with Germany is growing faster than with other European countries. It is likely that in bilateral trade, FDI and skills training, Germany will be a valuable partner for India in the coming decades. Modi was fully cognizant of this reality and courted Germany assiduously.

In comparison, in the past two decades, Indian PMs have required a fair amount of prodding to visit the UK. This is because the bilateral dialogue often degenerates into issues of visas and job opportunities for Indian students in the UK, which are limited. Additionally, due to the UK's current priorities, it cannot be of much assistance to India in terms of technical and financial support in manufacturing. India is fairly well positioned in the information and communications fields and has chosen to be cautious in the financial sector with the bulk of it in the public sector, unlike in the UK. Consequently, there is less of a fit between the Indian economy and that of the UK compared with France where some of its industry is still in the public sector or with Germany which boasts of highly specialized manufacturing firms.

Despite the lack of complementarity between the Indian and UK economies, the people-to-people relations are strong with perhaps about 2 million people of Indian origin residing in that country. The people of Indian origin in the UK have political and business linkages with India. Modi visited the UK in November 2015, and on the substantive side, the discussions probably included containment of anti-India elements and the return of Indian economic offenders who are based in the UK.

The EU is a repository of technical expertise in pharmaceutical products, the agriculture sector and renewable energy. Due to an incident involving the killing of two Indian fishermen in 2012, and two Italian marines consequently being placed in Indian custody, India–EU meetings were held up for a while. The Italian foreign minister Federica Mogherini had become the EU high representative for foreign affairs. Given the time taken for this case to wend its way through Indian courts, Mogherini said that 'the issue has the potential to impact the overall European Union-India relations'.[30]

Modi visited Brussels in March 2016 for an India–EU summit and a bilateral visit to Belgium. A trade agreement between India and the EU is stuck because the latter feels an agreement with a long negative list of excluded items does not serve any purpose. The Indian point of view is that a trade agreement between the world's largest and second-largest democracies has significance much beyond economics. Given the differences in perceptions and the anxieties about what ought to be included (for example, the EU does not want easier entry of Indian information technology specialists, and India has concerns about lower import duties on cars), there was again no progress on the India-EU trade agreement during Modi's tenure between 2014 and 2019.

Modi visited Russia four times to attend bilateral summits or multilateral meetings under the rubric of the BRICS and SCO groupings. His government gave enough indications to Russia that it feels that India's relationship with that country is special because of the extensive collaboration in the fields of nuclear power and sophisticated military technology and equipment. However, Modi's frequent visits to the US and the strengthening of the Indo-US relationship was viewed in Russia as a downgrading of India's traditional ties with them. Russia has made overtures to Pakistan, particularly because it could be helpful in containing extremist sentiments in Central Asia from gaining ground. Large numbers of Central Asia nationals move in and out of Russia to meet the shortage of semi-skilled labour. Russia's move towards engaging with the Taliban has become more significant with Trump announcing further reductions of US troops in Afghanistan.

Despite Russia's concern about India's growing friendships with the West, Modi kept the Russian side sufficiently engaged. However, earlier Indian governments and that of Modi have not prepared enough for eventual changes in Russia's current leadership. These will possibly result in a reduction in

Russia's ability and willingness to provide spares for dated military equipment India had sourced from that country.

Economy and Institutions

The Modi's government emphasis on rebooting the Indian economy was issue and innovation specific, and not geared towards systemic reforms. It promoted many eye-catching and far-reaching schemes, and all these taken together should create employment and raise government's tax revenues over time. However, there was no discernible underlying economy-wide logic to the steps taken by Modi's government. For instance, no progress was made to reform labour and land markets, improve India's trade competitiveness or address the underlying ills that afflict India's PSBs.

The Planning Commission, set up in 1950, was shut down after sixty-five years by Modi's government at the end of December 2014. In its place, in the same offices, with most of the earlier support staff, the NITI Aayog started functioning from 1 January 2015. According to Modi's public comments, he felt that the Planning Commission's inputs were not even-handed or based on adequate understanding of the constraints at the level of state governments. The newly formed NITI Aayog was meant to be a government think tank and not be involved in release of funds for state governments. However, it has not established itself in the last four and a half years as a source of in-depth studies and/or as an unbiased commentator. Shortly after it was constituted, the NITI Aayog was tasked to finalize reports of three subgroups of chief ministers on Central government sponsored schemes such as skill development and Swachh Bharat (Clean India). It seems that on this occasion the NITI Aayog 'played their role more as agents of the Central government than as technical advisers'.[31]

Earlier governments have kicked the problem of large, loss-making public-sector enterprises down the road. For example, FCI, Air India, BSNL and Mahanagar Telephone Nigam Limited (MTNL) are overstaffed and have consistently made losses over the last several decades. The FCI acquires foodgrains at government-determined MSPs and stores them. It has tentatively begun acquiring pulses but at market prices. The controversies about the inordinately high volumes of FCI stocks driven by knee-jerk acquisition of foodgrains at MSPs, wastage due to inadequate storage space and allegations of corruption involving FCI officials are legion. The Modi government did set up a committee headed by a former agriculture minister to look into reforming FCI. At the time of writing in May 2019, it was not at all clear what, if any, FCI-related reforms were being implemented.

The Ministry of Civil Aviation did try to sell a minority stake in Air India, but the terms were not palatable to potential buyers, and the government did not receive a single bid. Even if privatization was not politically feasible or considered appropriate, it was high time for the Modi government to sell parts of these loss-making institutions and make them board rather than government driven. It has to be borne in mind though that when Modi took over, serious charges of corruption against Central government ministers and senior officials were meandering through Indian courts or being investigated by Central government agencies.

A major problem inherited by the Modi government was the huge overhang of NPAs in the banking system. The PSBs needed to recover at least a fraction of the large amounts that were loaned between 2007 and 2012 to energize lending which had slowed down considerably by 2014. The existing legislation, including the SARFAESI Act, had proved inadequate to rein in recalcitrant borrowers who did not service their debts and clung on to their pledged assets. With this as background, a huge policy success of the Modi government was the passing of the Insolvency and Bankruptcy Code (Amendment) Act (IBC) in May 2016. Under this Act, lending banks can take borrowers to the National Company Law Tribunal (NCLT) in a time-bound, well-defined manner. An Insolvency and Bankruptcy Board of India (IBBI) was set up to certify insolvency professionals. The NCLTs are now ruling on auctioning of assets or change in management-ownership based on assessments made by professional resolution specialists. However, as in all other disputes Indian high courts and the Supreme Court have the final say and court proceedings can drag on indefinitely.

Fortunately for Modi's government, Aadhaar, a key prerequisite for reforms that has touched the lives of many, was ready for use in 2014. By April 2016, about a billion people had been registered under Aadhaar.[32] Moving back two years, the biometric data of around 700 million people was available with Aadhaar by May 2014. At around the same time, in 2014, the number of active mobile phone users had increased to half of India's entire population. By 2018, mobile plus fixed phone numbers had crossed a billion, and there were over 460 million broadband Internet users.

Building on this huge base of mobile users and holders of Aadhaar card, Modi announced a financial inclusion campaign, later called the Pradhan Mantri Jan Dhan Yojana (PM People's Money Plan), in his first Independence Day speech on 15 August 2014. It was claimed by Modi's government that by June 2016, about 220 million new accounts were opened. These accounts were to be linked to Aadhaar cards and mobile phones in what was called the

JAM (acronym for Jan Dhan, Aadhaar and Mobile) trinity. Even discounting for exaggerations in government-sponsored publicity about JAM, it is likely that this linkage across bank accounts, personal biometrics of Aadhaar and mobile phone numbers to promote financial inclusion was indeed achieved for millions of individuals. However, the continuing challenge is to help account holders to keep their accounts active by depositing cash benefits in them. This has proved to be difficult since the household sector's net financial savings as a percentage of GDP did not rise in the last few years and, in fact, declined marginally from 7.2 per cent in 2013–14 to 7.1 per cent in 2017–18.[33]

One out of several reasons for the consumer boom in the USA in the 1950s was the availability of easy consumer credit for household goods. In India, in the past, banks and NBFCs (non-banking financial companies) were reluctant to provide low-value consumer credit and loans have been available mostly for housing, cars or two-wheelers. Increased lending for low-cost items could help create credit history for millions of Indians—namely, those who honour their debt obligations and others who do not—which would then be available to lending institutions. This has already happened to a considerable extent through the spread of online shopping. The next stage could be to expand such lending to individuals in semi-rural and rural areas for instalment-based purchases of air conditioners, computers, mobile phones, bicycles and so on, leading to virtuous widening circles of easier access to consumer goods. It appears that after the initial publicity about JAM, subsequent steps to widen consumer lending were not taken with adequate urgency as the government took up a number of new initiatives with eye-catching acronyms to attract voter attention.

Demonetization

Demonetization was announced by Modi without any forewarning on 8 November 2016. It caused considerable anxiety among those who depend on wages in cash and those who own small businesses with transactions in cash. Micro, small and medium enterprises (MSMEs), whose employees are mostly part of the cash economy, were hit hard. Marginal farmers and those living in the less accessible parts of the country were also impacted adversely except where they reverted to age-old systems of informal credit based on family or social relationships but possibly at higher rates of interest. The export sector was impacted adversely because some of the small-scale units which provide inputs of goods and services function almost entirely on a cash basis.[34]

Despite these difficulties for the average Indian, there was considerable initial support for demonetization which was ostensibly meant to unearth unaccounted wealth stored in cash and increase tax collection. As it turned out, about 99.3 per cent of the cash in circulation came back to the banks.[35] If reducing the size of the unaccounted cash economy was the objective, the government should have printed enough 100-rupee notes to make up for the cash shortfall of demonetized 500-rupee and 1000-rupee notes. Instead, it inexplicably issued 2000-rupee notes. The Eurozone and the US governments have gradually phased out high-denomination notes to bring down tax evasion and reduce illegal activities. Even if secrecy was of paramount importance, Modi's government should have been able to find ways to print the required numbers of 100-rupee notes quietly. Atal Bihari Vajpayee's government was able to keep the May 1998 nuclear weapons tests secret from the intelligence agencies of developed countries.

Finance Minister Arun Jaitley reported in his budget speech of 1 February 2017 that after demonetization, of the cash deposits made in bank accounts, 10.5 million accounts belonged to companies and individuals, and the average deposit size was Rs 0.5 million. In another 14.8 million accounts, again held by companies and individuals, the average deposit size was Rs 33 million. It is unlikely that individual account holders would store Rs 0.5 million in cash, much less Rs 33 million. As of May 2019, the Modi government had not made public, in summary form or otherwise, the tax returns of individuals or companies that held such large cash balances. Analysis of tax returns as compared to the size of cash deposits was also not available on the website of the Ministry of Finance.

In the same February 2017 budget, the finance minister provided for issuance of anonymous electoral bonds. This was claimed to be in keeping with the avowed objectives of the Modi government to root out corruption and make funding of political parties more transparent. On the contrary, the issuance of such bonds has increased the probability of quid pro quo deals between big business and whichever party is in power.

It is widely agreed among non-government economists that the country lost about 1 per cent in GDP growth in 2017 due to demonetization. This is growth that has been forgone forever. In a nutshell, Modi wasted an immense amount of his personal political capital in the demonetization exercise. By the end of its term, the government was not able to make a convincing case that the benefits were commensurate with the economic pain inflicted on the many who are involuntarily part of the unorganized cash economy.

Direct taxes as a percentage of GDP went up marginally in the period 2014–18 from about 5.7 to 6.0. This better income tax compliance could at a stretch be attributed to the fear factor caused by the government's warnings and the demonetization exercise. Comparatively, indirect taxes as a fraction of GDP increased more, from 4.4 to 6 per cent.[36]

Goods and Service Tax (GST)

A nationwide goods and services tax (GST) to replace a range of indirect taxes levied by the Central and state governments was under discussion for over ten years when Modi took over. In the past though, the BJP was obstructionist, and Modi, as chief minister of Gujarat, had opposed GST. It is to the credit of Finance Minister Arun Jaitley and Modi's government that they were able to get the GST legislation involving constitutional amendment finally passed by both houses of Parliament by 8 August 2016. The state governments have since agreed on the GST rates to be applied,[37] although major items of consumption such as liquor and petroleum products were exempted.

Modi's government was heavily criticized for the multiple GST rates, the shortcomings in the GST software, and the consequent complications in the implementation of this hugely significant reform. A change so systemic and nationwide was bound to cause complications. However, at least some of the glitches in implementation should have been anticipated by the Ministry of Finance. Closer and quicker attention was needed to help those who did not get their GST refunds on taxes paid on inputs, in time. Smaller businesses needed more time to file their GST returns as they gradually mastered the intricacies of the involved soft-copy forms. It was particularly important to help smaller exporters receive their refunds to maintain production since they easily lose credibility with importers if they do not adhere to delivery schedules. In response to complaints from various quarters, the government did relax deadlines for filing GST returns. All things considered, the fact that GST was finally implemented will be seen as a major achievement of Modi's government as this brought to fruition the efforts of many others who had worked since the 1970s towards making India a single market.

Competitive and Cooperative Federalism

India is a Union of states with a powerful Central government as designed by the framers of the Constitution. Modi did not press the accelerator on broader economy-wide reforms to promote both competitive and cooperative federalism. For instance, he needed to do more on reforming the factor markets of land and labour. The NDA did not have a majority in the Rajya Sabha, and given the opposition of the Congress and other parties to most NDA legislative proposals, it was not possible for Modi's government to effect changes in land or labour-related legislation. However, a beginning was made at the state government level in the BJP-ruled state of Rajasthan. In Rajasthan the law was amended to make it easier to lay off workers in firms with less than 300 workers. Earlier the threshold was 100 workers. Subsequently, Maharashtra and Madhya Pradesh followed Rajasthan.

Instead of this tentative beginning of labour market reform in three states being expanded to other states, it was abandoned amidst the din of state assembly elections. Modi and the BJP may have lost interest in labour reforms or were perhaps never convinced about the need for systemic changes in labour laws.

Even though a few items which are heavily consumed have been kept out of the purview of GST, the empowered group of state finance ministers played a crucial role in arriving at a consensus on GST-related matters. On 12 September 2016, the notification for the GST Council, with the Union finance minister as the chairperson and with the finance ministers of all the states under Article 279A as members, came into effect. For all practical purposes, the GST Council has replaced the empowered group of state finance ministers.

It is likely that in the future there will be differences of opinion between the GST Council and the Finance Commission. This was already evident in the discomfort of some state government representatives on the council with the terms of reference of the Fifteenth Finance Commission. This has to do with the weightage given to population in allocation of funds across the various states. Southern states feel that their success in lowering birth rates would work against them as compared to northern states such as UP and Bihar where the rate of growth of population has been higher. Given that these differences could snowball over time, the Modi government could have sought the views of the GST Council on correlation between population and allocation of funds.[38]

Since Rajiv Gandhi's years as PM, steps were taken to devolve administrative and financial powers to local bodies and panchayats. The 73rd and 74th Amendments of the Constitution, which went into effect in 1993, enabled the setting up of panchayat and municipal bodies. However, 'even after nearly 26 years [in 2019] of the amendment of the Constitution, many states have failed to confer the responsibilities listed in the Eleventh and Twelfth Schedules to the local bodies. Similarly, their track record in transferring powers of taxation has been poor, with the exceptions of states such as Kerala and Karnataka.'[39] As of end May 2019, Modi's government had not pushed governments even in BJP-ruled states to devolve greater financial powers to local bodies or build professional capacities in them.

From May 2014 till December 2018, the BJP was in power on its own or in coalitions in Gujarat, Maharashtra, Madhya Pradesh, Rajasthan, Chhattisgarh, Jharkhand, Bihar, Karnataka and Himachal Pradesh.[40] The BJP lost power in Karnataka, Rajasthan, Madhya Pradesh and Chhattisgarh by end 2018. However, it won by a huge margin in India's largest state, Uttar Pradesh. It had more than four years to effect changes. Modi could have initiated healthy competition among the BJP-ruled states on land, labour reforms and greater devolution of financial autonomy to local bodies to serve as a model for non-BJP-ruled states.

Economic Indicators and Estimation Controversies

Moving on to economic indicators, in January 2015 the CSO changed the base year for estimating the country's GDP and related numbers from 2004–05 to 2011–12.[41] The CSO also dropped the earlier practice of estimating GDP[42] at factor cost and changed it to using GVA (gross value added). The GDP growth rates for all years from 2011 to 2018 are higher with the use of 2011–12 as the base year. Given these changes, comparisons on GDP growth rates, debt and related numbers between the pre-Modi and post-Modi years cannot be made with any confidence. The Modi government's credibility about GDP growth rate estimates would have been higher if it had set up an independent group of experts to provide a template for estimation of national income and related numbers.

The fiscal and other deficit numbers in Table 11.1 in the Appendices show that the gross fiscal deficit as a proportion of GDP decreased by 0.5 per cent to 3.5 per cent and primary deficit halved from 0.94 to 0.43 per cent between 2014–15 and 2017–18. These numbers do not tell the whole story and understate the true extent of the deficits in the Modi years. This is because a part of the recapitalization support provided to PSBs was through government bonds. This ruse has been used often in the past by the Central government as it is 'cash neutral'. The principal amount to be repaid does not show up in the fiscal deficit number in the year in which such assistance is provided. Unlike companies, the Central government's budgets are cash and not accrual based. As for gross capital formation, this has decreased from 33.5 to 30.6 per cent between 2014–15 and 2016–17, and capital outlays remained range bound between 1.3 and 1.6 per cent of GDP.

As of May 2019, the CSO was part of MoSPI. The NSSO too receives administrative and funding support from MoSPI. By contrast, the National

Statistical Commission (NSC) was expected to be independent of government and was set up under an executive order dated 1 June 2005 with non-government experts and government nominees as members. Simmering controversies over India's unemployment numbers boiled over with the resignation of two independent members of the NSC at the beginning of 2019.[43] These two NSC members were reported to be aggrieved because the higher than expected unemployment numbers which were cleared by them in December 2018 were not released by government.[44] This controversy about the extent of unemployment dented the government's credibility needlessly. Most working-age Indians who are not employed in the public or private sector are underemployed to various degrees in informal jobs. It is difficult without extensive and reliable sample surveys to come to definitive conclusions about the precise extent to which underemployment has changed over time and in which regions of the country.

It is important for CSO to continue to function within a Central government ministry, namely MoSPI, and to get government agencies to provide the required numbers consistently and on a timely basis. And going forward, the NSSO should be subsumed within the NSC and provided a separate budget.[45]

Modi inherited an overvalued Indian rupee, and this overvaluation increased further between May 2014 and December 2018. During this period, the Real Effective Exchange Rate (REER) of the rupee went up by another 10 per cent. This was only one of several factors that had a dampening impact on India's exports. India's exports to GDP dropped from 16.9 per cent in 2013 to 11.9 per cent in 2018. Despite this, the current account deficit remained below 2 per cent. This was primarily because the price of crude oil dipped from over US $100 per barrel in 2008 to an average of around US $50 during the years 2014–19. In a counterproductive protectionist move in the 2018–19 budget, the Modi government raised import duties on a range of products. This was a backward step in government's thinking about trade in goods since there has been a slow yet steady reduction in customs duties since the economic reforms of the 1990s.

On a positive note, FDI, although low in absolute terms for an economy of India's size, kept growing steadily. It was around US $16 billion in 2013–14 and had risen to US $37.4 billion by 2017–18.[46] It is likely that this rise in FDI was at least partly due to the Modi government's efforts to improve the ease of doing business.

During the course of 2018, Modi's government was involved in an unnecessary controversy with the RBI about the amount that would be transferred from the latter's reserves to government. The MoF and RBI also appeared to be in disagreement about allowing weaker PSBs to restart lending. The Modi government was concerned that long-term lending had frozen for the first three years it was in power, and in 2018 it was limping back. Reading between the lines, it appears that MoF would have liked the RBI to show even greater regulatory forbearance towards the PSBs with lower capital adequacy and allow them to restart lending. Unfortunately, the differences led to the resignation of RBI Governor Urjit Patel on 11 December 2018. Patel was appointed by Modi's government, and this has happened only once before in independent India in the mid-1950s.

An important reform during the Modi years for which the RBI deserves the bulk of the credit is the setting up of a Monetary Policy Committee (MPC) which sets short-term benchmark interest rates. The publishing of the minutes of MPC meetings has made the setting of interest rates more transparent than before. The Modi government has helped in this reform as the government's nominees on the RBI board have been supportive of this change.

BJP's absolute majority in the Lok Sabha and Modi's unquestioned supremacy within the BJP gave him the elbow room to take a fresh look at India's economic policies. In particular, Modi needed to focus more on employment generation in the formal sector. On this score, the Modi government's first budget in July 2014 came as a big disappointment. There was little urgency about reviving long-term investment that would lead to job creation. It was already obvious by 2014 that large-volume, long-maturity loans had ground to a halt because of imprudent lending in the previous six years. Hence, other sources of funding were required even as PSBs needed to be nursed back to health.

In past decades, Indian governments have not pushed hard enough to widen the tax net. For instance, in financial year 2016–17, only 7781 companies declared profit before tax of Rs 100 million, and just 3.2 million individuals reported annual income above Rupees one million. In his budget speech of 2017, the finance minister concluded that 'we are largely a tax non-compliant society'.[47]

In 2014–15 direct taxes collected in India amounted to 5.7 per cent of GDP compared to an average of about 7.4 per cent for other emerging economies. The numbers for indirect taxes, as a fraction of GDP, was 10.1 per cent for India and 10.8 per cent for emerging economies.[48] In addition to policy measures to widen and deepen the Indian tax base, such collections depend on the sincerity of the rank-and-file-level tax personnel of the Central government. This in turn depends on the government's ability to motivate these officials and punish wrongdoers.

Accounting and Financial Sector Scams

Modi spoke specifically about the sorry fact of business and other professionals under-reporting their incomes. He upbraided and exhorted accountants at an Institute of Chartered Accountants of India (ICAI) event on 1 July 2017 in the following terms: 'Only 32 lakh (3.2 million) people in the country reveal their income to be more than ten lakh (1 million) rupees . . . after demonetization . . . thieves and robbers must have gone to some economic doctor . . . they have definitely taken the help of someone who needs to be identified. Don't you feel the need to identify such people, who are sitting among you, who supported these companies?'[49] The implementation of GST had been announced by Modi the previous night, and he was speaking in the context of a new beginning, not just for indirect taxes but also about income tax disclosures. However, Modi's government has not yet followed up by setting up a separate regulator for the accounting profession, with the ICAI continuing to be the watchdog.

A Banks Board Bureau (BBB) was set up in April 2016 to improve governance of PSBs. The BBB was part of the Modi government's 'Indradhanush' programme to reform PSBs. As the selection of PSB management and board members was earlier heavily influenced by political–economic considerations, the BBB was expected to make such appointments more merit based. In practice, however, the Ministry of Finance did not let go and kept final decision making to itself. This is yet another example of how the Modi government started off with a sound thought but failed to carry through with it. The sense one gets is that Modi intends to carry out systemic reforms but the political will fades when faced with entrenched opposition.

The cash flow and solvency problems of the non-bank finance company (NBFC) called Infrastructure Leasing and Financial Services (IL&FS) came to the surface in the first week of October 2018. This so-called strategically important NBFC had the chairpersons of two public-sector behemoths, the LIC and the SBI, on its board, and several government officers have worked in IL&FS on deputation. The first thought that may have come to many was the oft-quoted French expression '*plus ça change, plus c'est la même chose*' (the more things change, the more they stay the same). It was another case of 'crony' capitalism in which IL&FS had access to large volumes of loans without adequate scrutiny of the business models and creditworthiness of the hundreds of subsidiaries it had set up.[50] The credit rating of IL&FS was downgraded from AAA in June 2018 to junk status in a matter of just three months after it defaulted in September 2018 on some of its debts out of a total debt of Rs 910 billion. The representatives of LIC, SBI and senior figures in Indian industry who were IL&FS board members were asleep at the wheel at best or complicit at worst.

In the case of Punjab National Bank (PNB), the irresponsible lending to Nirav Modi came to light in mid-March 2018. Modi's government was proactive in taking action against PNB officials who were either incompetent or were involved in the wrongdoing. Till the end of its first term in May 2019, the Modi government had not carried out a systemic review of the shortcomings in regulatory oversight of the financial sector or made the selection processes for the heads of public-sector financial institutions and their boards transparently fair.

Power Sector

As of February 2019, the total installed electricity generation capacity in India was about 350 gigawatts of which renewable energy amounted to 21.2 per cent.[51] State electricity boards (SEBs) are near bankrupt because over the decades, they have been coerced by state governments into selling power at prices which were well below administratively determined purchase prices. In November 2015, Modi's government set up the Ujwal DISCOM[52] Assurance Yojana (UDAY) to help the SEBs recover. The principal motivation was to help distribution companies, which are burdened with a total debt of around Rs 4.5 trillion. Under UDAY, state governments were to issue bonds of up to 75 per cent of the debt of each SEB. The remaining 25 per cent was to be covered by debt securities issued by DISCOMs. However, the underlying irrationality was not addressed by Modi's government, which is that power tariffs have been subsidized for decades depending on the consumer.[53] For instance, the agriculture sector continues to receive highly subsidized power.[54]

Surface transportation infrastructure was given a significant push forward by Nitin Gadkari's Ministry of Road Transport and Highways, and Shipping. Transportation is a sector which the Modi government has pushed hard. The number of highway kilometres added in four years from 2014 to 2018 was an impressive 28,531 kilometres, which was reported to be faster than during the UPA years.[55] Similarly, railway track length has increased substantially by about 9500 kilometres of broad-gauge lines between 2014 and 2018.[56] However, the rate of laying tracks was only marginally faster than during the UPA years. The significant difference with the past is that as of end May 2019 there were no allegations of wrongdoing, and the momentum was building up for faster completion of a number of NHAI projects in the next few years.

The coal block allocations during the tenure of the Manmohan Singh government were subsequently cancelled by the Supreme Court.[57] The Modi government's energy minister Piyush Goyal carried out fresh auctions swiftly and without any controversy. Modi spoke eloquently on several occasions about the need for India to move fast on increasing its renewable energy production. India's per capita consumption of energy is way below that of developed countries and China. In the coming decades, India will move up on this scale of consumption of energy per capita. Depending almost wholly on coal and oil-based power generation would add to pollution at irresponsible levels. India's renewable energy production capacity in February 2019 was 75 gigawatts.[58] The target of 175 gigawatts (this number varies depending on the source) for renewable energy by 2022 is clearly unattainable. However, Modi's ambitious numbers gave all concerned targets to aim for, and was welcome news for Indians and for the rest of the world.

Healthcare—Ayushman and Education

Healthcare for most of the Indian population is patchy in both quality and reach. Low-cost government hospitals are overcrowded and inadequate in number. Private hospitals are mostly located in large metropolitan areas, and even with cross-subsidies between higher-income and poorer patients, the costs are way too high for those who are not covered by insurance.

In this overall context, the healthcare for all programme called Ayushman Bharat Yojana or Pradhan Mantri Jan Arogya Yojana (PMJAY) launched by Modi's government in partnership with the Ministry of Health on 23 September 2018 was a welcome initiative. The purpose was to make primary, secondary and tertiary healthcare affordable and hence accessible. It is too early at the time of writing to assess whether this programme would meet the healthcare needs of the poorest in the country and how the costs will be met on a sustainable basis. If it does work, even for a fraction of the intended beneficiaries, it should reduce anxiety levels among those covered since the current high cost of private healthcare can and does impoverish Indians. This is particularly true for those who are self-employed with meagre earnings and are not covered for such costs by insurance companies.

As for the spread of literacy and numeracy, although Modi's government did initiate multiple programmes, it did not pay sufficient attention to the difficulties of implementation. His government focused more on enhancing skills. However, even to acquire basic skills, workers have to be familiar with the three 'Rs'; they need to be able to fluently read and write and be conversant with basic arithmetic. If India is to take advantage of the many programmes that Modi has launched, the young, particularly among the poor, have to be better educated. Under the Aam Aadmi Party's (AAP) administration, government schools are said to have improved in the state of Delhi.[59] Teachers are being held accountable, and parents have been compelled to come to schools for meetings with teachers. Modi's government could have included what was perceived to work in the Delhi model in the states where it was in power.

Multiple Programmes, Acronyms and Slogans

One of the campaign promises that Modi made in 2014 was that his government would enhance employment opportunities for all. To this end, Modi pushed for a 'Make in India' campaign for the manufacturing sector.[60] Modi's government also paid special attention to improving the ease of doing business in India to boost domestic and foreign investment in job-creating ventures. However, the rent-seeking practices which feed off the existing labyrinthine systems of permissions are difficult to change. The underlying legislation and the innumerable rules and regulations need to be first amended or abolished.

Modi created a mismatch between expectations and reality by promising too much on jobs and self-employment; instead, demonetization was a setback for those employed in MSMEs. Other schemes such as 'Startup India' and 'Standup India' were floated to help new businesses started by small entrepreneurs, women, Dalits and other disadvantaged groups. However, these appeared to be more political slogans than adequately thought-out and sustainably funded programmes.

Modi launched the Swachh Bharat Abhiyan (Clean India Mission) on Mahatma Gandhi's 145th birth anniversary on 2 October 2014. The objectives were to make India free of open defecation by constructing 90 million toilets in rural India. This effort also included the cleaning up of urban areas. There can be no two opinions about the need for such a campaign. No other PM had chosen to speak as often about this issue. A conversation that I had in 2017 with a European couple who had lived in India for about four years and had travelled to every corner of the country brings home the point about how outsiders view India. Their plaintive question was 'why does India have to be so dirty?' In their understanding, it could not be an issue of scarce financial resources since with community efforts, at least neighbourhoods can be kept clean. It follows that Modi deserves the nation's thanks for exhorting Indians to take responsibility and do their bit to promote cleanliness around the country. There is also a positive economic aspect to this campaign since a cleaner India with a lower incidence of communicable diseases will reduce public health expenditure and also attract more tourists. On the whole, it was too early in May 2019 to assess the effectiveness and longer-term sustainability of the several programmes which were floated by Modi with a host of acronyms.

Agriculture Sector Distress and Farm Loan Waivers

Media reports have indicated that farmers around the country felt neglected by Modi's government. This led to agitations in several states including those ruled by the BJP/NDA such as Madhya Pradesh and Maharashtra. At its core, farmer dissatisfaction is based on the undeniable fact that their earnings are not commensurate with the hard work they put in. Uncertainties related to monsoons in areas which do not receive assured irrigation is a major worry for them. Much more extension work remains to be done to get farmers to insure their output against the vagaries of weather and equally importantly understand the mechanics of how to claim compensation. In some states, production of foodgrains, vegetables and farm products has increased well beyond demand, leading to lower prices. Another persistently intractable issue is that intermediaries between farmers and retail outlets strip away a large proportion of the final sale price of the produce including grains, vegetables and livestock.

High-yielding foodgrain seeds were introduced in the 1960s, and currently average productivity per hectare for wheat production is 3.2, 3.5 and 5.3 tons in India, China and the US respectively.[61] Counter-intuitively, the proportion of land on which rice is cultivated in states which receive relatively less rainfall has increased substantially between 1960 and 2014. In Punjab and Haryana, this number has risen from 6.4 to 36 per cent and 4 to 19 per cent respectively.[62] Such distortions are due to higher than warranted subsidies on power, enabling low-cost pumping of groundwater. The Modi government and the state governments of Punjab and Haryana needed to motivate farmers in these two states to move out of rice and on to cash crops.

Modi did not choose subject specialists to head the Ministry of Agriculture and affiliated bodies. India's agriculture sector reform process is literally stuck in the mud, and for the most part, during Modi's tenure, ad hoc steps were taken. One day, it was about insurance for farm produce without thinking through who would pay what proportion of the insurance premiums and exactly how compensation would be assessed and paid promptly. On another, it was about controls on exports or import tariffs to protect consumers from rising prices of agricultural products.

The Central and state governments in India are prompt in subsidizing final consumer prices while insisting on high prices for agricultural products. For instance, the UP state government insisted that farmers be paid a minimum price for their sugar cane, while sugar mill owners were told they had to sell processed sugar at controlled prices below the purchase price of sugar cane. A rational approach in UP and Maharashtra would have been to start weaning farmers away from growing sugar cane which consumes much more water than other crops.

A major part of the attention of all governments has been on protecting consumers from high prices of farm products. This has been the policy since Independence, and Modi's government did little that was different. Since farmers of one or more products are also consumers of a range of other farm products, government policy for obvious electoral reasons has favoured consumers.

Specific programmes were needed to provide direct minimum income support to farmers. Instead, during 2017 and 2018, state governments of UP, Rajasthan and Madhya Pradesh authorized waivers of agricultural loans. The continuing principal underlying reasons for farmer distress are that the average size of landholdings is too small, agriculture is not sufficiently mechanized, and too large a proportion of India's population is still engaged in farming. Successive governments have not been able to implement measures to improve and diversify the skills of the farming communities around the country so that they obtain employment in other sectors. Although five years are too short a time to achieve any measure of success, Modi's government did not make a beginning towards sustainable reforms in the agriculture sector.

Supreme Court and Central Bureau of Investigation (CBI)

Four senior judges of the Supreme Court took the unprecedented step of holding a press conference on 12 January 2018.[63] They expressed their sense of disquiet about the manner in which the then Chief Justice of India, Dipak Misra, was allocating cases among Supreme Court judges, that diverged from established practice. The media gossip was that Dipak Misra was allocating politically sensitive cases to judges who were junior to the four judges who held the press conference. For the public at large, it was a matter of considerable concern that Supreme Court judges had reached such a point of dissatisfaction with the chief justice that they had to go public with a press conference.

During the course of 2018, the ugly accusations and counter-accusations between Alok Verma and Rakesh Asthana, the head and deputy head of the CBI, did no credit to them or the institution. These two officers were appointed to their respective posts by the Modi government. On 23 October 2018, Verma stripped Asthana of all responsibilities. The Modi government then dismissed Verma the same day and melodramatically at midnight. This must have lowered the morale among the rank and file in CBI. The CBI had already come in for sharp criticism during the second term of Dr Manmohan Singh. The expectation was that Modi's government would strengthen this important investigative body and not expose it to fresh criticism and hence doubt in the minds of the electorate.

Reservations

Reservations for Dalits, STs and OBCs are currently applicable for seats/positions in government and publicly owned educational institutions, banks and other undertakings. Every now and then, demands have been raised by one or the other community such as Gujjars, Patels and Jats in Rajasthan, Gujarat and Haryana respectively for inclusion in the category of OBCs. It is to the credit of the Modi government that it resisted demands for reservations from these groups, since acceding to them was likely to lead to a snowballing of the same demand from other communities.

In January 2019, the Modi government piloted fresh legislation through both houses of Parliament for an additional 10 per cent reservation in government jobs and educational institutions for all those in the 'general' category whose families earn less than Rs 0.8 million per annum (that is, Rs 66,667 per month), and have less than 5 acres of land, among other criteria.[64] If the declarations for income tax purposes are correct (only 3.2 million returns are for income above Rs 1 million), a large number of Indian families will qualify for this additional 10 per cent reservation. This move pandered to a misunderstanding, deliberate or otherwise, that it is essentially through reservations in government jobs and educational institutions that the country will uplift the socially and economically disadvantaged. Affirmative action to help those who are at the bottom of the social and economic ladder is an absolute must. However, this has to be tempered increasingly with fair competition to promote excellence. Modi's government should have taken the politically more difficult route of explaining that the existing quota for OBCs needs to be gradually reduced and eliminated over say the next ten years, and similarly for Dalits and STs over time.

Societal Intolerance and Anxieties

In the last six years, four prominent social activists and rationalists (against superstitions) were murdered in India. They are rationalist Narendra Dabholkar in Pune on 20 August 2013, social activist Govind Pansare in Pune on 16 February 2015, Kannada scholar and author M.M. Kalburgi in Dharwad on 30 August 2015, and outspoken journalist Gauri Lankesh in Bengaluru on 5 September 2017. In each case, the media speculation was that they were killed by Hindu fundamentalists. These cases of murder are being investigated by the CBI or by Special Investigation Teams and the state-level Criminal Investigation Department (CID). It is likely that the views of these activists angered obscurantist elements who may have conspired to murder them.

According to media reports, in August 2018 the Maharashtra Anti-Terrorism Squad (ATS) arrested three persons belonging to right-wing radical organizations who were possibly involved in the murder of Dabholkar and Pansare.[65] At the time of writing, the investigations into these four killings have not been concluded. The Modi government needed to speak up more forcefully in favour of freedom of speech and against such hate killings.

The Koregaon Bhima instance of caste-related violence took place in Pune district at the beginning of January 2018. In June and August 2018, several prominent lawyers, journalists, academics and activists who support the rights of Dalits and tribals were arrested under the Unlawful Activities Prevention Act for having links with banned outfits.[66] As of end May 2019, some of those activists were still in jail, and the cases against them were being pursued by Maharashtra police. It is difficult for the lay Indian to understand what threat these few left-leaning individuals pose to the integrity of the country. It would help the image of the BJP–Shiv Sena coalition in Maharashtra and Modi's government, domestically and internationally, if the cases against the activists were to be explained by government officials through mass media.

Inter-religious Issues

On 28 September 2015, a fifty-two-year-old called Mohammad Akhlaq Saifi was killed and his son Danish seriously injured in their home in a village near Dadri in Uttar Pradesh. The accusation was that Akhlaq had killed a calf and there was beef in the refrigerator in his house. Accepting that the law in UP and select other states in India prohibits wilful killing of cattle and there are social sanctions against the consumption of beef, it was still a grave crime for a mob to enter Akhlaq's home and kill him and injure others. If the law meant to protect cattle in UP was violated in any way, the aggrieved parties could have filed a case with the local police and sought legal redressal.[67]

In another incident, Pehlu Khan, a fifty-five-year-old, was killed on 1 April 2017 near Alwar by so-called cow vigilantes when he was returning from Jaipur after purchasing dairy cattle.[68] On 3 December 2018, a police inspector and a villager were murdered in Bulandshahr, UP, by so-called protectors of cows. It is illegal and abominable that groups of people take the law into their hands, ostensibly to impose their religious beliefs about cattle on the rest of the population. An unanticipated fallout was that unwanted cattle strayed into agricultural fields and ate standing crops leading to distress in rural areas in UP.[69] A majority of the people in Asia and the West consume beef. At a minimum, these cattle-related killings have detracted from India's image as a forward-looking nation on the move, and possibly also reduced inward tourism.

Modi had said at a public rally on 8 October 2015 that 'Hindus and Muslims should fight poverty, not against each other'. However, several BJP members have continued to make intemperate remarks. For example, the comment made by the 2019 BJP campaigner for Bhopal, Pragya Thakur, that Nathuram Godse, Mahatma Gandhi's assassin, was a patriot.[70] Several prominent academics and commentators are also concerned that there is a continuing attempt to introduce incorrect facts and even outlandish concepts about India's past into school textbooks.

January–May 2019 and Beyond

The cascading rush of significant events in just the first five months of 2019 included: (a) the Central government's interim budget announcement on 1 February 2019 that an annual grant of Rs 6000 will be provided to all farmers who own less than 2 hectares of land;[71] (b) JeM's—a Pakistan-based terrorist organization—claim that it was responsible for a suicide bomber attack in the Pulwama district of Jammu and Kashmir on 14 February 2019 which killed forty Central Reserve Police Force (CRPF) personnel; (c) India's missile attack on a JeM terrorist training centre in Balakot, Pakistan at 3.30 a.m. on 26 February 2019; (d) Pakistan's retaliation by sending warplanes into Indian airspace on 27 February 2019; (e) appointment of Justice P.C. Ghose as the first Lokpal on 19 March 2019; (f) India's destruction of one of its own satellites on 27 March 2019 with a ballistic missile interceptor; (g) yet another powerful bomb explosion on 9 April 2019 in Dantewada district in Chhattisgarh, attributed to so-called Maoist extremists in this state, which killed a member of the state legislative assembly and four security guards; and (h) announcement of general election results on 23 May 2019, and BJP-led Modi government's return to power with more than an absolute majority on its own.

Taking a step back from this relentless barrage of events, as of end of May 2019, the economic environment did not look promising, with a noticeable downturn in the profitability of the private sector. There was a gradual slackening of rural demand, stemming from lower prices of agricultural products and, to an extent, excess production. Sales of tractors, cars and two-wheelers were also down in the last two quarters.[72]

Overall, economic growth has slowed down, and in Modi's second term the government will need a competent and highly driven team. William Easterly, a former World Bank economist, and many others have argued persuasively that a focus on economic growth is of paramount importance for developing countries to reduce poverty sustainably.[73]

An important element in India's higher growth strategy has to be to push for increased exports of goods. As a proportion of GDP, Indian exports of goods in 2017 had shrunk to 11.7 per cent which is well below the same number in 2004 when it was about 16.9 per cent.[74] Clearly, the efforts till now to create conditions for greater ease of business, higher FDI and for India to be included in value chains—which are prerequisites to make the pricing of quality goods competitive internationally—have not been adequately implemented. The growth in the exports of IT services as a fraction of GDP also came down somewhat from 3.9 per cent in 2008 to 2.98 per cent in 2017. However, it is production of goods, not services, which involves employment of larger numbers of workers. Consequently, the Modi government in its second term needs to pay particular attention to promoting production of quality goods.

In the past, Indian corporate borrowers managed to strip assets and yet retain control of their companies after reneging on their debt service obligations to PSBs. It is in this context that the RBI had issued a circular on 12 February 2018 that set out a timetable over which impaired assets had to be immediately recognized and legal action initiated with the National Company Law Tribunal after 180 days. Under a Supreme Court order of 2 April 2019,[75] this RBI circular was set aside as unconstitutional, and it was left to the Central government to direct RBI on individual cases.

Even a cursory examination of this Supreme Court judgment[76] indicates that the balance of power in cases of debt default has again shifted in favour of borrowers. The logic which permeates this judgment is that RBI should not follow a 'one size fits all' approach for debt default cases. This flies in the face of the principle that all cases of bankruptcy should be dealt with impartially in exactly the same manner, particularly because borrowers of large amounts are able to get lender consortiums to be more 'understanding' in return for 'inducements'.

Another order of the Supreme Court of June 2018 on reservations in promotions for Dalits and OBCs or 'promotion quotas' in government has been discussed widely in the media.[77] The Central government was asked by the Supreme Court to ensure that administrative efficiency should not be compromised even as fair practices are followed in promotions. Separately, the Allahabad High Court had ruled that reservation quotas for universities should be calculated department-wise and not for the whole university. The Supreme Court upheld the Allahabad High Court judgment on 22 January 2019.[78] Perhaps with an eye to garnering voter support in the April–May 2019 general election Modi's government announced that it would bring in legislative changes to overturn the Supreme Court judgment. However, the Central government had not initiated a bill till the end of its first term in May 2019.

Five years since the Lokpal legislation came into force in January 2014, no Lokpal had been appointed by the end of calendar year 2018. After protests from a few non-governmental organizations (NGOs), the Central government constituted a search committee, at the end of September 2018, to propose names for a Lokpal and members. On 17 January 2019, the Supreme Court took it upon itself to ask the search committee to finalize names by end February 2019. A selection committee headed by the prime minister with the Chief Justice of India and the 'leader' of the Opposition as members finally selected P.C. Ghose, former Supreme Court judge, as the Lokpal on 19 March 2019. The other Lokpal members have also been selected. Lokayuktas were to be appointed by state governments, but several states had not done so by end May 2019.

On 14 February 2019, a twenty-two-year-old Kashmiri suicide bomber rammed his vehicle laden with explosives into a convoy of vehicles carrying CRPF personnel. In this attack, forty CRPF men were killed.[79] The Pakistan-based JeM claimed responsibility for this terrorist attack. The decibel levels in the Indian media rose to feverish levels with most calling for retaliatory action while a few counselled restraint and urged greater attention to reducing the sense of alienation that many in Kashmir feel from India.

In the early hours of 26 February 2019, Modi's government launched a missile attack from the air on Balakot located in the Khyber Pakhtunkhwa province in Pakistan. Balakot was said to harbour JeM terrorists who were preparing for another attack on India. Modi's government claimed that 'in this operation, a very large number of JeM terrorists, trainers, senior commanders and groups of jihadis who were being trained for fidayeen action were eliminated'.[80]

According to Indian media reports, a day later, on 27 February 2019, twenty Pakistani air force jets entered Indian airspace in Kashmir. The Indian air force scrambled MiG fighter planes to counter this attack, and one Indian MiG aircraft was brought down during the air battle.[81] The Indian pilot of this MiG fighter plane was taken into custody by Pakistani authorities. He was subsequently handed back to India via the Wagah border on 2 March 2019. The Indian government has claimed that one F-16 fighter was brought down during the encounter between the fighter planes of the two countries on 27 February.[82]

Irrespective of the precise veracity of the details about the Indian missile strike on Balakot and subsequent events, this was an inflection point in India's relations with Pakistan. It is the first time that India has retaliated against a target within that country since 1971. India had not resorted to a counter-attack of any sort on Pakistani soil, even after the Pakistan-supported terrorist killings in Mumbai in November 2008.

The usual argument has been that since Pakistan possesses nuclear weapons, any overt Indian government attack on Pakistani targets could lead to a nuclear counter-attack. Of course, Pakistan made it somewhat easier this time compared to November 2008. In 2008, despite any number of confirmations that the attack had been planned and carried out with the support of the Pakistani establishment, there was no claim by any Pakistan-based outfit that it was responsible for the attack.[83] On the contrary, for the February 2019 attack, the JeM claimed responsibility making it just that bit easier for India to retaliate.

The subsequent UN declaration of Masood Azhar as a global terrorist at the end of April 2019 was a foreign policy success for Modi's government.[84] China, with its veto power in the UN, had resisted such a classification for Masood Azhar. The Masood Azhar–led JeM's claim that it was responsible for the Pulwama attack had convinced the other four permanent members of the UNSC that he should be branded as a global terrorist and it was only China that held out till April 2019.

The second BRI (Belt and Road Initiative) forum summit meeting took place in Beijing in the last week of April 2019.[85] India did not participate and there is no compelling economic or strategic reason for India to allow China to claim such a BRI-related leadership role around the world. At a bilateral level, India has not reached a comprehensive agreement on its border with China, and the latter continues to lay claim to large areas within India such as the state of Arunachal Pradesh.

Legacy

Modi took over as PM in May 2014 at a difficult juncture for the Indian economy. He inherited PSBs laden with bad debts and power producer–electricity distribution companies groaning under the weight of debt they could not service. Inflation was high, fiscal deficits were elevated, and there was a run on the rupee in September 2013. Additionally, there was a pervasive view that Manmohan Singh's government was either a spectator or abettor of widespread corruption, and there was impatient dissatisfaction among the young because employment opportunities in the formal sector were inadequate.

On the positive side for Modi when he became PM, a significant proportion of the population was already registered under Aadhaar. Implementation of the MGNREGA, which was passed to provide limited yet assured employment to the rural unemployed, had started and was working well. On the foreign policy front, the hard and delicate work of rapprochement with the US was complete, with the conclusion of the 123 Agreement. Relations with the other four permanent members of the UNSC (Russia, China, France and the UK) were on a sound footing, and economic interactions with Japan and Germany were on the rise.

In overall terms, the foreign-policy-related performance of Modi's government was at a high level in content and breadth of coverage. This was particularly impressive given that he had no direct experience of foreign policy at a national level earlier. Modi's principal strength was that he was perceived abroad as the unquestioned leader within his party with an absolute majority in the Lok Sabha. However, Modi placed more emphasis than warranted on personal diplomacy and particularly on rhetoric about India's relations with Pakistan. The latter gave an inaccurate sense of parity between India and Pakistan.

In de facto terms, Sushma Swaraj, the minister of external affairs in Modi's government, was more the minister for the erstwhile Ministry of Overseas Indian Affairs (MOIA) than MEA. Modi would have done better to entrust MEA to someone who had his full confidence and could have shared the burden of travel to distant capitals. All Indian PMs have necessarily taken a close interest in foreign relations. At the same time, an able Indian foreign minister can take on the administrative burden of managing the foreign office, that is, the MEA, and would have the time to visit distant countries to which the PM may not have the time to travel except in transit. The MOIA was formally merged with the MEA in 2016. This was a rational decision taken by Modi's government since matters related to overseas Indians should logically be managed by the MEA.

India's relations with neighbours such as Bhutan, Bangladesh and Myanmar improved marginally, and those with Sri Lanka remained the same. However, Nepal's anxieties as a landlocked nation could have been handled better, and the relationship with Pakistan deteriorated considerably. By contrast, Modi's efforts at wooing the G7 were viewed positively in those countries. To a considerable extent, this was because these nations were looking to a further opening up of India as a market for their goods and services, particularly defence equipment. Although relations did not remain as close as before, the Modi government did enough with Russia for it to remain a reliable supplier of sophisticated defence equipment and classified technologies. The modus vivendi with China needed to be further fine-tuned for it to have a restraining influence on Pakistan. One inducement for China could have been to allow their goods and products to have greater access to the Indian market with reciprocal adjustments to be made by China to facilitate imports of Indian IT services.

In foreign relations, personal chemistry and summitry can help push bilateral ties to higher levels of engagement. However, when there are substantial differences about borders or divergences in strategic and economic interests, personal diplomacy is less effective. This became amply evident in the cases of Pakistan, China and the US during Modi's years as PM.

Modi took the view that the Indian PM needs to visit and engage with the leadership in smaller countries such as Mauritius, Fiji and the Maldives. This undoubtedly gave a boost to India's relationship with those countries. However, as these smaller countries face pulls and pressures from major powers, visit diplomacy does not necessarily lead to lasting benefits. A more efficient time management strategy was for Modi to have met with these leaders on the sidelines of the annual UN General Assembly meetings.

As the star BJP election campaigner, Modi continued to travel ceaselessly from mid-2014 to May 2019 to campaign during the state assembly elections of several large states such as UP, Karnataka, Gujarat, Madhya Pradesh and Rajasthan, and for the Lok Sabha elections. Modi needed to delegate at least some of this campaigning and spend more time checking on the implementation of his government's multiple initiatives. In politics that means allowing others to rise within the party including those who could in the future replace Modi. That is a risk that effective leaders have to take when they groom potential successors. To put this suggestion in perspective, even Jawaharlal Nehru did not measure up adequately in this matter.

A not so centralized mode of functioning would have enabled the government to be alerted whenever it was veering off course or policies were not being effectively followed. This was particularly true about the implementation of primary health and education targets. In both these fields, it is state governments that supervise subordinate bodies. However, it appears that Modi did not spend enough time coordinating and monitoring efforts with all chief ministers in these two vital fields.

Modi's yoga initiative was typical of his high personal energy and fitness levels. He was unique among Indian PMs and senior political figures in that he personally participated in community yoga popularization drives on live television. Modi used yoga astutely to promote India's image as a non-threatening nation which promotes physical and mental wellness through time-tested methods.

Modi was acutely conscious of the importance of keeping up with the latest technologies. This was evident in his election campaign for the Lok Sabha elections in 2014 and was abundantly clear in his interactions with heads of globally significant cutting-edge technology companies such as Microsoft, Google and Facebook. It was less evident that Modi had interacted enough with heads of high-technology companies in India and the Indian Institutes of Technology.

The Modi government's final approval for Rafale fighter aircraft imports from France was questioned by Opposition political parties and in the Indian media on various grounds. The deal showed up the inability of Hindustan Aeronautics Limited (HAL) or the French side's unwillingness to accept it as a reliable partner. This was a reminder about the slow pace at which India's domestic defence production capabilities have grown. While it was too short a period for Modi to have set up sophisticated defence manufacturing, it does not appear that his government gave sufficient attention to this matter.

The Lalit Modi episode, and the dubious manner in which he was in touch with the BJP chief minister of Rajasthan and the external affairs minister, was not satisfactorily explained by Modi's government. Indian authorities rarely reach closure on allegations of financial wrongdoing, impropriety or conflict of interest at high political levels. Coming as Modi did, after the scam-ridden years of UPA, enhanced transparency on such issues was expected from his administration.

Modi's punishing schedule included much more domestic and foreign travel than his predecessor. Additionally, the responsibilities he bore as PM were heavier than others before him since several of his ministers had relatively little experience of working in the Central government. All things considered, Modi placed too heavy a load on himself. The PMO appears to have centralized much of the government's decision making. This was an unfortunate throwback to the years when Indira Gandhi was PM.

By any standards, Modi was a superbly efficient manager. Modi's government made faster progress in the building of national highways and railway tracks. The auction bidding process for coal blocks was free of controversy, and electricity distribution companies are recovering gradually. However, power-sector reforms were again not systemic enough to do away with undeserving subsidies. PSBs are limping back to health, but again, no sustainable reforms were attempted to make them less vulnerable to pulls and pressures from whoever is ruling in Delhi.

On a broader note, Modi was unable to show the qualities of an all-embracing leadership required to take India, a country of multiple minorities, forward as one nation. For instance, the choice of UP's chief minister did not reflect a forward-looking mindset for the BJP or for Modi. Cow vigilantes have heartlessly hounded even those who are engaged in the leather-processing and buffalo meat exporting sectors. At the root of this issue are eating habits based on religious beliefs which should be personal and not extended to those who have different practices. The instances of vigilante justice may have been avoided if the norms and rules for transportation of cattle and disposal of their carcasses had been widely publicized by the Central and the BJP-ruled state governments.

Modi tended to adopt a transactional approach on governance issues. This can be effective under some circumstances, but is not enough or appropriate at all times. To be a transformational leader, he needed to have had at least some around him who could speak the truth to power and inform him about what was going well and what was not working.

On the perceived divide between India and Bharat, Modi leaned definitively towards Bharat. His personal origins are humble, and although he speaks English fluently, he seems to be more comfortable in Gujarati and Hindi. Modi used to dress in typically Indian clothes as an RSS and BJP worker. However, since becoming the chief minister of Gujarat and later PM, he preferred bandhgala suits in foreign locations and churidars and sleeveless jackets plus matching kerchiefs.

To summarize, a number of significant and uplifting steps were taken by the Narendra Modi government; for example, to promote cleanliness, implement GST, and float an as yet untested scheme called Ayushman Bharat to provide universal health coverage and to provide easier access to loans for smaller businesses. At the same time, among the touchy and difficult issues confronting the Narendra Modi government after five years in power are doubts about commitment to interfaith harmony, announcements of income support without mention of bringing down non-merit subsidies and higher levels of reservations. This is a complex mix of challenges, and it will take considerable skill on Modi's part to sustain optimism among the masses over the next five years, after securing an even more lopsided victory in the May 2019 elections.

As for the 3 Cs, on Character, the Supreme Court has not indicated that Modi had any direct responsibility for the 2002 communal riots. Modi's compassion for the economically weak and socially marginalized was evident in his frenetic and even frantic pushing for JAM which should help in direct transfer of cash benefits, cooking gas cylinder connections, housing and toilets for lower income households. Although political opponents and naysayers remain unconvinced that these and other welfare initiatives have succeeded in any substantive manner, the fact is that all public outreach programmes in India take time to grow roots. Modi's commitment was abundantly evident from the impossibly long hours that he has so visibly put in at work. However, Modi concentrated more on starting any number of specific programmes rather than trying to implement systemic reforms. Minority communities had reason to be vocal in expressing their disquiet about physical insecurity. On the remaining 2 Cs, Modi scored at extremely high levels on Competence and with large sections of the population on Charisma. In fact, Modi's charisma is evident from the warm reception he gets from crowds at his public meetings in many parts of the country.

EPILOGUE

'. . . And in these words that I have relayed
From other shoulders,
Is man's cruel experience
And the maulings of history.'[1]

Hiren Bhattacharya

As Mark Tully puts it, there are 'No full stops in India'.[2] I would go further and say that there are no colons, semicolons or even commas. It is invariably a downpour of conscience-stirring events which the media gushes about with short-lived interest. It is unclear which significant issues have been resolved, and experts rarely reach a consensus on the consequences for the country. The jackboots of time march on, and most Indians do not have the luxury of looking back as fresh events overtake yesterday's 'big' news.

The Indian electorate, with 900 million eligible voters in the general elections of April–May 2019, was by far the largest anywhere in the world. The voting, at 67.11 per cent, was the highest ever in any Indian general election since Independence. In recent years, television programmes in regional languages have come to be increasingly viewed on smartphones. By the time of the elections, perhaps over 90 per cent of Indian voters got their news and entertainment in the vernacular, with emphasis on issues of local interest, and often on hand-held phones. It has to be a matter of celebration that, despite the cynicism that was amply evident in the selection of candidates and statements made by several party leaders, the elections were held without evidence of widespread fraud or violence. The BJP got a clear majority, winning 303 out of 543 seats, and the participation of women was higher than in earlier elections.[3] Prime Minister Narendra Modi and his ministers took their oath of office on 30 May 2019 in the forecourt of Rashtrapati Bhavan.

A sobering thought is that India's elected representatives are much wealthier than average Indians, and many have serious charges against them, including criminal records. Another regret about the 2019 elections was that voter alienation was high in Kashmir as was evident from the extremely low polling percentages. Given the tense security environment there, the assembly elections could not be held simultaneously. The law and order situation for average Indians in several states, including Delhi, continues to be a matter of concern.

If the hugely favourable 2019 election results for BJP are an indication that development issues are to the fore, rather than communal–caste polarization, this is indeed a welcome trend. It appears from the election results that affiliations with the doctrinaire Left are weaker than before. This is a trend in other democracies as well, and 'strong' individuals rather than parties seem to appeal to voters. Perhaps due to language differences, southern states remained unimpressed by the Modi juggernaut.

A significant lesson from the 2019 elections is that if the Congress remains coterie ridden and feudally run, its days are numbered. The decline of the Congress in north India began in the 1980s with the rise of caste-based parties in Uttar Pradesh and Bihar. West Bengal was the bastion of the Left and then the Trinamool Congress (TMC). Currently, the Congress is near insignificant in that state, Tamil Nadu and Andhra Pradesh. It is unfortunate for the country that a national party has been gradually whittled down to scrambling to form governments in only three large states: Madhya Pradesh, Rajasthan and Karnataka. For a vibrant democracy, India needs at least two truly national parties.

The English-speaking elite based in India usually has one or more family members settled in the West. They can speak in the vernacular but find it difficult to write more than a few pages in any regional Indian language.[4] Most Indian academics, senior government officials, bankers, writers and media personalities belong to this group. By contrast, current BJP leaders and those of regional parties prefer to speak and write in Indian languages. However, textbooks in the physical sciences are almost exclusively available only in English in India. As for the social sciences, most of the seminal work is again available only in English. Textbooks will need to be translated to regional Indian languages, and this will take time. To have a window to what is being published around the world, a robust working knowledge of English is essential.

For India to succeed in tomorrow's world, the English-speaking classes and those who are more fluent in regional languages need to become more like each other. The former cannot merely talk among themselves. And the latter cannot move the country forward if they keep harking back to a distant, possibly mythical, glorious past. Some among those who speak only in the vernacular suggest that they alone are true Indians. This kind of inverse snobbery could lead to unhelpful divisions.

Going forward, after May 2019, systemic efforts will be necessary to meet India's social, economic and foreign policy challenges. Those who were from 'subaltern'[5] India are now firmly in power in Delhi. They were already in charge in several states, first in the south, and since the mid-1980s, in northern states too. However, a mere changing of the political elite would achieve little in addressing the glaring inequities and discrimination in part-obscurantist, semi-feudal, rural India and its congested urban slums. Indian leadership should be less cynical and more open in discussing and arriving at remedies based on consensus.

Turning to the Indian economy, farming and related activities employ the largest fraction of the country's population. Instead of the usual unwinnable game of micro-managing prices, the government's policies need to be rationalized and farmers supported to store, transport and sell their products at cost-plus prices. Leasing of land needs to be fully legalized for farming lots to be larger, enabling greater mechanization which would result in higher productivity and more income from farming. A prerequisite is digitization of landownership records to make leasing less risky for landowners.

Most rural households have family members working informally in urban areas. The national average for farm income of rural households as a proportion of total income was about 60 per cent in 2012–13.[6] The average hides wide divergences across states, and this number is at 30, 34, 69 and 76 per cent for West Bengal, Kerala, UP and Madhya Pradesh, respectively. However, according to a NABARD report in 2016–17, only 34 per cent of the income of agricultural households came from 'cultivation'.[7] It is unlikely that the share of farming income could have nearly halved, from 60 to 34 per cent in just four years from 2012–13 to 2016–17. Even assuming that the share of farming income for rural households has decreased substantially, non-farming income comes from a variety of *informal*-sector jobs. The single most important economic challenge for India is to get surplus labour in the agriculture sector out of farming and gainfully employed in industry, and more generally in the formal sector. One of the enabling steps is for the Central government to work with state governments to move agriculture from the state to the concurrent list in the Constitution.

The growing disparity in incomes and wealth has to be addressed. In 1930s India, the fraction of income earned by the top 1 per cent was 21 per cent of the total. This number came down to 13 per cent by the mid-1950s and 6 per cent by the mid-1980s. From then on, and particularly after the 1990s, the share of income for the top earners has grown steadily. A saving grace has been that concurrently the annual rate of growth of real income for all earners has risen steadily from 0.7 per cent in the 1970s to 4.7 per cent post-2000.[8]

The poor in India have been fed the myth by most political parties that they can be provided with quality primary education, subsidized healthcare, foodgrains, fertilizers, power and other benefits, including employment opportunities in the formal sector. This would just not be possible without sustained higher economic growth. Of course, the poor cannot wait for the Indian economy to grow. Even as income and other support are provided through direct bank transfers (DBT), there has to be a single-minded focus at the Centre and in the states to push for growth. This requires land, labour and financial market reforms, focus on water conservation and higher investments in infrastructure. Infrastructure includes not just roads, bridges, railways tracks, ports and power, but also rainwater harvesting, solar and wind power, irrigation canals and better power–grid connectivity.

As for the importance of keeping up with technological innovation, both (vernacular) Bharat and (English-speaking) India need to anticipate the ever-increasing mechanization of industry and agriculture. It may take decades for this to spread fully to agriculture, but the use of robots has been increasing in industry, even in labour-surplus India. It is likely that at least for the next two decades, manual labour would continue to be required in construction and road building. Greater emphasis on technical knowledge is the way forward in India as advanced countries are moving towards enhanced use of artificial intelligence.

For success of their initiatives, all Indian governments necessarily depend on the quality of those at senior and junior levels in political, constitutional, official and judicial positions. Since the Indira Gandhi years of the early 1970s, Indian prime ministers have invariably appointed pliable personalities to such positions. Retired civil service officers with little domain knowledge are often appointed to constitutional and statutory positions. The net has not been cast wide enough throughout the country in selecting people to head these bodies, and officials are rewarded for loyalty rather than expertise. Matters have reached a point where the Supreme Court has recorded its disappointment with the CBI. It is more than high time that selection to oversight and regulatory positions should also include those who have excelled in the private sector, academics and professionally.

A crucially important pillar of the Indian state is the independence and quality of its judiciary. It has to be a matter of serious concern that over the past several decades, the Indian judiciary has increasingly encroached on the turf of the executive. It also appears that considerations of religion, caste and region are followed too rigidly in the selection of judges. At a very minimum, there should be a cooling-off period for judges to accept any form of remunerative appointment after retirement. Unless the Central government plays favourites and waives rules, retired civil servants have to comply with such a requirement.[9]

Often, the government of the day appears to be relieved if courts take over and it can stonewall aggrieved parties by saying that the matter is sub judice.[10] As of 30 June 2016, the backlog of pending cases in the district and subordinate courts, high courts and the Supreme Court amounted to 2.8 crore, 40 lakh and 63,000 respectively.[11] If the lack of judges, staff and office space are continuing constraints, the Supreme Court should not spend as much time as it has, for instance, with the affairs of the Board of Control for Cricket in India (BCCI). The Supreme Court even has to accept cases related to disagreements between tenants and landlords. For instance, on 17 April 2017, it set aside a judgment of the Himachal Pradesh High Court on the grounds that 'the contents of the impugned order' were incomprehensible.[12] This case exposed the systemic flaws in the appointment of judges. In another instance, a strangely worded judgment passed on 24 July 2003 by Dipak Misra, the then chief justice of the Madhya Pradesh High Court, involved the singing of the national anthem. Readers can assess for themselves if this judgment made any more sense than that of the Himachal Pradesh High Court.[13]

A disproportionate assets case against Jayalalithaa started in 1996, and the final judgment was delivered by the Supreme Court twenty-one years later in February 2017, after she had passed away.[14] Lalu Prasad Yadav was chief minister in Bihar and also the cabinet minister for railways in the Central government. Accusations against him first surfaced around 1997, and he was convicted on charges of corruption sixteen years later in 2013 and is currently in jail.[15] These inordinate delays in court judgments, even for such high-profile cases, raise grave doubts about the efficacy of India's justice system.

In the India of 2019, the judiciary appears to have become the new royalty. Even though the Parliament enacted a law to set up a National Judicial Appointments Commission (NJAC), it was struck down by the Supreme Court as unconstitutional.[16] There is danger in this apparent accumulation of executive power by the judiciary. A future Indian government may refuse to respect a Supreme Court judgment, which would result in a constitutional crisis. The government, principal Opposition parties and the judiciary can sit down behind closed doors to work out boundaries for each other.

India's domestic and foreign policy strengths stem from its large geographical size and a relatively young population. These two factors, coupled with growing consumer markets, make it an attractive destination for investments and sale of products and services. Indian governments will have to deal with increasing protectionist tendencies in the developed West, including the United States. It follows that India has to nurture and develop domestic markets, and focus even more on Asia's relatively younger consumers and rising per capita incomes.

Since the Vajpayee years, there has been a gradual shift towards the US in India's foreign policy. Hence, despite the issues raised by President Trump's indiscriminate rattling of the trade and technology[17] cage, the overall trend is towards closer relations with the US. India would have to walk the tightrope of increasing economic, technological and defence interaction with the US without raising Russian hackles. A recent example, for which a balancing act is required, is the US threat to impose sanctions on India under its Countering America's Adversaries through Sanctions Act (CAATSA) if India goes ahead to purchase of the S-400 Triumf air defence system from Russia. Over the last decade, Russia has moved closer to China as they both cannot, at least not right now, stand up to US financial and technical hegemony individually on their own.

It remains to be seen if India can keep China at bay in South Asia while strengthening ties within SAARC (Pakistan is necessarily an exception because of its abetment of terrorism) and with BIMSTEC[18] nations. It will also be a challenge for India to expand trade and investment relationships with ASEAN countries without participating in China's Belt and Road Initiative (BRI). Foreign policy efforts would have to be geared towards attracting investment, and, if possible, classified and high-technology tie-ups with Japan, Germany and France.

The West, led by the US, relies on NATO for collective security, and the G7 grouping of high per capita income countries, again led by the US, for coordination on economic issues. India, Russia and China do not cooperate on security matters in any way comparable to NATO. The Russia–India–China (RIC) meetings at the level of foreign ministers are more for exchange of information, and there are no mechanisms for institutionalized follow-up. On the other hand, the BRICS group has set up a development bank headquartered in Shanghai. Another grouping, the SCO, is again headquartered in China. The SCO's members include China, Russia, India, Pakistan and four Central Asian nations excluding Turkmenistan. The primary unstated focus of China and Russia in SCO is to keep the West's economic and strategic tentacles from gaining any hold over the huge oil and gas reserves or the existing and potential military–intelligence facilities in Central Asian countries. India had close historical connections with Central Asian nations and should enhance economic cooperation with this group of countries, including buying/leasing of rights to fossil fuel and mineral resources.

A four-nation informal formation, of which India is ostensibly a part, is the so-called Quad comprising the US, Japan, Australia and India. The US would like to coordinate efforts with the other three countries to contain China's maritime ambitions. A basic difficulty for coherence in this grouping is that India needs to maintain working relations with neighbouring China. China is the largest trading partner in goods for Japan and Australia, and hence the ability of these two countries to contain China's designs in and around the East and South China Seas is limited.[19]

*

It was inevitable that the widespread faith in the leaders of the newly independent India of the 1950s would not be sustained. Over the past seven decades, the proportion of the desperately poor has diminished sharply. At the same time, the norms of probity and fairness in governmental decision making have eroded more than what can be attributed merely to the fading memories of the freedom struggle. Effective political leadership is needed from the new Modi government to strengthen confidence in the good faith of those at high levels in the government, judiciary and media.

In Jnanpith Award–winning author U.R. Ananthamurthy's novel titled *Samskara*,[20] the principal character Praneshacharya is a priest married to an invalid. Praneshacharya is a Sanskrit scholar, well versed in the scriptures, and his life consists entirely of his temple duties and looking after his wife. When childless and wayward Naranappa who was cohabiting with a prostitute dies, differences of opinion arise within the conservative community in which Praneshacharya lives about how Naranappa's funeral rites should be conducted. The community looks to Praneshacharya to provide answers, and despite his knowledge of sacred texts and rituals, he is unable to resolve in his mind who should conduct the last rites and how these should be carried out. An implied suggestion of this multifaceted novel is that mere book knowledge and asceticism do not provide answers to everyday challenges.

Another Jnanpith Award winner V.S. Khandekar's many-layered novel *Yayati* recounts the author's version of a story about this mythological king in the Mahabharata. Yayati is married to Devyani and falls in love with Sharmishtha, his wife's maid. In the involved plot in Khandekar's novel, as distinct from the original mythological tale, Devyani is mean-spirited, and Sharmishtha, who is of royal descent, provides the love that Yayati craves. At a physical level, after Yayati has sired five sons from the two women, he declares 'my lust for pleasure in still unsatisfied'.[21] A simple truth from this complex novel is that the desire to indulge in never-ending physical pleasures could be compared to nations chasing ever-increasing levels of consumption and material well-being.

Praneshacharya's excessive dependence on religious texts to guide his community, or the relentless chasing of physical pleasures as was Yayati's wont as a king, are clearly not the appropriate models for leaders. Kings in the past or heads of government today cannot raise their countries to higher levels of well-being without the confidence and support of the people. The character and competence of the teams led by India's prime ministers will remain critically important in inspiring fellow citizens to rise above themselves. Finally, it is average Indians who will have a definitive bearing on the nation meeting its enduring quest for the basics, dignity and peace for all.

APPENDICES AND TABLES

TABLE 1.1

Length of Railway Tracks, 1947–2016

Total Track Kilometre				
Year	BG	MG	NG	Total
August 1947	*	*	*	55,000
March 1961	*	*	*	83,706
March 1966	*	*	*	92,474
March 1985	68,654	32,705	4765	106,124
March 1990	71,563	32,300	4566	108,429
March 1997	81,121	22,201	4038	107,360
March 1999	85,428	19,158	3827	108,413
March 2004	88,547	16,489	3450	108,486
March 2014	107,603	6609	2553	116,765
March 2016				119,630

Sources

1947: http://www.kportal.indianrailways.gov.in/index.php/history-of-railways

1961 and 1966: Indian Railways Annual Statistical Statement 2011–12. http://www.indianrailways.gov.in/railwayboard/uploads/directorate/stat_econ/pdf/IR_STATISTICAL_STATEMENTS_BI_2011_12/8.pdf

1970–71 to 2012–13: Indian railways key statistics 1970–71 to 2012–13

2014: Indian Railways Statistical Publications 2013–14

2016: Indian Railways Statistical Publications 2015–16

Track kilometre: The length of all running tracks including tracks in sidings, yards and crossings.

BG: Broad gauge (lines with 1.67 metre width)

MG: Meter Gauge (lines with 1 metre width)

NG: Narrow Gauge (lines with 0.762/0.610 metre width)

*Break-up of track lengths are not readily available for these years

TABLE 1.2

India's Exports and Share of Total Value of World Exports, 1951–70

Calendar Year	Indian Exports (US $ millions)	Indian Exports as Percentage of World Exports
1951	1,611	2.2
1952	1,295	1.8
1953	1,116	1.5
1954	1,182	1.5
1955	1,276	1.5
1956	1,300	1.4
1957	1,379	1.4
1958	1,221	1.3
1959	1,308	1.4
1960	1,331	1.2
1961	1,387	1.2
1962	1,403	1.1
1963	1,631	1.2
1964	1,749	1.2
1965	1,686	1.0
1966	1,606	0.89
1967	1,612	0.84
1968	1,760	0.82
1969	1,835	0.75
1970	2,026	0.72

TABLE 1.4

Sectoral Composition of the Indian Economy (per cent of GDP)

Year	Agriculture and Allied Activities	Industry	Services*
1950–51	51.9	11.1	34.6
1960–61	47.6	13.7	36.6
1970–71	41.7	16.0	40.9
1980–81	35.7	18.0	45.3
1990–91	29.5	20.6	49.6
2000–01	22.3	20.7	57.0
2010–11	14.6	20.3	65.1
2017–18	14.8	23.4	61.8

*Including government services, for example Railway Services.

Source RBI

TABLE 1.5
Income Tax Rates for the Highest Income Slab (per cent)*

1954–55	78.1
1955–56	84.4
1956–57	87.5
1960–61	70
1962–63	72.5
1971–72	85
1974–75	70
1977–78	60
1984–85	55
1985–86	50
1992–93	40
1997–98#	30

* Surcharge is excluded
# Continuing till 2017
Source: RBI staff study, 'Empirical Fiscal Research in India: A Survey' (pp. 14–15).

TABLE 1.6
Institutional and Non-Institutional Agricultural Credit

Agency	1951	1961	1971	1981	1991	2002	2013
INSTITUTIONAL	10.2	20.9	32	56.2	66.3	61.1	64
Government	–	6.2		4	5.7	1.7	1.3
Cooperative societies/ banks, etc.	6.2	12.5		27.6	23.6	30.2	28.9
Commercial banks	4	2.2		23.8	35.2	26.3	30.7
Insurance, provident funds	–	–		0.8	0.7	0.5	0.1
Other agencies	–	–		–	1.1	2.4	3
NON-INSTITUTIONAL	89.8	79.1	68	43.8	33.7	38.9	36
Moneylenders	39.8	25.3		17.2	17.5	26.8	29.6
Relatives	–	–		11.5	4.6	6.2	4.3
Traders	–	–		5.8	2.2	2.6	
Landlords	21.4	15		3.6	3.7	0.9	0.4
Others	28.6	38.8		5.7	5.7	2.4	1.7
TOTAL	100	100	100	100	100	100	100

Source: All India Debt and Investment Survey, Various Issues, NSSO.

TABLE 3.1
Indira Gandhi: 1970–77

Years	Gross fiscal deficit*	Net primary deficit*	Capital outlay*	Current Account Deficit*	Defence Expenditure*
1970–71	3.08	1.64	2.06	–1.0	2.98
1971–72	3.53	2.34	2.28	–1.0	3.42
1972–73	4.04	1.72	1.81	–0.6	3.48
1973–74	2.64	0.95	1.54	1.7	2.95
1974–75	2.97	0.83	2.10	–1.2	3.00
1975–76	3.49	1.23	2.59	–0.2	3.31
1976–77	4.07	1.27	2.00	1.0	3.26

Years	GDP growth rate (Per cent)	Gross Capital Formation*	CPI (Annual per cent)	GDP Deflator (Annual per cent)	Rupees per USD (average)	Exports*
1970–71	5.2	15.3	1.7	1.6	7.6	3.1
1971–72	1.6	16.8	1.6	5.3	7.5	3.2
1972–73	–0.6	15.8	10.4	10.8	7.7	3.7
1973–74	3.3	16.5	21.5	17.8	7.8	3.5
1974–75	1.2	18.6	34.4	16.7	7.9	4.1
1975–76	9.1	18.5	–3.9	–1.6	8.7	5
1976–77	1.7	18.1	–13.8	6.0	9.0	5.7

Notes: Applicable to all the tables from 3.1 to 11.1, as relevant.

GDP: Gross Domestic Product

* Indicates percentage of GDP

Gross Fiscal Deficit and Net Primary Deficit are for the Central government and do not include state governments

CPI: Consumer Price Inflation

TABLE 3.2

Indira Gandhi: 1980–84

Years	Gross fiscal deficit*	Net primary deficit*	Capital outlay*	Current Account Deficit*	Defence Expenditure*
1980–81	5.55	2.87	2.05	−1.5	2.94
1981–82	4.93	2.05	2.39	−1.7	2.99
1982–83	5.40	2.49	2.37	−1.7	3.13
1983–84	5.69	2.46	2.28	−1.5	3.11

Years	GDP growth rate (Per cent)	Gross Capital Formation*	CPI (Annual per cent)	GDP Deflator Annual per cent	Rupees per USD (average)	Exports*
1980–81	6.7	18.0	14.1	11.5	7.9	4.6
1981–82	6.0	21.8	12.4	10.8	9.0	4.5
1982–83	3.5	22.0	5.1	8.1	9.7	4.8
1983–84	7.3	20.0	11.4	8.6	10.3	4.6

Appendix 3.1
Definitions of Deficits

(a) *Revenue Deficit (RD)* is the difference between revenue receipts and revenue expenditure.

Revenue Account Gap = Revenue Deficit (RD) = Revenue Receipts (RR) – Revenue Expenditure (RE).

(b) *Capital Deficit* denotes the difference between capital receipts and capital disbursements.

Capital Account Gap = Capital Account Deficit (CAD) = Capital Receipts (CR) – Capital Disbursements (CD).

(c) *Conventional deficit (budgetary deficit or overall deficit)* is the difference between all receipts and expenditure, both revenue and capital.

Overall Gap = RD+CAD = (RR–RE) + (CR–CD) = [(RR+CR) – (RE+CD)].

(d) *Gross Fiscal Deficit (GFD)* is the difference between aggregate disbursements net of debt repayments and recovery of loans and revenue receipts and non-debt capital receipts.

Gross Fiscal Deficit (GFD)
= RE + [CD–(Discharge of Internal Debt (DID) + Repayment of Loans to Centre (RLC) + Recoveries of Loans & Advances (RLA)] – RR
= RE + [Capital Outlay (CO) + Loans & Advances by States (LAS) + DID+RLC –(DID +RLC+RLA)] –RR
= (RE–RR) + [CO+ (LAS–RLA) + (DID–DID) + (RLC–RLC)]
= RD+CO+ Net Lending (NL)

(e) *Net Fiscal Deficit (NFD)* is the gross fiscal deficit *less* net lending of the State Governments.

Net Fiscal Deficit (NFD) = GFD – (LAS–RLA).

(f) *Gross Primary Deficit (GPD)* is defined as GFD *minus* interest payments.

Primary Deficit (PD) = GFD – Interest Payment (IP).

(g) *Net Primary Deficit (NPD)* denotes net fiscal deficit (NFD) *minus* net interest payments.

Net Primary Deficit (NPD) = NFD – [(IP–Interest Receipts (IR)].

(h) *Primary revenue balance* denotes revenue deficit *minus* interest payments. Primary Revenue Balance (PRB) = RD – IP.

(i) *Net primary revenue balance* denotes revenue deficit *minus* net interest payments.

Net Primary Revenue Balance (NPRB) = RD – (IP–IR)

Source: Reserve Bank of India

GCF as a percentage of GDP: Gross capital formation consists of outlays on additions to the fixed assets of the economy plus net changes in the level of inventories. Fixed assets include land improvements (fences, ditches, drains, and so on); plant, machinery, and equipment purchases; and the construction of roads, railways, and the like, including schools, offices, hospitals, private residential dwellings, and commercial and industrial buildings. Inventories are stocks of goods held by firms to meet temporary or unexpected fluctuations in production or sales, and "work in progress.

GDP Growth Rate: Annual percentage growth rate of GDP at market prices based on constant local currency. Aggregates are based on constant 2010 U.S. dollars. GDP is the sum of gross value added by all resident producers in the economy plus any product taxes and minus any subsidies not included in the value of the products. It is calculated without making deductions for depreciation of fabricated assets or for depletion and degradation of natural resources.

TABLE 4.1
Morarji Desai and Charan Singh: 1977–80

Years	Gross Fiscal deficit*	Net Primary Deficit*	Capital Outlay*	Current Account Deficit*	Defence Expenditure*
1977–78	3.48	1.52	2.12	1.1	2.96
1978–79	4.98	1.37	2.11	−0.2	2.93
1979–80	5.08	1.75	1.94	−0.5	3.06

Years	GDP growth rate (Per cent)	Gross Capital Formation*	CPI (Annual per cent)	GDP Deflator (Annual per cent)	Rupees per USD (average)	Exports*
1977–78	7.3	18.2	10.5	5.6	8.6	5.3
1978–79	5.7	20.0	−2.2	2.5	8.2	5.0
1979–80	−5.2	21.0	9.4	15.7	8.1	5.2

TABLE 5.1
Rajiv Gandhi: 1984–85 to 1988–89

Years	Gross fiscal deficit*	Net primary deficit*	Capital outlay*	Current Account Deficit*	Defence Expenditure*
1984–85	6.79	3.49	2.63	−1.2	3.18
1985–86	7.55	3.67	2.64	−2.1	3.33
1986–87	8.13	4.06	2.86	−1.9	3.83
1987–88	7.34	3.51	2.52	−1.8	3.95
1988–89	7.08	3.08	2.35	−2.7	3.73

Years	GDP growth rate (Per cent)	Gross Capital Formation*	CPI (Annual per cent)	GDP Deflator (Annual per cent)	Rupees per USD (average)	Exports*
1984–85	3.8	21.5	0.3	7.9	11.9	4.8
1985–86	5.3	23.5	4.8	7.2	12.2	4.1
1986–87	4.8	23.5	4.7	6.8	12.8	4.2
1987–88	4.0	22.6	9.9	9.3	13.0	4.6
1988–89	9.6	23.8	12.7	8.2	14.5	4.9

TABLE 6.1
V.P. Singh and Chandra Shekhar: 1989–91

Years	Gross fiscal deficit*	Net primary deficit*	Capital outlay*	Current Account Deficit*	Defence Expenditure*
1989–90	7.10	2.88	2.35	−2.3	3.53
1990–91	7.61	3.06	2.07	−3.0	3.24

Years	GDP growth rate (Per cent)	Gross Capital Formation*	CPI (Annual per cent)	GDP Deflator (Annual per cent)	Rupees per USD (average)	Exports*
1989–90	5.9	23.9	5.4	8.4	16.6	5.8
1990–91	5.5	24.9	7.6	10.7	17.9	5.8

TABLE 7.1
P.V. Narasimha Rao: 1991–96

Years	Gross fiscal deficit*	Net primary deficit*	Capital outlay*	Current Account Deficit*	Defence Expenditure*
1991–92	5.39	1.33	1.64	–0.4	3.00
1992–93	5.19	1.50	1.73	–1.4	2.79
1993–94	6.76	2.73	1.47	–0.4	2.91
1994–95	5.52	1.15	1.42	–1.0	2.75
1995–96	4.91	0.88	1.15	–1.7	2.66

Years	GDP growth rate (Per cent)	Gross Capital Formation*	CPI (Annual per cent)	GDP Deflator (Annual per cent)	Rupees per USD (average)	Exports*	REER (Base Year: 2004–05=100)
1991–92	1.1	22.5	19.3	13.8	24.5	6.8	–
1992–93	5.5	24.2	12.4	9.0	30.6	7.7	–
1993–94	4.8	21.3	3.5	9.9	31.4	8.2	–
1994–95	6.7	23.2	11.9	10.0	31.4	8.3	103.96
1995–96	7.6	26.1	12.8	9.1	33.4	9.1	99.50

TABLE 8.1
I.K. Gujral and Deve Gowda: 1996–98

Years	Gross fiscal deficit*	Net primary deficit*	Capital outlay*	Current Account Deficit*	Defence Expenditure*	Forex Reserves*
1996–97	4.70	0.64	1.00	–1.2	2.55	6.8
1997–98	5.66	1.45	1.11	–1.3	2.73	7.2

Years	GDP growth rate (Per cent)	Gross Capital Formation*	CPI (Annual per cent)	GDP Deflator (Annual per cent)	Rupees per USD (average)	Exports*	REER (Base Year: 2004–05=100)
1996–97	7.5	22.1	7.7	7.6	35.5	8.8	99.34
1997–98	4.0	24.5	3.4	6.5	37.2	8.7	102.58

TABLE 9.1
A.B. Vajpayee: 1998–2004

Years	Gross fiscal deficit*	Net primary deficit*	Capital outlay*	Current Account Balance*	Defence Expenditure*
1998-99	6.29	1.78	1.04	-1.0	2.81
1999-00	5.18	1.66	1.19	-1.0	3.05
2000-01	5.46	1.90	1.14	-0.6	3.04
2001-02	5.98	2.17	1.13	0.7	3.02
2002-03	5.72	2.12	1.15	1.3	2.92
2003-04	4.34	1.06	1.20	2.3	2.76

Years	GDP growth rate (Per cent)	Gross Capital Formation*	CPI (Annual per cent)	GDP Deflator (Annual per cent)	Rupees per USD (average)	Exports	REER (Base Year: 2004-05=100)
1998-99	6.2	23.5	11.0	8.0	42.1	8.2	94.46
1999-00	8.8	26.8	4.4	3.1	43.3	8.3	95.98
2000-01	3.8	24.1	-0.3	3.6	45.7	9.9	101.02
2001-02	4.8	25.6	1.1	3.2	47.8	9.4	100.91
2002-03	3.8	25.0	3.2	3.7	48.4	10.6	95.97
2003-04	7.9	26.1	3.9	3.9	46	11.1	97.44

TABLE 9.2
PMGSY Road Length Completed since 2000–01

Year	Road Length Completed (Km)[1]
2000–01	1,837
2004–05	61,923
2014–15	419,372
2017–18	550,622

[1] Pradhan Mantri Gram Sadak Yojana, Online Management, Monitoring and Accounting System (OMMAS). Refer: http://omms.nic.in/

TABLE 9.3
Exports of Software Services as a Percentage of GDP and Export of Goods, 1998–2017

Year	Exports of IT Software Services (US $ billion)	Exports of Software Services as a percentage of GDP	Exports of Software Services as a percentage of Exports of Goods
1998	2.6	0.63	7.83
1999	4.0	0.88	10.76
2000	6.3	1.37	14.23
2001	7.6	1.58	17.24
2002	9.6	1.89	18.21
2003	12.8	2.13	20.05
2004	17.7	2.53	21.19
2005	23.6	2.92	22.89
2006	31.3	3.40	24.76
2007	40.3	3.36	24.70
2008	46.3	3.90	24.99
2009	49.7	3.75	27.81
2010	59	3.56	23.62
2011	62.2	3.41	20.33
2012	65.9	3.60	21.93
2013	69.5	3.74	22.10
2014	73.1	3.59	23.56
2015	74.2	3.53	28.27
2016	74.4	3.27	26.95
2017	77.3	2.98	25.48

Note: Export of Software Services are divided into two major categories: (i) Computer Services exports which include IT services as well as Software Product Development; and (ii) ITES/BPO services (including engineering services).

TABLE 9.4
Exports of Goods as a Percentage of GDP, 1998–2017

(Current US $)

Year	Export of Goods (US $ billion)	Exports of Goods as percentage of GDP
1998	33.2	8
1999	36.8	8.1
2000	44.5	9.6
2001	43.8	9.2
2002	52.7	10.4
2003	63.8	10.7
2004	83.5	11.9
2005	103.1	12.7
2006	126.4	13.7
2007	163.1	13.6
2008	185.3	15.6
2009	178.8	13.5
2010	249.8	15.1
2011	306	16.8
2012	300.4	16.4
2013	314.4	16.9
2014	310.3	15.2
2015	262.3	12.5
2016	275.9	12.1
2017	303.5	11.7

Sources: Handbook of Statistics on Indian Economy, RBI, https://rbi.org.in/Scripts/ PublicationsView.aspx?id=7704; World Bank, https://data.worldbank.org/indicator/NY.GDP. MKTP.KD?locations=IN; Directorate General of Foreign Trade (DGFT), http://commerce-app.gov.in/eidb/ergnq.asp.

TABLE 10.1
Manmohan Singh: 2004–14

Years	Gross Fiscal Deficit*	Net Primary Deficit*	Capital Outlay*	Current Account Balance*	Defence Expenditure*	Forex Reserves*
2004-05	3.88	0.98	1.61	-0.3	2.92	20.2
2005-06	3.96	0.95	1.49	-1.2	2.84	18.7
2006-07	3.32	0.55	1.40	-1.0	2.61	21.6
2007-08	2.54	-0.59	2.14	-1.3	2.42	25.8
2008-09	5.99	2.80	1.35	-2.3	2.63	21.2
2009-10	6.46	3.40	1.50	-2.8	2.98	21.1
2010-11	4.80	1.89	1.69	-2.8	2.79	18.4
2011-12	5.91	2.99	1.58	-4.2	2.65	16.1
2012-13	4.93	1.93	1.47	-4.8	2.54	16
2013-14	4.48	1.28	1.50	-1.7	2.47	16.4

Years	GDP growth rate (Per cent)	Gross Capital Formation*	CPI (Annual per cent)	GDP Deflator (Annual per cent)	Rupees per USD (average)	Exports*	REER (Base Year: 2004–05=100)
2004-05	7.9	32.5	2.6	5.7	44.9	11.8	100.00
2005-06	9.3	34.3	3.9	4.2	44.3	12.6	105.17
2006-07	9.3	35.9	7.8	6.4	45.2	13.6	104.3
2007-08	9.8	38.0	7.5	5.8	40.3	13.4	112.76
2008-09	3.9	35.5	10.2	8.7	46.0	15.4	102.32
2009-10	8.5	36.3	13.9	6.1	47.4	13.4	101.97
2010-11	10.3	36.5	10.0	9.0	45.6	15.0	114.91
2011-12	6.6	39.0	8.2	8.5	47.9	17.0	111.51
2012-13	5.5	38.7	10.0	7.9	54.4	16.8	104.95
2013-14	6.4	33.8	9.4	6.2	60.5	17.2	112.77

TABLE 11.1
Narendra Modi: 2014–17

Years	Gross fiscal deficit*	Net primary deficit*	Capital outlay*	Current Account Balance*	Defence Expenditure*
2014-15	4.10	0.94	1.35	-1.3	2.50
2015-16	3.89	0.81	1.65	-1.1	2.41
2016-17	3.52	0.34	1.62	-0.6	2.47
2017-18	3.54	0.43	1.49	-1.9	2.5

Years	GDP growth rate (Per cent)	Gross Capital Formation*	CPI (Annual per cent)	GDP Deflator (Annual per cent)	Rupees per USD (average)	Exports	REER (Base Year 2004–05=100)
2014-15	7.4	33.5	5.8	3.3	61.1	15.6	120.02
2015-16	8.0	32.3	4.9	2.1	65.5	12.7	122.71
2016-17	8.2	30.6	4.5	3.5	67.1	12.4	125.17
2017-18	7.0	-	3.6	3.1	64.4	11.9	129.87
2018-19	6.8						

Sources: The sources listed here are the same for all the tables, from 3.1 to 11.1, for the respective heads.
Gross fiscal deficit: RBI, https://rbi.org.in/Scripts/PublicationsView.aspx?id=18699.
Net primary deficit: Ibid.
Capital outlay: Ibid.
Current Account
Deficit: RBI https://rbi.org.in/Scripts/PublicationsView.aspx?id=18703.
Defence Expenditure: World Bank.
Forex Reserves: RBI.
Gross Capital Formation: RBI.
CPI: RBI https://rbi.org.in/Scripts/PublicationsView.aspx?id=18698.
GDP Deflator: World Bank https://data.worldbank.org/indicator/ny.gdp.defl.kd.zg
Rupees per USD: RBI https://rbi.org.in/Scripts/PublicationsView.aspx?id=18607
Exports: RBI https://rbi.org.in/Scripts/PublicationsView.aspx?id=18703
REER: RBI.

NOTES

Prologue: The Promise of India Endures

1. The road in central Delhi that connects Rashtrapati Bhawan (currently the Indian President's house) at the top of Raisina hill at one end to India Gate at the other. Rashtrapati Bhawan was the British viceroy's residence prior to independence, and Rajpath was called Kingsway.

2. Former chief economic adviser in the Ministry of Finance, and World Bank economist.

3. As of October 2017, there were twenty-nine states and seven union territories (administered by the Central government).

4. The cabinet committees on economic affairs, on security and on political affairs are all headed by the PM, and their members include the home minister, external affairs minister and finance minister. The committees on economic affairs and on security also include the minister of defence.

5. Tables 1, 2, 3 and 4 at the end of this Prologue list India's prime ministers, finance and foreign ministers since 1947 and the ruling party's strength in Parliament.

6. *Choices: Inside the Making of India's Foreign Policy*, S. Menon, former foreign secretary and national security adviser, Penguin, 2017.

7. The prime minister was the ex-officio chairman of the Planning Commission. When Narendra Modi became PM in 2014, this body was replaced by the National Institution for Transforming India (NITI) Aayog (Commission).

8. The National Judicial Appointments Committee (NJAC) Act and the enabling Constitutional Amendment Act came into force in April 2015. However, the NJAC Act was struck down by the Supreme Court in October 2015 on the grounds that it was inconsistent with the basic structure of the Constitution which provides for independence of the judiciary.

9. In the 1951 Tennessee Williams play, the original line is 'deliberate cruelty is unforgivable'.
10. *Butter Chicken in Ludhiana: Travels in Small Town India* by Pankaj Mishra. It was first published in 1995, and now, more than two decades later, the state of our urban areas is more distressing than amusing.
11. *An Uncertain Glory: India and Its Contradictions*, Jean Dreze and Amartya Sen, Princeton University Press, 2013.
12. *What Is History?*, E.H. Carr, Cambridge University, 1961.
13. The film was based on a 1946 novel authored by Nikos Kazantzakis.
14. Millennials are those who were born in the 1980s or early 1990s, and this word was coined by investment bankers.
15. For sufficient numbers of people to be aware of this book, it needs to be translated into regional languages. Currently, about 8 per cent of Indians over eighteen years of age can read English (author's estimate based on the number of copies of English-language newspapers sold daily plus those who get their news in English from the Internet).

Acknowledgements

1. Specific reference to Bijoy Chandra Bhagwati: *Planter Raj to Swaraj, Freedom Struggle and Electoral Politics in Assam 1826–1947*, Amalendu Guha, Indian Council of Historical Research, 1977, republished by Tulika Books in 2006, p. 144.
2. *Planter Raj to Swaraj*, p. 241.
3. Congress leader and later chief minister of Assam, 1970–72.
4. Specific reference: *Gopinath Bardoloi, The Assam Problem and Nehru's Centre*, Nirode K. Barooah, Bhabani Print & Publications, Guwahati, November 2010, p. 229.
5. Details mentioned in *Strangers in the Mist* authored by Sanjoy Hazarika. Originally published in 1994 and republished by Penguin.
6. British admiral's daughter who was Gandhi's follower and renamed Mirabehn by him.

Introduction

1. *Employment, Growth and Development, Essays on a Changing World Economy*, Deepak Nayyar, Routledge Taylor and Francis Group, 2017. *Contours of the World Economy 1-2030 AD: Essays in Macro-Economic History*, Angus Maddison, Oxford, 2007.
2. Minto, Mary Caroline Grey Elliot-Murray-Kynynmound, 1934. India, Minto and Morley, 1905–1910; compiled from the correspondence between the viceroy and the secretary of state, London: Macmillan.

3. *Journal of Asian Studies*, Vol. 74, No. 1, February 2015.
4. *Power, Performance and Bias: Evaluating the Electoral Quotas for Scheduled Castes in India*, Francesca Refsum Jensenius, Spring 2013.
5. In Mysore there were reservations for backward classes in civil services as far back as 1874.
6. After 1947 the reservation of legislative seats for Dalits was originally intended to last for ten years. However, reservations for the Lok Sabha have been extended every ten years, and the last such extension was in 2009.
7. *The Discovery of India* was authored by Nehru while he was in prison in Ahmednagar Fort between August 1942 and March 1945 (Nehru was jailed nine times by the British). This book includes a recounting of India's heritage of thousands of years of civilizational and beneficial trade linkages with neighbouring countries and distant corners of the world.
8. *War and Diplomacy in Kashmir, 1947–48*, Chandrasekhar Dasgupta, Sage Publications, 2002.
9. The Indian Air Force was called the Royal Indian Air Force till 1950, and the last British commander in chief of the Indian Air Force was Air Marshal Gerald Gibbs who served till March 1954. The first Indian air marshal was Subroto Mukherjee, who served from April 1954 till he retired in March 1955.
10. The last British naval officer to head the Indian navy was Vice Admiral Sir Stephen Hope Carlill, and he served till April 1958. Vice Admiral R.D. Katari was the first Indian national to head the Indian navy, and he served from April 1958 till June 1962.
11. The Pakistani armed forces were also headed by British officers in 1947. However, Jinnah refused to accept Mountbatten as governor general.

Chapter I: Pandit Jawaharlal Nehru: Unparalleled Nation Builder, Caring Yet Distant Leader

1. Nehru was born on 14 November 1889 in Allahabad, Uttar Pradesh, to a wealthy lawyer father. He had a very privileged upbringing and was sent to Harrow in England when he was barely eleven. Nehru returned to India in his early twenties after completing a Tripos at Cambridge and being called to the bar in London. On his return to India, he spent a few years practising law in Allahabad before coming under the influence of Mahatma Gandhi and immersing himself in the freedom struggle. He was forty-seven years old when he lost his wife Kamala Nehru to tuberculosis in 1936.
2. *Sunday Standard* (*Indian Express on Sunday*), 17 August 1958.
3. Many had expressed doubts about one India, and Churchill is said to have remarked that British India should be broken up into Hindustan, Pakistan and Princes-stan.

4. *Patel: A Life*, Rajmohan Gandhi, Navajivan Publishing House, 1990.
5. Rajmohan Gandhi's article on p. 15 of the *Indian Express* dated 28 October 2018.
6. For example, *A Collector's Piece*, S.N. Mitra (1933 batch—served in Assam and West Bengal), A Writers Workshop Greybird Book, 1997. Mitra was the deputy commissioner in Tezpur, Assam, in the early 1940s and had jailed my father in that town during the Quit India period. In the 1960s, he was our house guest in Delhi on more than one occasion.
7. Constituent Assembly Debates, Nehru Memorial Museum and Library (NMML), Teen Murti, New Delhi.
8. *Amritsar: Mrs Gandhi's Last Battle*, Mark Tully and Satish Jacob, Jonathan Cape, 1986.
9. As mentioned to me by M. Rasgotra at his residence in New Delhi on 29 November 2017. He was India's foreign secretary and high commissioner to the UK during his long and distinguished career.
10. Nehru's younger sister who served as India's ambassador to the USSR and the US and high commissioner to the UK.
11. As mentioned to me on 30 November 2017 at his residence in New Delhi. K.S. Bajpai was secretary (East) in the Ministry of External Affairs and India's ambassador to the US, China and Pakistan. Mr Bajpai joined the Indian Foreign Service in 1952 and retired in 1986.
12. The RBI was owned by private shareholders since 1935 and was nationalized in January 1949. It continued to be the currency authority of the Government of Pakistan till April 1948 when the Reserve Bank of Pakistan was set up. Prior to Independence, decision making in RBI was driven by the interests of its private shareholders who appointed RBI's central board. RBI was nationalized in 1949 and thereafter took on the mantle of India's central bank.
13. Details: *Indian Fiscal Federalism*, Y.V. Reddy and G.R. Reddy, Oxford University Press, 2019.
14. *Indian Fiscal Federalism*, Y.V Reddy and G.R. Reddy, Oxford University Press, 2019, p. 193.
15. *India: Planning for Industrialization: Industrialization and Trade Policies since 1951*, Jagdish N. Bhagwati and Padma Desai, published on behalf of the Development Centre of the OECD by Oxford University Press, 1970.
16. This argument is attributed to Raul Prebisch and Hans Singer who developed it between 1945 and 1949. Hans Singer's paper 'Post-war price relations between underdeveloped and industrialised countries' was published in February 1949. This paper concluded that the terms of trade for developing countries declined steadily from 1876 to 1948. Separately, Prebisch presented a paper to this effect in May 1949 at a United Nations Economic Commission for Latin America and the Caribbeans meeting in Havana.

17. *The Bombay Plan*, Edited by Sanjaya Baru and Meghnad Desai, Rupa, 2018.

18. 'Commands and Controls: Planning for Indian Industrial Development, 1951-1990', Rakesh Mohan and Vandana Aggarwal, *Journal of Comparative Economics*, 1990, Vol. 14, Issue 4, pp. 681–712.

19. *The Commanding Heights: The Battle between Government and the Marketplace that Is Remaking the Modern World*, Daniel Yergin and Joseph Stanislaw, 1998.

20. Per capita income at 1948–49 prices. Source: *Aspects of Indian Economic Development, A Book of Readings*, with an Introduction by Pramit Chaudhuri, University of Sussex, George Allen & Unwin Ltd, 1971, p. 30.

21. 'Over the past decade economists have been intensely scrutinized for their intellectual failings in the run-up to the 2007–08 crisis . . . Economists understand even less about economic growth than about business cycles. But the profession has done little to address this failure or to understand its implications.' 14–20 April 2018 issue of the *Economist*, p. 67.

22. The members of this committee of economists were: V.K.R.V. Rao, D.R. Gadgil, C.N. Vakil, H.L. Dey, P.S.N. Prasad, Gyan Chand, E. Da Costa, K.T. Shah and Radha Kamal Mukherjee. Their report was classified as 'Secret' at the time it was submitted, and has been sourced from the Nehru Papers at the NMML, Teen Murti, New Delhi.

23. *India's Tryst with Destiny: Debunking Myths that Undermine Progress and Addressing New Challenges*, Jagdish Bhagwati and Arvind Panagariya, HarperCollins, 2012.

24. Defined in the same letter as lack of food, clothes and shelter—the familiar '*roti, kapda aur makan*'.

25. *The Course of My Life*, C.D. Deshmukh, Orient Blackswan Private Limited, 1974.

26. *Nehru: A Contemporary's Estimate*, Walter Crocker, Oxford University Press, 1966.

27. *Adam Smith: What He Thought and Why It Matters*, Jesse Norman, Penguin, 2018.

28. 'The moral component evaluates one's own action in terms of what would happen, if, hypothetically, this action were adopted by others. Such moral preferences have important implications for economic behaviour. They motivate individuals to contribute to public goods, to give fair offers when they could get away with cheap offers, and to contribute to social institutions and act in environmentally friendly ways even if their individual impact is negligible.' Ingela Alger and Jorgen W. Weibull, 'Morality—Evolutionary Foundations and Policy Implications', 3 June 2016, http://pubdocs.worldbank.org/en/543241464122153185/Weibull-PAPER.pdf

29. Published in 2009 by Penguin.

30. *The Clash of Economic Ideas: The Great Policy Debates and Experiments of the Last Hundred Years*, Lawrence H. White, Cambridge University Press, 2012.

31. Council for Mutual Economic Assistance (COMECON). Members were the USSR, Bulgaria, Czechoslovakia, Poland, Hungary and Romania.

32. There were three finance ministers from 1947 to 1950.
33. Private papers of John Mathai, Microfilm Division, NMML, Delhi.
34. Milton Friedman's 'Memorandum to the Government of India' dated 5 November 1955. This memorandum was published in *Foundations of India's Political Economy: Towards an Agenda for the 1990s*, Subroto Roy and William James, Sage Publications, New Delhi.
35. *Glimpses of Indian Economic Policy: An Insider's View*, I.G. Patel, Oxford University Press, 2002, p. 44.
36. Using 2004 as the base year, the real effective exchange rate (REER) of the Indian rupee was overvalued by about 30 per cent at the end of 2018.
37. On the Under-invoicing of Imports, Jagdish Bhagwati, Bulletin of the Oxford University Institute for Economics and Statistics, 26 November 1964 and Fiscal Policies, the Faking of Foreign Trade Declarations and the Balance of Payments, February 1967.
38. This Act was later replaced by the Foreign Trade (Development and Regulation) Act, 1992, and the chief controller of imports and exports was renamed director general of foreign trade.
39. National Bureau of Economic Research (NBER) publication, Title: 'An Overview: 1950–70', Chapter authors: Jagdish N. Bhagwati, T.N. Srinivasan. http://www.nber.org/chapters/c4508.
40. Net national product is the market value of a nation's goods and services minus depreciation.
41. C.D. Deshmukh, an ICS officer of the Central Provinces and Berar (Madhya Pradesh) cadre of the 1918 batch, was secretary of the central board of the RBI from 1939 to 1941, deputy governor RBI from 1941 to 1943 and governor RBI from 1943 to 1949. Deshmukh was one of the five members of the Planning Commission when it was first set up in 1950. He was finance minister from 1950 to 1956.
42. Winner of the Nobel Prize in Economics in 1979.
43. *Glimpses of Indian Economic Policy: An Insider's View*, I.G. Patel, Oxford University Press, 2002.
44. Source: *Aspects of Indian Economic Development*, edited by Pramit Chaudhuri, George Allen & Unwin/Blackie (India), 1971, pp. 18 and 33
45. Companies get around this law by employing contractual workers.
46. Published on behalf of the Development Centre of the Organization for Economic Cooperation and Development, Paris, by Oxford University Press, 1970.
47. 'The Political Economy of Trade and Foreign Investment Policies in India: 1950–2006', Arvind Panagariya, NCAER Golden Jubilee Volume.
48. From one pound, which was equal to $4.03, down to $2.80.
49. Currency peg arrangements were in vogue universally till 1971 when the US dollar parity with gold was abandoned by the administration of President Richard Nixon.

50. Indian Public Finance Statistics, 2017.

51. Direct taxes are 'progressive' since these depend on the level of income. Indirect taxes are easier to collect since these are levied at points of sale or purchase. However, indirect taxes are 'regressive' since these impact lower-income groups to same extent as the rich.

52. Orient Blackswan Private Limited, July 1974.

53. IDA and IMF loans are denominated in Special Drawing Rights (SDRs) which, before the euro replaced the Eurozone currencies, was mostly made up of US dollar, pound sterling, Japanese yen, Deutsche Mark and Swiss franc. IDA loans carried well below market rates of interest and before 1987 could be very long-term and up to fifty years in maturity. However, these loans have turned out to be extremely expensive for developing-country borrowers including India because of the embedded exchange rate risk. The principal amounts of IDA loans have risen to multiples of the original loans, as measured in the recipient country currencies because these have depreciated steadily over the last sixty years against the major reserve currencies, namely the US dollar, JPY and the euro (earlier Deutsche Mark).

54. The World Bank is made up of the International Bank for Reconstruction and Development (IBRD), IDA, International Finance Corporation (IFC) and Multilateral Investment Guarantee Agency (MIGA). IDA does not have any separate personnel like IFC and MIGA. IDA loans are based on contributions by developed countries such as the USA, Japan, Germany, Switzerland, the UK and France.

55. Source: World Bank (http://pubdocs.worldbank.org/en/804131447347453530/WBAR15-LendingData-rev.pdf)

56. The circumstances and numbers on bilateral and multilateral assistance received by India in the first two decades are available in a paper titled 'The Aid-India Consortium, the World Bank, and the International Order of Asia, 1958-1968' by Shigeru Akita of Osaka University. *Asian Review of World Histories 2:2* (July 2014), pp. 217–48 © 2014, The Asian Association of World Historians doi: http://dx.doi.org/10.12773/arwh.2014.2.2.217 217.

57. http://documents.worldbank.org/curated/en/164191468034447809/pdf/804800WP0India0m0Box379801B00OUO090.pdf

58. *Nice Guys Finish Second*, B.K. Nehru, Viking Books, 1997.

59. These two external assistance numbers are from a lecture delivered by Dr Y.V. Reddy, then governor, Reserve Bank of India, at Osmania University, Hyderabad on 16 December 2006.

60. *Nehru: A Contemporary's Estimate*, Walter Crocker, Oxford University Press, 1966.

61. A.M. Rosenthal was the *New York Times* (*NYT*) South Asia correspondent in Delhi from 1954 to 1958. He was the executive editor of the *NYT* from 1977 to 1988.

62. After scouring through records in the NMML, several accounts of the Nehru years and the first four volumes RBI's record, I have not found a single reference by Nehru to the Aid India Consortium or to bilateral assistance from Western countries.

63. *How India Sees the World: From Kautilya to Modi: Kautilya to the 21st Century*, Shyam Saran, 2017.

64. 'The Soft Power of India', Chinmaya R. Gharekhan, *The Hindu*, 19 April 2018, http://www.thehindu.com/opinion/lead/the-soft-power-of-india/article23590348.ece?homepage=true

65. Ibid.

66. *Nehru: A Contemporary's Estimate*, by Walter Crocker, Oxford University Press, 1966.

67. As reported in the *Indian Express*, 16 August 1961.

68. It is only in 1966 after Nehru had passed away and Indira Gandhi was PM that the Punjab Reorganisation Act was passed, and Punjab and Haryana were separated and a few areas went to Himachal Pradesh.

69. The *Journal of Imperial and Commonwealth History*, Vol. 38, No. 3, September 2010, pp. 441–469.

70. I succeeded him as India's high commissioner (HC) in London about six decades later and had exactly the same office in Aldwych House. According to the longest-serving local employees in the high commission, Menon's eccentric habits included spending the night in the room adjacent to the HC's office, and he was often on a diet of just coffee and biscuits.

71. Menon was India's defence minister from 1957 to 1962.

72. Ramachandra Guha in the Magazine section of *The Hindu* dated 1 August 2004, https://www.thehindu.com/thehindu/mag/2004/08/01/stories/2004080100290300.htm

73. As mentioned to the author by K.S. Bajpai in a conversation at the latter's residence in Friend's Colony, New Delhi, on 30 November 2017.

74. In 2018 developed countries continue to jostle for influence in the Congo which has huge deposits of copper, gold, diamonds and uranium.

75. *Outside the Archives*, Y.D. Gundevia.

76. *India's Nuclear Bomb: The Impact on Global Proliferation*, George Perkovich, University of California Press, 1999.

77. After the Independence of India Act was passed in the UK in July 1947 the princely states of India regained their paramountcy and technically had the right to accede to India or Pakistan or even seek autonomy. Most princely states joined the Indian union, but a few including the state of Jammu and Kashmir, Junagadh, Travancore, Hyderabad, Bhopal and Jodhpur chose to defer their decision.

78. *War and Diplomacy in Kashmir, 1947-48*, C. Dasgupta, Sage, 2001.

79. Ibid.

80. Ibid.

81. Source on details of Indian military equipment: *India's Wars, A Military History, 1947-1971*, Arjun Subramaniam, Harper Collins, 2016.

82. Dulles to George C. Marshall, 23 November 1948, Foreign Relations 5, Pt 1, pp. 459–60, quoted in *War and Diplomacy in Kashmir, 1947–48*.

83. Details on the lead-up to Maharaja Hari Singh's accession to India and the role of Sheikh Abdullah are available in *India After Gandhi* by Ramachandra Guha.

84. *War and Diplomacy in Kashmir, 1947–48*, C. Dasgupta.

85. 'Radical Land Reforms Were Key to Sheikh Abdullah's Towering Influence in Kashmir', David Devadas, The Wire, https://thewire.in/government/radical-land-reforms-key-sheikh-abdullahs-towering-influence-kashmir. 'Sheikh Abdullah and Land Reforms in Jammu and Kashmir', Anirudh Kumar Prasad, *Economic and Political Weekly*, Vol. 49, Issue No. 31, 2 August 2014.

86. This bilateral agreement was meant to protect minorities in both countries, enable the return of abducted women during Partition and of property to rightful owners.

87. *Syama Prasad Mookerjee, Life and Times*, Tathagata Roy, Penguin Books, 2012.

88. Article titled 'The Logic of History' by Jagmohan in *Business Standard* dated 14 June 2013, https://www.business-standard.com/article/beyond-business/the-logic-of-history-106112301093_1.html

89. Charges against Sheikh Abdullah were withdrawn and he and others in custody were released in 1964 a few months before Nehru passed away in May 1964. It is an indication that the two leaders were not estranged at a personal level, since Abdullah stayed with Nehru at his Teen Murti House residence in Delhi for a few days immediately after his release.

90. 'A Short History of Elections in Kashmir', *The Caravan*, 25 November 2014, https://caravanmagazine.in/vantage/short-history-elections-kashmir

91. Nehru passed away on 27 May 1964.

92. Gandak is a major river in Nepal and a tributary of the Ganga.

93. *Present at the Creation: My Years at the State Department*, Dean Acheson, 1969, W.W. Norton.

94. Set up in 1954, and among today's ASEAN members, Thailand and the Philippines were members of SEATO.

95. Set up in 1955.

96. Trumbo wrote the scripts for *Spartacus, Exodus* and *Roman Holiday*.

97. *Outside the Archives*, Y.D. Gundevia.

98. Ibid.

99. U-2 aircraft were supersonic and flew at 70,000 feet. One such U-2, which had taken off from Peshawar in Pakistan, was shot down by the USSR on 1 May 1960. Till then the US had assumed that U-2s were undetectable.

100. *JFK's Forgotten Crisis: Tibet, the CIA and the Sino-Indian War*, Bruce Riedel, HarperCollins, 2015.

101. Pakistan, without Bangladesh, is larger than France, and its population of 193 million is more than the combined population of Germany and France which adds up to about 150 million.
102. The agreement to share Indus waters was signed in Karachi on 19 September 1960 by Nehru and President Ayub Khan.
103. Source: https://www.thehindu.com/news/national/jawaharlal-nehru-on-permanent-unsc-membership-no-question-of-a-seat-being-offered-and-india-declining-it/article26536197.ece?utm_campaign=socialflow&fbclid=IwAR1qY-9g-L9j_njNV7YWnSipt5QKrxqTaNL33yzpZ6LRm9TyL9cW33wymBQ
104. *JFK's Forgotten Crisis*, Bruce Riedel.
105. *Nice Guys Finish Second*, B.K. Nehru, Viking Books, 1997.
106. David C. Engerman, Professor of History, Brandeis University, discussed his book *The Price of Aid: The Economic Cold War in India* on 23 February 2018 at Brookings, New Delhi. Professor Engerman's response to my question whether India could have achieved a meeting of minds on economic ties in 1961 on the lines of the US-China understanding of 1971 was that India did not present the US with a counter to Russia. Professor Engerman was perhaps forgetting that in 1961 China was not yet publicly estranged from the USSR, not a member of the UN or the Bretton Woods institutions, and for the US establishment was a communist menace to the 'free' world. To that extent, and on Nehru's terms, India could have been an economic counter-example to communist China.
107. Recounted to me by M. Rasgotra at his residence in New Delhi on 29 November 2017. Rasgotra was present at this meeting between Nehru and the US billionaires.
108. First mention of such a military-industrial complex in the US was made in the farewell speech of US President Dwight D. Eisenhower on 17 January 1961.
109. *JFK's Forgotten Crisis,* Bruce Riedel.
110. A now retired Indian foreign secretary commented with a wry smile while we were both working in the Ministry of External Affairs in New Delhi that it is bilateral ties which can be used to further vital national interests, and discussions at the UN are more suited to promote values.
111. *A Life in Diplomacy*, M. Rasgotra (former foreign secretary), Penguin, 2015.
112. The French left Pondicherry in 1954.
113. Turkey has been a member of NATO since 1952. West Germany and Spain became members of NATO in 1955 and 1982.
114. *Outside the Archives*, Y.D. Gundevia.
115. The heads of government of four permanent members of the UNSC—President Dwight D. Eisenhower of the US, Premier Nikolai A. Bulganin and Politburo member N.S. Khrushchev of the USSR, Prime Minister Anthony Eden of the UK and Prime Minister Edgar Faure of France attended this conference in Geneva on 18 July 1955. The principal topic on the agenda was how to scale down the Cold War.

116. Nehru Papers, NMML, Teen Murti, New Delhi. The record of discussions at this 21 June 1955 meeting was drawn up by P.N. Kaul.
117. Justice Radhabinod Pal from India submitted the sole dissenting note in the Tokyo trials of Japan's war crimes during the Second World War. Justice Pal's point was that all the defendants were not guilty and that a spirit of revenge rather than justice had marred the work of the tribunal of which he was a member. The controversial Yasukuni Shrine in Tokyo has a monument dedicated to Justice Pal within its precincts.
118. *Outside the Archives*, Y.D. Gundevia.
119. The 2008 novel *Sea of Poppies* by Amitav Ghosh provides a sensitive portrayal about opium cultivation in India and transportation over the seas to China.
120. In 1899 the British Indian government proposed this line to China via Claude MacDonald, the British envoy to that country.
121. As of May 2019, Indian troops have moved up to the LAC and so have Chinese troops, and hence there is no consistent 20 kilometres of buffer zone any longer. The LAC is somewhat different from the Line of Control (LoC) which is a demarcated line between India and Pakistan.
122. This letter is discussed in J.N. Dixit's, *Makers of India's Foreign Policy: From Raja Ram Mohun Roy to Yashwant Sinha*, HarperCollins, 2004.
123. Panikkar was the Indian ambassador in China from May 1950 to September 1952.
124. *JFK's Forgotten Crisis,* Bruce Riedel.
125. *The Noodle Maker of Kalimpong: The Untold Story of My Struggle for Tibet*, Gyalo Thondup (Anne E. Thurston), Random House, December 2014.
126. Chiang Kai-shek was Thondup's sponsor when he went to study in China in 1939, and they met several times including in 1950 in Taiwan. Thondup claims to have met Zhou Enlai in January 1957and Field Marshal He Long over dinner at the Chinese Embassy in Delhi, Thondup calls Zhou a 'xiao bailian' which is used by the Chinese to "describe someone who is understanding and sincere on the outside and inwardly, crafty, sly and full of tricks". Thondup mentions in *The Noodle Maker of Kalimpong* that he met Deng Xiaoping in Beijing in 1979.
127. Thondup says that he also met R.N. Kao, head of the Research and Analysis Wing (R&AW), after this external intelligence agency was set up by Indira Gandhi in 1968.
128. *The Noodle Maker of Kalimpong*, Thondup.
129. *JFK's Forgotten Crisis*, Bruce Riedel.
130. 'When Nehru Turned Down CIA's Proposal to Base Snooper Planes in Charbatia' *India Today*, 31 December 1983, https://www.indiatoday.in/magazine/cover-story/story/19831231-when-nehru-turned-down-cias-proposal-to-base-snooper-planes-at-charbatia-804557-2014-01-31
131. Nehru Papers, NMML, Teen Murti, New Delhi.

132. Communist China and the Soviet Union use their PMs to talk to heads of government in countries such as India. The fact was and is that the PM in China is not the head of government. The general secretary of the CPSU in the USSR era and now the President, and similarly Mao at that time and now the General Secretary Xi Ping, are the heads of government. It is not clear why Nehru did not insist that all substantive meetings and communications be with Mao and not the number two.

133. *India-China Boundary Issues, Quest for Settlement*, Ranjit Singh Kalha, Indian Council for World Affairs, Pentagon Press, 2014.

134. Ibid.

135. Nehru papers, NMML, Teen Murti, New Delhi.

136. *China's India War*, Bertil Lintner, Oxford University Press, 2018.

137. Former finance minister who resigned in 1950 and was followed by C.D. Deshmukh.

138. Source: Private papers of John Mathai, Microfilm Division, NMML.

139. This phrase is attributed to Rabindranath Tagore. Also the title of a book authored by Sunil Khilnani. Published by Farrar, Straus and Giroux, 1997.

Chapter II: Lal Bahadur Shastri: War and Peace during Short Tenure

1. Shastri was born in Mughalsarai near Varanasi in UP on 2 October 1904. He was from a family of modest means, and his father was a schoolteacher. He was a self-contained personality with an aura of quiet assurance. Unlike Nehru and many others at the forefront of Indian politics in the 1940s–50s, Shastri's education was entirely in India. His full name was Lal Bahadur Shrivastava, and Shastri was the title accorded to him after he graduated from Kashi Vidyapeeth, Varanasi, in 1925.

2. *Selected Speeches of Prime Minister Lal Bahadur Shastri*, Publications Division, Ministry of Information & Broadcasting, Government of India, 1974.

3. Source: *Aspects of Indian Economic Development*, edited by Pramit Chaudhuri, George Allen & Unwin/Blackie (India), 1971, pp. 18, 33.

4. W.D. Hopper, 'Distortions of Agricultural Development Resulting from Government Prohibitions', in *Distortions of Agricultural Incentives*, ed. T.W. Schultz (Bloomington, Ind., 1978), pp. 69–78.

5. *Sunday Standard*, 16 August 1964.

6. The leaders of the agitation were advised by senior political leaders across party lines that their demand should be based on a separate language and not on religious grounds. Since before Independence, the consensus in the Congress party had been that states should be reorganized on the basis of language, not religion. *Multilingualism in India*, Debi Pattanayak, Orient Longman, January 2007.

7. *The China-Pakistan Axis: Asia's New Geopolitics*, Andrew Small, Random House Publishers, 2015, p. 47.
8. During the Cold War era, the US and the USSR tried to whittle each other down and carve out their respective areas of influence. However, on issues such as non-proliferation of nuclear weapons, the two countries coordinated their efforts. Similarly, there was possibly a meeting of minds between the two superpowers that they did not want either India or Pakistan to win too decisively. Keeping the conflict in Kashmir brewing at low intensity made the otherwise antagonistic USA and USSR fancy their chances of fostering greater dependence on themselves for arms purchases and transfer of technology.
9. P.C. Bhattacharya was the RBI governor from March 1962 to June 1967. Of the fifty-one years from 1967 to 2018, economists have held the position of RBI governor for only twenty-four years. The remaining years, and earlier, from 1935 to 1967, RBI was headed by ICS or IAS officers.

Chapter III: Indira Gandhi: End of Innocence Yet Remarkable Achievements

1. English translation from Hadi Hasan's *A Golden Treasury of Persian Poetry* published by the Indian Council of Cultural Relations (ICCR) with a foreword by Zakir Husain, April 1966.
2. Indira Gandhi was born in Allahabad on 19 November 1917 to Jawaharlal and Kamala Nehru, and she was an only child. She was taught at home by tutors and attended schools in Allahabad and Geneva. She also studied at the Visva-Bharati University in Santiniketan and at Somerville College, Oxford University.
3. The Teen Murti (Three Statues) monument in front of Nehru's residence was built in 1922 to honour soldiers from the princely states of Mysore, Jodhpur and Hyderabad who fought and beat the Ottoman army under British command in and close to Haifa.
4. *Indira Gandhi: A Personal and Political Biography*, Inder Malhotra, Hodder & Stoughton, 1989.
5. *Indira: The Life of Indira Nehru Gandhi*, Katherine Frank, HarperCollins, 2010.
6. *Indira Gandhi: A Personal and Political Biography*, Inder Malhotra.
7. On a lighter note, the Syndicate should have known better given P.G. Wodehouse's following observation about women in *Uneasy Money*: 'At the age of eleven or thereabouts women acquire a poise and an ability to handle difficult situations which a man, if he is lucky, manages to achieve in his late seventies.'
8. This is the sense a reader gets from the following books: *Indira Gandhi: A Personal and Political Biography*, Inder Malhotra, Hay House India. *First Draft: Witness to the Making of Modern India*, B.G. Verghese, Tranquebar, 2010.
9. *The Political Economy of Trade and Foreign Investment Policies in India: 1950–2006*, Arvind Panagariya, NCAER Golden Jubilee Volume. Singh had advocated

adjustment of the rupee exchange rate downwards to more realistic levels. To that extent, Indian exports would have become more competitive in international markets.

10. *Glimpses of Indian Economic Policy: An Insider's View*, I.G. Patel, Oxford, India, 2003.

11. *Glimpses of Indian Economic Policy: An Insider's View*, I.G. Patel, pp. 102–07.

12. P.N. Haksar was among the several sincere, left-of-centre nationalists who were educated in England in the 1920s–30s and chose to return to India. Most of them were lawyers, a few were scientists and a handful chose careers in the private sector. Haksar was at the India League in London along with V.K. Krishna Menon. The India League promoted awareness in local circles about the injustice of colonial rule in India. Haksar joined the Indian Foreign Service in 1947.

13. The chief economic advisers in the Ministry of Finance during 1967–69 and 1970–72 were V.K. Ramaswamy and Ashok Mitra respectively.

14. *Intertwined Lives: P.N. Haksar and Indira Gandhi*, Jairam Ramesh, Simon & Schuster, 2018.

15. The V.T. Dehejia Committee, which was formed in October 1968, found that short-term bank lending for working capital purposes was often diverted to acquire fixed and longer-term assets. That is, bank lending was deliberately and irresponsibly long and not repayable on demand. In finance terminology, the 'modified duration' of loans was much too long compared to the duration of the sources of funding, namely demand deposits.

16. In April 1980, after IG had come back as PM, another six private banks were nationalized.

17. D.R. Gadgil was the deputy chairman of the Planning Commission from 1967 to 1971.

18. *Glimpses of Indian Economic Policy: An Insider's View*, I.G. Patel, 2003; *First Draft: Witness to the Making of Modern India*, B.G. Verghese, 2010, p. 121; and Time magazine article on the subject dated 3 December 1965, http://www.time.com/time/magazine/article/0,9171,842253-1,00.html

19. RBI's Master Circulars on Priority Sector Lending. https://www.rbi.org.in/scripts/BS_ViewMasCirculardetails.aspx?id=9815

20. *Aspects of Indian Economic Development*, Pramit Chaudhuri, George Allen and Unwin, 1971.

21. DMK first came to power in Tamil Nadu in 1967 and supported IG on abolition of privy purses for princes and nationalization of banks.

22. The Communist Party of India (Marxist) or CPI(M) came to power in West Bengal in 1977.

23. In the US, the federal and state-level anti-trust laws are meant to ensure fair competition, if necessary, break up monopolies and cartels, and prevent price gouging of consumers.

24. The MRTP Act and corresponding commission were replaced by the Competition Act of 2002 and the Competition Commission.

25. *Indira Gandhi, Letters to an American Friend 1950–1984* (Selected with commentary from correspondence with Dorothy Norman), edited by Helen and Kurt Wolff, 1985.

26. Coal India was set up in 1975.

27. *Indira Gandhi: A Personal and Political Biography*, Inder Malhotra, Hay House India, 2014.

28. *First Draft: Witness to the Making of Modern India*, B.G. Verghese, Tranquebar Press, 2010, pp. 186, 200–19.

29. *The KGB and the World: The Mitrokhin Archive II*, Christopher Andrew, Allen Lane, Penguin Group, 2005.

30. *Indira Gandhi: A Personal and Political Biography*, Inder Malhotra, Hay House, 2014.

31. *The Sanjay Story*, Vinod Mehta, Jaico Publishing House, 1978, republished by HarperCollins, 2012, pp. 76–92.

32. Phonetic version of the acronym for the US oil giant Standard Oil, or SO. In 1972, after regulatory action restricted ESSO's operations in the US, it was bought out by Exxon.

33. 'Political Economy of Petroleum Sector Deregulation', in *India Transformed: 25 Years of Economic Reforms*, Vikram Singh Mehta, Penguin, 2017, p. 316.

34. *All the Shah's Men*, Stephen Kinzer, John Wiley & Sons, 2003.

35. See Appendix 3.1 for definitions of the various measures of government deficits.

36. See the editorial by T.N. Ninan in *Business Standard*, 12 January 2019, titled 'Still a Fudget: Why the Union Budget Remains Someone's Version of the Facts', www.business-standard.com/article/opinion/still-a-fudget-why-the-union-budget-remains-someone-s-version-of-the-facts-119011100595_1.html. Two of my articles in the *Business Standard* about the care with which government's budget numbers should be read are at: www.business-standard.com/article/opinion/jaimini-bhagwati-accrual-based-budgeting-108062001013_1.html; and www.business-standard.com/article/opinion/jaimini-bhagwati-demystifying-the-budget-115021901259_1.html.

37. The Arab embargo on oil exports was meant to hurt Western countries which were perceived to have supported Israel in the Yom Kippur war of October 1973.

38. Source: https://www.indiabudget.gov.in/bspeech/bs197071.pdf

39. For details and analysis: 'Thirty Years of Tax Reform', Shankar Acharya, *Economic and Political Weekly*, 14 May 2005.

40. Covered in Chapter 4.

41. Under the Janata government, the P.C. Alexander Committee on import-export policies was set up in 1978, and the V. Dagli Committee on 'controls and subsidies' started work in 1979.

42. *India Today*, 15 April 1981.
43. See n. 59 in Chapter I. The SDR's value has been usually somewhat more than that of the US dollar. As of 30 May 2019, 1 SDR was equal to 1.38 US dollar (Source: IMF).
44. *Indira Gandhi: A Personal and Political Biography*, Inder Malhotra, Hay House India.
45. Congress (Organisation) or Congress (O) was formed after the Congress party broke up in November 1969 when Indira Gandhi was expelled from the party. Congress (O) had leaders such as Morarji Desai from Gujarat, K. Kamaraj from Tamil Nadu, Veerendra Patil from Karnataka and Bhola Paswan Shastri from Bihar.
46. *Indira Gandhi: A Personal and Political Biography*, Inder Malhotra, Hay House India, 2014.
47. In a conversation with me on 23 October 2017. Chandrashekhar Dasgupta, an IFS officer, was India's ambassador to China and later to the European Union. He was awarded the Padma Bhushan in 2008.
48. I was then an undersecretary-level officer, designated officer on special duty (press relations), in the Ministry of External Affairs. My responsibilities included managing anything and everything that the Indian press and about 950 persons from radio, television and print media from abroad needed. During this summit, I was busy trying to get responses, in addition to attending to logistical and administrative arrangements, to the innumerable requests from the media for interviews with heads of government.
49. As foreign minister in the Janata government headed by Prime Minister Morarji Desai.
50. M.C. Chagla was the foreign minister. IG was preoccupied with consolidating her tenuous hold on power, and Chagla, as a legal luminary, was probably not adequately aware of the longer-term potential for economic linkages with these countries.
51. *The Blood Telegram: Nixon, Kissinger and a Forgotten Genocide*, Gary J. Bass, Vintage Books, 2013.
52. *Times of India*, 16 August 1971.
53. Archer Blood was the US consul general in Dacca during those fateful years at the end of the 1960s and the beginning of the 1970s. The title of this book refers to a telegram sent by Archer Blood to the US State Department detailing the then ongoing genocide in East Pakistan (Bangladesh).
54. *A History of Assam*, Sir Edward Albert Gait, Calcutta, Thacker, Spink and Co., 1906.
55. Ambassador K.S. Bajpai speaking to the Association of Indian Diplomats on 27 November 2018 at Sapru House. In 1970, Ambassador Bajpai was the Indian political officer in Sikkim.

56. Signed by the negotiators G. Parthasarathy, on behalf of Indira Gandhi, and Mirza Mohammad Afzal Beg, on behalf of Sheikh Abdullah on 13 November 1974 in New Delhi. Text of the accord is at: https://www.mainstreamweekly. net/article3395.html

57. 'How Many Times Must We Lose the Valley?', Omair Ahmed, The Wire, https://thewire.in/politics/kashmir-valley-1987-militancy. 'History of Electoral Fraud Has Lessons for BJP in J&K', *Times of India*, 22 November 2014. https:// timesofindia.indiatimes.com/blogs/gray-areas/history-of-electoral-fraud-has-lessons-for-bjp-in-jk/

58. *Bangladesh: The Unfinished Revolution,* Lawrence Lifschultz and Kai Bird, Zed Books, 1979.

59. Pakistan's ambassador to the US, 1959–63, foreign secretary from 1963 till 1967, and later minister of state for foreign affairs when Z.A. Bhutto became President of Pakistan in December 1971.

60. *Indira Gandhi, the Emergency and Indian Democracy*, P.N. Dhar, Oxford University Press, 2000.

61. *Indira Gandhi, the Emergency and Indian Democracy*, P.N. Dhar, p. 203.

62. Ibid, p. 194.

63. Ibid., p. 209.

64. *Across Borders: Fifty Years of India's Foreign Policy*, J.N. Dixit, Picus Books, 1998, p. 96.

65. *Intertwined Lives*, Jairam Ramesh.

66. *American Prometheus: The Triumph & Tragedy of J. Robert Oppenheimer*, Kai Bird & Martin J. Sherwin, 2009.

67. NSG was set up as a multilateral group to prevent the export of materials, equipment and technology which could be used to build nuclear weapons. The principal members of the NSG are the USA, Russia (USSR in 1974), China, France, the UK, Japan, Canada and South Korea.

68. The Missile Technology Control Regime (MTCR) was set up much later in 1987 by the G7 countries. The MTCR is meant to control the proliferation of missile and drone technology which can carry more than 500 kilograms and travel further than 300 kilometres.

69. *Indira Gandhi, the Emergency and Indian Democracy*, P.N. Dhar.

70. For example, the railway strike organized by George Fernandes who was the president of the All India Railwaymen's Federation and Navnirman Andolan of 1974 in Gujarat.

71. It lasted until 21 March 1977.

72. *India After Gandhi*, Ramachandra Guha, Macmillan, 2007, provides details of the circumstances under which the Emergency was declared.

73. The provisions under this chapter do not apply to managers and administrators or to the armed forces and police.

74. *Times of India*, 16 August 1976.
75. Lalu Prasad Yadav of Bihar was jailed under this Act, and thumbing his nose at Indira Gandhi, he named one of his daughters Misa.
76. In 1973, Justice A.N. Ray was rewarded with the position of chief justice, superseding three others, after he was the lone judge to dissent in a ten-to-one Supreme Court verdict which struck down the 1969 Bank Nationalisation Act.
77. P.N. Bhagwati was appointed chief justice in 1985 when Rajiv Gandhi was PM.
78. Subsequently, during the Janata government years, 1977–80, the then Law Minister Shanti Bhushan piloted the 43rd and 44th Amendments of the Constitution. These two amendments more or less restored the status quo ante. The 44th Amendment revoked MISA and also took it out from the 9th schedule of the Constitution where it had been placed in 1971 to put it outside judicial review. In a reinforcement of a reversion of the legal framework to a pre-1970s India, in July 1980 in the Minerva Mills versus Union of India case, the Supreme Court ruled that certain parts of the 42nd Amendment, which was enacted during the Emergency in 1976, were unconstitutional since these provisions give precedence to the Directive Principles over fundamental rights of individuals.
79. *The Dramatic Decade: The Indira Gandhi Years*, Pranab Mukherjee, Rupa Publications, 2015.
80. To gain the electoral support of illegal migrants from Bangladesh in Assam, the Congress-led UPA government of Manmohan Singh amended the 1964 tribunal order, making Assam exempt from this directive. In 2005, the Supreme Court struck down the 1983 IMDT Act as unconstitutional.
81. *Amritsar: Mrs Gandhi's Last Battle*, Mark Tully and Satish Jacob, 1985.
82. *Indira Gandhi, Letters to an American Friend 1950–1984* (Selected with commentary from correspondence with Dorothy Norman), edited by Helen and Kurt Wolff, Harcourt Brace Jovanovich Publishers, 1985.
83. Turning and turning in the widening gyre / The falcon cannot hear the falconer; / Things fall apart; / the centre cannot hold; . . . / The best lack all conviction, while the worst / Are full of passionate intensity. ('The Second Coming'— William Butler Yeats)
84. *Amritsar: Mrs Gandhi's Last Battle*, Mark Tully and Satish Jacob, Jonathan Cape, 1986.
85. *India's Long Road: The Search for Prosperity*, Vijay Joshi, Allen Lane, Penguin Random House India, 2016.
86. *Intertwined Lives: P.N. Haksar and Indira Gandhi*, Jairam Ramesh, Simon & Schuster, 2018.
87. Widow of Rajni Patel, a well-known lawyer in Mumbai, who joined the Congress in the late 1960s and was reportedly close to Indira Gandhi.
88. Author of Indira Gandhi's biography titled *Indira: The Life of Indira Nehru Gandhi*, HarperCollins, 2002.

89. High-school physics: a compass does not point to the true North if there is a magnet in its immediate vicinity.
90. *Indira Gandhi: Tryst with Power*, Nayantara Sahgal, Penguin Books, 2012.
91. 'New Economic Policies: A Historical Perspective', *Economic and Political Weekly*, Vol. 27, No. 1/2, 4–11 January 1992, pp. 41–46.
92. It is rumoured that Pupul Jayakar, who was a personal friend, helped in the selection of saris for IG.

Chapter IV: Morarji Desai: Sincere Yet Inflexible and Outmoded

1. Morarji Desai was born on 29 February 1896 in Bhadeli village, Bulsar district (erstwhile Bombay Presidency) which is now in Gujarat, and his father was a schoolteacher. Desai went to high school in Valsad, Gujarat, and graduated from Wilson College, Bombay (Mumbai). He passed away on 10 April 1995.
2. Congress (O), Bharatiya Janata Party and Bharatiya Kranti Dal.
3. *Times of India*, 16 August 1977.
4. *Glimpses of Indian Economic Policy: An Insider's View*, I.G. Patel.
5. *Trilateral Nuclear Proliferation: Pakistan's Euro-Chinese Bomb*, Arvind Virmani, Institute for Defence Studies and Analyses, New Delhi, December 2006, IDSA Monograph Series, p. 40.
6. *Across Borders: Fifty Years of India's Foreign Policy*, J.N. Dixit, Picus Books, 1978.
7. The Brzezinski Interview with *Le Nouvel Observateur* (1998). The University of Arizona, https://dgibbs.faculty.arizona.edu/brzezinski_interview. Translated from the French by William Blum and David N. Gibbs. This translation was published in Gibbs, 'Afghanistan: The Soviet Invasion in Retrospect,' *International Politics* 37, No. 2, 2000, 241–42.
8. Charan Singh was born in a peasant family in Noorpur, UP, on 23 December 1902. He graduated with a science degree and was also trained in law, and all his education was in UP. He passed away on 29 May 1987.

Chapter V: Rajiv Gandhi: Forward-looking Yet Catastrophically Error-prone

1. RG was born on 20 August 1944. He went to Doon School in Dehradun and studied engineering at Trinity College, Cambridge, from 1962 to 1965. However, he did not earn a degree at Cambridge. He then went on to Imperial College in London to study mechanical engineering but again did not get a degree. RG returned to India in 1966, the year his mother became prime minister. Thereafter, he learnt to fly at the Delhi flying club and joined the government-owned Indian Airlines as a pilot in 1970. He married Sonia Maino in 1968, and his son Rahul and daughter Priyanka were born in 1970 and 1972, respectively.

2. Video recordings of the speech are available on YouTube and also at: https://scroll.in/video/1558/watch-rajiv-gandhi-make-his-infamous-big-tree-falls-speech-justifying-the-1984-anti-sikh-riots. A report is at https://www.dnaindia.com/india/report-when-a-big-tree-falls-the-earth-shakes-how-rajiv-gandhi-justified-1984-anti-sikh-riots-2697259

3. In 2006 while he was a member of the Rajya Sabha.

4. Arun Nehru was the same age as RG, a contemporary at Doon School, and related to him. Arun was a private-sector executive when he was persuaded by Indira Gandhi to join the Congress party. He was elected to the Lok Sabha in 1980, and in 1984, and was a minister of state for energy and later home from 1984 to 1986 in RG's government.

5. Details in a report titled 'Who Are the Guilty? Report of a Joint Inquiry into the Causes and Impact of the Riots in Delhi from 31 October to 10 November 1984', People's Union for Democratic Rights, People's Union for Civil Liberties, http://www.unipune.ac.in/snc/cssh/HumanRights/04%20COMMUNAL%20RIOTS/B%20-%20ANTI%20-%20SIKH%20RIOTS/01%20-%20DELHI/a.pdf

6. 'Between Rhetoric and Reality', Manoj Mitta, *The Hindu*, 20 December 2018, www.thehindu.com/opinion/op-ed/between-rhetoric-and-reality/article25783934.ece

7. *Amritsar: Mrs Gandhi's Last Battle*, Mark Tully and Satish Jacob.

8. Towards the end of the 1970s, it was noticed that in Lok Sabha constituencies such as Mangoldoi the number of voters had risen far too quickly. This, and the visual evidence of the entrants from Bangladesh, led to the 'Assam Agitation' spearheaded first by the AASU and later the All Assam Gana Sangram Parishad (AAGSP). AAGSP converted later to the AGP. The agitation was at its height from 1979 to 1985. The massacres in Nellie and Khoirabari were horrific examples of extreme violence against alleged foreign settlers.

9. This amendment has since been challenged and the case is pending with the Supreme Court.

10. *One Life Is Not Enough*, K. Natwar Singh, Rupa Publications, 2014.

11. SICA was enacted by Parliament to identify sick or potentially sick companies and then decide if these needed to be closed or could be helped to recover. The underlying logic was that if a company could not be nursed back to health, it was best to close it and use whatever assets could be recovered for profitable investment elsewhere.

12. A concept elaborated upon by Austrian economist Joseph Schumpeter, who moved to the US and taught at Harvard University, in his 1942 work *Capitalism, Socialism and Democracy*.

13. Several specific cases are discussed in 'Corporate Rescue in India: The Influence of the Courts', *Journal of Corporate Law Studies*, Vol. 1, 2015, Oxford Legal

Studies Research Paper 37/2014, Kristin van Zwieten, University of Oxford, Faculty of Law.

14. SICA was finally repealed in 2003. However, such was the labyrinthine working of the processes of the political executive, civil servants and office-bearers in BIFR that it was only thirteen years later in 2016 that the repeal of SICA was notified. The excuse was that since cases already in the pipeline needed to be resolved, BIFR could not be shut down. The inordinate delay was also attributed to a perceived conflict between SICA and the Companies Law.

15. Sam Pitroda's article titled 'Development, Democracy and the Village Telephone' in the *Harvard Business Review* of November–December 1993 details the role that he played in bringing about this phone revolution in India. This article also mentions that Pitroda received Indira Gandhi's support and strong backing from RG.

16. J.L. Ford, S. Sen and Hong Xu Wei, *FDI and Economic Development in China 1970–2006, A Cointegration Study*, Department of Economics, University of Birmingham, 2010.

17. http://www.worldbank.org/en/news/feature/2010/07/16/foreign-direct-investment-china-story.

18. *India Transformed: 25 Years of Economic Reforms*, Edited by Rakesh Mohan, Penguin-Viking, 2017, p. 57.

19. *Across Borders: Fifty Years of Indian Foreign Policy*, J.N. Dixit. *One Life Is Not Enough*, K. Natwar Singh.

20. 'Thirty Years of Tax Reform in India', Shankar Acharya, *Economic and Political Weekly*, 14 May 2005.

21. *First Draft: Witness to the Making of Modern India*, B.G. Verghese, Tranquebar Press, 2010, pp. 345–46.

22. *The Hindu* dated March 2013, www.thehindubusinessline.com/blogs/blog-nramakrishnan/congress-i-and-the-cag/article4504238.ece

23. 'One year after that prime ministerial promise, the Joint Parliamentary Committee (JPC) probing the Bofors scandal came up with its findings last fortnight which, in effect, said the Rs 1,700 crore deal for buying 400 of the 155 mm Bofors field guns was as lily-white as could be.' *India Today* dated 15 May 1988, https://www.indiatoday.in/magazine/special-report/story/19880515-bofors-inquiry-joint-parliamentary-committee-report-reveals-more-than-it-conceals-797272-1988-05-15

24. Record of discussions in the Lok Sabha on this matter on 1 April 1992 is at: https://eparlib.nic.in/bitstream/123456789/10295/1/10_III_01041992_p298_p368_t290.pdf

25. Mikhail Sergeyevich Gorbachev was the general secretary of the Communist Party of the CPSU between 1985 and 1991.

26. *Nuclear Signalling in South Asia: Revisiting A.Q. Khan's 1987 Threat*, Carnegie Endowment for International Peace, P.R. Chari, 14 November 2013, https://carnegieendowment.org/2013/11/14/nuclear-signaling-in-south-asia-revisiting-a.-q.-khan-s-1987-threat-pub-53328

27. *One Life Is Not Enough*, K. Natwar Singh.

28. Even the 1972 Shimla Agreement between India and Pakistan did not specify the precise border between the two countries in the Siachen glacier region.

29. *One Life Is Not Enough*, K. Natwar Singh.

30. The history of distrust between Sri Lankan Tamils and the majority Sinhala community goes back to Sri Lanka's independence from the British in 1948. At that time, the Tamils were better educated than the Sinhalas, and a disproportionately high proportion of Tamils occupied senior positions in the Sri Lankan government. The resulting Sinhala resentment led to discrimination against Tamils including in admission to educational institutions and employment in government. For instance, The Official Languages Act, 1956, recognized Sinhalese as the only official language. Gradually, the less militant Tamil organizations, such as the Tamil United Liberation Front (TULF), were sidelined by the extremist Liberation Tigers of Tamil Eelam (LTTE) as the former were seen as ineffective in reversing discrimination against Tamils. Source: 'The Liberation Tigers of Tamil Eelam and the Lost Quest for Separatism in Sri Lanka', Neil DeVotta, *Asian Survey*, Vol. 49, No. 6, November/December 2009, pp. 1021–51, University of California Press.

31. 'The Best Guerrilla of All', *Outlook*, Anita Pratap, 5 June 2000, https://www.outlookindia.com/magazine/story/the-best-guerrilla-of-all/209492. 'Indira Gandhi Helped Train Tamil Rebels and Reaped Whirlwind', Akshaya Mishra, 23 May 2011, Firstpost, https://www.firstpost.com/world/indira-gandhi-helped-train-tamil-rebels-and-reaped-whirlwind-13913.html. 'RAW in Sri Lanka', *Economic and Political Weekly*, Rita Manchanda, Vol. 28, No. 19, 8 May 1993.

32. 'DMK & ADMK play politics, Tamil Tigers Say Thank You', *Economic Times*, 10 October 2008, https://economictimes.indiatimes.com/news/politics-and-nation/dmk-admk-play-politics-tamil-tigers-say-thank-you/articleshow/3578468.cms?from=mdr

33. *One Life Is Not Enough*, K. Natwar Singh and author's conversation with Mr Kuldip Sahdev at his residence in New Delhi on 2 January 2018.

34. *One Life Is Not Enough*, K. Natwar Singh, Rupa Publications, 2014 and author's conversation with Mr Kuldip Sahdev at his residence in New Delhi on 2 January 2018.

35. The Bofors story had broken on 16 April 1987.

36. In conversation with me on 2 January 2018 at India International Centre in New Delhi. Gharekhan was joint secretary and later additional secretary in the PMO from 1981 to 1986.

37. In conversation with me on 2 January 2018 at the India International Centre in New Delhi.

38. *Road to Nandikadal* by Sri Lankan Major General Kamal Gunaratne, http://www. newindianexpress.com/world/2016/sep/12/Arming-LTTE-against-Indian-Army-was-most-unfavorable-and-dangerous-Maj.-Gen-Gunaratne-1518394.html

39. In conversation with me at Kuldip Sahdev's residence in New Delhi on 2 January 2018.

40. *Across Borders: Fifty Years of India's Foreign Policy*, J.N. Dixit, Picus Books, 1998.

41. *Half Lion: How P.V. Narasimha Rao Transformed India*, Vinay Sitapati, Penguin-Viking, 2016.

42. IG returned to the Lok Sabha from Chikmagalur in Karnataka in November 1978. Soon thereafter, she travelled to the UK via Moscow. She was received by a junior Soviet official, which irritated her. *Indira Gandhi: A Personal and Political Biography*, Inder Malhotra, Hay House India, 2014.

43. 'Role of Arun Nehru, Rajiv in Opening Masjid Ignored', *The Hindu*, 25 November 2009, https://www.thehindu.com/news/national/Role-of-Arun-Nehru-Rajiv-in-opening-masjid-ignored/article16894059.ece. 'How Rajiv Gandhi Blundered on Ayodhya: Baba Said "Bachcha" Let It Happen and "Bachcha" Did', Firstpost, Ajay Singh, 19 January 2016, https://www.firstpost.com/politics/the-errors-that-rajiv-gandhi-made-by-unlocking-doors-to-the-ram-janmabhoomi-temple-in-ayodhya-2603582.html

44. See note 65 in Chapter 3.

45. Mani Shankar Aiyar was the driving force in the PMO in the setting up of Panchayati Raj bodies.

46. 'How Mufti Mohammed Sayeed Shaped the 1987 Elections in Kashmir', Praveen Donthi, 23 March 2016, *The Caravan*, https://caravanmagazine.in/vantage/mufti-mohammad-sayeed-shaped-1987-kashmir-elections. 'Jammu and Kashmir Assembly Poll: NC–Congress (I) Alliance Sweeps a Massive Win', Inderjit Badhwar, *India Today*, 15 April 1987, https://www.indiatoday.in/magazine/cover-story/story/19870415-jammu-kashmir-assembly-poll-nc-congressi-alliance-sweeps-a-massive-win-799831-1987-04-15

Chapter VI: V.P. Singh: Downward Game Changer

1. Vishwanath Pratap Singh was born on 25 June 1931 and passed away on 27 November 2008. He was adopted by the Raja of Manda and studied at Allahabad and Pune universities. Singh began his political career as a Congress party member of the legislative assembly of Uttar Pradesh in 1969. He was elected to the Lok Sabha in 1971, and went on to become the commerce minister in Indira Gandhi's cabinet during the Emergency in 1976–77 and CM of UP in 1980 and commerce minister again in 1983.

2. Leaders of the Janata Dal constituent parties were chief ministers in five states at this time. In Uttar Pradesh—Mulayam Singh Yadav, Bihar—Lalu Prasad Yadav, Gujarat—Chimanbhai Patel, Orissa—Biju Patnaik and Haryana—Om Prakash Chautala.

3. Chandra Shekhar was jailed during the Emergency. Subsequently, he left the Congress party and was the president of the Janata Party in 1977.

4. The mood of the times, and that Devi Lal had supported Singh and then they fell out, is recounted in this *India Today* item dated 15 August 1990 by Inderjit Badhwar, https://www.indiatoday.in/magazine/cover-story/story/19900815-for-janata-dal-and-v.p.-singh-the-recent-crisis-proves-to-be-a-damaging-one-812913-1990-08-15

5. I.G. Patel in *Economic and Political Weekly*, January 1992 issue.

6. The word used is classes and not castes, making it that much more difficult to identify who belongs to the 'Backward Classes'. The recommendations included: a) reservations in technical institutions for candidates from backward classes; reservations of 25 per cent in Class I, 33.5 per cent in Class II and 40 per cent in Class III and IV positions in government and public-sector institutions.

7. 'The Tyranny of Compulsory Identities', Sundeep Dougal, 13 May 2010, *Outlook*, https://www.outlookindia.com/blog/story/the-tyranny-of-compulsory-identities/2294

8. See Chapter IV on Morarji Desai for details.

9. 'Breaking Up My Country', *Outlook*, 8 June 2006, https://www.outlookindia.com/website/story/breaking-up-my-country/231503

10. National Sample Survey Organization (NSSO) data of 2007.

11. The C in OBC is classes and not castes. This took up the percentage of reservations for SCs, STs and OBCs to 49.5 per cent of all Central and state government and public-sector (defined as government ownership of 50 per cent or more) vacancies.

12. *Times of India*, 8 April 2008, https://timesofindia.indiatimes.com/india/Pilot-kept-out-to-prevent-caste-imbalance/articleshow/2933934.cms

13. 'Tribal War', Rohit Parihar, *India Today*, 29 May 2008, https://www.indiatoday.in/magazine/states/story/20080609-tribal-war-736454-2008-05-29; 'Eyewitness: What Happened in Sikandra', 28 May 2008, Rediff News, https://www.rediff.com/news/2008/may/28sld04.htm

14. In the 1992 Indira Sawhney case, the Supreme Court ruled that reservations shall not exceed 50 per cent barring exceptional circumstances. However, a 1994 Act passed by the Tamil Nadu legislature allows total reservations up to 69 per cent. This Tamil Nadu Act has been placed in the 9th Schedule of the Constitution and hence outside judicial review in any Indian court.

15. 'Mufti Sayeed's Darkest Hour, Militants Released for Abducted Daughter', Harinder Baweja, *Hindustan Times*, 8 January 2016, https://www.hindustantimes.

com/india/mufti-saeed-s-dark-hour-militants-released-for-abducted-daughter/
story-527VIWsrLi2F3kiQ1hTT4O.html

16. *Across Borders: Fifty Years of Indian Foreign Policy*, J.N. Dixit, Picus Books,
    pp. 212–13.

17. Chandra Shekhar (CS) was born on 17 April 1927 in Ibrahimpatti in Ballia
    district, Uttar Pradesh, and he did his master's in political science from Allahabad
    University. He was initially a member of the Praja Socialist Party and joined the
    Congress party in 1964. He was first elected to the Lok Sabha in 1967 and was
    member of a group of left-oriented Congress leaders who were nicknamed the
    'Young Turks'. He supported nationalization of banks and abolition of privy
    purses. In 1988 his party merged with others to fight the Congress. He passed
    away on 8 July 2007.

18. Chandra Shekhar claimed later that he had kept Rajiv Gandhi informed, and the
    latter had not expressed any disagreement.

Chapter VII: P.V. Narasimha Rao: Economic Reforms—Better Late than Never

1. Rao was born on 28 June 1921, and did his bachelor's degree from Osmania
   University and his master's in law from Nagpur University. Rao was widely read
   and spoke several Indian and foreign languages. He participated in India's freedom
   struggle and was a member of the Congress party since before Independence.

2. *Half Lion: How P.V. Narasimha Rao Transformed India*, Vinay Sitapati, Penguin
   Viking, 2016. *1991: How P.V. Narasimha Rao Made History*, Sanjaya Baru, Aleph
   Book Company, 2016. In Sitapati's book Rao is described more as half-lion and
   half-fox rather than the literal meaning of Narasimha. This characterization of
   Rao is accurate. Rao was many things to many people, and changed his views and
   persona depending on the twists and turns in his long and eventful political career.

3. *Half Lion*, Vinay Sitapati.

4. The crucial roles played by successive RBI governors and officials in the ministries
   of industry, finance and commerce are cited in detail in *India Transformed: 25
   Years of Economic Reforms*, edited by Rakesh Mohan, Penguin-Viking, 2017.

5. Manmohan Singh inducted Dr Rakesh Mohan and Dr Arvind Virmani as
   economic advisers in the Planning Commission when he was deputy chairman
   during 1985–87. Separately, Dr Shankar Acharya was hired as economic
   adviser in the Ministry of Finance in the 1980s. Dr Jayanta Roy was hired as
   an economic adviser in the Ministry of Commerce in 1989. Montek Singh
   Ahluwalia had joined Prime Minister Rajiv Gandhi's office in 1985. All of
   them were earlier employed with the World Bank. These are a few of the highly
   qualified economists who were fortuitously working in the Government of India
   since the 1980s, and they were of immense assistance to Rao and Manmohan
   Singh in thinking through and implementing the required reforms.

6. *Times of India*, 16 August 1991.

7. Source for per capita numbers at current prices in 1990 and 2016: IMF World Economic Outlook Database, April 2018.

8. *India Transformed: 25 Years of Economic Reforms*, edited by Rakesh Mohan, Penguin-Viking, 2017, pp. 11–33.

9. *The Intelligent Person's Guide to Liberalization*, Amit Bhaduri and Deepak Nayyar, Penguin Books, 1995.

10. A simple yet reasonably reliable measure of changes in the rupee's value between two points of time is its Real Effective Exchange Rate (REER).

11. The areas that remained in the public sector were: atomic energy and related minerals, coal, iron and manganese ore and mining of copper, lead and zinc, gold and silver, mineral oil and arms and ammunition.

12. Reservations for small-scale industries were sharply reduced in 2002, and the final few were taken off the reserved list in 2015.

13. *Essays on Macroeconomic Policy and Growth in India*, Shankar Acharya, Oxford University Press, 2006.

14. Further details: 'Thirty Years of Tax Reform in India', Shankar Acharya, *Economic and Political Weekly*, 14 May 2005.

15. M. Narasimham was governor of the RBI for about six months from May to November 1977. He was replaced by I.G. Patel who went on to serve for five years.

16. Budget and RBI: New Directions, address by Dr Y.V. Reddy, deputy governor, Reserve Bank of India, at Administrative Staff College of India, Hyderabad, on 8 March 1997. RBI press release dated 15 January 1997, https://rbi.org.in/Scripts/BS_PressReleaseDisplay.aspx?prid=18556

17. Under CRR, all banks have to maintain a specified percentage of total bank deposits in a current account with the RBI.

18. SLR is the ratio of the liquid assets that banks have to maintain as a percentage of their demand plus time liabilities. Assets are considered to be liquid if these are in cash, gold or RBI-approved securities.

19. In May 2019 the same two ratios were 4 and 19.5 per cent.

20. Primary dealers create markets in government securities, and their purchases and sales provide a basis for market-driven interest rates.

21. In 2000 the Indian government under Atal Bihari Vajpayee did consider seeking the identities of the companies which invested in India out of Mauritius. However, this led to a sharp sell-off in Indian equity markets, and the government backed off from renegotiating the treaty with Mauritius. This was finally done by Modi's government on 10 May 2016 without any disruption in Indian financial markets.

22. For details: 'India's External Economic Challenges in the 1990s' in *Essays on Macroeconomic Policy and Growth in India*, Shankar Acharya, Oxford University Press, 2006.

23. *The Scam: Who Won, Who Lost, Who Got Away: From Harshad Mehta to Ketan Parekh*, Sucheta Dalal and Debashis Basu. Kensource Information Service Pvt. Ltd.

24. *Indian Fiscal Federalism*, Y.V. Reddy and G.R. Reddy, Oxford University Press, 2019, pp. 152–59.

25. *India Transformed: 25 Years of Economic Reforms*, edited by Rakesh Mohan, Penguin-Viking, 2017.

26. *India's Tryst with Destiny: Debunking Myths that Undermine Progress and Addressing New Challenges*, Jagdish Bhagwati and Arvind Panagariya, HarperCollins, 2012, provides a review of the Indian economy from Independence till end 2011.

27. Reflected in the arguments of Amit Bagchi and Deepak Nayyar in *The Intelligent Person's Guide to Liberalization*, Penguin, 2000, which was critical of the post-1991 reforms.

28. Review of the pro-temple view in the book *In Search of Ram Rajya, A Journey through UP Politics* by Manjula Lal is at www.outlookindia.com/website/story/book-on-up-politics-pegs-ayodhya-dispute-to-two-centuries-ago/298300

29. The Wire, 6 December 2018, https://thewire.in/history/babri-masjid-asi-excavation-ayodhya-ram-temple

30. *Half-Lion* by Vinay Sitapati.

31. On 21 March 2013, the Supreme Court upheld the death sentence against Yakub Memon as one of those held responsible for the Bombay bomb blasts. Among the other accused, Dawood Ibrahim and Tiger Memon are reportedly in hiding in Pakistan. Yakub Memon was executed on 30 July 2015.

32. *Hindustan Times* item titled 'When Babri Fell, Bombay Burned', dated 3 May 2017 is at https://www.hindustantimes.com/mumbai-news/when-babri-fell-bombay-burned/story-2toyr59uA8zdxbVfqKZxqJ.html

33. The Supreme Court order written by Justice Verma and dated 6 October 1993 mentions that the following two issues were under its consideration: '(1) Primacy of the opinion of the Chief Justice of India in regard to the appointments of Judges to the Supreme Court and the High Court, and in regard to the transfers of High Court Judges/Chief Justices; and (2) Justiciability of these matters, including the matter of fixation of the Judge-strength in the High Courts.' The full order is at https://indiankanoon.org/doc/753224/

34. Controversies about judges of the Supreme Court continue after the introduction of the collegium system, and charges of corruption have increased. For example, in 2012 Justice J.S. Verma and others suggested that former Chief Justice of India K.G. Balakrishnan should step down from the National Human Rights Commission because there were financial corruption allegations against him. Details in 'Probe Former Chief Justice of India K.G. Balakrishnan', Moneylife, 10 May 2012, https://www.moneylife.in/article/probe-former-cji-kg-balakrishnan-supreme-court/25566.html and *The Hindu*, https://www.

thehindu.com/news/national/allegations-against-justice-balakrishnan-being-probed-centre/article2987376.ece

35. *Business Standard* item titled 'Rao, 18 Others Told to Face Trial in JMM Bribery Case', 13 September 1997, https://www.business-standard.com/article/economy-policy/rao-18-others-told-to-face-trial-in-jmm-bribery-case-197091301104_1.html. *India Today* article titled 'Jharkhand Mukti Morcha Bribery Scandal: In 1993, Corruption Got Institutionalised in India', dated 26 December 2005 by Fali S. Nariman, https://www.indiatoday.in/magazine/cover-story/story/20051226-jharkhand-mukti-morcha-bribery-scandal-in-1993-corruption-got-institutionalised-in-india-786386-2005-12-26

36. Rao vs State: A Critique by Balwant Singh Malik, https://www.ebc-india.com/lawyer/articles/9808a1.htm. *Hindustan Times* article titled 'Can Parliamentary Privilege Protect Tainted Leaders? Supreme Court to Hear', dated 8 March 2019 by Bhadra Sinha, https://www.hindustantimes.com/india-news/can-parliamentary-privilege-protect-tainted-leaders-supreme-court-to-hear/story-Jb5DkzyPQNQHyQqTJtJOhM.html. Details of Supreme Court judgment of 17 April 1998 at https://indiankanoon.org/doc/45852197/

37. 'On the Nuclear Edge', Seymour M. Hersh, *New Yorker*, 21 March 1993, https://www.newyorker.com/magazine/1993/03/29/on-the-nuclear-edge

38. Operation Gibraltar was the code name for Pakistan's move into Kashmir in August 1965 with the expectation that the local population would rise in revolt against India's rule in J&K. The opposite happened as the local population informed security agencies about the infiltrators.

39. Under Jyoti Basu and later under Buddhadev Bhattacharjee, CPI(M) was in power in West Bengal for thirty-four years from 1977 till 2011.

40. *Choices: Inside the Making of India's Foreign Policy*, Shivshankar Menon, Penguin.

41. https://edition.cnn.com/2013/09/15/world/asia/tiananmen-square-fast-facts/index.html; https://www.britannica.com/event/Tiananmen-Square-incident

42. One of the several ways to measure the intensity of earthquakes which was developed in the 1970s to replace the Richter scale methodology of the 1930s.

43. Article in *The Hindu* titled 'Nellie: India's Forgotten Massacre,' dated 14 December 2008, by Harsh Mander, https://www.thehindu.com/todays-paper/tp-features/tp-sundaymagazine/Nellie-Indiarsquos-forgotten-massacre/article15402276.ece

44. Congress chief minister Hiteswar Saikia took over on 27 February 1983.

45. *Economic Times* 'Chandraswami, the Rise and Fall of a High Flyer', https://economictimes.indiatimes.com/news/politics-and-nation/chandraswami-the-rise-and-fall-of-a-high-flyer/articleshow/58811428.cms. 'Spiritual Guru Chandraswami, Once Close to PM Narasimha Rao, Dies at 66', *India Today*, https://www.indiatoday.in/india/story/spiritual-guru-chandraswami-godman-dead-978773-2017-05-23

46. Penguin Books, January 2000.
47. *Half-Lion* by Vinay Sitapati.

Chapter VIII: Deve Gowda and I.K. Gujral: Prime Ministers of Wobbly, Short-lived Coalitions

1. Deve Gowda was born on 18 May 1933 in a farming family in Haradanahalli village, Hassan district in Karnataka. He has a diploma in civil engineering and joined the Congress in 1953. He joined the Congress (O) when the Congress split and was imprisoned during the Emergency in Bangalore. Deve Gowda has been elected repeatedly to the state assembly and was a minister in Ramakrishna Hegde's Janata Party government in Karnataka. Later, Deve Gowda was chief minister of Karnataka from December 1994 to May 1996.
2. P. Chidambaram had left the Congress party to form the Tamil Maanila Congress (TMC) along with G.K. Moopanar. TMC won a few seats in the 1996 elections, and Chidambaram was the finance minister in Gowda's government.
3. He was born on 4 December 1919 in a village called Parri Darvaiza in undivided Punjab and he studied in colleges affiliated with the University of Punjab. Gujral participated in the freedom struggle and was jailed in 1942 during the Quit India movement.

Chapter IX: Atal Bihari Vajpayee: Decisive, Balanced Yet Susceptible

1. These lines from Vajpayee's 'Yaksha Prashna' are derived from a mythical tale from the Mahabharata. In this story Yama (the Hindu God of Death) asks Yudhishthira, the eldest of the Pandava brothers, what is it about the world that surprises him the most. Yudhishthira replies the fact that humans see others around them die and yet, they conduct themselves as if they themselves will never die.
2. Vajpayee was born on 25 December 1924 in Gwalior. He did his schooling there and graduated from the same city, and did his master's in political science from DAV College in Kanpur. He joined the Rashtriya Swayamsevak Sangh (RSS) in 1939 and the BJS in 1951.
3. *India's Nuclear Bomb*, George Perkovich, University of California Press, 1999, p. 259.
4. At that time, I was the lead specialist for derivatives in the World Bank treasury. Jessica Einhorn was the treasurer of the World Bank and was aware that I was an Indian Foreign Service officer. She remarked to me with a mischievous smile one morning that her husband Robert Einhorn (specialist in nuclear matters in the Arms Control and Disarmament Agency of the US State Department) had mentioned to her that day that the US government had detected preparations for

another Indian nuclear test and was able to dissuade India from going ahead in the nick of time.

5. Source: Ambassador Rakesh Sood in conversation with the author.

6. Brajesh Mishra, an Indian Foreign Service officer, was a close confidant of Atal Bihari Vajpayee and adviser to him. Mishra became the first Indian national security adviser in September 1998 and held that position till the end of Vajpayee's term in May 2004.

7. Details about the meeting as conveyed by Ambassador Rakesh Sood who was the joint secretary (disarmament) in the Ministry of External Affairs at that time.

8. *Engaging India: Diplomacy, Democracy and the Bomb*, Strobe Talbott, Brookings, 2004.

9. As recounted to me by Rakesh Sood on 6 August 2018. He participated in the official-level discussions between India and Pakistan prior to Vajpayee's visit to Lahore. Rakesh Sood was India's ambassador to Afghanistan, Nepal and France.

10. A significant difference with the 1988 Non-Nuclear Aggression Agreement (NNAA) between India and Pakistan was that the two countries had declared themselves as nuclear weapon powers after the tests in May 1998.

11. *Engaging India: Diplomacy, Democracy and the Bomb*, Strobe Talbott, Brookings Institution, 2004, pp. 176–78.

12. 'IC 814 Hijack: How Jaish-e-Mohammed Chief Masood Azhar's Brother Planned Indian Airlines Hijack in 1999', *Financial Express*, 6 March 2019, https://www.financialexpress.com/india-news/kandahar-ic indian-airlines-flight-814-hijack-1999-december-masood-azhar-rauf-pulwama-jem/1506554/. 'The Release of Three Wanted Terrorists in Kandahar Marked Yet Another Low Point in the Blood-splattered Recent History of Kashmir. In a New Book, A.S. Dulat Recalls How It Happened', Kaveree Bamzai, 3 July 2015, *India Today*, https://www.indiatoday.in/magazine/books/story/20150713-dulat-kandahar-hijack-raw-kashmir-vajpayee-years-book-review-820027-2015-07-03

13. 'Vajpayee's "Insaniyat, Jamhooriyat" Won Hearts in Kashmir', Fayaz Wani, *New Indian Express*, 17 August 2018, http://www.newindianexpress.com/nation/2018/aug/17/vajpayees-insaniyat-jamhooriyat-won-hearts-in-kashmir-1858939.html

14. http://edition.cnn.com/2001/WORLD/asiapcf/south/07/17/agra.summit.analysis/

15. 'Parliament Attack Anniversary: What Happened on 13 December 2001,' NDTV, edited by Richa Taneja, 13 December 2018, www.ndtv.com/india-news/parliament-attack-anniversary-what-happened-on-december-13-2001-1962002

16. *Economic Times*, https://economictimes.indiatimes.com/news/defence/jems-ghazwa-e-hind-brought-india-pakistan-on-brink-of-war-twice-in-20-yrs/articleshow/68242129.cms?from=mdr; and *The Hindu*, https://www.thehindubusinessline.com/news/national/timeline-major-terror-attacks-on-security-forces-in-jammu-and-kashmir-since-1999/article26278836.ece

17. *Descent into Chaos: How the War against Islamic Terrorism Is Being Lost in Pakistan, Afghanistan and Central Asia*, Ahmed Rashid, Allen Lane, 2008; also, *The Great Game: On Secret Service in High Asia*, Peter Hopkirk, John Murray, 1990.

18. https://www.theguardian.com/uk-news/2016/jul/06/iraq-inquiry-key-points-from-the-chilcot-report

19. There has been considerable slippage in even attempting to achieve these objectives from around 2007–08 when Dr Manmohan Singh was PM.

20. Background and details are available at the following two sources: https://www.imf.org/external/pubs/ft/fandd/1998/06/imfstaff.htm; and 'Who Triggered the Asian Financial Crisis?', Michael R. King, *Review of International Political Economy*, Vol. 8, Issue 3, 2001, pp. 438–66.

21. Full report of the task force is at https://www.prsindia.org/sites/default/files/bill_files/kelkar_direct_taxes.pdf

22. Although there has been some progress, in 2019 India is still behind middle-income countries in life and health insurance coverage.

23. Dr Kelkar was the chairman of the Thirteenth Finance Commission, and one of the important recommendations of this commission was for the Central government to offer financial support to state governments to arrive at a consensus on a nationwide GST system.

24. Denominated in US dollars, yen and the Deutschmark group which included the Swiss franc.

25. While RBI's holdings of foreign exchange reserves are in the major hard currencies, namely US dollar, euro, yen and British pounds, it would be reasonable to guess that since the US dollar has the largest and most liquid government debt markets, India's reserves are to a large extent invested in US dollar–denominated debt securities.

26. From 1999 to 2002, I was the joint secretary for capital markets, external commercial borrowings and pension reforms in the department of economic affairs, Ministry of Finance.

27. Derivatives can be used to speculate by effectively going long or short on stocks or other financial instruments. The buyer or seller of exchange-traded futures or options has to pay margin money to the exchange in line with movements of stock prices.

28. Mr Yashwant Sinha was FM for most of the time that I served in the MoF. Mr Sinha and Mr Jaswant Singh exchanged places after the UTI scam of 2001. Mr Sinha moved across Rajpath to South Block to become the external affairs minister, and Mr Jaswant Singh became the finance minister.

29. *The Hindu, Business Line,* 13 June 2002, https://www.thehindubusinessline.com/2002/06/13/stories/2002061302650100.htm

30. Subramanyam was an executive director in IDBI immediately prior to becoming chairman UTI on 12 August 1998.

31. Currently chairman of the Housing Development Finance Corporation Limited and well known in Mumbai for decades as a financial-sector expert.

32. These included the chairpersons of IDBI, LIC, SBI, and an RBI deputy governor.

33. The ACC consists of the PM, the minister concerned, in this case, the FM, and the home minister.

34. It is ironic that in October 2018 the Central government appointed G.N. Bajpai as a board member of IL&FS. IL&FS has defaulted on several of its borrowings and cast a long shadow over the health of the entire non-bank finance company (NBFC) sector.

35. As mentioned earlier in this chapter I had briefed Finance Secretary Ajit Kumar in person immediately after Subramanyam had left my room on 29 June 2001.

36. This so-called cash-neutral mechanism works in the interim period because the Indian government does not follow accrual-based accounting, and its budget and other financial statements are cash based.

37. Though a substantial digression, I have included this detailed account of UTI-related events of 2000–2002 so that readers can judge for themselves how and why egregious mistakes are made in India's public-sector-dominated financial sector which have to be ultimately paid for by taxpayers.

38. A Rakesh Mohan Committee had made this recommendation in 1996.

39. Pradhan Mantri Gram Sadak Yojana, Online Management, Monitoring and Accounting System (OMMAS). Refer http://omms.nic.in/. Table 9.2 in the Appendices provides the PMGSY road length completed since 2000–01.

40. Source: International Energy Agency. All numbers are for 2016.

41. Companies have to follow accrual-based accounting, while Railways and the Central government use cash-flow-based accounting. Accrual-based accounting considers contingent liabilities and provides a more accurate picture of the financial health of the entity concerned.

42. The situation has remained the same as of May 2019.

43. In 2008 the allocation of telecom licences was done on a first come, first served basis. *Economic Times*, '2G Spectrum Allocation Case: The Key Accused Who Were Acquitted', 21 December 2017.

44. https://www.forbes.com/sites/saritharai/2016/01/06/india-just-crossed-1-billion-mobile-subscribers-milestone-and-the-excitements-just-beginning/#30eaa1a07db0

45. From the tables, it can be seen that exports as a percentage of GDP stagnated during 2010–2014 and have gone down steadily since then to 11.7 per cent, which was the level achieved as far back as 2004.

Chapter X: Manmohan Singh: Long-lasting Achievements Yet PM in Name

1. Dr Singh was born on 26 September 1932 in Gah (Punjab, now in Pakistan), and his family moved to Amritsar post-Partition. He studied economics in Hindu College, Amritsar, and Punjab University, Hoshiarpur, and obtained his master's degree in 1954. He went on to complete his tripos in economics at

St John's College, Cambridge University, by 1957. Dr Singh did his doctorate at Oxford University, and his thesis was on 'India's export performance, 1951–1960, export prospects and policy implications'.

2. Atal Bihari Vajpayee had opted to include the All India Anna Dravida Munnetra Kazhagam (AIADMK) in his government's NDA coalition. AIADMK did not win a single Lok Sabha seat in the 2004 elections.

3. US law does not allow naturalized citizens to be head of government in that country.

4. *The Accidental Prime Minister: The Making and Unmaking of Manmohan Singh*, Sanjaya Baru, Penguin, 2014.

5. As in the case of the Mahatma Gandhi National Rural Employment Guarantee Act (MGNREGA).

6. *Business Standard*, 14 June 2013, https://www.business-standard.com/article/economy-policy/manmohan-is-politically-shrewd-dr-ig-patel-104052001025_1.html

7. *Economic Times*, 12 April 2014, https://economictimes.indiatimes.com/news/politics-and-nation/pm-had-little-control-over-cabinet-sonia-decided-on-files-writes-manmohan-singhs-ex-media-advisor-sanjay-baru/articleshow/33615246.cms

8. Also known as the 123 Agreement. An exception had to be made to Section 123 of the United States Atomic Energy Act of 1954 to permit nuclear cooperation with a nuclear weapon power, namely India, which had chosen not to be a signatory to the 1968 Non-proliferation of Nuclear Weapons Treaty (NPT). See the chapters on Morarji Desai and Vajpayee for the historical details.

9. This is George W. Bush, son of former US President George H.W. Bush. Bush Junior was US President from January 2001 to January 2009. Bush Senior was President from January 1989 to January 1993.

10. M.K. Narayanan joined the Indian Police Service (IPS) in 1955 and was director IB from 1987 to 1990. He was the Indian NSA from 2005 to 2010.

11. I was posted in the Ministry of External Affairs in Delhi at that time and had a ringside view of the efforts made by MEA to get the 123 Agreement concluded.

12. By 2016, India had signed similar civil nuclear agreements with fourteen countries.

13. *Five Past Midnight in Bhopal: The Epic Story of the World's Deadliest Industrial Disaster*, Dominique Lapierre and Javier Moro, English edition 2001.

14. Cooperation with Russia was 'grandfathered' under India's 1988 agreement with the USSR to set up two VVER 1000 megawatt (water-cooled light water reactors) at Kudankulam in Tamil Nadu. The same agreement has been expanded to cover another four reactors proposed for this site.

15. South Africa was not yet a member of this group.

16. Covered in the 15 June 2005 edition of the *New York Times*, www.nytimes. com/2005/06/15/world/asia/gandhis-moscow-flight-raises-questions-in-india.html

17. As of May 2019, there were eight SCO members and the other six, in addition to India and Pakistan, were China, Russia, Kazakhstan, Kyrgyzstan, Turkmenistan and Uzbekistan. The SCO is a multilateral organization which focuses mostly on economic, technical, environmental and counterterrorism-related coordination among its members.

18. By then I was the Indian ambassador to the European Union, Belgium and Luxembourg.

19. Later NSA in David Cameron's government and UK ambassador to the US since 2016.

20. *Choices: Inside the Making of India's Foreign Policy*, Penguin-Viking, November 2016. In November 2008, Menon was the foreign secretary.

21. So called because of a 1893 agreement between Mortimer Durand, a British civil servant, and Abdur Rahman Khan, the Afghan ruler at that time. The line became the border between Afghanistan and British India and is about 2430 kilometres long. Afghanistan was the only country to vote against the admission of Pakistan into the United Nations after the emergence of the latter as a nation in 1947 because it did not accept the Durand Line as the Afghanistan–Pakistan border.

22. The UK Foreign and Commonwealth Office's director general (political). Later Mr Sedwill was the equivalent of the Indian home secretary in the UK and was appointed cabinet secretary in October 2018.

23. Source: IMF

24. https://www.middleeastmonitor.com/20180907-gulf-military-spending-to-hit-100bn-by-2019/

25. The armed forces of the three European countries are much better equipped and they are members of NATO, which provides a guarantee of collective security.

26. Borrowed from P.G. Wodehouse's description of how the mind of Bertie Wooster, one of the principal characters in his hilarious novels, 'boggled' at the thought of having to confront any tricky situation without the help of his trusted valet Jeeves.

27. V. Prabhakaran, who headed the LTTE insurgency against the Sri Lankan state, was killed in May 2009. The LTTE wanted to create an independent Tamil state including the north and east of Sri Lanka where the Tamil-speaking population is in a majority.

28. 'India-EU Attempts to Restart Free Trade Talks Stumble on Old Issues', *Business Line*, Amiti Sen, 7 December 2018, https://www.thehindubusinessline.com/economy/india-eu-attempts-to-re-start-free-trade-talks-stumble-on-old-issues/article25692022.ece

29. Lehman's shutdown on 15 September 2008 set in motion collapses or near collapses of several other US banks and other financial institutions such as the

insurance giant AIG. Subsequently, the US government provided financial assistance under the Troubled Asset Relief Programme (TARP) to help stabilize its financial system.

30. www.business-standard.com/article/opinion/jaimini-bhagwat-how-about-an-asian-investment-bank-108012501076_1.html

31. Even if this institution were based in India, China would still have had a dominant say since it would have been the highest contributor to the US $100 billion of capital allocated to set up this institution. Twenty per cent of this amount is paid in, and the rest in callable. In comparison, as of December 2018, the World Bank has a total subscribed capital of US $269 billion, and the largest shareholder is the United States with 17.25 per cent of the subscribed capital. The paid-in capital is a small fraction of total capital, and the remaining much larger fraction which is callable is to be sought from member countries only in case of need.

32. Set up by the five-member BRICS grouping consisting of Brazil, Russia, India, China and South Africa.

33. Higher GDP growth rates do not necessarily result in preferred outcomes for all sections of Indians. However, this number does serve as a first-order approximation of what a country is achieving in raising the per capita income of its citizens.

34. National Institution for Transforming India (NITI); 'aayog' is 'commission' in Hindi. The erstwhile Planning Commission was replaced by the NITI Aayog after Narendra Modi became prime minister in May 2014.

35. *Towards Economic Crisis (2012–14) and Beyond*, Shankar Acharya, Academic Foundation, 2015.

36. Following the 2008 financial-sector crisis, the central banks of the US, the UK, Japan and the Eurozone (European Central Bank or ECB headquartered in Frankfurt) embarked on what came to be known as unprecedented monetary policies (UMPs). These central banks bought their own government and privately issued debt securities to provide solvency and liquidity support to their flailing private-sector financial institutions. Interest rates in hard currencies plummeted to unprecedented low levels and even turned negative in some countries. Low returns on hard-currency debt investments and the easy availability of liquidity resulted in higher foreign investor purchases of Indian government debt securities and stocks.

37. 'India and the Global Crisis, Global Economics in Extraordinary Times', Shankar Acharya, Peterson Institute for International Economics, Washington DC, November 2012.

38. Three-time chief minister of Puducherry, elected thrice to the Lok Sabha and governor of Jharkhand and Kerala. He passed away in 2012.

39. *India's Tryst with Destiny*, Jagdish Bhagwati and Arvind Panagariya, Collins Business, 2012, Chapter 10, 'Infrastructure'.

40. Government expenditure well above revenue results in fiscal deficits which can lead to inflation. Excessive fiscal deficits and short-term borrowings in hard currencies can lead to a balance of payments crisis. This is what happened to India during 1989–91.

41. Robert Vadra is Sonia Gandhi's son-in-law. He has been accused of acquiring farmland in Haryana at low prices, then having land use converted to urban, and later selling this land at much higher prices. It is alleged that this was done with the covert help of B.S. Hooda, then chief minister of the state. *Times of India*, 1 September 2018, https://timesofindia.indiatimes.com/india/land-grab-case-fir-registered-against-robert-vadra-former-haryana-cm-bhupinder-hooda/articleshow/65638269.cms

42. The right of governments to acquire private property, with due compensation, for public use.

43. 'The Distribution of Firm Size in India: What Can Survey Data Tell Us?', ADB Economics Working Paper Series, Rana Hasan and Karl Robert L. Jandoc, No. 213, August 2010; also, 'Labour Costs in India's Organized Manufacturing Sector', Jessica R. Sincavage, Carl Haub and O.P. Sharma, *Monthly Labour Review*, May 2010, https://www.bls.gov/opub/mlr/2010/05/art1full.pdf

44. The Modi government finally repealed SICA on 25 November 2016 after passing the Insolvency and Bankruptcy Act in July 2016.

45. 'Confront the Harsh Reality: The Only Way We Can Really Help Farmers Is to Take Most of Them Out of Farming', Arvind Panagariya, 10 January 2019, *Times of India*.

46. http://www.agricoop.nic.in/sites/default/files/NCF3.pdf

47. Sources: Policy Research Working Paper 6258, 'What Does Debt Relief Do for Development? Evidence from India's Bailout Program for Highly-Indebted Rural Households', Martin Kanz, November 2012, The World Bank Development Research Group Finance and Private Sector Development Team, http://documents.worldbank.org/curated/en/589181468044056902/pdf/wps6258.pdf; Statement 4 of Expenditure Budget 2008–09, Volume 1, p. 15, Government of India, https://www.indiabudget.gov.in/ub2008-09/eb/stat04.pdf

48. 'Status of Genetically Modified (GM) crops in India', Uttara Shankar, Project Associate, TERI, 2016, https://www.teriin.org/library/files/GM-crops-in-India.pdf

49. US company which was at the forefront as a supplier of GM seeds and was acquired by Bayer in 2018.

50. 'Suresh Kalmadi Arrested', *The Hindu*, Vinay Kumar, 25 April 2011, https://www.thehindu.com/news/national/Suresh-Kalmadi-arrested/article14696689.ece

51. https://www.ndtv.com/india-news/coal-scam-case-in-detailed-judgment-huge-relief-for-manmohan-singh-1696214

52. 'Did ex-PM Manmohan Singh Forgo Duties as Coal Minister? Deputy Approved Coal Block Allocation, Says Probe', Meetu Jain, *Business Today*, 6 December 2017, https://www.businesstoday.in/current/economy-politics/manmohan-singh-coal-minister-deputy-approved-coal-block-allocation-scam/story/265387.html

53. 'Coal Scam Case: IAS Officers Feel Betrayed by H.C. Gupta Conviction—They Feel Coal and 2G Scams Show How They've Been Scapegoats While Political Masters Walk Free', Subhomoy Bhattacharjee, *Business Standard*, 20 May 2017, https://www.business-standard.com/article/economy-policy/is-h-c-gupta-being-made-a-scapegoat-in-the-coal-scam-117051900632_1.html; and 'IAS Officers to Extend Support to Convicted ex-Coal Secretary Gupta', *Times of India*, Surojit Gupta, 2 December 2018, https://timesofindia.indiatimes.com/india/ias-officers-association-to-extend-support-to-convicted-ex-coal-secretary-gupta/articleshow/66902204.cms

54. 'CAG Submits Report on 2G Spectrum to Govt: Vinod Rai', *Economic Times*, 10 November 2010, https://economictimes.indiatimes.com/news/politics-and-nation/cag-submits-report-on-2g-spectrum-to-govt-vinod-rai/articleshow/6900822.cms

55. *Not Just an Accountant: The Diary of the Nation's Conscience Keeper*, Vinod Rai, Rupa Publications, 2014.

56. 'What Was the 2G Spectrum Scam? 10 Things to Know', *India Today*, 21 December 2017, https://www.indiatoday.in/fyi/story/what-is-2g-scam-in-india-2g-scam-verdict-upa-a-raja-cbi-judge-op-saini-verdict-things-to-know-1113444-2017-12-21

57. Press interaction with Dr Singh, *The Hindu*, https://www.thehindu.com/news/resources/Prime-Minister-Manmohan-Singhs-interaction-with-Editors-of-the-Electronic-Media-on-Feb.16-2011/article15446992.ece

58. https://www.deccanherald.com/content/139607/manmohan-singh-weak-kneed-jayalalithaa.html

59. https://www.outlookindia.com/newswire/story/bofors-court-pulls-up-cbis-malafide-intentions/707452

60. In 2018 this amount has ballooned to Rupees 221 billion including penalties and interest.

61. A detailed article about this case in The Wire is at https://thewire.in/business/air-india-well-researched-scandal

62. 'Supreme Court Strikes Down Thomas Appointment as CVC', J. Venkatesan, 3 March 2011, https://www.thehindu.com/news/national/Supreme-Court-strikes-down-Thomas-appointment-as-CVC/article13729316.ece

63. 'Coal Scam: "Ashwani Kumar Did Call Me for a Meeting to Examine Draft Status Reports," Says Ranjit Sinha', Aman Sharma, *Economic Times*, 3 May 2013, https://economictimes.indiatimes.com/news/politics-and-nation/coal-

scam-ashwani-kumar-did-call-me-for-a-meeting-to-examine-draft-status-report-says-ranjit-sinha/articleshow/19847710.cms

64. https://www.outlookindia.com/magazine/story/a-new-found-agency/285354

65. 'Mahesh Kumar Struck Rs 10 Crore Deal for Post: FIR', Devesh K. Pandey and Jiby Kattakayam, *The Hindu*, 5 May 2013, https://www.thehindu.com/news/national/mahesh-kumar-struck-rs-10-crore-deal-for-post-fir/article4684202.ece

66. 'ED Attaches "Bribe" Cash Seized from Former Rail Min Pawan Bansal's Nephew', *Economic Times*, 7 May 2019, https://economictimes.indiatimes.com/news/politics-and-nation/ed-attaches-bribe-cash-seized-from-former-rail-min-pawan-bansals-nephew/articleshow/69218037.cms

67. According to the Lokpal Act, it can have a maximum of eight members. Of this number, 50 per cent have to be judicial members and 50 per cent must be SCs, STs, OBCs, other minorities and women.

68. In 2004 the Congress party had won 145 Lok Sabha seats, and in 2009 its tally rose to 206.

69. During Vajpayee's tenure as PM, a mechanism called Group of Ministers (GoM) was devised to get a few of the ministers who were directly involved with the issues under consideration to make their recommendations. The cabinet committees are larger bodies, and it was felt that the smaller GoMs would first thrash out contentious issues so that the cabinet committees would be able to take final decisions faster.

70. 'Modi Govt Abolishes All EGoMs, GoMs', Shishir Sinha, *Business Line*, 24 November 2017, https://www.thehindubusinessline.com/economy/Modi-Govt-abolishes-all-EGoMs-GoMs/article20788283.ece

71. *The Accidental Prime Minister* by Sanjaya Baru.

72. 'Rahul Gandhi Trashes Ordinance, Shames Government', *Times of India*, 28 September 2013, https://timesofindia.indiatimes.com/india/Rahul-Gandhi-trashes-ordinance-shames-government/articleshow/23180950.cms

73. 'The Lalu Factor Behind Rahul Gandhi's Ordinance Rap', Shantanu Bhattacharji, *Business Standard*, 27 September 2013, https://www.business-standard.com/article/politics/the-lalu-factor-behind-rahul-gandhi-s-ordinance-rap-113092700666_1.html

Chapter XI: Narendra Modi: Result Oriented, Charismatic Orator and Controversial

1. Narendra Modi was born on 17 September 1950 in Vadnagar in Gujarat into a family of modest means. Modi was an RSS worker (*pracharak*), and in that capacity he travelled extensively within India and to several countries including the US.

2. Except that after Indira Gandhi became PM in 1967, there was a split in the Congress party and she depended on CPI members to cross the halfway mark in the Lok Sabha.

3. 'Economic Freedom of the States of India', https://object.cato.org/sites/cato.org/files/economic-freedom-india-2013/economic-freedom-states-of-india-executive-summary.pdf

4. 'Did Gujarat's Growth Rate Accelerate under Modi?', Maitreesh Ghatak and Sanchari Roy, *Economic & Political Weekly*, Vol. 49, Issue No. 15, 12 April 2014.

5. 12 January 2011, https://www.ndtv.com/photos/business/vibrant-gujarat-2011-lures-investors-8950#photo-112986; also, *Economic Times* 12 January 2013, https://economictimes.indiatimes.com/news/politics-and-nation/india-inc-praises-narendra-modi-at-vibrant-gujarat-summit-congress-plays-down-the-uproar/articleshow/17988483.cms

6. Kar sevaks is a term for activists who offer their services free for a Hindu cause.

7. 'The Facts from Godhra', *Frontline*, Vol. 19, 10 July–2 August 2002, https://frontline.thehindu.com/static/html/fl1915/19150110.htm; also, *India Today*, 20 March 2019, https://www.indiatoday.in/india/story/2002-godhra-train-burning-case-court-sentences-convict-yakub-pataliya-to-life-imprisonment-1482446-2019-03-20

8. *The Hindu* dated 20 April 2018, https://www.thehindu.com/news/national/the-2002-gujarat-riots-cases-and-their-statuses-so-far/article23617950.ece

9. 'Supreme Court Relief for Gujarat Riots Victim Bilkis Bano', Anupama Katakam, 2 May 2019, https://frontline.thehindu.com/dispatches/article27014150.ece

10. *Narendra Modi: A Political Biography*, Andy Marino, HarperCollins, 2014.

11. *Malevolent Republic: A Short History of the New India*, K.S. Komireddi, C. Hurst & Co., 2018.

12. Livemint, 10 June 2013. https://www.livemint.com/Politics/P60JH8i6a3oxUgsfinOcVM/Narendra-Modi-to-head-BJPs-election-campaign-committee-Raj.html

13. Regional parties such as Trinamool Congress in West Bengal, AIADMK in Tamil Nadu and Naveen Patnaik's BJD in Orissa won thirty-four, thirty-seven and twenty seats respectively.

14. Pathankot is located in Punjab close to the India–Pakistan border, and the distance by road to Chandigarh is about 230 kilometres.

15. Chronology of events provided in *The Hindu* article dated 3 January 2016, https://www.thehindu.com/news/national/Pathankot-attack-All-terrorists-dead/article13982714.ece; also, 'The Next Pathankot', Sumit Ganguly, *Foreign Affairs*, 6 January 2016, https://www.foreignaffairs.com/articles/india/2016-01-06/next-pathankot

16. Uri is situated in the Indian state of Jammu and Kashmir near the LoC, and the distance by road to Srinagar is 108 kilometres. '17 Soldiers, 4 Militants Killed in Uri Army Base Terror Attack, Live Mint, 16 September 2016, https://www.livemint.com/Politics/TUmQJ8kOTaQxr0Oira2RuN/Militants-attack-Armys-battalion-HQ-10-Army-men-injured.html

17. For example, Burhan Muzaffar Wani, who had come to be well known in social media in Kashmir, was killed on 8 July 2016, along with two others. They were said to belong to Hizbul Mujahideen which is categorized as a terrorist group by India, the EU and the US.

18. Waters from the three eastern tributaries of the Indus, namely, Ravi, Beas and Sutlej, were assigned fully to India under the India-Pakistan Indus Water Treaty of 1960. *Business Today*, 7 December 2018, https://www.businesstoday.in/top-story/govt-nod-to-ravi-dam-project-in-punjab-to-help-india-arrest-access-water-flowing-into-pakistan/story/298334.html

19. *The Hindu*, 24 July 2016, https://www.thehindu.com/news/national/otherstates/JampK-gets-10-of-Central-funds-with-only-1-of-population/article14506264.ece

20. RBI, https://rbi.org.in/scripts/PublicationsView.aspx?Id=18277; and https://www.prsindia.org/parliamenttrack/budgets/jammu-and-kashmir-budget-analysis-2018-19

21. *Economic Times*, 11 July 2018, https://economictimes.indiatimes.com/news/defence/the-indian-army-also-has-its-own-kashmir-story-to-tell/articleshow/58678889.cms

22. www.ohcr.org/Documents/Countries/IN/DevelopmentsInKashmirJune2016ToApril2018.pdf

23. The Madhesis live in the outer terai regions of that country, and they speak Maithili and Bhojpuri more than Nepalese. In local parlance, the people living on both sides of the India–Nepal border in the terai area have a '*roti-beti ka rishta*' (relationships that involve exchanges of foodgrains and daughters in marriage).

24. *The Hindu*, 27 January, 2018, https://www.thehindu.com/news/national/what-is-the-doklam-issue-all-about/article22536937.ece; also, *Washington Post*, 30 August 2017, https://www.washingtonpost.com/news/worldviews/wp/2017/08/30/who-blinked-in-china-india-military-standoff/?noredirect=on&utm_term=.7ebdc1c2a110

25. *New York Times*, 12 May 2019, https://www.nytimes.com/2019/05/12/us/politics/trump-us-china-economy.html

26. Twenty-nine heads of government and state and representatives from 130 countries and most major international organizations participated in these May 2017 meetings in Beijing.

27. 2011 census data, http://censusindia.gov.in/Census_And_You/age_structure_and_marital_status.aspx

28. 'Rafale Fighter Jet Deal: Chronology of Events', Times Now, 10 April 2019, https://www.timesnownews.com/india/article/rafale-fighter-jet-deal-chronology-of-events/397774

29. *Business Standard*, 10 May 2019, https://www.business-standard.com/article/current-affairs/sc-reserves-verdict-on-petitions-seeking-review-of-verdict-on-rafale-deal-119051001221_1.html

30. *The Hindu*, 6 May 2016, https://www.thehindu.com/opinion/op-ed/no-longer-at-sea/article8561775.ece

31. *Indian Fiscal Federalism*, Y.V. Reddy and G.R. Reddy, Oxford University Press, 2019.

32. Press Information Bureau release dated 4 April 2016, http://pib.nic.in/newsite/PrintRelease.aspx?relid=138555

33. RBI Annual Report 2017–18, p. 17.

34. 'Demonetisation: All Cost and Little Benefit', *Economic Times*, 2 September 2018, https://economictimes.indiatimes.com/news/economy/policy/demonetisation-all-cost-and-little-benefit/articleshow/65639832.cms?from=mdr

35. 'Over 99 Per Cent Demonetised Currency Returned to Banks', *India Today*, 30 August 2018, https://www.indiatoday.in/india/story/over-99-per-cent-demonetised-currency-returned-to-banks-rbi-report-1327126-2018-08-30

36. RBI Annual Report 2017–18, p. 66, https://rbidocs.rbi.org.in/rdocs/AnnualReport/PDFs/0ANREPORT201718077745EC9A874DB38C991F580ED14242.PDF

37. The five rates in per cent, as initially decided, were 0, 5, 12, 18 and 28.

38. State governments often feel that the Central government does not consult them enough on centrally sponsored schemes (CSSs). With the GST Council set up as a constitutional body, it is an appropriate institution to work as a coordinator with the National Development Council and the Finance Commission.

39. *Indian Fiscal Federalism*, Y.V. Reddy and G.R. Reddy, Oxford University Press, 2019, pp. 20–21.

40. Except for Gujarat, Maharashtra and Karnataka, the others are Hindi-speaking states.

41. *Economic Times*, 29 November 2018, https://economictimes.indiatimes.com/news/et-explains/all-you-wanted-to-know-about-the-ongoing-gdp-data-row/articleshow/66863249.cms?from=mdr

42. 'Measuring India's GDP Growth: Unpacking the Analytics & Data Issues behind a Controversy that Refuses to Go Away', National Council of Applied Economic Research (NCAER), 12–13 July 2016, http://www.ncaer.org/events/ipf-2016/IPF-2016-Paper-RNagaraj-TNSrinivasan.pdf

43. *Economic Times*, Kirtika Suneja, 30 January 2019, https://economictimes.indiatimes.com/news/economy/policy/2-more-members-of-nsc-quit-on-feeling-sidelined/articleshow/67748951.cms

44. Details at https://www.businesstoday.in/current/economy-politics/2-non-govt-national-statistical-commission-members-resign-over-delay-in-release-of-nsso-data/story/314979.html

45. A reconstituted National Statistical Commission (NSC) could be given statutory status with fixed tenure for its members. Such an NSC would be fully independent of MoSPI and the NITI Aayog.

46. RBI Annual Report 2017–18, p. 245.

47. Extract from finance minister's budget speech on 1 February 2017: 'As against estimated 42 million persons engaged in organised sector employment, the number of individuals filing return for salary income are only 17.4 million. As against 56 million informal sector individual enterprises and firms doing small business in India, the number of returns filed by this category are only 18.1 million . . . Of the 7.6 million individual assesses who declare income above Rupees 0.5 million, 5.6 million are in the salaried class. The number of people showing income more than Rupees 5 million in the entire country is only 0.172 million. We can contrast this with the fact that in the last five years, more than 12.5 million cars have been sold, and number of Indian citizens who flew abroad, either for business or tourism, is 20 million in the year 2015.' https://www.indiabudget.gov.in/ub2017-18/bs/bs.pdf

48. Economic Survey 2015–16, p. 108.

49. Full speech available at Prime minister's official website.

50. Details at https://www.moneycontrol.com/news/business/economy/flashback-2018-when-ilfs-nearly-sank-the-financial-system-3300731.html; also, https://thewire.in/business/ilfs-downfall-banking-india-economy

51. Government of India, Ministry of Power, https://powermin.nic.in/en/content/power-sector-glance-all-india

52. Electricity Distribution Company.

53. Government of India, Ministry of Power, Central Electricity Authority (CEA) Report, p. 31, http://www.cea.nic.in/reports/monthly/executivesummary/2018/exe_summary-03.pdf

54. World Bank, https://www.worldbank.org/en/news/feature/2018/12/17/new-report-power-sector-distortions-cost-india-billions

55. https://timesofindia.indiatimes.com/india/nda-pips-upa-ii-in-building-roads-but-most-are-2-lanes/articleshow/66112824.cms; also, https://www.businesstoday.in/sectors/infra/modi-government-constructed-73-percent-more-highways-compared-upa-last-4-years/story/279060.html

56. https://indianexpress.com/article/india/four-years-of-modi-government-railways-piyush-goyal-5187436/

57. 'Supreme Court Quashes Allocation of 214 Coal Blocks', The Hindu, Krishnadas Rajagopal, https://www.thehindu.com/news/national/supreme-court-quashes-allocation-of-all-but-four-of-218-coal-blocks/article6441855.ece

58. https://www.ibef.org/industry/renewable-energy.aspx

59. 'AAP Government Fixed a Broken State Schooling System, But Glitches Remain', Outlook, 27 May 2019, https://www.outlookindia.com/magazine/story/india-news-a-for-aaplause-b-for-boos/301297

60. The Hindu Business Line, 4 October 2019, https://www.thehindubusinessline.com/opinion/columns/a-clean-up-for-make-in-india/article22992083.ece

61. OECD-FAO Agricultural Outlook (2017 Edition).

62. Numbers for 1998 and 2014 are from the Directorate of Economics and Statistics, Ministry of Agriculture and Farmer Welfare, Govt. of India, http://eands.dacnet.nic.in/. Data for 1964 is from *Indian Agriculture: Four Decades of Development* by G.S. Bhalla and Gurmail Singh.

63. *New Indian Express*, 12 January 2018, http://www.newindianexpress.com/nation/2018/jan/12/four-senior-sc-judges-call-unprecedented-press-conference-all-you-need-to-know-as-it-happened-1751713.html

64. https://economictimes.indiatimes.com/news/politics-and-nation/after-lok-sabha-rajya-sabha-approves-quota-bill-for-economically-weak-in-general-category/articleshow/67455461.cms

65. *Economic Times*, 11 August 2018, https://economictimes.indiatimes.com/news/politics-and-nation/maharashtra-ats-arrests-three-for-planning-terror-attack/articleshow/65361533.cms

66. 2 September 2018, https://scroll.in/article/892850/from-pune-to-paris-how-a-police-investigation-turned-a-dalit-meeting-into-a-maoist-plot

67. *The Hindu*, 14 July 2016, https://www.thehindu.com/news/national/FIR-for-cow-slaughter-ordered-against-Dadri-lynching-victim-Akhlaqs-family/article14488640.ece

68. *India Today*, 6 April 2017, https://www.indiatoday.in/india/story/alwar-gau-rakshak-attack-murder-cattle-farm-owner-pehlu-khan-969763-2017-04-06

69. *Economic Times*, 20 January 2019, https://economictimes.indiatimes.com/news/politics-and-nation/what-made-rural-india-abandon-its-cattle-in-droves/articleshow/67604493.cms

70. *Hindustan Times*, 16 May 2019, https://www.hindustantimes.com/lok-sabha-elections/outrage-as-bjp-s-pragya-calls-mahatma-killer-godse-a-patriot/story-mUy7Tnk8X5hL08veZxQHoM.html

71. Interim budget presented by acting finance minister Piyush Goyal, https://www.indiabudget.gov.in/ub2019-20/bs/bs.pdf

72. Live Mint, 29 May 2019, https://www.livemint.com/news/india/the-macroeconomic-dilemma-for-india-s-new-government-1559029581234.html

73. *The Elusive Quest for Growth*, William Easterly, MIT Press, 2001.

74. Handbook of Statistics on Indian Economy, RBI, https://rbi.org.in/Scripts/PublicationsView.aspx?id=7704; World Bank, https://data.worldbank.org/indicator/NY.GDP.MKTP.KD?locations=IN; Directorate General of Foreign Trade (DGFT): http://commerce-app.gov.in/eidb/ergnq.asp

75. *Economic Times*, 3 April 2019, https://economictimes.indiatimes.com/industry/banking/finance/banking/supreme-court-strikes-down-rbis-february-12-circular-on-defaulting-firms-calls-it-illegal/articleshow/68682597.cms

76. *Business Standard*, 3 April 2019, https://www.business-standard.com/article/economy-policy/sc-order-on-rbi-circular-might-prolong-the-debt-resolution-process-119040201175_1.html

77. For example, *Times of India* editorial, dated 7 June 2018.

78. *Indian Express,* dated 23 January 2019.

79. 'Pulwama Attack 2019', *India Today*, 16 February 2019, https://www. indiatoday.in/india/story/pulwama-attack-2019-everything-about-jammu-and-kashmir-terror-attack-on-crpf-by-terrorist-adil-ahmed-dar-jaish-e-mohammad-1457530-2019-02-16

80. Foreign secretary's statement, https://mea.gov.in/Speeches-Statements.htm?dtl/ 31089/statement+by+foreign+secretary+on+26+february+2019+on+the+ strike+on+jem+training+camp+at+balakot

81. *Business Standard*, 28 February 2019, https://www.business-standard.com/ article/news-ians/pakistan-targeted-military-installations-lied-on-use-of-f-16-services-119022801118_1.html

82. *The Hindu*, 14 April 2019, https://www.thehindu.com/news/national/did-india-shoot-down-an-f-16-of-the-pakistan-air-force/article26830937.ece

83. 'Pakistan Intelligence Services "Aided Mumbai Terror Attacks"', *Guardian*, 18 October 2010, https://www.theguardian.com/world/2010/oct/18/pakistan-isi-mumbai-terror-attacks

84. *Business Standard*, 1 May 2019, https://www.business-standard.com/article/ pti-stories/un-decision-to-declare-masood-azhar-global-terrorist-big-success-for-india-pm-modi-119050101065_1.html

85. https://www.bloomberg.com/news/articles/2019-04-28/xi-jinping-s-wins-and-losses-at-his-second-belt-and-road-forum

Epilogue

1. The poem 'These My Words' is by Hiren Bhattacharya (translated from Assamese by D.N. Bezboruah) and included in *Another India: An Anthology of Contemporary Indian Fiction and Poetry*, selected and edited by Nissim Ezekiel and Meenakshi Mukherjee, Penguin, 1990.

2. *No Full Stops in India*, Mark Tully, Penguin, 1992.

3. http://loksabhaph.nic.in/Members/AlphabeticalList.aspx

4. 'In India, Who Speaks in English, and Where?', *Mint*, 15 May 2019. https://www.livemint.com/news/india/in-india-who-speaks-in-english-and-where-1557814101428.html

5. Literal meaning: An army officer whose rank is below that of a captain. Used here in the sense of those who were earlier from weaker economic and/or social groupings.

6. *Economic and Political Weekly*, Vol. 54, No. 21, 25 May 2019, https://www.epw. in/journal/2019/21/special-articles/factors-contributing-income-inequalities-among.html

7. https://www.nabard.org/PressReleases-article.aspx?id=25&cid=554&NID=43

8. Lucas Chancel and Thomas Piketty, *Indian Income Inequality, 1922-2015: From British Raj to Billionaire Raj?*, Wid.world Working Paper Series No. 2017/11 July 2017, http://wid.world/wp-content/uploads/2017/12/ChancelPiketty2017WIDworld.pdf

9. Arghya Sengupta, *Independence and Accountability of the Higher Indian Judiciary*, Cambridge University Press, 2019.

10. A satirical 2010 film called *Peepli Live* is unnervingly close to reality about passing the buck to the judiciary.

11. *Court News*—Quarterly Newsletter of the Supreme Court.

12. https://www.livelaw.in/sc-sets-aside-hc-judgment-poor-english/

13. Justice Dipak Misra's judgment is at https://indiankanoon.org/doc/1836522/. Justice Misra later became the Chief Justice of India from August 2017 to October 2018.

14. https://www.thehindubusinessline.com/news/national/disproportionate-assets-case-a-timeline-of-events/article9541095.ece

15. https://www.thehindu.com/news/national/fodder-scam-case-sc-rejects-bail-to-lalu-prasad-yadav/article26789802.ece

16. https://www.thehindu.com/specials/in-depth/njac-vs-collegium-the-debate-decoded/article10050997.ece

17. US measures against Chinese telecommunications equipment and smartphone giant Huawei, suspected of being an espionage accomplice, include cutting off its linkages with all US companies. China has been developing its own capabilities in quantum computing and artificial intelligence. Currently, Huawei depends on US companies for supply of microchips and is probably preparing to manufacture such chips in China.

18. Bay of Bengal Initiative for Multi-sectoral Technical and Economic Cooperation set up in 1997. Members are Bangladesh, India, Myanmar, Sri Lanka, Thailand, Nepal and Bhutan.

19. *Foreign Policy*, 23 July 2018, https://foreignpolicy.com/2018/07/23/india-is-the-weakest-link-in-the-quad/

20. U.R. Ananthamurthy, *Samskara: A Rite for a Dead Man*, Oxford University Press, 1976.

21. V.S. Khandekar, *Yayati: A Classic Tale of Lust*, Orient Paperbacks, 1959.

SELECT BIBLIOGRAPHY

Acharya, Shankar. 'Thirty Years of Tax Reform'. *Economic and Political Weekly*, Vol. 40, Issue No. 20, 14 May 2005.

———. *Essays on Macroeconomic Policy and Growth in India*. New Delhi: Oxford University Press, 2006.

Acheson, Dean. *Present at the Creation: My Years at the State Department*. New York: W.W. Norton, 1969.

Ananthamurthy, U.R. *Samskara: A Rite for a Dead Man*. New Delhi: Oxford University Press, 1976.

Barooah, Nirode K. *Gopinath Bardoloi: The Assam Problem and Nehru's Centre*. Guwahati: Bhabani Print and Publications, 2010.

Baru, Sanjaya. *The Accidental Prime Minister: The Making and Unmaking of Manmohan Singh*. New Delhi: Penguin Books India, 2014.

———. *1991: How P.V. Narasimha Rao Made History*. New Delhi: Aleph Book Company, 2016.

Bass, Gary J. *The Blood Telegram: Nixon, Kissinger and a Forgotten Genocide*. New York: Knopf Doubleday, *2013.*

Bhaduri, Amit, and Deepak Nayyar. *The Intelligent Person's Guide to Liberalization*. New Delhi: Penguin, 2000.

Bhagwati, Jagdish, and Arvind Panagariya. *India's Tryst with Destiny: Debunking Myths that Undermine Progress and Addressing New Challenges*. Noida: HarperCollins Publishers India, 2012.

Bhagwati, Jagdish, and Padma Desai. *India: Planning for Industrialization, Industrialization and Trade Policies since 1951*. Published on behalf of the Development Centre of the OECD by Oxford University Press, 1970.

Carr, E.H. *What Is History*. Cambridge: University of Cambridge Press, 1961.

CATO. *Economic Freedom of the States of India*, Washington, DC: CATO Institute.

Chaudhuri, Pramit. *Aspects of Indian Economic Development, A Book of Readings*. London: University of Sussex, George Allen & Unwin Ltd, 1971.

Crocker, Walter. *Nehru: A Contemporary's Estimate*. New York: Oxford University Press, 1966.

Dasgupta, Chandrasekhar. *War and Diplomacy in Kashmir, 1947-48*. New Delhi: Sage Publications, 2002.

Deshmukh, C.D. *The Course of My Life*. Mumbai: Orient Blackswan Private Limited, 1974.

Dhar, P.N. *Indira Gandhi, the Emergency and Indian Democracy*. New Delhi: Oxford University Press, 2000.

Dixit, J.N. *Across Borders: 50 Years of India's Foreign Policy*. New Delhi: Picus Books, 1998.

Easterly, William. *The Elusive Quest for Growth*. Cambridge, Massachusetts: MIT Press, 2001.

Ezekiel, Nissim and Meenakshi Mukherjee. Selected and edited. *Another India: An Anthology of Contemporary Indian Fiction and Poetry*. Penguin Books India, 1990.

Frank, Katherine. *Indira: The Life of Indira Nehru Gandhi*. London: HarperCollins, 2010.

Gait, Edward Albert. *A History of Assam*. Calcutta: Thacker Spink and Co, 1906.

Gandhi, Rajmohan. *Patel: A Life*. Ahmedabad: Navajivan Publishing House, 1990.

Ghatak, Maitreesh and Sanchari Roy. 'Did Gujarat's Growth Rate Accelerate under Modi?' *Economic and Political Weekly*, Vol. 49, Issue No. 15, 12 April 2014.

Guha, Amalendu. *Planter Raj to Swaraj: Freedom Struggle and Electoral Politics in Assam 1826-1947*. New Delhi: Indian Council of Historical Research, 1977. New Delhi: Tulika Books, 2006.

Guha, Ramachandra. *India After Gandhi*. New Delhi: Pan Macmillan India, 2007.

Gunaratne, Kamal. *Road to Nandikadal: True Story of Defeating Tamil Tigers*. Colombo: Kamal Gunaratne, 2016.

Gundevia, Y.D. *Outside the Archives*. New Delhi: Orient Longman Limited, 1987.

Guyot-Rechard, Berenice. *Shadow States, India, China and the Himalayas, 1910-1962*. Cambridge: Cambridge University Press, 2017.

Hasan, Rana, and Karl Robert L. Jandoc. 'The Distribution of Firm Size in India: What Can Survey Data Tell Us?' ADB Economics Working Paper Series, No. 213, August 2010.

Joshi, Vijay. *India's Long Road: The Search for Prosperity*. New Delhi: Oxford University Press, 2016.

Kalha, Ranjit. *India-China Boundary Issues: Quest for Settlement*. New Delhi: Indian Council for World Affairs and Pentagon Press, 2014.

Khandekar, V.S. *Yayati: A Classic Tale of Lust*. Delhi: Orient Paperbacks 1959.

Khosla, Madhav. Edited. *Letters for a Nation from Jawaharlal Nehru to His Chief Ministers 1947-1963*. New Delhi: Allen Lane, Penguin Books India, 2014.

Kinzer, Stephen. *All the Shah's Men*. New Jersey: John Wiley & Sons, 2003.

Komireddi, K.S. *Malevolent Republic: A Short History of New India*. London: C. Hurst & Co. 2018.

Lifshultz, Lawrence, and Kai Bird. *Bangladesh: The Unfinished Revolution*. London: Zed Books, 1979.

Lintner, Bertil. *China's India War*. New Delhi: Oxford University Press, 2018.

Malhotra, Inder. *Indira Gandhi, A personal and Political Biography*. London: Hodder & Stoughton, 1989.

Marino, Andy. *Narendra Modi, A Political Biography*. Noida: HarperCollins Publishers India, 2014.

Mehta, Vinod. *The Sanjay Story*. Mumbai: Jaico Publishing House, 1978. Noida: HarperCollins Publishers India, 2012.

Menon, Shivshankar. *Choices: Inside the Making of India's Foreign Policy*. Gurgaon: Penguin Books India, 2017.

Mohan, Rakesh, and Vandana Aggarwal. 'Commands and controls: Planning for Indian industrial development, 1951-1990.' *Journal of Comparative Economics*, Vol. 14, Issue 4, pp. 681–712, 1990.

Mohan, Rakesh. Edited. *India Transformed: 25 Years of Economic Reforms*. Gurgaon: Viking/Penguin, 2017.

Mukherjee, Pranab. *The Dramatic Decade, The Indira Gandhi Years*. New Delhi: Rupa Publications, 2015.

Nagaraj, R., and T.N. Srinivasan. 'Measuring India's GDP Growth: Unpacking the Analytics and Data Issues behind a Controversy that Refuses to Go Away'. National Council of Applied Economic Research (NCAER), 12–13 June 2016. Mumbai: Indira Gandhi Institute of Development Research. India Policy Forum, Yale University.

Nehru, B.K. *Nice Guys Finish Second*. New Delhi: Penguin, 1997.

Norman, Dorothy. *Indira Gandhi, Letters to an American Friend, 1950-1984*. A. Helen and Kurt Wolff, 1985.

Norman, Jesse. *Adam Smith: What He Thought and Why It Matters*. London: Penguin Random House, 2018.

Patel, I.G. 'New Economic Policies'. *Economic and Political Weekly*, Vol. 27, Issue No. 1-2, 4 January 1992.

Patel, I.G. *Glimpses of Indian Economic Policy, An Insider's View*. New Delhi: Oxford University Press, 2002.

Perkovich, George. *India's Nuclear Bomb*. Oakland: University of California Press, 1999.

Ramesh, Jairam. *Intertwined Lives: P.N. Haksar and Indira Gandhi*. New Delhi: Simon & Schuster, 2018.

Rao, P.V. Narasimha. *The Insider*. New Delhi: Penguin Books India, 2000.

Rasgotra, M. *A Life in Diplomacy*. New Delhi: Penguin Books India, 2015.

Reddy, Y.V., and G.R. Reddy. *Indian Fiscal Federalism*. New Delhi: Oxford University Press, 2019.

Riedel, Bruce. *JFK's Forgotten Crisis: Tibet, the CIA, and the Sino-Indian War*. Noida: HarperCollins Publishers India, 2015.

Sahgal, Nayantara. *Indira Gandhi: Tryst with Power*. New Delhi: Penguin Books India, 2012.

Saran, Shyam. *How India Sees the World*. New Delhi: Juggernaut Publication, 2017.

Sen, Amartya, and Jean Dreze. *An Uncertain Glory: India and Its Contradictions*. New Jersey: Princeton University Press, 2013.

Singh, K. Natwar. *One Life is Not Enough: An Autobiography*. New Delhi: Rupa Publications, 2014.

Sitapati, Vinay. *Half Lion: How P.V. Narasimha Rao Transformed India*. Gurgaon: Viking/Penguin Books India, 2016.

Subramaniam, Arjun. *India's Wars, A Military History 1947-1971*. Noida: HarperCollins Publishers India, 2016.

Talbott, Strobe. *Engaging India, Diplomacy, Democracy and the Bomb*. Brookings: Brookings Institution Press, 2004.

The Journal of Imperial and Commonwealth History. Vol. 38, No. 3, September 2010, pp. 441–69.

Thondup, Gyalo, and Anne E. Thurston. *The Noodle Maker of Kalimpong: The Untold Story of My Struggle for Tibet*. London: Random House, December 2014.

Tully, Mark, and Satish Jacob. *Amritsar: Mrs Gandhi's Last Battle*. London: Jonathan Cape, 1986.

van Zwieten, Kristin. 'Corporate Rescue in India: The Influence of the Courts'. *Journal of Corporate Law Studies*, Vol. 1. Oxford Legal Studies Research Paper 37/2014. Oxford: University of Oxford, Faculty of Law, 2015.

Verghese, B.G. *First Draft to the Making of Modern India*. New Delhi: Tranquebar Press, 2010.

White, Lawrence H. 'Indian Planning and Development Economics'. In *The Clash of Economic Ideas: The Great Policy Debates and experiments of the Last Hundred Years*. Cambridge: Cambridge University Press, 2012.

INDEX

Aadhaar (personal identity card with
   biometrics registration), 240, 254,
   272–73, 292
Abdullah, Farooq, 97, 108, 148, 154
Abdullah, Sheikh, 34–35, 36, 37–38, 70
Abid Hussain Committee on Trade Policies.
   See Committee on Trade Policies
Advani, L.K., 155, 157, 195, 207, 213, 259
Afghanistan and India, relations, 38, 197,
   226, 253–54; Soviet invasion of, 102,
   136, 179; United States' intervention, 43,
   100, 120, 137–38, 147, 175, 197, 268
Afro-Asian Conference, Bandung, 1955, 49
agricultural debt waiver and debt relief
   scheme (ADWDRS), 247
agriculture under Indira Gandhi, 79–80,
   85; Jawaharlal Nehru, 22, 23–24; Lal
   Bahadur Shastri, 68; Narendra Modi,
   284–85
Ahluwalia, Montek Singh, 132–33, 242, 244
Aid India Consortium, 26–27, 77
Air India, 232, 251, 271, 272
Akali Dal, 109, 117, 187
Aksai Chin, under Chinese occupation, 50,
   52, 53, 57, 91
All Assam Students' Union (AASU), 107,
   127
All India Anna Dravida Munnetra Kazhagam
   (AIADMK), 110, 205, 230, 249
Allahabad High Court, 290; judgment, 1975,
   103–05

Ambedkar, B.R., 2–3
anti-Sikh riots, Delhi, 1984, 124–25, 149,
   180, 214
Appointments Committee of the Cabinet
   (ACC), 166, 203, 207
Armed Forces (Special Powers) Act (AFSPA),
   1948, 2
Arunachal Pradesh, 57, 91, 137, 266, 292;
   territory lost to China, 42
Asian Development Bank (ADB), 200, 241
Asian Investment Bank (AIB), 234–35
Assam Accord (1985), 127
Assam agitation, 107, 124, 127
Assam Gana Parishad (AGP), 127
Association of Southeast Asian Nations
   (ASEAN), 49, 91, 146, 176, 266, 304;
   India, free trade agreement, 233;
atomic energy and strategic implications;
   Nehru, 32–33
Atomic Energy Commission (AEC), 32
Ayushman Bharat Yojana (Pradhan Mantri
   Jan Arogya Yojana (PMJAY)), 282–83
Azhar, Masood, 194, 291

Babri Masjid, 147, 149, 161, 171–72;
   demolition, 160, 180, 181, 214
Backward Classes Commission, First, 152–53
Backward Classes Commission, Second
   (Mandal Commission), 118, 122,
   153–54, 157
badla system, 168–69, 201–02